teach®
yourself

hindi
rupert snell with
simon weightman

For over 60 years, more than
50 million people have learnt over
750 subjects the **teach yourself**
way, with impressive results.

be where you want to be
with **teach yourself**

The publisher has used its best endeavours to ensure that the URLs for external websites referred to in this book are correct and active at the time of going to press. However, the publisher and the author have no responsibility for the websites and can make no guarantee that a site will remain live or that the content will remain relevant, decent or appropriate.

For UK order enquiries: please contact Bookpoint Ltd, 130 Milton Park, Abingdon, Oxon, OX14 4SB. Telephone: +44 (0) 1235 827720. Fax: +44 (0) 1235 400454. Lines are open 09.00–17.00, Monday to Saturday, with a 24-hour message answering service. Details about our titles and how to order are available at www.teachyourself.co.uk

For USA order enquiries: please contact McGraw-Hill Customer Services, PO Box 545, Blacklick, OH 43004-0545, USA. Telephone: 1-800-722-4726. Fax: 1-614-755-5645.

For Canada order enquiries: please contact McGraw-Hill Ryerson Ltd, 300 Water St, Whitby, Ontario, L1N 9B6, Canada. Telephone: 905 430 5000. Fax: 905 430 5020.

Long renowned as the authoritative source for self-guided learning – with more than 50 million copies sold worldwide – the **teach yourself** series includes over 500 titles in the fields of languages, crafts, hobbies, business, computing and education.

British Library Cataloguing in Publication Data: a catalogue record for this title is available from the British Library.

Library of Congress Catalog Card Number: on file.

First published in UK 1989 by Hodder Education, part of Hachette Livre UK, 338 Euston Road, London, NW1 3BH.

First published in US 1989 by The McGraw-Hill Companies, Inc.

This edition published 2003.

The **teach yourself** name is a registered trade mark of Hodder Headline.

Copyright © 2003 Rupert Snell and Simon Weightman

Typeset by Transet Limited, Coventry, England.
Printed in Great Britain for Hodder Education, part of Hachette Livre UK, 338 Euston Road, London, NW1 3BH, by Cox & Wyman Ltd, Reading, Berkshire.

Hachette Livre UK's policy is to use papers that are natural, renewable and recyclable products and made from wood grown in sustainable forests. The logging and manufacturing processes are expected to conform to the environmental regulations of the country of origin.

Impression number   25 24 23 22 21 20
Year   2012 2011 2010 2009 2008

CONTENTS

INTRODUCTION

This course is designed to enable those with no previous knowledge of Hindi to learn to read, write and converse in the language with confidence and enjoyment. The course has also proved effective as teaching material for both class tuition and individual study.

The Hindi presented in this course is primarily colloquial and practical. To start by learning a very formal linguistic register, such as the purists might prefer, would be to invite looks of incredulity (and incomprehension) during everyday encounters with Hindi-speakers.

An advantage of the colloquial approach is that it gives greater access to Urdu, Hindi's sister-language. Hindi and Urdu share a virtually identical grammar and much of their vocabulary. In the higher registers they do part company, because Hindi looks to the classical Indian language of Sanskrit for its higher vocabulary, script and general cultural orientation, while Urdu looks to Persian and Arabic for these things. But at the everyday spoken level, Hindi and Urdu are virtually identical, and you should not be surprised if you are complimented on your spoken 'Urdu' when you complete this course in 'Hindi'!

How to use the course

The course is divided into 18 units, each of which is based on (usually two) dialogues which exemplify and bring to life the new grammar introduced in that particular unit. Transliteration in the roman script is provided for the first five units and for all words in the Hindi-English glossary. The dialogues form a kind of soap opera based on the life of a Delhi family; the English translations are deliberately close and literal, so as to function as a key to the Hindi. The book ends with some additional material in the appendixes, together with a Key to the exercises and complete Hindi-English and English-Hindi glossaries.

Once you have worked carefully through the introductory section on script and pronunciation, taking help from the cassette and/or a native speaker if possible, you should turn to Unit 1. Familiarise yourself with the vocabulary of the first dialogue (given beneath it) before reading the dialogue and working towards an understanding of it by means of the translation; then work through the grammatical explanations and the examples; alternatively, you may prefer to start with the grammar sections, and then turn back to the dialogue. Either way, learning the dialogues by heart will give you a sound basis for conversations of your own. When you have completed the whole unit in this way, learn the vocabulary (no short cuts here – this is essential!), and then do the exercises, checking your work against the key. Don't forget to revise earlier sections as you progress through the book.

The grammatical explanations are meant to be as accessible and non-technical as possible. A book of this kind cannot aim to be exhaustive, but the main grammatical structures of Hindi are all presented here. Learn as much as possible by heart and augment your vocabulary from other sources whenever you can. Hindi is not a particularly difficult language to learn and you will find your efforts amply rewarded by the warm reactions of the Hindi-speaking world. A note on further learning material is included in Exercise 18b.3, which you can read in translation in the Key to the exercises.

Acknowledgements

The authors wish to thank Dr A.S. Kalsi, Mr M.D. Mundhra and Dr R.D. Gupta for their invaluable comments and suggestions on the Hindi text.

RS and SCRW

Acknowledgements to the new edition

The number of students, teachers and other readers whose suggestions over the last decade have influenced the content of this second edition is too great for them all to be named individually. I am however particularly indebted to my friend Dr A.S. Kalsi for his close reading of the new text and for teaching me Hindi as we teach it together at the School of Oriental and African Studies; such colleagues are among the greatest boons of academic life. Professor Frances Pritchett of the University of Columbia also deserves special thanks.

The Macintosh fonts 'Jaisalmer' (Devanagari) and 'Taj' (roman with diacriticals) have been kindly provided by their designer, Professor K.E. Bryant of the University of British Columbia; and the illustrations to the dialogues are by Kavita Dutta. Sue Hart, of Hodder & Stoughton, has been the most supportive of commissioning editors. Many thanks to these people.

RS

The dialogues: meet the Kumar family

The 37 dialogues tell the story of the Kumar family, who live in Delhi, and their paying guest Pratap, who is from London; many of the exercises also form part of the same narrative.

Pratap (21) has come to India to study Hindi at a private college run by Sharma ji. Pratap's divorced mother Anita, living in London, has arranged for him to stay as a paying guest with the Kumars. The Kumar family consists of the strong-willed Kamala and her obedient husband Prakash, their daughter Sangeeta (19), sons Rishi (14) and Raj (12) and Prakash's elderly but spry mother, whom everybody addresses as Dadi ji ('Grandma'). Tensions between Kamala and Prakash are not helped by their shared concern about the future of Sangeeta: they would like to see her married, but she strongly cherishes her independence. Sweet-natured Dadi ji, meanwhile, has a calming effect on the whole family.

Prakash's younger brother, the aspiring author Arun, often stays with them; he speaks a rather Sanskritised or formal Hindi (whereas his co-author Prem speaks a Hindi liberally sprinkled with English). Suresh, a neighbour of the Kumars, is another frequent visitor; he is closer to Kamala than to Prakash.

Prakash works in a company recently taken over by Mr Khanna, who has a rather pathetic office peon called Chotu. Khanna's younger sister Pinkie is a close friend of Sangeeta Kumar. Khanna's son Harish, like Pratap, admires Sangeeta from afar; but Sangeeta's heart is engaged elsewhere.

THE HINDI SCRIPT AND SOUND SYSTEM

Hindi is written in the Devanagari script, which is also used by Marathi and Nepali and is the main script for Sanskrit (India's classical language). Devanagari is pronounced as it's written, so 'what you see is what you get'. This makes it quite easy to learn. The script is written from left to right and has no capital letters.

Vowels have two forms: an independent *character* used when a vowel stands at the beginning of a syllable, and a dependent *sign* used for a vowel immediately following a consonant. Here's an example:

आ is the independent character form of the long vowel *ā*, pronounced as in the English word 'calm'. Placed before the consonant म *m* it forms the word आम *ām*, 'mango'. But in the name 'Ram', the same vowel sound is written with its dependent form (the sign ा), because the vowel now follows 'r' (र) as part of the syllable *rā*: hence राम *Rām*.

Consonants that are *not* followed by a dependent vowel sign are automatically followed by the short vowel *a*, pronounced as in 'alive'. It's called the 'inherent vowel' because it is *inherent* in the consonant character. This is why the Hindi consonants in the following table are transliterated *ka, kha, ga* etc. and not *k, kh, g* etc. The inherent vowel can be cancelled by writing the sign ् (called *virām* or *halant*) below the consonant: क *ka*, क् *k*.

You may have noticed that no inherent vowel was shown just now after the *m* character in the name राम; this is because the inherent vowel is dropped at the end of a word (and sometimes elsewhere, as we shall see later on). But this dropping doesn't occur in Sanskrit, where the name राम has two full syllables – *Rāma*, not *Rām*.

Two important contrasts lie at the heart of correct Hindi pronunciation. First, you must distinguish between 'dental' and 'retroflex' consonants. Dental consonants are pronounced with the tip of the tongue touching the upper teeth, giving a 'soft' sound: Hindi तीन *tīn* 'three' has much softer consonants than English 'teen'. Retroflex consonants are pronounced with the tongue curled back to touch the roof of the mouth, which it touches further back than in English, giving a 'hard' sound: Hindi लूट *lūṭ* has a harder 't' than English 'loot' (which, incidentally, derives from the Hindi word). To Hindi-speakers, English consonants sound more retroflex than dental; so they'll pronounce 'David' as डेविड *ḍeviḍ*.

The second important contrast is in the amount of breath that's released when a consonant is pronounced: 'aspirated' consonants contrast with 'unaspirated' ones. The same effect sometimes occurs in English: put your hand in front of your mouth and say 'pit, spit' loudly (when alone!), and you'll probably feel that the 's' reduces the aspiration accompanying the adjacent 'p'. Hindi has several pairs of aspirated/unaspirated consonants; English-speakers must try hard to curb their aspiration in pronouncing the unaspirated ones (practise saying 'Panjab' and 'Pakistan' with minimum aspiration in the 'p').

When pronouncing Hindi vowels, English-speakers must take care to avoid English-style diphthongs: words like से *se* ('from') and को *ko* ('to') are pure vowels that can be held unchanged as long as you have breath to hold them (try it!); they must not be pronounced like 'say' and 'Co', in which the quality of the vowel changes as you utter it.

You should now practise the shapes of the Devanagari characters. Using lined paper, begin on the left of each character and follow through to the right, completing the character with the headstroke, which should fall on the printed line; your words should hang from the printed line like washing put out to dry, not standing on the lower line as the Roman script does. Maintain the overall proportions of the characters carefully, not letting them get too straggly; each one should fill two-thirds of the space between your printed lines.

The Devanagari syllabary

Independent vowel characters

अ *a*　　　आ *ā*　　　इ *i*　　　ई *ī*

उ *u*　　　ऊ *ū* ·　　ऋ *ṛ*

ए *e*　　　ऐ *ai*　　　ओ *o*　　　औ *au*

Consonants

क *ka*	ख *kha*	ग *ga*	घ *gha*	(ङ *ṅ*)*
च *ca*	छ *cha*	ज *ja*	झ *jha*	(ञ *ñ*)*
ट *ṭa*	ठ *ṭha*	ड *ḍa*	ढ *ḍha*	ण *ṇa*
त *ta*	थ *tha*	द *da*	ध *dha*	न *na*
प *pa*	फ *pha*	ब *ba*	भ *bha*	म *ma*
य *ya*	र *ra*	ल *la*	व *va*	
श *śa*	ष *ṣa*	स *sa*	ह *ha*	

*These bracketed forms rarely occur and can be ignored for now.

Dependent vowel signs, based on क as an example

क *ka*	का *kā*	कि *ki*	की *kī*
कु *ku*	कू *kū*	कृ *kṛ*	
के *ke*	कै *kai*	को *ko*	कौ *kau*

The Devanagari script and phonetics

The phonetic organisation of the Devanagari script was laid down by the grammarians of ancient India, who codified the Sanskrit language in order to preserve the effectiveness of its sacred mantras or prayer formulae. As a result, the main block of consonants from क *ka* to म *ma* has a very precise layout: the vertical columns show the *manner* of articulation (voiceless unaspirated and aspirated; voiced unaspirated and aspirated; nasal) while the horizontal rows show the *place* of articulation in the mouth (velar, palatal, retroflex, dental, labial).

Some Devanagari characters have 'dotted' versions which show sounds not occurring in Sanskrit. Thus the guide to pronunciation that follows includes seven characters that don't appear in the syllabary: क़ *qa*, ख़ *kha*, ग़ *ga*, ज़ *za*, ड़ *ṛa*, ढ़ *ṛha*, and फ़ *fa*. These characters are not distinguished in dictionary order from their undotted equivalents; and the dots are often omitted in both handwriting and print.

Vowels

Shown first in their independent forms, then in their dependent forms, again using the consonant क् by way of example.

अ	*a*	क	*ka*	as in 'alive'; inherent in any consonant not bearing a dependent vowel sign
आ	*ā*	का	*kā*	as in 'palm'
इ	*i*	कि	*ki*	as in 'hit'
ई	*ī*	की	*kī*	as in 'heat'
उ	*u*	कु	*ku*	as in 'foot'
ऊ	*ū*	कू	*kū*	as in 'fool'
ऋ	*ṛ*	कृ	*kṛ*	as 'ri' in 'critic'; in Sanskrit loanwords only
ए	*e*	के	*ke*	as in French *é*; a pure vowel sound, *not* a diphthong as in English
ऐ	*ai*	कै	*kai*	as in 'hen'
ओ	*o*	को	*ko*	as in the first part of 'o' in 'hotel'; a pure vowel sound, *not* a diphthong as in English

औ   *au*   कौ   *kau*   as in 'off'

A consonant can support only one dependent vowel. When two vowels appear in sequence, the second is written in its independent form: हुआ *huā*, जाओ *jāo*, लिए *lie*, कई *kaī*, दाऊद *dāūd*, etc.

The character र *ra* is something of a maverick; *ru* and *rū* have special forms – रु *ru*, and रू *rū*.

Velar consonants (produced in the throat)

क	*ka*	as in 'skit', with minimal release of breath
क़	*qa*	a 'k' sound produced further back than क *ka*
ख	*kha*	aspirated form of क *ka*: as in 'kit', but more aspirated
ख़	*kha*	as 'ch' in Scottish 'loch', or German 'Bach'
ग	*ga*	as in 'gift'
ग़	*ga*	a 'g' sound produced further back than ग *ga*
घ	*gha*	aspirated form of ग *ga*: as in 'dog-house'
ङ	*ṅ*	used only with a velar consonant; as in 'ink'; it is rarely seen in Hindi but is included here for completeness

Palatal consonants (produced at the palate)

च	*ca*	as in 'cheese', but with less release of breath
छ	*cha*	aspirated form of च *ca*: as in 'pitch-hook'
ज	*ja*	as in 'jeer'
ज़	*za*	as in 'zip'
झ	*jha*	aspirated form of ज *ja*: as in 'large house'.
ञ	*ñ*	used only with a palatal consonant; as in 'inch' – rarely seen, but included here for completeness

Retroflex consonants (tongue curls back to touch the palate: 'hard' sounds)

ट	*ṭa*	as in 'train', but harder
ठ	*ṭha*	aspirated form of ट *ṭa*; as in 'at home'
ड	*ḍa*	as in 'drum', but harder

ड़	*ṛa*	a flapped hard 'r'– the tongue makes a ड *ḍa* sound as it moves past the palate
ढ	*ḍha*	aspirated form of ड *ḍa*
ढ़	*ṛha*	flapped equivalent of ढ *ḍha*
ण	*ṇa*	the retroflex nasal; a hard 'n' sound

Dental consonants (tongue touches the upper teeth: 'soft' sounds)

त	*ta*	as in 'at' within the phrase 'at the'
थ	*tha*	aspirated form of त *ta*
द	*da*	as in 'breadth'
ध	*dha*	aspirated form of द *da*
न	*na*	the dental nasal: as in 'anthem'

Labial consonants (produced with the lips)

प	*pa*	as in 'spin', with minimal release of breath
फ	*pha*	like 'p' in 'pin', but more aspirated, as in 'top-hat'
ब	*ba*	as in 'bin'
भ	*bha*	aspirated form of ब *ba*: as in 'club-house'
म	*ma*	as in 'mother'

Semi-vowels etc.

य	*ya*	as in 'yet', but less tense
र	*ra*	as in 'roll'
ल	*la*	a dental 'l'; softer than the first 'l' in 'label', and *much* softer than the second
व	*va*	between English 'v' and 'w'; the teeth don't touch the lip as in 'vest', but neither are the lips rounded as in 'west'

Sibilants

श	*śa*	as 'sh' in 'ship'
ष	*ṣa*	a retroflex 'sh'; usually not distinguished from श *śa* in pronunciation (found in Sanskrit loanwords only)
स	*sa*	as in 'sip'

Aspirate

ह *ha*   This 'h' sound is always fully voiced, as in 'ahead'. It often 'lightens' an adjacent *a* vowel: both vowels in महल *mahal* ('palace') are similar to the 'e' in 'melt'.

Visarga

Visarga looks like a colon with widely spaced dots; it occurs without a headstroke within or at the end of a word, and is pronounced as ह *ha*. It's transliterated as *ḥ*, as in दुःख *duḥkh*, छः *chaḥ*. Mostly limited to Sanskrit loanwords.

Conjunct characters

Just when you thought you had mastered the script, along come the conjunct characters! When two consonants come in succession with no vowel between them, they are physically joined together as a 'conjunct'. In the word *sthān* ('place') for example, no vowel separates the 's' from the 'th', so स *sa* is reduced to a special half-form, स् *s*, which is attached to the following थ *th* to form स्थ *stha* (स्थान *sthān*). Without the conjunct, the word would be read as '*sathān*'.

Most conjuncts are formed on this principle; but some are a little more complicated, and some don't resemble either of their component parts.

As already noted, र *ra* is a bit of a wild card. As the first member of a conjunct it appears in the 'flying' form ˘ above the headstroke, as in धर्म *dharm* (let's be very clear: the 'r' *precedes* the 'm' here). It's written at the very end of the syllable that it precedes in pronunciation: शर्मा *śarmā*, बर्फ़ी *barfī*. As the second member of a conjunct its characteristic sign is ╱ as in प्र *pra*; but its location changes according to its partner:

प्र gra   ट्र ṭra   ड्र ḍra   त्र tra   श्र śra   स्र sra   ह्र hra

The common conjuncts are shown in the following tables. In the first column the consonants are written initially with the *halant* sign ╷ introduced earlier; it cancels the inherent vowel. This list is meant for reference: have a look through it to familiarise yourself with the basic principle, but don't feel you have to learn all the forms immediately. You will pick them up gradually, as you encounter them.

To begin with, here are all the conjuncts that appear in Unit 1

क् + य = क्य

क् + र = क्र, क्र

ग् + र = ग्र

च् + च = च्च

च् + छ = च्छ

त् + थ = त्थ

न् + द = न्द

प् + र = प्र

र् + त = र्त

र् + फ़ = र्फ़

र् + म = र्म

स् + त = स्त

And here is a list of the 100 most common conjuncts, numbered for convenience. (Two forms are regarded as independent characters in their own right: क्ष (क् + ष), pronounced 'ksha'; and ज्ञ (ज + ञ), pronounced 'gya'.)

1	क्	+	क	=	क्क	5	क्	+	र	=	क्र
2	क्	+	ख	=	क्ख	6	क्	+	ल	=	क्ल
3	क्	+	त	=	क्त, क्त	7	क्	+	व	=	क्व
4	क्	+	य	=	क्य	8	क्	+	श	=	क्श

9	क्	+	ष	=	क्ष	32	त्	+ त् + व	=	त्व
10	क्	+ ष् + म	=	क्ष्म	33	त्	+	थ	=	त्थ
11	क्	+	स	=	क्स	34	त्	+	न	=	त्न
12	ख्	+	य	=	ख्य	35	त्	+	म	=	त्म
13	ग्	+	द	=	ग्द	36	त्	+	य	=	त्य
14	ग्	+	न	=	ग्न	37	त्	+	र	=	त्र
15	ग्	+	र	=	ग्र	38	त्	+	व	=	त्व
16	ग्	+	ल	=	ग्ल	39	त्	+	स	=	त्स
17	ग्	+	व	=	ग्व	40	द्	+	ग	=	द्ग
18	घ्	+	र	=	घ्र	41	द्	+	द	=	द्द
19	च्	+	च	=	च्च	42	द्	+	ध	=	द्ध
20	च्	+	छ	=	च्छ	43	द्	+	भ	=	द्भ
21	ज्	+	ञ	=	ज्ञ	44	द्	+	म	=	द्म
22	ज्	+	र	=	ज्र	45	द्	+	य	=	द्य
23	ट्	+	ट	=	ट्ट	46	द्	+	र	=	द्र
24	ट्	+	ठ	=	ट्ठ	47	द्	+	व	=	द्व
25	ट्	+	र	=	ट्र	48	ध्	+	य	=	ध्य
26	ड्	+	ड	=	ड्ड	49	ध्	+	व	=	ध्व
27	ड्	+	र	=	ड्र	50	न्	+	त	=	न्त
28	ण्	+	ट	=	ण्ट	51	न्	+	द	=	न्द
29	ण्	+	ठ	=	ण्ठ	52	न्	+ द् + र	=	न्द्र
30	त्	+	क	=	त्क	53	न्	+	न	=	न्न, न्न
31	त्	+	त	=	त्त	54	न्	+	य	=	न्य

55	न्	+	ह	=	न्ह	78	श्	+	क	=	श्क
56	प्	+	त	=	प्त	79	श्	+	च	=	श्च, श्र
57	प्	+	न	=	प्न	80	श्	+	य	=	श्य
58	प्	+	प	=	प्प	81	श्	+	र	=	श्र
59	प्	+	य	=	प्य	82	श्	+	व	=	श्व, श्व
60	प्	+	र	=	प्र	83	ष्	+	ट	=	ष्ट, ष्ट
61	प्	+	ल	=	प्ल	84	ष्	+ ट् + र		=	ष्ट्र
62	ब्	+	ज	=	ब्ज	85	ष्	+	ण	=	ष्ण
63	ब्	+	द	=	ब्द	86	स्	+	क	=	स्क
64	ब्	+	ध	=	ब्ध	87	स्	+	ट	=	स्ट
65	ब्	+	र	=	ब्र	88	स्	+	त	=	स्त
66	भ्	+	य	=	भ्य	89	स्	+ त् + र		=	स्त्र
67	भ्	+	र	=	भ्र	90	स्	+	थ	=	स्थ
68	म्	+	न	=	म्न	91	स्	+	न	=	स्न
69	म्	+	र	=	म्र	92	स्	+	प	=	स्प
70	र्	+	त	=	र्त	93	स्	+	य	=	स्य
71	र्	+	थ	=	र्थ	94	स्	+	र	=	स्र
72	र्	+	म	=	र्म	95	ह्	+	न	=	ह्न
73	र्	+	फ	=	र्फ	96	ह्	+	म	=	ह्म
74	र्	+	व	=	र्व	97	ह्	+	य	=	ह्य
75	र्	+	स	=	र्स	98	ह्	+	र	=	ह्र
76	ल्	+	म	=	ल्म	99	ह्	+	ल	=	ह्ल
77	व्	+	र	=	व्र	100	ह्	+	व	=	ह्व

Nasalised vowels, and conjuncts beginning with *n* or *m*

Any Hindi vowel (except ऋ *ṛ*) can be nasalised – some of the breath flows through the nose. Nasalised vowels bear the sign ⁀, a moon and a dot, called *candrabindu* (*candra* 'moon', *bindu* 'dot', logically enough!). This is transliterated with a tilde (~) as in मुँह *mūh* 'mouth, face', and हाँ *hā̃* 'yes'.

Any vowel sign that protrudes above the headline eclipses the *candra* moon, so the *bindu* dot has to appear alone – नहीं *nahī̃* 'no', हैं *haĩ* 'are'. Some people replace *candrabindu* with *bindu* for all nasalised vowels, writing हां for हाँ *hā̃*. Should you do this? नहीं *nahī̃* 'No'! Should you write *candrabindu* in full where there's no superscript vowel? हाँ *hā̃* 'Yes'!

The *bindu* dot has a second function: it can replace any of the nasal consonants (ङ, ञ, ण, न, म) when they appear as the *first* member of a conjunct. Note its position in the following:

रंग	=	रङ्ग	*raṅg*	colour
पंजाब	=	पञ्जाब	*pañjāb*	Panjab
अंडा	=	अण्डा	*āṇḍā*	egg
हिंदी	=	हिन्दी	*hindī*	Hindi
लंबा	=	लम्बा	*lambā*	long, tall

Both spellings are correct and either may be used freely – although in the first two pairs, the simple *anusvār* forms (रंग, पंजाब) are *much* more common than their complicated alternatives. In this book, no special symbol is used for *anusvār*: both हिन्दी and हिंदी are transliterated as '*hindī*'.

Pronunciation

Do try to use the cassette, or better still get help from a native speaker, when practising pronunciation. Some watchpoints:

1   Short and long vowels in the pairs *a/ā*, *i/ī*, *u/ū* must be clearly distinguished, especially the *a/ā* pair as in कम *kam* 'less' / काम *kām* 'work'; दल *dal* 'political party' / दाल *dāl* 'lentils'.

2   A doubled consonant is 'held' momentarily – as in English 'night train', whose 't...t' is held to distinguish it from 'night

rain'. So बच्चा *baccā* 'child' sounds different from बचा *bacā* 'survived'. The same effect occurs with repeated sounds in adjacent words: उस से *us se* 'from that' sounds different from उसे *use* 'to that'.

3   As we've seen, the inherent vowel is not pronounced at the end of a word. But there's an exception: it may be lightly pronounced when the word ends in a conjunct. Thus मित्र *mitr(a)* 'friend', अवश्य *avaśy(a)* 'of course'.

4   There are occasions when an inherent vowel is not pronounced in the *middle* of a word, even though the spelling involves no conjunct. As a general rule, the inherent vowel remains silent in the second syllable of a word whose third character either includes a vowel sign (thus समझ *samajh* 'understanding', but समझा *samjhā* 'understood') or is followed by a fourth syllable (thus मानव *mānav* 'human being', but जानवर *jānvar* 'animal'). This rule does not apply when the second or third syllable of the word has a conjunct.

5   Inherent vowel + य *ya*, as in समय *samay* 'time' and जय *jay* 'victory', is pronounced *ai* (indeed, the spellings समै *samai* and जै *jai* were once current).

6   The pattern of stress across a sentence is more even in Hindi than in English – emphasis is usually carried by the addition of 'particles' (short indeclinable words) rather than through the voice.

Punctuation and other signs

The 'full stop' is a vertical line (।) called *daṇḍ* 'stick' or *kharī pāī* 'perpendicular line'. Other punctuation follows English usage.

In writing abbreviations, a small circle (०) follows the first entire *akṣar* or syllable of the abbreviated word:

उ० प्र०	=	उत्तर प्रदेश Uttar Pradesh
पं० गो० ना० शर्मा	=	पंडित गोपाल नारायण शर्मा
		Pandit Gopal Narayan Sharma

The ० is dropped when the initials cohere as an acronym:

भाजपा	=	भारतीय जनता पार्टी
		Bharatiya Janata Party
नभाटा	=	नवभारत टाइम्स
		NavBharat Times (newspaper)

Sometimes abbreviations are merely transliterations of the English:

यू० पी०	=	(*yū. pī.*)	UP
जी० एन० शर्मा	=	(*jī. en. śarmā*	G.N. Sharma
बी० जे० पी०	=	(*bī. je. pī*	BJP

English 'o' sounds as in 'chocolate' or 'sorry' are pronounced by some Hindi speakers as similar to *ā*; and Devanagari spellings of such sounds may use a special *candra* character (without dot) over the vowel: चॉकलेट, सॉरी.

Alternative spellings

ए *e* following a vowel in verb endings can have different forms (the standard form is shown in the left-hand column):

जाए *jae*	=	जाये *jāye,* जाय *jāy* may go
जाइए *jāie*	=	जाइये *jāiy* please go
चाहिए *cāhie*	=	चाहिये *cāhiye* needed

The use of conjuncts in loans from Persian is not fully standardised:

उमर *umar*	=	उम्र *umr* age
गरम *garam*	=	गर्म *garm* warm, hot
परदा *pardā*	=	पर्दा *pardā* curtain, purdah

Numerals

०	१	२	३	४	५	६	७	८	९
0	1	2	3	4	5	6	7	8	9

The so-called 'Arabic' numerals (which originated in India!) are used at least as commonly as the Devanagari numerals.

Dictionary order

The dictionary order of the script follows the pattern shown in the Devanagari syllabary section, reading horizontally. Three principles apply:

1   Syllables with *candrabindu* or *anusvār* precede those without: गाँव *gā̃v* 'village' precedes गाड़ी *gāṛī* 'train, car', and तंग *tang* 'narrow' precedes तक *tak* 'up to'.

2   Non-conjunct forms precede conjunct forms: छाता *chātā* 'umbrella' precedes छात्र *chātr* 'pupil', and बचा *bacā* 'survived' precedes बच्चा *baccā* 'child'.

3   'Dotted' forms (e.g. क़ *qa*, ड़ *ṛa*, ज़ *za*) are not distinguished in sequence from 'undotted' equivalents (क *ka*, ड *ḍa*, ज *ja*).

Note: Transcriptions of the Hindi sounds on the cassette are given at the beginning of the Key to the exercises on page 260.

1 | I AM PRATAP
मैं प्रताप हूँ

In this unit you will learn how to
- greet and identify people
- ask and answer 'yes/no' questions
- ask people how they are
- use adjectives

1a   Pratap, from London, meets his Delhi host

प्रताप	नमस्ते । मैं प्रताप हूँ । क्या आप कमला जी हैं ?
कमला	जी हाँ, मैं कमला हूँ । नमस्ते । यह लड़का राज है ।
प्रताप	नमस्ते राज । तुम ठीक हो ?
राज	जी हाँ, शुक्रिया, मैं ठीक हूँ । क्या आप अँग्रेज़ हैं ?
प्रताप	जी नहीं, मैं अँग्रेज़ नहीं हूँ, हिन्दुस्तानी हूँ ।

राज	अच्छा, आप हिन्दुस्तानी हैं !
प्रताप	जी हाँ । क्या वह गाड़ी जापानी है ?
राज	नहीं, वह जापानी नहीं है, वह मारुति है ।

Pratāp	*namaste. maĩ Pratāp hũ. kyā āp Kamalā jī haĩ?*
Kamalā	*jī hā̃, maĩ Kamalā hũ. namaste. yah laṛkā Rāj hai.*
Pratāp	*namaste Rāj. tum ṭhīk ho?*
Rāj	*jī hā̃, śukriyā, maĩ ṭhīk hũ. kyā āp āgrez haĩ?*
Pratāp	*jī nahĩ, maĩ āgrez nahĩ hũ, hindustānī hũ.*
Rāj	*acchā, āp hindustānī haĩ!*
Pratāp	*jī hā̃. kyā vah gāṛī jāpānī hai?*
Rāj	*nahĩ, vah jāpānī nahĩ hai, vah Māruti hai.*

नमस्ते	*namaste*	hello	हो	*ho*	are
मैं	*maĩ*	I	शुक्रिया	*śukriyā*	thank you
हूँ	*hũ*	am	अँग्रेज़	*āgrez*	English
क्या	*kyā*	question-marker	जी नहीं	*jī nahĩ*	no
आप	*āp*	you (formal)	नहीं	*nahĩ*	not
जी	*jī*	respect-marker	हिन्दुस्तानी	*hindustānī*	Indian
हैं	*haĩ*	are	अच्छा	*acchā*	good, really?, I see!
यह	*yah*	this	हाँ	*hā̃*	yes
लड़का ^m	*laṛkā*	boy	वह	*vah*	it, that
है	*hai*	is	गाड़ी ^f	*gāṛī*	car
तुम	*tum*	you (familiar)	जापानी	*jāpānī*	Japanese
ठीक	*ṭhīk*	all right	मारुति ^f	*māruti*	Maruti (make of car)

Pratap	Hello, I am Pratap. Are you Kamala ji?
Kamala	Yes, I'm Kamala. Hello. This boy is Raj.
Pratap	Hello Raj. Are you OK?
Raj	Yes, thank you, I'm OK. Are you English?
Pratap	No, I'm not English, I'm Indian.
Raj	Oh, you're Indian!
Pratap	Yes. Is that car Japanese?
Raj	No, it's not Japanese, it's a Maruti.

Grammar

1.1   Personal pronouns and the verb 'to be'

SINGULAR			PLURAL		
मैं हूँ	*maĩ hũ*	I am	हम हैं	*ham haĩ*	we are
तू है	*tū hai*	you are (intimate)	तुम हो	*tum ho*	you are (familiar)
			आप हैं	*āp haĩ*	you are (formal)
यह है	*yah hai*	he, she, it, this is	ये हैं	*ye haĩ*	these, they are; he, she is (formal)
वह है	*vah hai*	he, she, it, that is	वे हैं	*ve haĩ*	those, they are; he, she is (formal)

Hindi has a subtle system of 'honorific' levels – like French tu/vous, or German du/Sie. There are three second-person pronouns, each with its own verb form as shown in the table.

तू *tū*   indicates great intimacy and is used in addressing a close loved one or a small child.

तुम *tum*   is informal and casual and is used with a person expecting no formality or deference – a friend, child or servant.

आप *āp*   is relatively formal; it indicates the respect one shows towards equals (and above!) and is the natural choice in conversations with all people not falling into the previous categories.

Both तुम *tum* and आप *āp* are grammatically plural; but either may indicate several people (numerical plural) or a single individual (honorific plural).

The honorific system extends into the third person: when referring to a person whom you would address face-to-face as आप *āp*, use the plural forms ये *ye* / वे *ve*.

यह *yah* and its plural ये *ye* refer to a subject that's nearby, while वह *vah* (which is often pronounced '*vo*') and वे *ve* refer to a subject that's more remote – rather like English 'this' and 'that'. Unless a specific sense of 'nearness' is involved, use वह/ वे *vah/ve*.

The honorific system can indicate disdain as well as respect: to use
a lower-grade honorific than expected by the person you're talking
to can imply severe disrespect. So you must observe the usages of
others and learn from them. When in doubt, stick to आप *āp*!

मैं गुजराती हूँ ।	*maĩ gujarātī hū̃.*	I am Gujarati.
वह जर्मन है ।	*vah jarman hai.*	He/she is German.
हम पंजाबी हैं ।	*ham panjābī haĩ.*	We are Panjabi.
तुम अँग्रेज़ हो ?	*tum ãgrez ho?*	You're English?
आप हिन्दुस्तानी हैं ।	*āp hindustānī haĩ.*	You are Indian.
वे भारतीय हैं ।	*ve bhāratīy haĩ.*	They are Indian. (or He/she is Indian.)

1.2   Questions and answers

Questions expecting a 'yes/no' answer are formed by simply
prefixing a statement with क्या *kyā*:

तुम ठीक हो ।	*tum ṭhīk ho.*	You're OK. (statement)
क्या तुम ठीक हो ?	*kyā tum ṭhīk ho?*	Are you OK? (question)

In speech, a question can be conveyed by a rising tone, as in English:

तुम ठीक हो ?	*tum ṭhīk ho?*	You're OK?

▶ 1b   Kamala shows Pratap his room

प्रताप	यह कमरा बहुत बड़ा है ! क्या दूसरे कमरे छोटे हैं ?
कमला	जी नहीं । सिर्फ़ एक कमरा छोटा है, दूसरे बड़े हैं ।
प्रताप	क्या यह बड़ी अलमारी ख़ाली है ?
कमला	जी हाँ, ज़रूर, दोनों अलमारियाँ ख़ाली हैं ।
प्रताप	और यहाँ एक मेज़ और दो कुरसियाँ हैं । क्या पंखा नहीं है ?
कमला	पंखा नहीं है; लेकिन खिड़की काफ़ी बड़ी है ।
प्रताप	बहुत अच्छा । कमरा साफ़ और बहुत हवादार है ।

Pratāp	*yah kamrā bahut baṛā hai! kyā dūsre kamre choṭe haĩ?*
Kamalā	*jī nahī̃. sirf ek kamrā choṭā hai, dūsre baṛe haĩ.*

Pratāp	kyā yah baṛī almārī <u>kh</u>ālī hai?
Kamalā	jī hã, zarūr, donõ almāriyã <u>kh</u>ālī haĩ.
Pratāp	aur yahã ek mez aur do kursiyã haĩ. kyā pankhā nahĩ hai?
Kamalā	pankhā nahĩ hai; lekin khiṛkī kāfī baṛī hai.
Pratāp	bahut acchā. kamrā sāf aur bahut havādār hai.

कमरा^m	kamrā	room	और	aur	and
बहुत	bahut	very	यहाँ	yahã	here
बड़ा	baṛā	big	मेज़^f	mez	table
दूसरा	dūsrā	other	दो	do	two
छोटा	choṭā	small	कुरसी^f	kursī	chair
सिर्फ़	sirf	only	पंखा^m	pankhā	fan
एक	ek	one, a	लेकिन	lekin	but
अलमारी^f	almārī	cupboard	खिड़की^f	khiṛkī	window
ख़ाली	<u>kh</u>ālī	empty, vacant	काफ़ी	kāfī	quite
ज़रूर	zarūr	of course	साफ़	sāf	clean
दोनों	donõ	both	हवादार	havādār	airy

Pratap	This room is very big! Are the other rooms small?
Kamala	No. Only one room is small, the others are big.
Pratap	Is this big cupboard empty?
Kamala	Yes, of course, both cupboards are empty.
Pratap	And here there's a table and two chairs. Isn't there a fan?
Kamala	There's no fan; but the window is quite big.
Pratap	Very good. The room is clean and very airy.

Grammar

1.3 Nouns

Hindi nouns are either masculine or feminine; the gender of every new noun must be learnt. There is no definite article 'the'; एक *ek*, the number 'one', sometimes functions as the indefinite article 'a'.

Masculine nouns are of two types: those ending -*ā* in the singular, changing to -*e* in the plural; and all others, which are the same in both singular and plural.

Masculine type 1

| लड़का | *laṛkā* | boy | लड़के | *laṛke* | boys |
| कमरा | *kamrā* | room | कमरे | *kamre* | rooms |

Masculine type 2

| मकान | *makān* | house | मकान | *makān* | houses |
| आदमी | *ādmī* | man | आदमी | *ādmī* | men |

Not all nouns ending in *-ā* are masculine: many Sanskrit loanwords such as आशा *āśā* 'hope' and भाषा *bhāṣā* 'language' (and names like कमला *Kamalā*) are feminine. A few masculines ending in *-ā* belong to type 2 and therefore don't change in the plural; these are mostly relationship terms like पिता *pitā* 'father', चाचा *cācā* 'uncle' – but also राजा *rājā* 'king'.

Feminine nouns are also of two types: those ending *-ī*, *-i* or *-iyā* in the singular, all changing to *-iyā̃* in the plural; and all others, which add *-ẽ* in the plural.

Feminine type 1

लड़की	*laṛkī*	girl	लड़कियाँ	*laṛkiyā̃*	girls
प्रति	*prati*	copy (of book)	प्रतियाँ	*pratiyā̃*	copies
चिड़िया	*ciṛiyā*	bird	चिड़ियाँ	*ciṛiyā̃*	birds

Feminine type 2

| मेज़ | *mez* | table | मेज़ें | *mezẽ* | tables |
| माता | *mātā* | mother | माताएँ | *mātāẽ* | mothers |

Feminine nouns ending *-ū* are of type 2, but shorten the *-ū* to *-u-* in the plural: बहू *bahū* 'daughter-in-law', बहुएँ *bahuẽ* 'daughters-in-law'.

 आदमी   *ādmī* 'man' derives from Arabic and means 'descendant of Adam'; compare मानव *mānav* 'man, human being', derived from Sanskrit and meaning 'descendant of Manu' (the progenitor of the world in Hindu belief).

1.4 Adjectives

Adjectives agree with the nouns they qualify. They are of two types: those that inflect (change their endings), and those that are invariable.

Inflecting adjectives follow the pattern of बड़ा *baṛā* 'big': *-ā* masculine singular, *-e* masculine plural, *-ī* feminine singular and plural.

बड़ा लड़का	*baṛā laṛkā*	big boy
बड़े लड़के	*baṛe laṛke*	big boys
बड़ी लड़की	*baṛī laṛkī*	big girl
बड़ी लड़कियाँ	*baṛī laṛkiyā̃*	big girls
छोटा मकान	*choṭā makān*	small house
छोटे मकान	*choṭe makān*	small houses
छोटी मेज़	*choṭī mez*	small table
छोटी मेज़ें	*choṭī mezē̃*	small tables

Invariable adjectives, of course, remain unchanged:

ख़ाली कमरा	*khālī kamrā*	vacant room
ख़ाली कमरे	*khālī kamre*	vacant rooms
लाल कुरसी	*lāl kursī*	red chair
लाल कुरसियाँ	*lāl kursiyā̃*	red chairs
सुन्दर मकान	*sundar makān*	beautiful house
सुन्दर मकान	*sundar makān*	beautiful houses
साफ़ मेज़	*sāf mez*	clean table
साफ़ मेज़ें	*sāf mezē̃*	clean tables

One or two adjectives ending *-ā*, such as बढ़िया *baṛhiyā* 'excellent', are invariable; these are marked 'inv.' in the Glossary.

1.5 The simple sentence

A typical sentence begins with the subject and ends with the verb. The question-word क्या *kyā* usually precedes the subject; the negative नहीं *nahī̃* precedes the verb.

क्या यह मूर्ति है ?	*kyā yah mūrti hai?* Is this a statue?
यह मूर्ति नहीं है । पत्थर है ।	*yah mūrti nahī̃ hai. patthar hai.*
	It's not a statue. It's a stone.

The last example shows how a pronoun can be dropped if its reference is entirely clear: [यह] पत्थर है *[yah] patthar hai*. Similarly a verb can be dropped when negated: मैं अमरीकन नहीं [हूँ], रूसी हूँ *maĩ amrīkan nahī̃ [hū̃], rūsī hū̃* 'I'm not American, I'm Russian'.

Word order: note the very important difference in meaning between the following:

यह कमरा बड़ा है।	*yah kamrā baṛā hai.*	This room is big.
यह बड़ा कमरा है।	*yah baṛā kamrā hai.*	This is a big room.

The first sentence answers the question 'What is this room like?', and gives the information 'big'; the second answers the question 'What is this?', and gives the information 'a big room'.

☑ **EXERCISE 1a**   Fill the gap with हूँ *hū̃*, हो *ho*, है *hai*, or हैं *haĩ*. Then translate.

१   वह आदमी पंजाबी... ।

२   क्या ये आदमी पाकिस्तानी... ?

३   राज, तू अच्छा लड़का नहीं... ।

४   मैं जर्मन नहीं... , रूसी... ।

५   हम लोग हिन्दू नहीं... , लेकिन यह आदमी हिन्दू... ।

६   पीटर, क्या तुम अँग्रेज़... ? नहीं, मैं जर्मन... ।

७   क्या तुम दोनों अँग्रेज़... ? नहीं, हम अमरीकन... ।

८   सुशीला गुजराती... , लेकिन सुशील और रवि दोनों पंजाबी... ।

९   क्या आप प्रताप...ˑ ? जी हाँ, मैं प्रताप... ।

१०   क्या वे दो आदमी जर्मन... ? नहीं, वे अँग्रेज़... ।

1   *vah ādmī panjābī... .*
2   *kyā ye ādmī pākistānī... ?*
3   *Rāj, tū acchā laṛkā nahī̃... .*
4   *maĩ jarman nahī̃... , rūsī... .*
5   *ham log hindū nahī̃... , lekin yah ādmī hindu... .*
6   *Pīṭar, kyā tum ãgrez... ? nahī̃, maĩ jarman... .*
7   *kyā tum donõ ãgrez... ? nahī̃, ham amrīkan... .*
8   *Suśīlā gujarātī... , lekin Suśīl aur Ravi donõ panjābī... .*
9   *kyā āp Pratāp... ? jī hā̃, maĩ Pratāp... .*
10   *kyā ve do ādmī jarman... ? nahī̃, ve ãgrez... .*

EXERCISE 1b   Translate this entry from Pratap's diary.

रविवार, १५ जनवरी

कमला और प्रकाश कुमार बहुत अच्छे लोग हैं । तीन बच्चे हैं — एक लड़की,
संगीता, और दो लड़के, ऋषि और राज । संगीता बहुत सुन्दर है ।ऋषि बड़ा
है, राज छोटा है । दादी जी बूढ़ी हैं लेकिन बहुत अच्छी हैं ।मकान साफ़ है और
बग़ीचा बहुत सुन्दर है । मेरा कमरा काफ़ी बड़ा है । एक पलंग, दो अलमारियाँ
(दोनों ख़ाली), एक छोटी मेज़, दो कुरसियाँ हैं । पंखा नहीं है, लेकिन कमरा
हवादार है । एक सफ़ेद मारुति गाड़ी और दो-तीन पुरानी साइकिलें हैं ।

ravivār, 15 janvarī
Kamalā aur Prakāś Kumār bahut acche log haĩ. tīn bacce haĩ – ek laṛkī,
Saṅgītā, aur do laṛke, Ṛṣi aur Rāj. Saṅgītā bahut sundar hai. Ṛṣi baṛā
hai, Rāj choṭā hai. dādī jī būṛhī haĩ lekin bahut acchī haĩ. makān sāf hai aur
bagīcā bahut sundar hai. merā kamrā kāfī baṛā hai. ek palaṅg, do almāriyā̃
(donõ khālī), ek choṭī mez, do kursiyā̃ haĩ. paṅkhā nahī̃ hai, lekin kamrā
havādār hai. ek safed Māruti gāṛī aur do-tīn purānī sāikilē haĩ.

Vocabulary

अँग्रेज़ ^{m, f}	*āgrez*	English person	क्या	*kyā*	(question-marker)
अच्छा *acchā*		good, nice; really?, o I see!	ख़ाली	*khālī*	empty, vacant
अमरीकन	*amrīkan*	American	खिड़की ^f	*khiṛkī*	window
अलमारी ^f	*almārī*	cupboard	गाड़ी ^f	*gāṛī*	car
आदमी ^m	*ādmī*	man, person	गुजराती	*gujarātī*	Gujarati
आप	*āp*	you (formal)	चाचा ^m	*cācā*	paternal uncle
आशा ^f	*āśā*	hope	चिड़िया ^f	*ciṛiyā*	bird
और	*aur*	and	छोटा	*choṭā*	small
एक	*ek*	one, a	जनवरी ^f	*janvarī*	January
कमरा ^m	*kamrā*	room	ज़रूर	*zarūr*	of course, certainly
काफ़ी	*kāfī*	quite	जर्मन	*jarman*	German
कुरसी ^f	*kursī*	chair	जापानी	*jāpānī*	Japanese
			जी	*jī*	(respect-marker)

अँग्रेज़ ^{m, f} *āgrez* English person
अच्छा *acchā* good, nice; really?, o I see!
अमरीकन *amrīkan* American
अलमारी ^f *almārī* cupboard
आदमी ^m *ādmī* man, person
आप *āp* you (formal)
आशा ^f *āśā* hope
और *aur* and
एक *ek* one, a
कमरा ^m *kamrā* room
काफ़ी *kāfī* quite
कुरसी ^f *kursī* chair

क्या *kyā* (question-marker)
ख़ाली *khālī* empty, vacant
खिड़की ^f *khiṛkī* window
गाड़ी ^f *gāṛī* car
गुजराती *gujarātī* Gujarati
चाचा ^m *cācā* paternal uncle
चिड़िया ^f *ciṛiyā* bird
छोटा *choṭā* small
जनवरी ^f *janvarī* January
ज़रूर *zarūr* of course, certainly
जर्मन *jarman* German
जापानी *jāpānī* Japanese
जी *jī* (respect-marker)

जी नहीं　*jī nahī̃*　no
जी हाँ　*jī hā̃*　yes
ठीक　*ṭhīk*　all right, OK
तीन　*tīn*　three
तुम　*tum*　you (familiar)
तू　*tū*　you (intimate)
दादी ^f　*dādī*　grandmother
दूसरा　*dūsrā*　other, second
दो　*do*　two
दोनों　*donō̃*　both
नमस्ते　*namaste*　hello; goodbye
नहीं　*nahī̃*　not
पंखा ^m　*pankhā*　fan
पंजाबी　*panjābī*　Panjabi
पत्थर ^m　*patthar*　stone
पलंग ^m　*palang*　bed
पाकिस्तानी　*pākistānī*　Pakistani
पिता ^m　*pitā*　father
पुराना　*purānā*　old (of things)
प्रति ^f　*prati*　copy
बग़ीचा ^m　*bagīcā*　garden
बच्चा ^m　*baccā*　child
बड़ा　*baṛā*　big
बहुत　*bahut*　very
बहू ^f　*bahū*　daughter-in-law
बूढ़ा　*būṛhā*　elderly
भारतीय　*bhāratīy*　Indian
भाषा ^f　*bhāṣā*　language
मकान ^m　*makān*　house
माता ^f　*mātā*　mother

मानव ^m　*mānav*　human being
मारुति ^f　*māruti*　Maruti (car make)
मूर्ति ^f　*mūrti*　statue, image
मेज़ ^f　*mez*　table
मैं　*maī̃*　I
यह　*yah*　this, he, she, it
यहाँ　*yahā̃*　here
ये　*ye*　these, they; he, she (formal)
रविवार ^m　*ravivār*　Sunday
राजा ^m　*rājā*　king
रूसी　*rūsī*　Russian
लड़का ^m　*laṛkā*　boy
लड़की ^f　*laṛkī*　girl
लाल　*lāl*　red
लोग ^{m. pl}　*log*　people
वह　*vah*　that, he, she, it
वे　*ve*　those, they; he, she (formal)
शुक्रिया　*śukriyā*　thank you
सफ़ेद　*safed*　white
साइकिल ^f　*sāikil*　bicycle
साफ़　*sāf*　clean
सिर्फ़　*sirf*　only
सुन्दर　*sundar*　beautiful
हम　*ham*　we
हवादार　*havādār*　airy
हाँ　*hā̃*　yes
हिन्दुस्तानी　*hindustānī*　Indian
हिन्दू　*hindū*　Hindu
हूँ　*hū̃*　am; है *hai* is; हैं *haĩ* are;
हो *ho*　are

2 | QUESTIONS AND ANSWERS

सवाल और जवाब

In this unit you will learn how to

■ ask and answer questions about quality and number
■ describe things
■ use adjectives
■ use conversational conventions

2a   Pratap in his Hindi teacher's office

प्रताप	अध्यापक जी, यहाँ कितने विद्यार्थी हैं ?
शर्मा जी	अभी चौदह हैं – नौ लड़कियाँ और पाँच लड़के ।
प्रताप	यह "टीच योरसेल्फ़ हिन्दी" कैसी किताब है ? क्या यह अच्छी है ?
शर्मा जी	हाँ, बुरी नहीं है । लेकिन सस्ती नहीं है, काफ़ी महँगी है ।
प्रताप	क्या ये शब्दकोश भी महँगे हैं ?
शर्मा जी	नहीं, बिलकुल नहीं । बहुत सस्ते हैं ।

प्रताप	और वह मोटी किताब क्या है ? क्या वह भी शब्दकोश है ?
शर्मा जी	नहीं नहीं, वह शब्दकोश नहीं है, रामायण है !

Pratāp	*adhyāpak jī, yahā̃ kitne vidyārthī haĩ ?*
Śarmā jī	*abhī caudah haĩ – nau laṛkiyā̃ aur pā̃c laṛke.*
Pratāp	*yah 'ṭīc yorself hindī' kaisī kitāb hai? kyā yah acchī hai?*
Śarmā jī	*hā̃, burī nahī̃ hai. lekin sastī nahī̃ hai, kāfī mahā̃gī hai.*
Pratāp	*kyā ye śabdkoś bhī mahā̃ge haĩ?*
Śarmā jī	*nahī̃, bilkul nahī̃. bahut saste haĩ.*
Pratāp	*aur vah moṭī kitāb kyā hai? kyā vah bhī śabdkoś hai?*
Śarmā jī	*nahī̃ nahī̃, vah śabdkoś nahī̃ hai, rāmāyaṇ hai!*

अध्यापक ^m	*adhyāpak*	teacher	सस्ता *sastā*	cheap
कितना	*kitnā*	how much/many	महँगा *mahā̃gā*	expensive
विद्यार्थी ^{m, f}	*vidyārthī*	student	शब्दकोश ^m *śabdkoś*	dictionary
अभी	*abhī*	at the moment, just now	भी *bhī*	also, too
चौदह	*caudah*	fourteen	बिलकुल *bilkul*	quite
नौ	*nau*	nine	बिलकुल नहीं *bilkul nahī̃*	not at all
पाँच	*pā̃c*	five	मोटा *moṭā*	fat, thick
कैसा	*kaisā*	of what kind, what like	क्या *kyā*	what
किताब ^f	*kitāb*	book	रामायण ^m *rāmāyaṇ*	Ramayan
बुरा	*burā*	bad		(epic poem)

Pratap	Teacher ji, how many students are there here?
Sharma ji	At the moment there are 14 – nine girls and five boys.
Pratap	What kind of book is this *Teach Yourself Hindi*? Is it good?
Sharma ji	Yes, it's not bad. But it's not cheap, it's quite expensive.
Pratap	Are these dictionaries also expensive?
Sharma ji	No, not at all. They're very cheap.
Pratap	And what is that thick book? Is it a dictionary too?
Sharma ji	No no, it's not a dictionary, it's the Ramayan!

Grammar

2.1 Interrogative words

Interrogative words – often beginning 'wh' in English – begin with क् *k* in Hindi:

क्या	*kyā*	what?
कौन	*kaun*	who?
कैसा/ कैसी/ कैसे	*kaisā/kaisī/kaise*	of what kind?
कितना/ कितनी/ कितने	*kitnā/ kitnī/ kitne*	how much, how many?

 क्या *kyā* 'what?' has a different role here from the 'yes-no' question-maker role that we met in 1.2.

यह क्या है ?	*yah kyā hai?*	What is this?
तुम कौन हो ?	*tum kaun ho?*	Who are you?
मौसम कैसा है ?	*mausam kaisā hai?*	What's the weather like?
कितने विद्यार्थी हैं ?	*kitne vidyārthī haĩ?*	How many students are there?

 मौसम *mausam*, an Arabic loanword, is the ultimate source of the English word 'monsoon'.

2.2 Agreement of adjectives with mixed genders

A plural adjective qualifying a group of people of mixed gender is masculine:

| ऋषि और संगीता लंबे हैं । | *Ṛṣi aur Saṅgītā lambe haĩ.* Rishi and Sangeeta are tall. |
| राज और कमला दुबले नहीं हैं । | *Rāj aur Kamalā duble nahī̃ haĩ.* Raj and Kamala are not thin. |

With inanimate nouns of mixed gender, a plural adjective agrees with the nearest noun:

| ये चप्पलें और जूते गंदे हैं । | *ye cappalē aur jūte gande haĩ.* These sandals and shoes are dirty. |
| वे काग़ज़ और चिट्ठियाँ पुरानी हैं । | *ve kāgaz aur ciṭṭhiyā̃ purānī haĩ.* Those papers and letters are old. |

In the first sentence, गंदे *gande* agrees with masculine plural जूते *jūte*; and in the second sentence, पुरानी *purānī* agrees with feminine plural चिट्ठियाँ *ciṭṭhiyā̃*.

> ❗ Learning a new noun *with* an adjective helps you learn the noun's gender: अच्छी किताब *acchī kitāb*, बड़ा मकान *baṛā makān*, and so on.

💬 2b   Pratap's little problem

प्रताप	हलो राज, क्या हाल है ? सब ठीक है ?
राज	हाँ, सब ठीक है । और आप कैसे हैं ?
प्रताप	मैं भी अच्छा हूँ, शुक्रिया । ऋषि और संगीता कैसे हैं ?
राज	ऋषि अच्छा है, लेकिन संगीता अच्छी नहीं है ।
प्रताप	क्यों ? क्या बात है ? क्या वह बीमार है ?
राज	नहीं, वह नाराज़ है क्योंकि... क्योंकि आप यहाँ हैं !
प्रताप	अच्छा ? यह बहुत बुरी बात है ! पर संगीता क्यों परेशान है ?
राज	मालूम नहीं । लड़की है, न ?

Pratāp	*halo Rāj, kyā hāl hai? sab ṭhīk hai?*
Rāj	*hā̃, sab ṭhīk hai. aur āp kaise haĩ?*
Pratāp	*maĩ bhī acchā hū̃, śukriyā. Ṛṣi aur Saṅgītā kaise haĩ?*
Rāj	*Ṛṣi acchā hai, lekin Saṅgītā acchī nahī̃ hai.*
Pratāp	*kyō? kyā bāt hai? kyā vah bīmār hai?*
Rāj	*nahī̃, vah nārāz hai kyõki... kyõki āp yahā̃ haĩ!*
Pratāp	*acchā? yah bahut burī bāt hai ! par Saṅgītā kyō pareśan hai?*
Rāj	*mālūm nahī̃. laṛkī hai, na?*

हलो	*halo* hello	क्योंकि *kyõki* because
हाल ^m *hāl* condition, state		पर *par* but
सब *sab* everything, all		परेशान *pareśan* troubled, upset
क्यों *kyō* why		मालूम नहीं *mālūm nahī̃* [I] don't know
बात ^f *bāt* matter, thing		
बीमार *bīmār* ill		न *na* not; isn't that so?
नाराज़ *nārāz* angry, displeased		

Pratap	Hello Raj, how're things? Everything OK?
Raj	Yes, everything's OK. And how are you?
Pratap	I'm well too, thank you. How are Rishi and Sangeeta?
Raj	Rishi is well, but Sangeeta isn't all right.
Pratap	Why? What's the matter? Is she ill?
Raj	No, she's in a huff because... because you're here!
Pratap	Really? This is a very bad thing! But why is Sangeeta upset?
Raj	[I] don't know. She's a girl, isn't she?

Grammar

2.3   Some conversational features

The greetings नमस्ते *namaste* or नमस्कार *namaskār*, often said formally with the hands folded in front of the chest, mean 'Hello', 'Good morning', 'Goodbye' etc.

The word जी *jī* following a surname means roughly 'Mr' (e.g. शर्मा जी *śarmā jī* 'Mr Sharma'), although its tone is rather more cordial. जी *jī* can also be used with first names, both male and female, equivalent in formality to use of the pronoun आप *āp*; it is often attached to terms of relationship – पिताजी *pitājī* 'Father', माताजी *mātājī* 'Mother' etc. जी *jī* also occurs alone, roughly in the sense 'sir' (but with either gender), and the loanwords सर *sar* 'sir' and मैडम *maiḍam* 'madam' are also common. साहब *sāhab* is an alternative to जी *jī*, especially common with Muslim names.

भाई *bhāī* 'brother' is used in addressing males of similar age to oneself; the more formal भाई साहब *bhāī sāhab* is useful in addressing strangers. Similarly बहिन जी *bahin jī* for females.

श्री *śrī* and श्रीमती *śrīmatī* mean 'Mr' and 'Mrs' respectively. श्री *śrī* also means 'lord'(with a deity): श्री कृष्ण *śrī kṛṣṇa* 'Lord Krishna'.

क्या हाल है? *kyā hāl hai?* means literally 'What's [your] condition?' – a colloquial alternative to the more literal आप कैसे (कैसी) हैं? *āp kaise (kaisī) haĩ ?* 'How are you?'.

Honorific usages such as आप *āp* are innately polite, often making equivalents for 'please' and 'thank you' redundant. In formal contexts you will hear कृपया *kṛpayā* 'please' and धन्यवाद *dhanyavād* 'thank you', while प्लीज़ *plīz* 'please' and शुक्रिया *śukriyā* 'thanks' have a more colloquial ring. मेहरबानी है *meharbānī hai* (literally 'it is [through your] kindness') also means 'thank you'.

अच्छा *acchā* 'good' bears various meanings, depending on tone: 'Good!', 'Really?' 'Ah, I see!' etc.

मालूम नहीं *mālūm nahī̃* '[I] don't know' (lit. 'not known') is introduced more fully in 4.4.

The negative न *na* after a verb invites confirmation, as in 'is it not so?' – तुम ठीक हो, न? *tum ṭhīk ho, na?* 'You're all right, aren't you?'. It's like the French 'n'est ce pas?'.

As well as meaning 'and', और *aur* means 'more, else, other': और कौन? *aur kaun?* 'who else?'; और क्या *aur kyā* 'what else/of course'; और लोग *aur log* 'more/other people'. In this meaning, और *aur* is stressed in speech.

The position of भी *bhī* 'also' is essential – *it qualifies the word(s) immediately preceding it:*

ऋषि भी होशियार है ।	*Ṛṣi bhī hośiyār hai.* Rishi too is clever.
ऋषि होशियार भी है ।	*Ṛṣi hośiyār bhī hai.* Rishi is clever too. [as well as e.g. tall]

2.4   More on adjectives and nouns

Remember that the pronouns आप *āp* and तुम *tum* are grammatically plural, even when referring to just one person. So adjectives agreeing with them must also be in the plural. The question आप कैसे (कैसी) हैं? *āp kaise (kaisī) haĩ?* 'How are you?' can, as in English, address one person or a group of people.

Adding the pluralising word लोग *log* 'people' will specify a *numerical* plural:

हम लोग बहुत ख़ुश हैं ।	*ham log bahut khuś haĩ.* We are very happy.
तुम लोग कैसे हो ?	*tum log kaise ho?* How are you lot?
वे लोग पागल हैं ।	*ve log pāgal haĩ.* They (those people) are crazy.

A masculine noun of type 1 (see 1.3) will show its *-e* plural in honorific plurals as well as numerical ones: thus तुम लड़के *tum laṛke* means both 'you boy' and 'you boys'. By contrast, feminine nouns show plural forms in numerical plurals only.

तुम अच्छे बेटे हो ।	*tum acche beṭe ho.*
	You are a good son/good sons.
तुम अच्छी बेटी हो ।	*tum acchī beṭī ho.*
	You are a good daughter.
तुम अच्छी बेटियाँ हो ।	*tum acchī beṭiyā̃ ho.*
	You are good daughters.

EXERCISE 2a.1 Answer these questions on Dialogue 2a.

१ शर्मा जी कौन हैं ?

२ कितने छात्र और छात्राएँ हैं ?

३ क्या "टीच योरसेल्फ़ हिन्दी" सस्ती किताब है ?

४ क्या शब्दकोश महँगे हैं ?

५ रामायण कैसी किताब है – क्या वह पतली है ?

1 *Śarmā jī kaun haĩ?*

2 *kitne chātr aur chātrāẽ haĩ?*

3 *kyā 'ṭīc yorself hindī' sastī kitāb hai?*

4 *kyā śabdkoś mahãge haĩ?*

5 *rāmāyaṇ kaisī kitāb hai – kyā vah patlī hai?*

EXERCISE 2a.2 Translate Pratap's postcard home.

सोमवार १६ जनवरी; नई दिल्ली

यहाँ सब ठीक है । शर्मा जी अच्छे आदमी हैं, पर काफ़ी सख़्त भी हैं । हम १४ छात्र हैं । दूसरे छात्र ज़्यादातर अँग्रेज़, जर्मन या अमरीकन हैं । दो जापानी लड़कियाँ भी हैं । दोनों बहुत दुबली-पतली हैं ! दिल्ली सुन्दर है लेकिन हवा साफ़ नहीं है – बहुत गंदी है । प्रदूषण बहुत ख़राब है । पर आज मौसम ठीक है । वहाँ मौसम कैसा है ?

प्रताप

somvār 16 janvarī; naī dillī

*yahā̃ sab ṭhīk hai. Śarmājī acche ādmī haĩ, par kāfī sa<u>kh</u>t bhī haĩ. ham
14 chātr haĩ. dūsre chātr zyādātar āgrez, jarman yā amrīkan haĩ. do
jāpānī laṛkiyā̃ bhī haĩ. donō bahut dublī-patlī haĩ! dillī sundar hai
lekin havā sāf nahī̃ hai – bahut gandī hai. pradūṣaṇ bahut <u>kh</u>arāb hai.
par āj mausam ṭhīk hai. vahā̃ mausam kaisā hai?*

Pratāp

✔ **EXERCISE 2b.1** Translate.

1 Sangeeta is tall; Rishi is tall too.
2 The teacher is strict; he's crazy too.
3 The new fan is cheap; and it's good too.
4 These shoes are dirty; the sandals are dirty too.
5 That girl is fat; she's beautiful too.
6 These newspapers are good; they're cheap too.

✔ **EXERCISE 2b.2 Convert singular to numerical plural, as shown.**

वह बूढ़ा आदमी दुबला-पतला है। > वे बूढ़े आदमी दुबले-पतले हैं।

vah būṛhā ādmī dublā-patlā hai. > ve būṛhe ādmī duble-patle haĩ.

१ यह बच्चा अच्छा नहीं है, बीमार है।

२ मैं लंबा नहीं हूँ, छोटा हूँ। (हम...)

३ वह किताब कैसी है ? क्या वह अच्छी है ?

४ वह मेज़ साफ़ नहीं है, बहुत गंदी है।

५ यह नया अख़बार बहुत अच्छा नहीं है।

६ यह शब्दकोश सस्ता है। हाँ, और काफ़ी अच्छा भी है।

1 *yah baccā acchā nahī̃ hai, bīmār hai.*
2 *maĩ lambā nahī̃ hū̃, choṭā hū̃. (ham...)*
3 *vah kitāb kaisī hai? kyā vah acchī hai?*
4 *vah mez sāf nahī̃ hai, bahut gandī hai.*
5 *yah nayā akhbār bahut acchā nahī̃ hai.*
6 *yah śabdkoś sastā hai. hā̃, aur kāfī acchā bhī hai.*

Vocabulary

अख़बार ^m *akhbār* newspaper

अध्यापक ^m *adhyāpak* teacher

अभी *abhī* at the moment, right now

आज *āj* today

और *aur* more, else, other

काग़ज़ ^m *kāgaz* paper; a piece of paper

कितना *kitnā* how much/many

किताब ^f *kitāb* book

कृपया *kṛpayā* please

कैसा *kaisā* of what kind, what like, how

कौन *kaun* who

क्या *kyā* what

क्यों *kyõ* why

क्योंकि *kyõki* because

ख़राब *kharāb* bad

ख़ुश *khuś* happy

गंदा *gandā* dirty

चप्पल ^f *cappal* sandal

चिट्ठी ^f *ciṭṭhī* letter, note, chit

छात्र ^m *chātr* student

छात्रा ^f *chātrā* female student

जवाब ^m *javāb* answer

जूता ^m *jūtā* shoe; pair of shoes

ज़्यादातर *zyādātar* mostly, most

दिल्ली ^f *dillī* Delhi

दुबला *dublā* thin; दुबला-पतला *dublā-patlā* thin, slight of build

धन्यवाद *dhanyavād* thank you

न *na* not; is it not so?

नमस्कार *namaskār* hello; goodbye

नया (नए, नई) *nayā (nae, naī)* new

नाराज़ *nārāz* angry, displeased

नौ *nau* nine

पतला *patlā* thin

पर *par* but

परेशान *pareśān* troubled, upset

पाँच *pā̃c* five

पागल *pāgal* mad, crazy

प्रदूषण ^m *pradūṣaṇ* pollution

बहिन ^f *bahin* sister

बात ^f *bāt* matter, thing

बिलकुल *bilkul* completely

बिलकुल नहीं *bilkul nahī̃* not at all

बीमार *bīmār* ill

बुरा *burā* bad

बेटा ^m *beṭā* son

बेटी ^f *beṭī* daughter

भाई ^m *bhāī* brother

भी *bhī* also, too

महँगा *mahãgā* expensive

मालूम नहीं *mālūm nahī̃* [I] don't know

मेहरबानी ^f *meharbānī* kindness

मैडम ^f *maiḍam* madam

मोटा *moṭā* fat, thick

मौसम ^m *mausam* weather

या *yā* or

रामायण^m *rāmāyaṇ* Ramayan (epic poem)

लंबा *lambā* tall, high

विद्यार्थी^{m, f} *vidyārthī* student

शब्दकोश^m *śabdkoś* dictionary

श्री *śrī* Mr; Lord (with deity)

श्रीमती *śrīmatī* Mrs

सख़्त *sakht* strict, severe

सब *sab* everything, all

सर *sar* sir

सवाल^m *savāl* question

सस्ता *sastā* cheap

साहब^m *sāhab* Mr; sir

सोमवार^m *somvār* Monday

सोलह *solah* sixteen

हलो, हेलो *halo , helo* hello

हवा^f *havā* air

हाल^m *hāl* condition, state

हिन्दी^f *hindī* Hindi

3 ROOMS IN THE HOUSE
घर में कमरे

In this unit you will learn how to
■ describe locations – 'in', 'on' etc.
■ use a fuller range of pronouns
■ develop conversational skills

3a Pratap's mother phones from London

अनीता	कैसे हो प्रताप ? तुम्हारी तबियत ठीक है न ? और वह मकान कैसा है ?
प्रताप	बिलकुल ठीक हूँ माँ । और यह घर भी बुरा नहीं है ।
अनीता	कुमार परिवार कितना बड़ा है ? सिर्फ़ पति-पत्नी हैं, या बच्चे भी हैं ?
प्रताप	परिवार में कई लोग हैं – प्रकाश और कमला, दादी जी, एक लड़की और दो लड़के ।
अनीता	अच्छा, काफ़ी बड़ा परिवार है ! मकान में कितने कमरे हैं ?
प्रताप	नौ बड़े कमरे हैं, और एक छोटा । सब कमरों में सामान नया है ।
अनीता	और तुम्हारा कमरा ? कमरे में पंखा वग़ैरह है न ?
प्रताप	हाँ, अब मेज़ पर नया पंखा है । और फ़र्श पर नई दरी भी है ।

Anītā	*kaise ho Pratāp? tumhārī tabiyat ṭhīk hai na? aur vah makān kaisā hai?*
Pratāp	*bilkul ṭhīk hū̃ mā. aur yah ghar bhī burā nahī̃ hai.*
Anītā	*Kumār parivār kitnā baṛā hai? sirf pati-patnī haĩ, yā bacce bhī haĩ?*
Pratāp	*parivār mẽ kaī log haĩ – Prakāś aur Kamalā, Dādījī, ek laṛkī aur do laṛke.*
Anītā	*acchā, kāfī baṛā parivār hai! makān mẽ kitne kamre haĩ?*
Pratāp	*nau baṛe kamre haĩ, aur ek choṭā. sāb kamrõ mẽ sāmān nayā hai.*
Anītā	*aur tumhārā kamrā? kamre mẽ pankhā vagairah hai na?*
Pratāp	*hā̃, ab mez par nayā pankhā hai. aur farś par naī darī bhī hai.*

तुम्हारा	*tumhārā*	your, yours	छह	*chah*	six
तबियत ^f	*tabiyat*	health	सारा	*sārā*	all, whole
घर ^m	*ghar*	house, home	सामान ^m	*sāmān*	furniture, things
परिवार ^m	*parivār*	family	वग़ैरह	*vagairah*	and so on, etc.
पति ^m	*pati*	husband	अब	*ab*	now
पत्नी ^f	*patnī*	wife	फ़र्श ^{m/f}	*farś*	floor
कई	*kaī*	several	दरी ^f	*darī*	floor rug, mat

Anita	How are you, Pratap? Your health is OK isn't it? And what's that house like?
Pratap	I'm absolutely fine, Mum. And this house too isn't bad.
Anita	How big is the Kumar family? Is it just husband and wife, or are there children too?
Pratap	There are six in the family – Prakash and Kamala, Grandma, a girl and two boys.
Anita	Oh, it's quite a big family. How many rooms are there in the house?
Pratap	There are nine big rooms and one small. And the furniture in all the rooms is new.
Anita	And your room? There's a fan etc. in the room isn't there?
Pratap	Yes, there's a new fan on the table now. And there's a new rug on the floor too.

Grammar

3.1 Simple postpositions

In English, words like 'in' and 'from' are called *pre*positions because they precede a noun or pronoun ('in the house'); in Hindi they *follow* a noun or pronoun, so they're called *post*positions (मकान में *makān mẽ*). There are five 'simple' or single-word postpositions:

में	*mẽ* 'in'	पर	*par* 'on'	तक	*tak* 'up to, as far as'
को	*ko* 'to' etc.	से	*se* 'by, with, from' etc.		

घर में *ghar mẽ* in the house   राम को *Rām ko* to Ram

मेज़ पर *mez par* on the table   रात को *rāt ko* at night

समय पर *samay par* on time   बस से *bas se* by bus

आज तक *āj tak* until today   आराम से *ārām se* with ease, easily

यहाँ तक *yahā̃ tak* up to here   भारत से *bhārat se* from India

3.2 Nouns with postpositions

Hindi has two main cases. In Units 1 and 2, all nouns were in the *direct* case, which is obligatory for verb subjects. But when a noun is followed by a postposition, it must transform into a different case, known as the *oblique* case. Thus all the nouns in 3.1 above, shown with postpositions, are by definition in the oblique; but no change is apparent, because the nouns cunningly chosen there are all singular 'type 2' nouns (see 1.3), whose oblique form is identical to the direct singular.

For example, the word घर *ghar* 'house' remains the same in the following two sentences, although its case changes: in the first sentence it's the subject of the verb and is therefore in the direct case, while in the second it is followed by a postposition and is therefore in the oblique case.

घर ख़ाली है ।   *ghar khālī hai.*   The house is vacant.

घर में सामान है ।   *ghar mẽ sāmān hai.*   There is furniture in
                                       the house.

Not all nouns are so user friendly. Masculine 'type 1' nouns like कमरा *kamrā* 'room' change their final -*ā* to -*e* in the oblique singular (कमरे *kamre*):

कमरा ख़ाली है ।   *kamrā khālī hai.*   The room is vacant.

कमरे में सामान है ।   *kamre mẽ sāmān hai.* There is furniture in
                                         the room.

Nouns of *all* classes change in the oblique plural, which ends in -*õ* (घरों में *gharõ mẽ*, कमरों में *kamrõ mẽ*):

घरों में सामान है ।   *gharõ mẽ sāmān hai.*   There is furniture in
                                         the houses.

कमरों में सामान है ।   *kamrõ mẽ sāmān hai.* There is furniture in
                                         the rooms.

The following table gives all the noun types in the direct and oblique cases, singular and plural:

DIRECT CASE	OBLIQUE CASE + POSTPOSITION
Masculine type 1	
लड़का *laṛkā* boy	लड़के से *laṛke se* from the boy
कमरा *kamrā* room	कमरे में *kamre mẽ* in the room
लड़के *laṛke* boys	लड़कों से *laṛkõ se* from the boys
कमरे *kamre* rooms	कमरों में *kamrõ mẽ* in the rooms
Masculine type 2	
मकान *makān* house	मकान में *makān mẽ* in the house
आदमी *ādmī* man	आदमी को *ādmī ko* to the man
हिन्दू *hindū* Hindu	हिन्दू को *hindū ko* to the Hindu
मकान *makān* houses	मकानों में *makānõ mẽ* in the houses
आदमी *ādmī* men	आदमियों को *ādmiyõ ko* to the men
हिन्दू *hindū* Hindus	हिन्दुओं को *hinduõ ko* to the Hindus
Feminine type 1	
लड़की *laṛkī* girl	लड़की से *laṛkī se* from the girl
मूर्ति *mūrti* image	मूर्ति में *mūrti mẽ* in the image
चिड़िया *ciṛiyā* bird	चिड़िया से *ciṛiyā ko* to the bird
लड़कियाँ *laṛkiyā̃* girls	लड़कियों से *laṛkiyõ se* from the girls
प्रतियाँ *pratiyā̃* copies	प्रतियों में *pratiyõ mẽ* in the copies
चिड़ियाँ *ciṛiyā̃* birds	चिड़ियों को *ciṛiyõ ko* to the birds
Feminine type 2	
मेज़ *mez* table	मेज़ पर *mez par* on the table
माता *mātā* mother	माता से *mātā se* from Mother
मेज़ें *mezẽ* tables	मेज़ों पर *mezõ par* on the tables
माताएँ *mātāẽ* mothers	माताओं से *mātāõ se* from the mothers

Before the oblique plural -ō ending, -ū nouns shorten to -u- (हिन्दू *hindū* > हिन्दुओं *hinduō*); and -ī nouns change to -iy- (आदमी *ādmī* > आदमियों *ādmiyō*).

मकान में कई कमरे हैं ।	*makān mē kaī kamre haī.* In the house there are several rooms.
दीवारों पर तस्वीरें हैं ।	*dīvārō par tasvīrē haī.* There are pictures on the walls.
फ़र्श पर दरी है ।	*farś par darī hai.* There is a rug on the floor.
अलमारियों में क्या है ?	*almāriyō mē kyā hai?* What's in the cupboards?

Word order: look back to the vital word-order point made in 1.5; then note how the sense 'there is...' is conveyed through a similar inversion of word order. Compare the following two sentences:

मेज़ पर क़लम है ।   *mez par qalam hai.*   There is <u>a pen</u> on the table.

This statement answers the question मेज़ पर क्या है ? *mez par kyā hai?* 'What is there on the table?'

क़लम मेज़ पर है ।   *qalam mez par hai.*   The pen is <u>on the table</u>.

This statement answers the question क़लम कहाँ है *qalam kahā̃ hai?* 'Where is the pen?'

In both Hindi sentences, the answer words (क़लम *qalam*, मेज़ पर *mez par*) replace the respective question words (क्या *kyā*, कहाँ *kahā̃*).

3b   Prakash has lost his glasses

प्रकाश	ऋषि, ओ ऋषि, तुम कहाँ हो ?
ऋषि	मैं अभी छोटे बाथरूम में हूँ, पिता जी । क्यों? क्या बात है ?
प्रकाश	तुम सुबह से वहाँ हो ? ख़ैर... मेरा चश्मा कहाँ है रे ?
ऋषि	बड़ी मेज़ पर नहीं है ? या उस छोटी अलमारी में, बड़े कमरे में ?

प्रकाश	नहीं है । शायद तुम्हारे कमरे में है ।
ऋषि	नहीं पिताजी, मेरे कमरे में सिर्फ़ मेरा चश्मा है, आपका नहीं ।
प्रकाश	और तुम्हारी दराज़ में भी नहीं है ?
ऋषि	जी नहीं, मेरी दराज़ में बहुत-सारी चीज़ें हैं, पर आपका चश्मा नहीं है ।

Prakāś	*Ṛṣi, o Ṛṣi, tum kahā̃ ho?*
Ṛṣi	*maĩ abhī choṭe bāthrūm mẽ hū̃, pitā jī. kyõ? kyā bāt hai?*
Prakāś	*tum subah se vahā̃ ho? khair... merā caśmā kahā̃ hai re?*
Ṛṣi	*baṛī mez par nahī̃ hai? yā us choṭī almārī mẽ, baṛe kamre mẽ?*
Prakāś	*nahī̃ hai. śāyad tumhāre kamre mẽ hai.*
Ṛṣi	*nahī̃ pitājī, mere kamre mẽ sirf merā caśmā hai, āpkā nahī̃.*
Prakāś	*aur tumhārī darāz mẽ bhī nahī̃ hai?*
Ṛṣi	*jī nahī̃, merī darāz mẽ bahut-sārī cīzẽ haĩ, par āpkā caśmā nahī̃ hai.*

ओ *o* o!	आपका *merā* your, yours
कहाँ *kahā̃* where?	चश्मा[m] *caśmā* glasses
बाथरूम[m] *bāthrūm* bathroom	रे *re* eh, hey
में *mẽ* in	पर *par* on
सुबह[f] *subah* morning	उस *us* that
से *se* since, from	शायद *śāyad* perhaps
वहाँ *vahā̃* there	दराज़[f] *darāz* drawer
ख़ैर *khair* well, anyway	बहुत-सारा *bahut-sārā* lots of
मेरा *merā* my, mine	चीज़[f] *cīz* thing

Prakash	Rishi, o Rishi, where are you?
Rishi	I'm in the small bathroom at the moment, Father. Why? What's the matter?
Prakash	Have you been there since morning? Anyway... where are my glasses, eh?
Rishi	Aren't they on the big table? Or in that small cupboard in the big room?
Prakash	They're not. Perhaps they're in your room.
Rishi	No, Father, in my room there's only my glasses, not yours.
Prakash	And aren't they in your drawer either?
Rishi	No, there are lots of things in my drawer, but your glasses aren't there.

Grammar
3.3   Adjectives in the oblique case

A noun before a postposition must be in the oblique case (3.2), and so must any adjective qualifying it. Inflecting adjectives like बड़ा *baṛā* 'big', ending in *-ā*, change to *-e* in the oblique (singular and plural); masculine adjectives not ending in *-ā* do not change. Similarly the feminine ending *-ī* (बड़ी *baṛī*) doesn't change in the oblique.

Note incidentally that the pronouns मेरा *merā* 'my, mine', तुम्हारा *tumhārā* 'your, yours' (relating to तुम *tum*) and आपका *āpkā* 'your, yours' (relating to आप *āp*) work just like adjectives, agreeing with the thing possessed (मेरा भाई, मेरी बहिन *merā bhāī, merī bahin* 'my brother, my sister'); they're introduced more fully in 6.2.

बड़े कमरे में	*baṛe kamre mē*	in the big room
बड़े कमरों में	*baṛe kamrõ mē*	in the big rooms
मेरे मकान में	*mere makān mē*	in my house
मेरे मकानों में	*mere makānõ mē*	in my houses
तुम्हारी अलमारी में	*tumhārī almārī mē*	in your cupboard
तुम्हारी अलमारियों में	*tumhārī almāriyõ mē*	in your cupboards
आपकी मेज़ पर	*āpkī mez par*	on your table
आपकी मेज़ों पर	*āpkī mezõ par*	on your tables
लाल दरवाज़े पर	*lāl darvāze par*	on the red door
लाल दरवाज़ों पर	*lāl darvāzõ par*	on the red doors

3.4 Pronouns in the oblique case

When a pronoun is followed by a postposition (3.1), it must of course take the oblique case (compare English: 'tell her' is correct, 'tell she' is not). Here are the pronouns with their oblique forms:

SINGULAR			PLURAL		
मैं *mai*	>	मुझ *mujh*	हम *ham*	>	हम *ham*
तू *tū*	>	तुझ *tujh*	तुम *tum*	>	तुम *tum*
—			आप *āp*	>	आप *āp*
यह *yah*	>	इस *is*	ये *ye*	>	इन *in*
वह *vah*	>	उस *us*	वे *ve*	>	उन *un*
कौन *kaun*	>	किस *kis*	कौन *kaun*	>	किन *kin*
क्या *kyā*	>	किस *kis*	क्या *kyā*	>	किन *kin*

Postpositions following pronouns may be written separately, or as one word: मुझ से *mujh se* / मुझसे *mujhse* ; आप को *āp ko* / आपको *āpko*.

> A verb subject *must* be in the direct case (compare English: 'he is' is correct, 'him is' is not). Test this rule by identifing the subject in each sentence of Dialogues 3a and 3b.

 EXERCISE 3a.1 Answer these questions on Dialogue 3a.

१   प्रताप कैसा है ?

२   कुमार परिवार में कितने लोग हैं, और वे कौन हैं ?

३   मकान में कितने कमरे हैं ? क्या वे सब बड़े हैं ?

४   कमरों में कैसा सामान है ?

५   पंखा कहाँ है ? वह कैसा है ?

६   क्या दरी पुरानी है ? वह कहाँ है ?

1   *Pratāp kaisā hai?*

2   *Kumār parivār mẽ kitne log haĩ, aur ve kaun haĩ?*

3   *makān mẽ kitne kamre haĩ? kyā ve sab baṛe haĩ?*

4   *kamrõ mẽ kaisā sāmān hai?*

5   *pankhā kahā̃ hai? vah kaisā hai?*

6   *kyā darī purānī hai? vah kahā̃ hai?*

EXERCISE 3a.2 Describe a room, using at least eight sentences based on the format of the descriptions in Dialogue 3a.

EXERCISE 3b.1 Translate.

1	this big room	in this big room	The boys are in this big room.
2	those black chairs	on those black chairs	The clothes are on those black chairs.
3	this dirty floor	on this dirty floor	There's a rug on this dirty floor.
4	these old tables	on these old tables	The books are on these old tables.
5	that big garden	in that big garden	There's a car in that big garden.
6	these new rooms	in these new rooms	Are there fans in these new rooms?
7	the old city	from the old city	Those girls are from the old city.
8	this little village	from this little village	Is that boy from this little village?
9	this clean kitchen	in this clean kitchen	There's a table in this clean kitchen.
10	those tall boys	from those tall boys	This letter is from those tall boys.

EXERCISE 3b.2 Using Dialogue 3b as your model, write a short dialogue in which Rishi asks his mother where his new book is.

Vocabulary

अब	*ab* now	इस *is* oblique of यह *yah*
आपका	*āpkā* your, yours	इन *in* oblique of ये *ye*
आराम ^m *ārām* rest, comfort;		उस *us* oblique of वह *vah*
आराम से	*ārām se* comfortably, easily	उन *un* oblique of वे *ve*
		ऐनक ^f *ainak* glasses

ओ _o_ o!

कपड़ा ^m _kapṛā_ cloth; garment

क़लम ^{m/f} _qalam_ pen

काला _kālā_ black

किस _kis_ oblique singular of **कौन** _kaun_ and of **क्या** _kyā_

किन _kin_ oblique plural of **कौन** _kaun_ and of **क्या** _kyā_

को _ko_ to, on, at

ख़ैर _khair_ well, anyway

गाँव ^m _gãv_ village

गुसलख़ाना ^m _gusalkhānā_ bathroom

घर ^m _ghar_ house, home

चश्मा ^m _caśmā_ glasses

चार _cār_ four

चीज़ ^f _cīz_ thing

छह _chah_ six

तक _tak_ up to, as far as

तबियत ^f _tabiyat_ health

तस्वीर ^f _tasvīr_ picture

तुझ _tujh_ oblique of **तू** _tū_

तुम्हारा _tumhārā_ your, yours

दरवाज़ा ^m _darvāzā_ door

दराज़ ^f _darāz_ drawer

दरी ^f _darī_ floor rug, mat

दस _das_ ten

दीवार ^f _dīvār_ wall

पति ^m _pati_ husband

पत्नी ^f _patnī_ wife

पर _par_ on

परदा ^m _pardā_ curtain

परिवार ^m _parivār_ family

फ़र्श ^{m/f} _farś_ floor

बस ^f _bas_ bus

बहुत-सारा _bahut-sārā_ lots of

बाथरूम ^m _bāthrūm_ bathroom

भारत ^m _bhārat_ India

मुझ _mujh_ oblique of **मैं** _maĩ_

में _mẽ_ in; **में से** _mẽ se_ from among, out of

मेरा _merā_ my, mine

रसोईघर ^m _rasoīghar_ kitchen

रात ^f _rāt_ night

रे _re_ eh, hey

लंदन ^m _landan_ London

वग़ैरह _vagairah_ etc., and so on

वहाँ _vahã_ there

शहर ^m _śahar_ town, city

शायद _śāyad_ perhaps

समय ^m _samay_ time

सामान ^m _sāmān_ furniture, things

सारा _sārā_ all, whole

सुबह ^f _subah_ morning

से _se_ by, since, from, with

4 | WHO WAS THAT HANDSOME MAN?

वह ख़ूबसूरत आदमी कौन था ?

In this unit you will learn how to

■ use the past tense
■ make comparisons
■ say you have a cold or fever
■ use the vocative case – 'O children!'

4a   Sangeeta's friend Suhas – just a friend?

पिंकी	संगीता, आज तुम क्लास में क्यों नहीं थीं ? तुम कहाँ थीं ?
संगीता	मैं घर पर थी; सुहास भी था । दूसरे लोग बाहर थे । हाँ, प्रताप भी था वहाँ ।
पिंकी	सुहास – वह ख़ूबसूरत आदमी ? वह कौन है – दोस्त या रिश्तेदार ?
संगीता	रिश्तेदार तो नहीं, वह मेरा बहुत पुराना दोस्त है ।
पिंकी	यह तुम्हारा दोस्त उम्र में तुमसे काफ़ी बड़ा है !

संगीता	हाँ मुझसे बड़ा तो है, पर बहुत प्यारा आदमी है ।
पिंकी	क्या वह दिल्ली से है ?　या विदेश से ?
संगीता	वे लोग पहले लंदन में थे – मेरा मतलब है, बाल-बच्चे भी थे... पर अब तो सुहास अकेला है ।
पिंकी	और सुहास सिर्फ़ तुम्हारा "दोस्त" है क्या ?
संगीता	हाँ पिंकी, वह सिर्फ़ मेरा दोस्त है – मेरा मित्र है, फ्रेंड है !

Pinkī	Sangītā, āj tum klās mẽ kyõ nahī̃ thī? tum kahā̃ thī?
Sangītā	maĩ ghar par thī; Suhās bhī thā. dūsre log bāhar the. hā̃, Pratāp bhī thā vahā̃.
Pinkī	Suhās – vah <u>kh</u>ūbsūrat ādmī? vah kaun hai – dost yā riśtedār?
Sangītā	riśtedār to nahī̃, vah merā bahut purānā dost hai.
Pinkī	yah tumhārā dost umr mẽ tumse kāfī baṛā hai!
Sangītā	hā̃ mujhse baṛā to hai, par bahut pyārā ādmī hai.
Pinkī	kyā vah dillī se hai? yā videś se?
Sangītā	ve log pahle landan mẽ the – merā matlab hai, bāl-bacce bhī the... par ab to Suhās akelā hai.
Pinkī	aur Suhās sirf tumhārā 'dost' hai kyā?
Sangītā	hā̃ Pinkī, vah sirf merā dost hai – merā mitr hai, freṇḍ hai!

क्लास ^{m/f} *klās* class	उम्र ^f *umr, umar* age
था, थी, थे, थीं *thā, thī, the, thī̃* was, were	प्यारा *pyārā* dear, lovely
घर पर *ghar par* at home	विदेश ^m *videś* foreign country; abroad
बाहर *bāhar* out; outside	पहले *pahle* previously
ख़ूबसूरत <u>kh</u>ūbsūrat beautiful, handsome	मतलब ^m *matlab* meaning
दोस्त ^{m, f} *dost* friend	बाल-बच्चे ^{m.pl} *bāl-bacce* children, family
रिश्तेदार ^{m, f} *riśtedār* relative	अकेला *akelā* alone
तो *to* so; as for (see 4.2)	मित्र ^{m, f} *mitr* friend

Pinkie	Sangeeta, why weren't you in college today? Where were you?
Sangeeta	I was at home; Suhas was there too. The others were out. Oh yes, Pratap was there too.
Pinkie	Suhas – that handsome man? Who is he – friend or relative?

Sangeeta	Not a relative, he's my very old friend.
Pinkie	This friend of yours is quite a lot older ('bigger in age') than you!
Sangeeta	Yes, he is older than me, but he's a very dear man.
Pinkie	Is he from Delhi? Or from abroad?
Sangeeta	They were in London before – I mean, there was a family with children... but now Suhas is alone.
Pinkie	And Suhas is just your 'friend'?
Sangeeta	Yes Pinkie, he's just my friend – my *mitra*, my 'friend'!

> सुहास सिर्फ़ तुम्हारा "दोस्त" है क्या ? *Suhās sirf tumhārā 'dost' hai kyā?*
> Here, क्या *kyā* is colloquially thrown in at the end.

Grammar

4.1 'was' and 'were'

Unlike the present tense, the past tense of the verb होना *honā* 'to be' distinguishes gender: वह था *vah thā* 'he was', वह थी *vah thī* 'she was'.

MASCULINE			FEMININE		
मैं था	*maĩ thā*	I was	मैं थी	*maĩ thī*	I was
तू था	*tū thā*	you were	तू थी	*tū thī*	you were
यह था	*yah thā*	this, he, it was	यह थी	*yah thī*	this, she, it was
वह था	*vah thā*	that, he, it was	वह थी	*vah thī*	that, she, it was
हम थे	*ham the*	we were	हम थीं	*ham thī̃*	we were
तुम थे	*tum the*	you were	तुम थीं	*tum thī̃*	you were
आप थे	*āp the*	you were	आप थीं	*āp thī̃*	you were
ये थे	*ye the*	they, these were; he was (hon.)	ये थीं	*ye thī̃*	they, these were; she was (hon.)
वे थे	*ve the*	they, those were; he was (hon.)	वे थीं	*ve thī̃*	they, those were; she was (hon.)

मैं कल दफ़्तर में था ।	*maĩ kal daftar mẽ thā.*	Yesterday I was in the office.
चाचा जी दुकान में थे ।	*cācā jī dukān mẽ the.*	Uncle was in the shop.
माँ भी घर पर नहीं थीं ।	*mā̃ bhī ghar par nahī̃ thī̃.*	Mum too wasn't at home.
दोनों बच्चे बीमार थे ।	*donõ bacce bīmār the.*	Both children were ill.
गोलियाँ मेज़ पर थीं ।	*goliyā̃ mez par thī̃.*	The pills were on the table.

4.2 तो *to* 'so'; 'as for'

The important little word तो *to* has two separate functions: (a) as a conjunction meaning 'so', and (b) to lend emphasis to a preceding word or phrase: वे तो *ve to*... 'as for them...'. It isn't a postposition, so it doesn't affect case. Its two uses are explained separately.

(a) At the beginning of a phrase, तो *to* means 'so', or 'then':

तो क्या दुकान बंद है ?	*to kyā dukān band hai?*	So is the shop closed?
अच्छा, तो तुम लन्दन से हो ?	*acchā, to tum landan se ho?*	Ah, then you're from London?

(b) Following a word or phrase, तो *to* contrasts that preceding item to some other item in the same context:

खाना तो गरम था, पर चाय एकदम ठंडी थी ।	*khānā to garam thā, par cāy ekdam ṭhaṇḍī thī.*	The <u>food</u> was hot, but the tea was completely cold.
खाना अच्छा तो था, पर महँगा भी था ।	*khānā acchā to thā, par mahãgā bhī thā.*	The food was <u>good</u>, but it was expensive too.

Often the contrasted item or situation is only implied:

कल तो वह घर पर था ।	*kal to vah ghar par thā.*	<u>Yesterday</u> he was at home. ['... but today?']

| कल वह घर पर तो था । | *kal vah ghar par to thā.* | Yesterday he <u>was at home</u>. ['... but he was busy'] |
| कल वह तो घर पर था । | *kal vah to ghar par thā.* | Yesterday <u>he</u> was at home. ['... but the others?'] |

This second use of तो *to* usually carries a subtle nuance; it is to be understood gradually, after seeing more examples.

4.3 Comparison of adjectives

Hindi has few special adjectives corresponding to the English comparative and superlative, 'taller, tallest'. Comparisons involve just an ordinary adjective and the comparing word से *se* 'than':

| संगीता राज से लम्बी है । | *Saṅgītā Rāj se lambī hai.* | Sangeeta is taller than Raj. |
| राज संगीता से मोटा है । | *Rāj Saṅgītā se moṭā hai.* | Raj is fatter than Sangeeta. |

Comparisons can be made more specific by adding a word for 'more' (और *aur* or ज़्यादा *zyādā*) before the adjective, as in ज़्यादा लंबा *zyādā lambā* 'taller' (lit. 'more tall'). This is also done when the object of comparison is not stated:

ऋषि संगीता से ज़्यादा लंबा है ।	*Ṛṣi Saṅgītā se zyādā lambā hai.*	Rishi is taller than Sangeeta.
ऋषि ज़्यादा लंबा है ।	*Ṛṣi zyādā lambā hai.*	Rishi is taller.
राज ज़्यादा मोटा है ।	*Rāj zyādā moṭā hai.*	Raj is fatter.

Comparisons involving the sense 'less' use the word कम *kam* 'little, less':

| चाँदी सोने से कम महँगा है । | *cā̃dī sone se kam mahãgī hai.* | Silver is less costly than gold. |
| ये चीज़ें कम महँगी हैं । | *ye cīzẽ kam mahãgī haĩ.* | These things are less expensive. |

Superlatives follow the pattern of सब से अच्छा *sab se acchā* 'best of all':

| मैं सब से लंबा हूँ । | *maĩ sab se lambā hū̃.* | I am the tallest. |

वह पहाड़ सब से ऊंचा है । *vah pahāṛ sab se ū̃cā hai.*   That mountain is
                                                                                              the highest.

4b   Khanna ji at the office

खन्ना जी	छोटू, क्या तुमको मालूम है कि रामदास कहाँ है ?
छोटू	खन्ना जी, रामदास घर पर है । उसको जुकाम है ।
खन्ना जी	अरे, वह कल भी बीमार था ! और प्रकाश कहाँ है ?
छोटू	सर, आज प्रकाश जी भी यहाँ नहीं हैं ।
खन्ना जी	क्यों ? क्या बात है ? क्या उसको भी जुकाम है ?
छोटू	कल तो उनको बुख़ार था । वे शायद आज भी बीमार हैं ।
खन्ना जी	या उसको काम पसंद नहीं है, शायद !
छोटू	वह बात नहीं है खन्ना जी – प्रकाश जी बहुत मेहनती आदमी हैं ।
खन्ना जी	तुम अच्छे लड़के हो छोटू, लेकिन तुमको कुछ नहीं मालूम है ।

Khannā jī	*Choṭū, kyā tumko mālūm hai ki Rāmdās kahā̃ hai?*
Choṭū	*Khannā jī, Rāmdās ghar par hai. usko zukām hai.*
Khannā jī	*are, vah kal bhī bīmār thā! aur Prakāś kahā̃ hai?*
Choṭū	*sar, āj Prakāś jī bhī yahā̃ nahī̃ haĩ.*
Khannā jī	*kyõ? kyā bāt hai? kyā usko bhī zukām hai?*
Choṭū	*kal to unko bukhār thā. ve śāyad āj bhī bīmār haĩ.*
Khannā jī	*yā usko kām pasand nahī̃ hai, śāyad!*
Choṭū	*vah bāt nahī̃ hai, Khannā jī – Prakāś jī bahut mehnatī ādmī haĩ.*
Khannā jī	*tum acche laṛke ho Choṭū , lekin tumko kuch nahī̃ mālūm hai.*

मालूम	*mālūm* known	बुख़ार^m	*bukhār*	fever
कि	*ki* that	काम^m	*kām*	work
जुकाम^m	*zukām* a cold	पसंद	*pasand*	liked, pleasing
अरे	*are* oh! what!	मेहनती	*mehnatī*	hardworking
कल	*kal* yesterday; tomorrow	कुछ नहीं	*kuch nahī̃*	nothing

Khanna ji	Chotu, do you know where Ramdas is?
Chotu	Khanna ji, Ramdas is at home. He's got a cold.
Khanna ji	What! He was ill yesterday too! And where's Prakash?
Chotu	Sir, Prakash ji is not here today either.
Khanna ji	Why? What's the matter? Has he got a cold too?

Chotu	Yesterday he had a fever. Maybe he's ill today as well.
Khanna ji	Or he doesn't like work, maybe!
Chotu	That's not it, Khanna ji – Prakash ji's a very hardworking man.
Khanna ji	You're a good lad, Chotu, but you don't know anything.

> Chotu looks up to Prakash, and refers to him in the honorific plural as 'Prakash ji'; but Khanna is Prakash's boss, and refers to him in the singular.

Grammar
4.4   Some constructions with को *ko*

The word को *ko* 'to' appears in many constructions of the type मुझ को ज़ुकाम है *mujh ko zukām hai* 'I have a cold' (literally 'to me there is a cold'). The important thing to note here is that ज़ुकाम *zukām* 'a cold', and *not* the person suffering from it, is the subject of the verb (here, है *hai*). It is essential to understand this vital principle, because you will encounter it many times in Hindi grammar. Notice here how the verb stays the same, agreeing with masculine singular ज़ुकाम *zukām* throughout the following sentences, although the sufferer changes:

दादीजी को ज़ुकाम था ।	*dādījī ko zukām thā.*	Granny had a cold.
दोनों भाइयों को ज़ुकाम था ।	*donō bhāiyō ko zukām thā.*	Both brothers had a cold.
सौ लोगों को ज़ुकाम था ।	*sau logō ko zukām thā.*	A hundred people had a cold.

Other nouns using the same construction are:

| बुख़ार *bukhār* (m) a fever | आशा *āśā* (f) hope |
| अफ़सोस *afsos* (m) regret | ख़ुशी *khuśī* (f) happiness |

तुम को बुख़ार था ।	*tum ko bukhār thā.*	You had a fever.
हम को अफ़सोस है कि तुम बीमार हो ।	*ham ko afsos hai ki tum bīmar ho.*	We're sorry that you're ill.
मुझ को आशा है कि वे ठीक हैं ।	*mujh ko āśā hai ki ve ṭhīk haĩ.*	I hope they're OK.
उन को ख़ुशी थी कि गाड़ी सस्ती थी ।	*un ko khuśī thī ki gāṛī sastī thī.*	They were pleased the car was cheap.

The adjectives मालूम *mālūm* 'known' and पसंद *pasand* 'pleasing' also feature in this construction (translating literally as 'X is known to me', 'X is pleasing to me' etc.).

उस को समोसे पसंद हैं ।	*us ko samose pasand haĩ.*	He likes samosas.
हाँ, मुझ को मालूम है ।	*hā̃, mujh ko mālūm hai.*	Yes, I know.
क्या उस को दाल पसंद है ?	*kyā us ko dāl pasand hai?*	Does he like daal?
हम को मालूम नहीं ।	*ham ko mālūm nahī̃.*	We don't know.

In the English sentence 'Do you know where Raj is?', the core question 'Where is Raj?' is inverted to 'where Raj is'. In Hindi, the core question राज कहाँ है? *Rāj kahā̃ hai?* remains *unchanged* within the longer sentence. In each of the following three sentences, the words following कि *ki* constitute the core question.

क्या तुमको मालूम है कि राज कहाँ है ?	*kyā tumko mālūm hai ki Rāj kahā̃ hai?*	Do you know where Raj is?
क्या उसको मालूम है कि मैं कौन हूँ ?	*kyā usko mālūm hai ki maĩ kaun hū̃?*	Does he know who I am?
मुझको नहीं मालूम कि यह क्या है ।	*mujhko nahī̃ mālūm ki yah kyā hai.*	I don't know what this is.

4.4   The vocative case

The vocative (the case used when addressing someone) is the same as the oblique, except that in the plural the ending -ओ -*o* is not nasalised.

बेटे	*beṭe!*	Son!
ओ बच्चो	*o bacco!*	O, children!
भाइयो-बहिनो	*bhāiyo-bahino!*	Brothers and sisters!

 EXERCISE 4a.1   Translate.

१   तुम्हारा पुराना पंखा इस नए पंखे से ज़्यादा मज़बूत था ।

२   बच्चों में से संगीता सबसे बड़ी है ।

३   क्या ऋषि राज से कम मोटा है ?

४   क्या संगीता पिंकी से ज्यादा होशियार है ?

५   आज प्रताप घर पर है लेकिन दूसरे लोग बाहर हैं – शायद बाज़ार पर ।

1   *tumhārā purānā pankhā is nae pankhe se zyādā mazbūt thā.*
2   *baccõ mẽ se Sangītā sabse baṛī hai.*
3   *kyā Ṛṣi Rāj se kam moṭā hai?*
4   *kyā Sangītā Pinkī se zyādā hośiyār hai?*
5   *āj Pratāp ghar par hai lekin dūsre log bāhar haĩ – śāyad bāzār par.*

EXERCISE 4a.2 Translate.

1   This man is taller than that girl.

2   Was your old car better than this new car?

3   Is my sister fatter than my brother?

4   I am taller than you but you are more beautiful than me.

5   She was taller than us; she was the tallest of all.

EXERCISE 4b.1 Translate.

1   Pinkie knows that Sangeeta wasn't in college today.

2   Who doesn't know that Suhas is older than Sangeeta?

3   Sangeeta is pleased that Pinkie likes Suhas.

4   Pratap was at home today; he knows who Suhas is.

5   Pratap knows that Sangeeta likes the new white Maruti.

6   Do you know where Kamala was yesterday?

7   We're sorry that your friends are ill.

8   I don't know who that man is.

EXERCISE 4B.2 Answer the following questions, in which you are addressed as तुम *tum*.

१   तुम्हारे कमरे में कितनी कुरसियाँ हैं ?

२   क्या तुम्हारे पड़ोसी हिन्दुस्तानी हैं ?

३   क्या तुम्हारी किताब तुम्हारी मेज़ पर है ?

४   क्या तुम्हारे कपड़े साफ़ हैं ?

५   क्या तुमको मालूम है कि तुम्हारे पड़ोसी अभी कहाँ हैं ?

६   तुम्हारी तबियत कैसी है ? क्या तुमको ज़ुकाम है ?

1   *tumhāre kamre mẽ kitnī kursiyā̃ haĩ?*

2   *kyā tumhāre paṛosī hindustānī haĩ?*

3   *kyā tumhārī kitāb tumhārī mez par hai?*

4   *kya tumhāre kapṛe sāf haĩ?*

5   *kyā tumko mālūm hai ki tumhāre paṛosī abhī kahā̃ haĩ?*

6   *tumhārī tabiyat kaisī hai? kyā tumko zukām hai?*

EXERCISE 4b.3 Write a postcard as from Pratap to Mohan (मोहन *Mohan*) in Varanasi (वाराणसी *vārāṇasī*). Pratap tells Mohan his reactions to Delhi. He hopes Mohan is well; he wants to know about Mohan's family, and whether he knows where the palace (महल *mahal*) is in Varanasi. Begin प्रिय... *priy...* ('Dear...'), and end आपका प्रताप *āpkā Pratāp*.

Vocabulary

अकेला	*akelā*	alone	कि	*ki*	that
अफ़सोस ^m	*afsos*	regret	कुछ नहीं	*kuch nahī̃*	nothing
अरे	*are*	oh! what!	क्लास ^{m/f}	*klās*	class
उम्र ^f	*umr, umar*	age	खाना ^m	*khānā*	food
एकदम	*ekdam*	completely	खुशी ^f	*khuśī*	happiness, pleasure
और	*aur*	more	खूबसूरत	*khūbsūrat*	beautiful,
कम	*kam*	less; little			handsome
कल	*kal*	yesterday; tomorrow	गरम	*garam*	warm, hot
काम ^m	*kām*	work	गोली ^f	*golī*	tablet, pill
कालेज ^m	*kālej*	college	घर पर	*ghar par*	at home

चाँदी ^f *cā̃dī* silver

चाचा ^m *cācā* paternal uncle

चाय ^f *cāy* tea

जुकाम ^m *zukām* a cold

ज़्यादा *zyādā* more, very

ठंडा *ṭhaṇḍā* cold

तो *to* so, etc. (see 4.2)

था, थी, थे, थीं *thā, thī, the, thī̃* was, were

दफ़्तर ^m *daftar* office

दाल ^f *dāl* daal, lentils

दुकान ^f *dukān* shop

दोस्त ^{m, f} *dost* friend

पड़ोसी ^{m, f} *paṛosī* neighbour

पसंद *pasand* liked, pleasing

पहले *pahle* previously

पहाड़ ^m *pahāṛ* hill, mountain

प्यारा *pyārā* dear, lovely

प्रिय *priy* dear

बंद *band* closed, shut

बाज़ार ^m *bāzār* market

बाल-बच्चे ^{m pl} *bāl-bacce* children, family

बाहर *bāhar* out; outside

बुख़ार ^m *bukhār* fever

मज़बूत *mazbūt* strong

मतलब ^m *matlab* meaning

महल ^m *mahal* palace

माँ ^f *mā̃* Ma, Mother

मालूम *mālūm* known

मित्र ^m *mitr* friend

मेहनती *mehnatī* hardworking

रिश्तेदार ^{m, f} *riśtedār* relative

वाराणसी ^f *vārāṇasī* Varanasi, Banaras

विदेश ^m *videś* foreign country; abroad

समोसा ^m *samosā* samosa

साल ^m *sāl* year

सोना ^m *sonā* gold

सौ *sau* hundred

होशियार *hośiyār* clever, intelligent

5 | PLEASE SIT HERE
यहाँ बैठिए

In this unit you will learn how to
- give commands
- make requests
- talk about ownership and possession
- use more pronouns

5a   Kamala's neighbour Suresh comes for lunch

कमला	आइए सुरेश । खाना तैयार है, बैठिए ।
सुरेश	शुक्रिया । अच्छा, तो तुम अकेली नहीं हो – राज भी है । दूसरे बच्चे कहाँ हैं ?
कमला	वे तो अभी बाहर हैं, खाँ मार्केट में । राज, तू बैठ । इधर मत बैठ, उधर बैठ ।
राज	अम्माँ, मुझको चाय दो, मुझको दूध पसंद नहीं ।
कमला	तू चाय मत पी, दूध पी । तू तो अभी बहुत छोटा है बेटा !
राज	सुरेश अंकल, अम्माँ से कहिए कि मैं छोटा बच्चा नहीं हूँ ।

सुरेश	नहीं राज, तुम तो बहुत बड़े आदमी हो ! कमला, राज साहब को चाय दो!
कमला	सुनिए सुरेश, राज बड़ा आदमी तो है, लेकिन बड़ा शैतान भी है !

Kamalā	*āie Sureś. khānā taiyār hai, baiṭhie.*
Sureś	*śukriyā. acchā, to tum akelī nahī̃ ho – Rāj bhī hai. dūsre bacce kahā̃ haĩ?*
Kamalā	*ve to abhī bāhar haĩ, khā̃ mārkeṭ mẽ. Rāj, tū baiṭh. idhar mat baiṭh, udhar baiṭh.*
Rāj	*ammā̃, mujhko cāy do, mujhko dūdh pasand nahī̃.*
Kamalā	*tū cāy mat pī, dūdh pī. tū to abhī bahut choṭā hai beṭā!*
Rāj	*Sureś ankal, ammā̃ se kahie ki maĩ choṭā baccā nahī̃ hū̃.*
Sureś	*nahī̃ Rāj, tum to bahut baṛe ādmī ho! Kamalā, Rāj sāhab ko cāy do!*
Kamalā	*sunie Sureś, Rāj baṛā ādmī to hai, lekin baṛā śaitān bhī hai!*

> **!** इधर मत बैठ, उधर बैठ *idhar mat baiṭh, udhar baiṭh* – an ideal sentence for practising the difference between dental and retroflex consonants!

(For convenience, this vocabulary listing shows commands in the forms found in the dialogue, not as infinitives.)

आइए	*āie* please come	दो	*do* give
तैयार	*taiyār* ready	दूध ^m ^{m}	*dūdh* milk
बैठिए	*baiṭhie* please sit	मत	*mat* don't
खाँ मार्केट ^m	*khā̃ mārkeṭ* Khan Market (in Delhi)	पी	*pī* drink
		अंकल ^{m}	*ankal* uncle
बैठ	*baiṭh* sit	कहिए	*kahie* please tell
इधर	*idhar* here, over here	शैतान ^{m}	*śaitān* devil
उधर	*udhar* there, over there		

Kamala	Come, Suresh. The food is ready. Please sit.
Suresh	Thanks. Ah, you're not alone, Raj is here too. Where are the other children?
Kamala	They're out at the moment, in Khan Market. Raj, you sit. Don't sit here, sit there.
Raj	Mum, give me tea, I don't like milk.
Kamala	Don't you drink tea, drink milk. You're still very young, son!

Raj	Suresh Uncle, tell Mum that I'm not a little kid.
Suresh	No Raj, you're a very big fellow! Kamala, give Raj Sahib tea!
Kamala	Listen Suresh, Raj is a big man, but he's a big devil too!

Grammar

5.1 The infinitive verb

The Hindi verb is listed (in dictionaries etc.) in the infinitive – बोलना *bolnā* 'to speak'. The infinitive consists of the stem बोल- *bol-* plus the infinitive ending -ना *-nā* (always written with full न, not as a conjunct).

The infinitive has a variety of grammatical uses. The stem too is the basis for many verb forms, so when you learn a new infinitive verb, find its stem form by removing the -ना *-nā* ending.

Here, in Devanagari 'alphabetical' order, are some of the most common verbs:

आना	*ānā*	to come	(से) पूछना	*pūchnā*	to ask (of)
करना	*karnā*	to do	बताना	*batānā*	to tell
(से) कहना	*kahnā*	to say (to)	बुलाना	*bulānā*	to call, invite
खाना	*khānā*	to eat	बैठना	*baiṭhnā*	to sit
चलना	*calnā*	to move, go	मारना	*mārnā*	to beat, hit
जाना	*jānā*	to go	लाना	*lānā*	to bring
देखना	*dekhnā*	to see, look	लिखना	*likhnā*	to write
देना	*denā*	to give	लेना	*lenā*	to take, receive
पढ़ना	*paṛhnā*	to read, study	सुनना	*sunnā*	to listen, hear
पीना	*pīnā*	to drink, smoke	होना	*honā*	to be, become

5.2 Commands and requests

Commands and requests convey very fully the 'politeness' hierarchy of the honorific system (1.1). As in English, they may be used with or without the pronoun: 'speak' or 'you speak'.

तू बोल *tū bol*	The तू *tū* command consists of the verb stem alone. Its brevity accentuates its lack of formality, implying intimacy or bluntness: सुन *sun* 'Listen!'; जा *jā* 'Go!'; दे *de* 'Give!'
तुम बोलो *tum bolo*	The तुम *tum* command consists of stem plus -ओ *-o.* आओ *āo* 'Come'; लिखो *likho* 'Write'; बैठो *baiṭho* 'Sit'.
आप बोलिए *āp bolie*	The आप *āp* command consists of stem plus -इए *-ie.* खाइए *khāie* 'Please eat'; कहिए *kahie* 'Please say'; पढ़िए *paṛhie* 'Please read'.
आप बोलिएगा *āp boliega*	An extra-polite variant of the आप *āp* command, to which it adds the ending -गा *-gā.* बैठिएगा *baiṭhiegā* 'Please be so kind as to sit'; कल आइएगा *kal āiegā* 'Kindly come tomorrow'; आप भी एक पत्र लिखिएगा *āp bhī ek patr likhiegā* 'You also should kindly write a letter'.
बोलना *bolnā*	The infinitive too can be used as a command – often a 'deferred' one, to be acted on at some time in the future. It has no specific place in the 'honorifics' hierarchy, but it lacks the deference of an आप *āp* command and is most at home in तुम *tum* contexts.

> **!** सुनिए *sunie* 'Please listen': this is a polite way of attracting someone's attention, like 'excuse me' in English.

Four common verbs have irregular आप *āp* commands:

करना *karnā*	>	कीजिए *kījie*	please do
लेना *lenā*	>	लीजिए *lījie*	please take
देना *denā*	>	दीजिए *dījie*	please give
पीना *pīnā*	>	पीजिए *pījie*	please drink

देना *denā* and लेना *lenā* are irregular in the तुम *tum* commands also:

| लेना *lenā* | > | लो *lo* | take |
| देना *denā* | > | दो *do* | give |

The negative for commands ('don't...') is न *na*, or, more forcefully, मत *mat*. And notice that the verbs कहना *kahnā* 'to say, tell' and पूछना *pūchnā* 'to ask' use the postposition से *se* with the person addressed (see the first two examples below). There's more on this in 15.3.

मुझसे कहो ।	*mujhse kaho.*	Tell me.
पापा से न पूछो ।	*pāpā se na pūcho.*	Don't ask Papa.
वह पान मत खा !	*vah pān mat khā!*	Don't eat that paan!
यह पैसा लो ।	*yah paisā lo.*	Take this money.
ध्यान से सुनिए ।	*dhyān se sunie.*	Please listen with care.
उनका नाम लिखिएगा ।	*unkā nām likhiegā.*	Kindly write their name.
लन्दन से ख़त लिखना ।	*landan se khat likhnā.*	Write a letter from London.

> **!** One or two commands have found their way into English: 'Let's have a dekko' (a look), from देखो *dekho*; and 'shampoo', from चाँपो *cā̃po* (चाँपना *cā̃pnā* 'to rub, massage').

5b Lost keys and lost tempers

ऋषि	राज, तुम्हें मालूम है कि अरुण चाचा की चाबियाँ कहाँ हैं ?
राज	कौनसी चाबियाँ ? गाड़ी की चाबियाँ या घर की ?
ऋषि	घर की । कल तो संगीता के कमरे में थीं, उसकी मेज़ पर । अब नहीं हैं ।

राज	तो मुझसे मत पूछो, संगीता से पूछो । मैं संगीता का नौकर हूँ क्या ?
ऋषि	नहीं राज, नौकर नहीं हो, तुम तो सचमुच "राजा" हो !
राज	और इस "ऋषि" को यह भी नहीं मालूम कि घर की चाबियाँ कहाँ हैं !
अरुण	अरे बच्चो ! झगड़ा मत करो ! मुझे घर की चाबियाँ जल्दी दो ।
ऋषि	उधर देखिए अंकल ! दरवाज़े की चाबी पापा की मेज़ पर पड़ी है ।

Ṛṣi	Rāj, tumhē mālūm hai ki Aruṇ cācā kī cābiyā̃ kahā̃ haĩ?
Rāj	kaunsī cābiyā̃? gāṛī kī cābiyā̃ yā ghar kī?
Ṛṣi	ghar kī. kal to Saṅgītā ke kamre mē thī̃, uskī mez par. ab nahī̃ hai.
Rāj	to mujhse mat pūcho, Saṅgītā se pūcho. maĩ Saṅgītā kā naukar hū̃ kyā?
Ṛṣi	nahī̃ Rāj, naukar nahī̃ ho, tum to sacmuc 'rājā' ho!
Rāj	aur is 'ṛṣi' ko yah bhī nahī̃ mālūm ki ghar kī cābiyā̃ kahā̃ hai!
Aruṇ	are bacco! jhagṛā mat karo! mujhe ghar kī cābiyā̃ jaldī do.
Ṛṣi	udhar dekhie aṅkal! darvāze kī cābī pāpā kī mez par paṛī hai.

तुम्हें *tumhē* = तुमको *tumko*		ऋषि ^m *ṛṣi* sage, seer	
चाबी ^f *cābī* key		झगड़ा ^m *jhagṛā* quarrel, row;	
का/की/के *kā/kī/ke* 's (apostrophe s)		झगड़ा करना *jhagṛā karnā* to quarrel	
कौनसा/सी/से *kaunsā/sī/se* which?		जल्दी *jaldī* quickly	
नौकर ^m *naukar* servant		पड़ा *paṛā* lying	
सचमुच *sacmuc* really		पापा ^m *pāpā* Papa, Father	

Rishi	Raj, do you know where Uncle Arun's keys are?
Raj	Which keys? The car keys or the house ones?
Rishi	The house ones. Yesterday they were in Sangeeta's room, on her table. They're not now.
Raj	So don't ask me, ask Sangeeta. Am I Sangeeta's servant?
Rishi	No Raj, you're not a servant, you really are a 'raja'!
Raj	And this 'rishi' [sage] doesn't even know where the house keys are!
Arun	Hey children! Don't squabble! Give me the house keys quickly.
Rishi	Look over there Uncle! The door key is lying on Papa's table.

Grammar

5.3   Possession with का *kā*

Possession is expressed through का – राम का नाम   *rām kā nām*,
'Ram's name' or 'the name of Ram'.   Being a postposition, it needs
a preceding noun or pronoun to be in the oblique case:

| बच्चे का कुत्ता | *bacce kā kuttā* | the child's dog |
| उन का घोड़ा | *un kā ghoṛā* | their horse |

But it also agrees adjectivally with the thing possessed:

| बच्चे की किताब | *bacce kī kitāb* | the child's book |
| उस बच्चे के खिलौने | *us bacce ke khilaune* | that child's toys |

In terms of function and word order, का *kā* is equivalent to the
English apostrophe 's'. When the thing possessed is in the oblique
case, then का *kā* will be too:

लड़के के कमरे में	*laṛke ke kamre mẽ*	in the boy's room
लड़के की कुरसी पर	*laṛke kī kursī par*	on the boy's chair
लड़कों के कमरे में	*laṛkõ ke kamre mẽ*	in the boys' room
लड़कों के कमरों में	*larkõ ke kamrõ mẽ*	in the boys' rooms
लड़कों की कुरसियों पर	*laṛkõ kī kursiyõ par*	on the boys' chairs

उस आदमी का बेटा विद्यार्थी है ।	*us ādmī kā beṭā vidyārthī hai.*	That man's son is a student.
उन लोगों के कपड़े बहुत गंदे हैं ।	*un logõ ke kapṛe bahut gande haĩ.*	Those people's clothes are very dirty.
उस घर के बग़ीचे में चार लंबे पेड़ हैं ।	*us ghar ke bagīce mẽ cār lambe peṛ haĩ.*	There are four tall trees in the garden of that house.
खन्ना की बहिन के कुत्ते का नाम चीकू है ।	*Khannā kī bahin ke kutte kā nām Cīkū hai.*	Khanna's sister's dog's name is Chikoo.

5.4 को *ko* with the indirect and direct object

को *ko* with the indirect object

In a sentence such as 'Give the key to Raj', 'key' is the direct object and 'Raj' is the indirect object. Hindi marks the indirect object with को *ko* – राज को चाबी दो *Rāj ko cābī do*.

The pattern remains the same even if को *ko* is not translatable by 'to': मुझ को वह ख़त दो *mujh ko vah khat do*, 'Give me that letter' (='Give that letter to me'); उस को भी बताओ *us ko bhī batāo* 'Tell him too'; in these sentences the indirect objects are 'me' and 'him' respectively.

हम को गरम खाना खिलाओ ।	*ham ko garam khānā khilāo.*	Serve us hot food.
धोबी को गंदे कपड़े देना ।	*dhobī ko gande kapṛe denā.*	Give the dirty clothes to the dhobi.
उनको मेरा नाम मत बता !	*unko merā nām mat batā!*	Don't tell them my name!

को *ko* with the direct object

A direct object is sometimes marked with को *ko* and sometimes not; the distinction is often quite subtle – not to say elusive! Usually, direct objects such as चाय *cāy* and समोसा *samosā* in these examples take no postposition – and hence remain in the direct case:

भैया, चाय लाओ ।	*bhaiyā, cāy lāo.*	Brother, bring tea.
समोसा खाओ ।	*samosā khāo.*	Have ('eat') a samosa.

Here, both 'tea' and 'samosa' are perceived as generic items – there is no focus on their individuality, no *specific* cup of tea or *individual* samosa is meant. But when an object is individualised, को *ko* may be added – the effect often being similar to adding the definite article 'the' in English:

पानी पियो ।	*pānī piyo.*	Drink water.
पानी को पियो ।	*pānī ko piyo.*	Drink the water.
एक कुरसी लाओ ।	*ek kursī lao.*	Bring a chair.
कुरसी को साफ़ करो ।	*kursī ko sāf karo.*	Clean the chair.

To some extent, then, को *ko* marks a *specific* direct object. So when referring to something that's already been mentioned, को *ko* will be used:

| यह किताब अच्छी है | *yah kitāb acchī hai* | This book's good |
| – इसको पढ़ो । | *– isko paṛho.* | – read it. |

The most specific thing of all is an individual, a person: so people who are verb objects (and pronouns standing for them) nearly always take को *ko*.

छोटू को मत मारना ।	*Choṭū ko mat mārnā.*	Don't hit Chotu.
पिताजी को बुलाइए ।	*pitājī ko bulāie.*	Call Father.
उनको जगाइए ।	*unko jagāie.*	Wake them up.

5.5   Alternative forms of the oblique pronoun + को *ko*

The oblique personal pronouns + को *ko* (e.g. उसको *usko*) have alternative forms as follows:

मुझको	*mujhko*	मुझे	*mujhe*
तुझको	*tujhko*	तुझे	*tujhe*
इसको	*isko*	इसे	*ise*
उसको	*usko*	उसे	*use*
हमको	*hamko*	हमें	*hamẽ*
तुमको	*tumko*	तुम्हें	*tumhẽ*
आपको	*āpko*	(no alternative form)	
इनको	*inko*	इन्हें	*inhẽ*
उनको	*unko*	उन्हें	*unhẽ*
किसको	*kisko*	किसे	*kise*
किनको	*kinko*	किन्हें	*kinhẽ*

The two forms are completely interchangeable, although the shorter forms tend to be favoured in colloquial style, or to avoid repetitiveness if there's another को *ko* elsewhere in the sentence. In the first of the following examples, मुझे *mujhe* is preferred to मुझको *mujhko*; and in the second, हमें *hamē* to हमको *hamko*.

मुझे अफ़सोस है कि	*mujhe afsos hai ki*	I'm sorry that you
तुमको ज़ुकाम है ।	*tumko zukām hai.*	have a cold.
हमें मालूम है कि	*hamē mālūm hai ki*	We know that he
उसको बुख़ार है ।	*usko bukhār hai.*	has fever.

EXERCISE 5a.1 Transpose तुम *tum* commands into आप *āp* commands and vice versa. Then translate.

१   यहाँ सिग्रेट न पियो ।   ६   पानी न पीजिए; काफ़ी लीजिए ।

२   ज़रा यहाँ ठहरो ।   ७   आइए । बताइए, क्या हाल है?

३   इस कमरे में बैठो ।   ८   गाड़ी को इधर लाइए ।

४   चाय पियो, फल खाओ ।   ९   उधर देखिए, वह नारा पढ़िए !

५   मुझे ऋषि के कपड़े दो ।   १०   दरवाज़े को बन्द कीजिए ।

1   *yahā̃ sigreṭ na piyo.*   6   *pānī na pījie; kāfī lījie.*
2   *zarā yahā̃ ṭhaharo.*   7   *āie. batāie, kyā hāl hai?*
3   *is kamre mē baiṭho.*   8   *gāṛī ko idhar lāie.*
4   *cāy piyo, phal khāo.*   9   *udhar dekhie, vah nārā paṛhie!*
5   *mujhe Ṛṣi ke kapṛe do.*   10 *darvāze ko band kījie.*

EXERCISE 5a.2 Transpose the infinitive commands into तू *tū* commands. Then translate.

१   कंबलों को गंदा मत करना ।

२   खाने को मत छूना ।

३   सरल हिन्दी बोलना ।

४   किताब में मेरा नाम न लिखना ।

५   घोड़े को मत मारना !

1   *kambalō ko gandā mat karnā.*
2   *khāne ko mat chūnā.*

3   *saral hindī bolnā.*

4   *kitāb mẽ merā nām na likhnā.*

5   *ghoṛe ko mat mārnā!*

 EXERCISE 5b.1 Rewrite the following sentences, removing को *ko* from the direct object. Then translate.

१   इन मोटे कंबलों को अलमारी में रखो ।

२   इस गरम समोसे को खाओ ।

३   उस बड़ी कुरसी को इस कमरे में लाइए ।

४   आज के अख़बार को पढ़ ।

५   चाचा जी के दरवाज़े को बन्द करना ।

1   *in moṭe kambalõ ko almārī mẽ rakho.*

2   *is garam samose ko khāo.*

3   *us baṛī kursī ko is kamre mẽ lāie.*

4   *āj ke akhbār ko paṛh.*

5   *cācā jī ke darvāze ko band karnā.*

EXERCISE 5b.2 Rewrite the following sentences, adding को *ko* to the direct object. Then translate.

१   ये नए खिलौने लो ।

२   ऋषि का पुराना कुरता पहनो ।

३   गाड़ी की चाबियाँ ढूँढ़ो ।

४   ये गंदे कपड़े धोना ।

५   यह थैला दराज़ में रखिए ।

1   *ye nae khilaune lo.*

2   *Ṛṣi kā purānā kurtā pahano.*

3   *gāṛī kī cābiyā̃ ḍhū̃ṛho.*

4   *ye gande kapṛe dhonā.*

5   *yah thailā darāz mẽ rakhie.*

EXERCISE 5b.3 Translate the questions, then answer them.

1   What is the name of Kamala's brother-in-law (देवर^m) ?

2   Is Rishi at home just now? (See Dialogue 5a.)

3   Who does not like milk?

4   Why does he not like milk?

5   Where were Sangeeta's uncle's keys yesterday?

6   Who knows where those keys are today?

7   Do you know where the Kumar family's house is?

8   In your opinion (ख़याल^m), are these questions (सवाल^m) simple?

Vocabulary

आना	*ānā* to come	चलना	*calnā* to move
इधर	*idhar* here, over here	चाबी^f	*cābī* key
उधर	*udhar* there, over there	छूना	*chūnā* to touch
ऋषि^m	*ṛṣi* sage, seer	जगाना	*jagānā* to arouse from sleep
कंबल^m	*kambal* blanket	ज़रा	*zarā* just, a little
करना	*karnā* to do	जल्दी	*jaldī* quickly, soon, early
(से) कहना	*kahnā* to say (to)	जाना	*jānā* to go
का/की/के	*kā/kī/ke* 's (indicating possession)	झगड़ा^m	*jhagṛā* quarrel, row;
		झगड़ा करना	*jhagṛā karnā* to quarrel
काफ़ी^f	*kāfī* coffee		
कुत्ता^m	*kuttā* dog	ठहरना	*ṭhaharnā* to stop, wait
कुरता^m	*kurtā* kurta, Indian shirt	ढूँढना	*ḍhū̃ṛhnā* to look for, find
कौनसा/सी/से	*kaunsā/sī/se* which?	तैयार	*taiyār* ready
ख़त^m	*khat* letter	थैला^m	*thailā* bag, cloth bag
ख़याल^m	*khayāl* opinion	दूध^m	*dūdh* milk
खाँ मार्केट^m	*khā̃ markeṭ* Khan Market (in Delhi)	देखना	*dekhnā* to see, look
		देना	*denā* to give
खाना	*khānā* to eat	देवर^m	*devar* husband's younger brother
खिलाना	*khilānā* to serve, give to eat		
खिलौना^m	*khilaunā* toy	धोना	*dhonā* to wash
घोड़ा^m	*ghoṛā* horse	धोबी^m	*dhobī* dhobi, washerman

ध्यान ^m   *dhyān* attention; ध्यान से
   dhyān se attentively

न   *na* don't (in commands)

नारा ^m   *nārā* slogan

नौकर ^m   *naukar* servant

पड़ा   *paṛā* lying

पढ़ना   *paṛhnā* to read, study

पान ^m   *pān* paan

पानी ^m   *pānī* water

पापा ^m   *pāpā* Papa, Father

पीना   *pīnā* to drink; to smoke

(से) पूछना   *pūchnā* to ask (of)

पेड़ ^m   *peṛ* tree

पैसा ^m   *paisā* money; paisa
   (hundredth of a rupee)

फल ^m   *phal* fruit

बंद करना   *band karnā* to close,
   shut

बताना   *batānā* to tell

बुलाना   *bulānā* to call, invite

बैठना   *baiṭhnā* to sit

बोलना   *bolnā* to speak

भैया ^m   *bhaiyā* brother

मत   *mat* don't (with commands)

मारना   *mārnā* to beat, hit

रखना   *rakhnā* to put, keep

लाना   *lānā* to bring

लिखना   *likhnā* to write

लेना   *lenā* to take, receive

शैतान ^m   *śaitān* devil

सचमुच   *sacmuc* really

सरल   *saral* simple

साफ़ करना   *sāf karnā* to clean

सिग्रेट ^f   *sigreṭ* cigarette

सुनना   *sunnā* to listen, hear

होना   *honā* to be, become

6 | WHAT DOES PRATAP DO?

प्रताप क्या करता है?

In this unit you will learn how to
- talk about regular activities
- ask what things are called in Hindi
- learn the remaining possessive pronouns
- discuss opinions and relationships

6a   Suresh asks Prakash about his household

सुरेश	प्रकाश, बताइए, आपका मेहमान प्रताप – वह क्या करता है ?
प्रकाश	वह विद्यार्थी है । एक प्राइवेट स्कूल में हिन्दी सीखता है ।
सुरेश	उसका प्रोनंसियेशन बहुत साफ़ है । हिन्दी में "प्रोनंसियेशन" को क्या कहते हैं – उच्चारण !
प्रकाश	हाँ, प्रताप अच्छा बोलता है । वैसे वह बहुत होनहार लड़का है ।
सुरेश	मालूम होता है कि संगीता उससे नफ़रत करती है; ऐसा क्यों है ?

प्रकाश	मैं नहीं जानता । पर संगीता सोचती है कि प्रताप उससे प्यार करता है ।
सुरेश	अच्छा ! एक बात और – राज हमेशा घर पर क्यों रहता है ? वह दिन भर क्या करता है ?
प्रकाश	खेलता है, खाता है, सोता है, शरारत करता है । बच्चा है, न?
सुरेश	यह अच्छी बात नहीं है कि लड़का घर पर अकेला रहता है ।
प्रकाश	अरे छोड़ो इन बातों को सुरेश ! *[मन में सोचता है – "तुम इन बच्चों के बाप हो क्या ?"]*

मेहमान ^m guest		सोचना to think
प्राइवेट स्कूल ^m private school		प्यार ^m love
सीखना to learn		हमेशा always
प्रोनंसियेशन ^m 'pronunciation'		रहना to stay
उच्चारण ^m pronunciation		दिन भर all day
अच्छा well		खेलना to play
वैसे actually		सोना to sleep
होनहार promising		शरारत ^f mischief
नफ़रत ^m hate, dislike		छोड़ना to leave
ऐसा thus, so, like this		मन ^m mind
जानना to know		बाप ^m father

Suresh	Prakash, tell me, your guest Pratap – what does he do?
Prakash	He's a student. He learns Hindi in a private school.
Suresh	His pronunciation is very clear. What's 'pronunciation' called in Hindi – *uccāraṇ*!
Prakash	Yes, Pratap speaks well. Actually he's a very promising boy.
Suresh	It seems Sangeeta dislikes him. Why is it so?
Prakash	I don't know. But Sangeeta thinks that Pratap loves her.
Suresh	I see! One more thing – why does Raj always stay at home? What does he do all day?
Prakash	He plays, eats, sleeps, makes mischief. He's a kid, isn't he?
Suresh	It's not good that the boy stays alone at home.
Prakash	Oh leave these things, Suresh! [Thinks to himself: 'Are you the father of these children?']

Grammar
6.1 The imperfective present tense

The imperfective tense describes regular events or habits: 'I speak Hindi', 'She lives in Delhi, 'We don't smoke'. The participle – बोलता 'speaks', from बोलना 'to speak' – is followed by हूँ / हो / है / हैं.

MASCULINE	FEMININE	
मैं बोलता हूँ	मैं बोलती हूँ	I speak
तू बोलता है	तू बोलती है	you speak
यह, वह बोलता है	यह, वह बोलती है	he, it, she speaks
हम बोलते हैं	हम बोलती हैं	we speak
तुम बोलते हो	तुम बोलती हो	you speak
आप बोलते हैं	आप बोलती हैं	you speak
ये, वे बोलते हैं	ये, वे बोलती हैं	they speak

मैं शुद्ध हिन्दी बोलता हूँ ।	I speak pure Hindi.
क्या श्रीमती खन्ना पंजाबी समझती हैं ?	Does Mrs Khanna understand Panjabi?
तुम कहाँ रहते हो ?	Where do you live?
प्रताप कभी कभी शराब पीता है ।	Pratap sometimes drinks.

In the negative, the auxiliary verb (हूँ / हो / है / हैं) can be dropped:

मैं सिग्रेट कभी नहीं पीता ।	I never smoke.
शर्मा जी गोश्त नहीं खाते ।	Sharma ji does not eat meat.
वह लखनऊ में नहीं रहती, दिल्ली में रहती है ।	She doesn't live in Lucknow, she lives in Delhi.

When this happens with a feminine plural, the participle becomes nasalised, compensating for the dropped nasalised auxiliary हैं:

दादी जी गोश्त खाती हैं / नहीं खातीं ।	Dadi ji eats meat / doesn't eat meat.
वे औरतें शराब पीती हैं / नहीं पीतीं ।	Those women drink / don't drink.

All these examples relate to *habitual* events. (Continuous activities, with '-ing' verbs in English (e.g. 'he is speaking'), have a separate tense: see Unit 8.) The imperfective tense is also used for ongoing states of mind:

वह सोचता है कि तुम्हारा उच्चारण अच्छा है ।	He thinks that your pronunciation is good.
मैं अक्सर अकेलापन महसूस करता हूँ ।	I often experience loneliness.

An idiomatic use of the imperfective is seen when someone who's just about to leave says अच्छा, मैं चलती हूँ 'Well, I'm off' – in which the 'leaving' is not 'habitual' at all. Similarly अभी आता हूँ 'I'm coming straightaway'.

Although expressions for time of day aren't introduced fully until 12.2, the expression कितने बजे 'at what time?' is useful in practising imperfective tenses. You can make up many sentences on the following models, using verbs such as आना 'to come', उठना 'to get up', खाना 'to eat', खेलना 'to play', जाना 'to go', and सोना 'to sleep'.

राज नौ बजे स्कूल जाता है ।	Raj goes to school at nine o'clock.
आप कितने बजे उठती हैं ?	What time do you get up?
मैं सात बजे उठती हूँ ।	I get up at seven o'clock.

Relating to the knowledge of a language, the verb आना 'to come' can be used in the imperfective construction हमें हिन्दी आती है, literally 'Hindi comes to us', i.e. 'We know Hindi'.

मुझको थोड़ी उर्दू आती है ।	I know a little Urdu.
तुमको कितनी भाषाएँ आती हैं ?	How many languages do you know?

Here's a useful way of asking the Hindi word for something:

इस लिपि को क्या कहते हैं ?	What's this script called? ('What do they call...?')
इसको देवनागरी कहते हैं ।	They call it Devanagari.

Using होता है (from होना 'to be') implies a general statement of lasting validity, whereas है alone is for a specific one-off statement.

अच्छी साड़ियाँ महँगी होती हैं ।	Good saris are expensive.
हाँ, लेकिन यह साड़ी सस्ती है ।	Yes, but this sari is cheap.

See also the difference of meaning between मालूम होता है and मालूम है:

मालूम होता है कि माँ नाराज़ हैं ।	It seems Mother's angry.
मुझे मालूम है कि माँ नाराज़ हैं ।	I know Mother's angry.

By now you're used to verb gender in the verb: masculine बोलता, feminine बोलती. When a mixture of genders is involved, agreement follows the rule given for adjectives in 2.2: if the subjects are people, then the plural verb is masculine; if they're inanimates, the verb takes its gender from the closest item.

कृष्ण और राधा खेलते हैं ।	Krishna and Radha play.
क्या जूते और चप्पलें सस्ती होती हैं ?	Are shoes and sandals cheap?

6.2 Possessive pronouns

As we've already seen with मेरा, तुम्हारा and आपका (3.3.), the possessive pronouns decline like adjectives – they agree with the thing possessed. An oblique pronoun + का can be written as two words or one: उसका or उस का, किसका or किस का. Here's the full list.

मैं	I	मेरा	my, mine
तू	you	तेरा	your, yours
यह	he, she, it	इसका	his, her, hers, its, of this
वह	he, she, it	उसका	his, her, hers, its, of that
हम	we	हमारा	our, ours
तुम	you	तुम्हारा	your, yours
आप	you	आपका	your, yours
ये	they	इनका	their, theirs
वे	they	उनका	their, theirs
कौन	who?	किसका	whose? (singular);
		किनका	whose? (plural)

तुम्हारा कुत्ता हमारे घर में है ।	Your dog is in our house.
तेरा पापा कहाँ है ?	Where's your father?
आपके हाथ में क्या है?	What is in your hand?
ये कपड़े किसके हैं ? मेरे तो नहीं हैं ।	Whose clothes are these? They're not mine.

Word order: look back at the points made about word order in 1.5 and 3.2, then see the difference between the following sentences:

यह मेरा दफ़्तर है ।	This is my office.
यह दफ़्तर मेरा है ।	This office is mine.

6b   **Pratap and Sangeeta**

प्रताप	संगीता, ऋषि अपने भाई से कितना बड़ा है ?
संगीता	राज सबसे छोटा है – सिर्फ़ बारह साल का है । ऋषि चौदह साल का है ।
प्रताप	और तुम, संगीता ? तुम्हारी उम्र कितनी है ? क्या तुम मुझसे बड़ी हो ?
संगीता	मैं उन्नीस साल की हूँ । मुझे मालूम नहीं कि तुम्हारी उम्र कितनी है ।
प्रताप	मैं तुम से थोड़ा बड़ा हूँ – इक्कीस साल का हूँ ।
संगीता	और लंबाई में भी तुम मुझसे बड़े हो । [व्यंग्य से] बहुत बहुत बधाइयाँ !
प्रताप	यह व्यंग्य क्यों, संगीता ? तुम मुझे क्यों नापसंद करती हो ?
संगीता	कौन कहता है कि मैं तुम्हें नापसंद करती हूँ ? मैं तुम्हारे बारे में तो सोचती भी नहीं !
प्रताप	तुम तो सिर्फ़ अपने बारे में सोचती हो, अपने दोस्तों के बारे में नहीं ।
संगीता	अच्छा, तो तुम अपने को मेरा दोस्त समझते हो? वाह!

अपना	one's own	लंबाई ^f	height
बारह	twelve	व्यंग्य ^m	sarcasm
साल ^m	year	बधाई ^f	congratulation
चौदह	fourteen	नापसंद करना	to dislike
उन्नीस	nineteen	के बारे में	about, concerning
थोड़ा	a little	समझना	to consider, reckon
इक्कीस	twenty-one	वाह	wonderful! bravo!

Pratap	Sangeeta, how much older is Rishi than his brother?
Sangeeta	Raj is the youngest – he's only 12. Rishi is 14.
Pratap	And you, Sangeeta? What's your age? Are you older than me?
Sangeeta	I'm 19. I don't know how old you are.
Pratap	I'm a little older than you – I'm 21.
Sangeeta	And you're taller than me ('greater in height') too. [*sarcastically*] Many congratulations!
Pratap	Why this sarcasm, Sangeeta? Why do you dislike me?
Sangeeta	Who says I dislike you? I don't even think about you!
Pratap	You only think about yourself, not about your friends.
Sangeeta	I see, so you consider yourself my friend! Wonderful!

 वह बारह साल का है – 'he's 12' ('of 12 years'); का agrees with the male subject. And why isn't साल in the oblique plural, सालों? Because the 12 years constitute a *single block of time* in which the separate years are not individualised. Similarly दस दिन में 'in ten days'.

Grammar
6.3 अपना 'one's own'

अपना 'one's own' is a reflexive pronoun – it means 'my, 'your', 'her' etc. depending on the subject of the clause. Compare the following:

राज अपने कमरे में है ।	Raj is in his [own] room.
राज उसके कमरे में है ।	Raj is in his [someone else's] room.

In the first sentence, the word 'his' refers back to Raj *as the subject of the clause*; that is, the words 'Raj' and 'his' refer to the same person. In such situations, Hindi uses अपना in place of any possessive pronoun (e.g. मेरा, तेरा, उसका).

मैं संगीता को अपनी किताब देता हूँ ।	I give Sangeeta my book.
सुहास संगीता को अपनी किताब देता है ।	Suhas gives Sangeeta his book.
संगीता सुहास को अपनी किताब देती है ।	Sangeeta gives Suhas her book.
हम अपने दोस्तों को ख़त लिखते हैं ।	We write letters to our friends.
वे अपनी भाषा क्यों नहीं बोलते ?	Why don't they speak their own language?

Now compare the following sentences very carefully:

मैं अपने भाई से लंबा हूँ ।	I am taller than my brother.
मेरा भाई बहुत लंबा नहीं है ।	My brother isn't very tall.
मैं और मेरा भाई दोनों मोटे हैं ।	My brother and I are both fat.

In the first sentence, 'my' refers to 'I' as subject; so अपना is used. In the second, 'My brother' is *itself* the subject, so अपना is *not* used. Similarly अपना is *not* used in the third sentence, because मेरा भाई is part of a *joint subject* ('my brother and I') rather than being a reference to a subject.

Using the possessive and the reflexive pronouns together, e.g. मेरा अपना, gives an emphatic sense – 'my own, my very own':

यह मेरी अपनी गाड़ी है ।	This is my very own car.
हिन्दी हमारी अपनी भाषा है ।	Hindi is our own language.

In a command, 'you' will *always* be अपना, because the subject of a command is 'you':

(तुम) अपनी किताब पढ़ो ।	(You) read your book.
मुझे अपने गंदे कपड़े दो ।	Give me your dirty clothes.
अपना ख़याल/ ध्यान रखना ।	Take care of yourself.

अपना takes some getting used to. As a *general* rule, use it if you can add the word 'own' to an English possessive ('her own car', 'our own house') without changing the fundamental sense of the phrase; the main exceptions to this are with the 'joint subject', as in मैं और मेरा भाई, always linked by 'and', and in commands.

6.4 Compound postpositions

These postpositions consist of two or more words, the first of which is the possessive के (or की if used with a feminine noun, e.g. तरफ़ 'direction'). Like the one-word 'simple postpositions' (3.1), they take the oblique case.

की तरफ़	towards	घर की तरफ़	towards home
के अंदर	inside	कमरे के अंदर	inside the room

के आगे	in front of, ahead of	डाकघर के आगे	in front of the post office
के ऊपर	on top of	बस के ऊपर	on top of the bus
के नीचे	beneath, below	मेज़ के नीचे	under the table
के/से पहले	before	शुक्रवार से पहले	before Friday
के पास	near	पेड़ों के पास	near the trees
के पीछे	behind	परदे के पीछे	behind the veil
के बाद	after	इसके बाद	after this
के बारे में	about, concerning	इस बात के बारे में	about this matter
के बाहर	outside	कमरे के बाहर	outside the room
के लिए	for	बच्चों के लिए	for the children
के यहाँ	at the place of	पिंकी के यहाँ	at Pinkie's place
के सामने	facing, opposite	तेरे घर के सामने	opposite your house

Compare these two phrases, based on के लिए 'for':

उनके लिए for them   मेरे लिए for me

The first phrase, उनके लिए, features के because के is part of the possessive form उनका/उनके 'their'. But in the second phrase, मेरे लिए, no का/के is apparent; this is because there is no का/के in the possessive form मेरा 'my'. Thus when used with pronouns ('for me, for her' etc.), compound postpositions are based on the *possessive* form of the pronoun (6.2):

मैं	→	मेरा	→	मेरे लिए	for me
तू	→	तेरा	→	तेरे लिए	for you
यह	→	इसका	→	इसके लिए	for him/her/it
वह	→	उसका	→	उसके लिए	for him/her/it
हम	→	हमारा	→	हमारे लिए	for us
आप	→	आपका	→	आपके लिए	for you
तुम	→	तुम्हारा	→	तुम्हारे लिए	for you
कौन	→	किसका	→	किसके लिए	for whom?
self	→	अपना	→	अपने लिए	for oneself

Some more examples:

की तरफ़	towards	हमारी तरफ़	towards us
की तरह	like	मेरी तरह	like me
के पीछे	behind	मेरे पीछे	behind me
के बारे में	about	अपने बारे में	about oneself
के साथ	with	मेरे साथ	with me

6.5 Pronouns revisited

Let us revise the pronoun types encountered so far.

Direct case personal pronouns such as मैं, तू, वह came in 1.1 with the verb 'to be' and should be very familiar by now. The oblique forms मुझ, तुझ, उस etc., to which they change when followed by a postposition, came in 3.4. Then in 5.5 we saw how the 'personal pronoun + को' formula has an alternative set: मुझे, तुझे उसे etc.

'Personal pronoun + को' constructions are very common: मुझको बुख़ार है 'I have fever'. In English the subject is 'I', but in Hindi it's बुख़ार. (Remember that a verb subject *must be in the direct case.*) You may find it helpful to think in terms of two general types of construction: a 'मैं' type (मैं बीमार हूँ) and a 'मुझको' type (मुझको बुख़ार है).

Possessive pronouns (मेरा, तेरा, उसका etc.) have just been introduced in 6.2, although some had slipped in earlier. They agree with the thing possessed (not the possessor): मेरा भाई, मेरी बहिन, मेरे चाचा; so they behave just like adjectives, as in बड़ा भाई, बड़ी बहिन etc.

Possessive pronouns are replaced by अपना when the possessor is also the verb subject: 'I read my book' must be मैं अपनी किताब पढ़ता हूँ because 'I' and 'my' both refer to the same person.

We have also encountered some interrogative pronouns: कौन 'who?', किस 'whom?', किसका 'whose?', क्या 'what?', कौनसा 'which?'. And we can look forward to meeting relative pronouns ('the man who...', 'the book which...' etc.) in Unit 13.

EXERCISE 6a.1 Answer the questions (6–10 are on the dialogues).

१   आप कहाँ रहते हैं / रहती हैं ?

२   आपके घर में कितने लोग रहते हैं ?

३   हिन्दी में "प्रोनंसियेशन" को क्या कहते हैं ?

४   आप कितनी भाषाएँ बोलते हैं / बोलती हैं ?

५   क्या आपके शहर में मकान महँगे होते हैं ?

६   प्रताप किसके घर में रहता है ?

७   उस घर में कितने लोग रहते हैं ?

८   प्रताप की माँ कहाँ रहती हैं, और उनका नाम क्या है ?

९   क्या राज दिन भर काम करता है ?

१०   कौन किसको नापसंद करता है ?

EXERCISE 6a.2 Translate this extract from Pratap's letter home.

प्रकाश कुमार एक बड़ी कंपनी में काम करते हैं; उनके मालिक का नाम खन्ना है । मालूम होता है खन्ना साहब बहुत बड़े आदमी हैं; प्रकाश जी उनसे डरते हैं (और शायद अपनी पत्नी कमला से भी !)। प्रकाश और कमला के दोनों बच्चे स्कूल जाते हैं; और उनकी लड़की संगीता कालेज जाती है । संगीता बहुत होशियार है लेकिन मुझसे तो ज़्यादा बात नहीं करती । मैं सोचता हूँ कि वह मुझको पसंद नहीं करती । उसकी सहेली पिंकी अक्सर यहाँ आती है; दोनों दिन भर गपशप करती हैं और ख़ूब हँसती हैं । पिंकी खन्ना की छोटी बहिन है; वह संगीता से बड़ी है, लेकिन दोनों में से संगीता ज़्यादा ख़ूबसूरत है । वह शायद भारत की सबसे सुन्दर लड़की है !

दादीजी अक्सर मुझसे पूछती हैं कि मेरे माँ-बाप क्या करते हैं, मेरे दोस्त कौन हैं, वग़ैरह । वे राज और ऋषि को बहुत हँसाती हैं – मुझको भी ! राज को वे बहुत प्यार करती हैं; उसको "मुन्ना" या "मेरा चाँद का टुकड़ा" कहती हैं । राज को ये नाम बिलकुल पसंद नहीं हैं । पर वह चुप रहता है । दादीजी को सब लोग प्यार करते हैं ।

EXERCISE 6b.1 Translate the English words, then translate the whole sentences into English.

१   प्रताप his अध्यापक से हिन्दी के बारे में अक्सर मुश्किल सवाल पूछता है ।

२   दादी हम को her बचपन के बारे में बताती हैं ।

३   ऋषि और his भाई their दादी के साथ बहुत हँसते हैं ।

४   मुन्ना, मैं your दादी हूँ; तू मुझे क्यों नहीं your खाना खिलाता है ?

५   ऋषि, तू your काम कर; फिर मुझे my खाना खिला ।

६   प्रकाश his बेटी से her सहेली के बारे में पूछता है ।

७   संगीता her पिता को her सहेली के बारे में बताती है ।

EXERCISE 6b.2 Translate.

They call me Rishi. Raj is my little brother; he's a bit crazy. He's not in his room at the moment, he's in my room. And I'm not in my room; I'm in his room! He doesn't know that I know that he's in my room. Here in his room there are several old newspapers, but I don't know whose they are; they're not his. Raj doesn't read books or newspapers. He plays with his friends but he doesn't talk to me. His friends are not my friends.

I like Pratap. I go to the cinema with him and we talk about films. It seems he's quite bright. He speaks good Hindi. Even his pronunciation is quite good. He doesn't speak like a foreigner.

Vocabulary

अकेलापन ^m loneliness	के पीछे behind
अक्सर often; usually	के बाद after
अच्छा well, proficiently	के बारे में about, concerning
अपना (one's) own	के बाहर outside
इक्कीस twenty-one	के यहाँ at the place of
उच्चारण ^m pronunciation	के लिए for
उठना to get up, rise	के साथ with, in company of
उन्नीस nineteen	के सामने facing, opposite
कंपनी ^f company, firm	(का) ख़याल रखना to take care of,
कभी कभी sometimes; कभी नहीं	mind
never	ख़ूब a lot, well
की तरफ़ towards	गपशप ^f gossip
की तरह like	गोश्त ^m meat
के अंदर inside	चाँद ^m moon
के आगे in front of, ahead of	चुप silent
के ऊपर on top of	चौदह fourteen
के नीचे beneath, below	छोड़ना to leave
के/से पहले before	जानना to know
के पास near	टुकड़ा ^m piece, bit

(से) डरना to fear	लंबाई ^f height, length
डाकघर ^m post-office	लखनऊ ^m Lucknow
तेरा your (from तू)	लिपि ^f script
थोड़ा a little	वाह (expresses admiration or
दिन ^m day; दिन भर all day	scorn) wonderful!
देवनागरी ^f Devanagari script	विदेशी ^{m, f} foreigner
(का) ध्यान रखना to take care of,	वैसे actually
mind	व्यंग्य ^m sarcasm
नफ़रत ^f hate, dislike	शराब ^f alcoholic, liquor
नापसंद करना to dislike	शरारत ^f mischief
प्यार ^m love, affection; (को/ से)	शुक्रवार ^m Friday
प्यार करना to love	शुद्ध pure, unmixed
फिर then; again	संस्कृत ^f Sanskrit
बचपन ^m childhood	सहेली ^f girl's female friend
बजे o' clock	साड़ी ^f sari
बधाई ^f congratulation	साल ^m year
(से) बात/बातें करना to talk, converse	सीखना to learn
बाप ^m father	से पहले before
बारह twelve	सोचना to think
मन ^m mind	सोना to sleep
महसूस करना to feel, experience	स्टेशन ^m station
मालिक ^m boss	हँसना to laugh
मुन्ना Munna (nickname for little	हँसाना to make laugh
boy)	हमारा our, ours
मुश्किल difficult	हमेशा always
मेहमान ^m guest	होनहार promising

7 | FATHER USED TO TEACH URDU

पिताजी उर्दू पढ़ाते थे

In this unit you will learn how to

- talk about regular activities in the past
- express needs and wants
- use ordinal numbers – first, second
- use several colloquial expressions

 7a **Grandmother's childhood in Kanpur**

संगीता	दादी जी, बचपन में आप लोग कानपुर में रहते थे न ?
दादी जी	हाँ बेटी, मेरे पिताजी किसी कालेज में उर्दू पढ़ाते थे । माँ भी पढ़ाती थीं ।
संगीता	आपके घर में कोई अँग्रेज़ी बोलता था ?
दादी जी	हाँ, पिताजी को कोई पाँच भाषाएँ आती थीं । पर हम लोग ज़्यादातर हिन्दी बोलते थे ।
संगीता	क्या आपके घर के नज़दीक कोई सिनेमा था ?
दादी जी	हाँ, हम लोग हर शनिवार को कुछ सहेलियों के साथ सिनेमा जाते थे ।

संगीता	अपनी सहेलियों के बारे में कुछ बताइए ।
दादी जी	एक मुसलमान डाक्टर की बेटी मेरी ख़ास सहेली थी । वह मुझसे कुछ बड़ी थी ।
संगीता	[*थोड़ी देर के बाद*] अच्छा दादी जी, मैं चलती हूँ । आपको कुछ चाहिए ?
दादी जी	नहीं बेटी, तेरी बूढ़ी दादी को कुछ नहीं चाहिए । तू जा, अपना काम कर ।

कानपुर m	Kanpur	**हर**	every, each
किसी	obl. of **कोई**; some, a certain	**शनिवार** m	Saturday
उर्दू f	Urdu	**कुछ**	some; somewhat; something
पढ़ाना	to teach	**मुसलमान**	Muslim
कोई	anyone; some, about; any	**डाक्टर** m	doctor
के नज़दीक	near	**ख़ास**	special, particular
सिनेमा m	cinema	**देर** f	delay, a while

Sangeeta	Grandma, in your childhood you people used to live in Kanpur, didn't you?
Dadi ji	Yes child, my father used to teach Urdu in some college. Mother used to teach too.
Sangeeta	Did anyone speak English in your home?
Dadi ji	Yes, Father knew some five languages. But we mostly spoke Hindi.
Sangeeta	Was there any cinema near your house?
Dadi ji	Yes , we used to go to the cinema every Saturday with some friends.
Sangeeta	Tell me something about your friends.
Dadi ji	A Muslim doctor's daughter was my special friend. She was a bit older than me.
Sangeeta	[*after a little while*] OK Grandma, I'm off. Do you need anything?
Dadi ji	No, child, your old Grandma doesn't need anything. Off you go, do your work.

Grammar
7.1 The past imperfective

This tense describes regular events or habits in the past: 'She used to speak Hindi'. The participle बोलता / बोलती / बोलते 'speaks' (6.1) is followed by the auxiliary था etc.

MASCULINE	FEMININE	
मैं बोलता था	मैं बोलती थी	I used to speak
तू बोलता था	तू बोलती थी	you used to speak
यह, वह बोलता था	यह, वह बोलती थी	he, it, she used to speak
हम बोलते थे	हम बोलती थीं	we used to speak
तुम बोलते थे	तुम बोलती थीं	you used to speak
आप बोलते थे	आप बोलती थीं	you used to speak
ये, वे बोलते थे	ये, वे बोलती थीं	they used to speak

मैं तुझे ख़त लिखता था ।	I used to write you letters.
तू कभी कभी जवाब देती थी ।	You sometimes used to reply.
किताबें सस्ती होती थीं ।	Books used to be cheap.
हम दोनों बहुत-सारी किताबें पढ़ते थे ।	We both used to read lots of books.

An imperfective verb with neither present nor past auxiliary (हूँ / था) tells of an action whose timescale is indefinite; this 'routine imperfective' narrates habitual events in the past, like the English 'I would...':

रविवार को हम लंबी सैर करते ।	On Sundays we would take a long walk.
शाम को मैं अक्सर सिग्रेट पीता ।	I would often smoke in the evening.

7.2   कोई and कुछ

These two essential words have several functions. Linger on these important paragraphs!

a)   As a *pronoun*, कोई means 'someone' and कुछ means 'something'. Thus the difference between the two *as pronouns* is a difference between human beings and inanimates:

ज़मीन पर कोई पड़ा था ।	There was someone lying on the ground.
ज़मीन पर कुछ पड़ा था ।	There was something lying on the ground.

b)   Hence in the negative, कोई नहीं means 'nobody', and कुछ नहीं means 'nothing':

घर में कोई नहीं है ।	There's nobody in the house.
घर में कुछ नहीं है ।	There's nothing in the house.

The negative नहीं may be written separately from कोई / कुछ :

यहाँ कोई गोश्त नहीं खाता है ।	Nobody here eats meat.

c)   As an *adjective* qualifying a singular 'countable' item (whether human or otherwise), कोई means 'some, a, a certain one', : कोई लड़का 'some boy', कोई गाड़ी 'some car'. As an equivalent to the English 'a', it is an alternative to एक:

डिब्बे में कोई अँग्रेज़ बैठा था ।	There was some Englishman sitting in the compartment.
कोई अख़बार फ़र्श पर पड़ी थी ।	Some newspaper was lying on the floor.

d)   The oblique of कोई is किसी, both as pronoun (किसी के लिए 'for someone') and as adjective (किसी लड़के के लिए ' for some boy', किसी वजह से 'for some reason'):

किसी से कहना कि मैं यहाँ खड़ा हूँ ।	Tell someone that I'm standing (waiting) here.
यह रोटी किसी बच्चे को दो ।	Give this bread to some child.

e)   In the plural, कोई and किसी both change to कुछ, qualifying a group of 'countable' items: कुछ लड़के 'some boys' (direct case), कुछ लड़कों के लिए 'for some boys' (oblique case). The word कई 'several' is partially a plural equivalent to कोई:

कुछ/कई विदेशी अच्छी हिन्दी बोलते हैं ।	Some/several foreigners speak good Hindi.
कुछ अँग्रेज़ों को सिर्फ़ अँग्रेज़ी आती है ।	Some English people only know English.

f)   As an *adjective*, कुछ also means 'some', qualifying a substance or thing that is either uncountable (like 'milk'), or is a composite whose component parts aren't relevant (like 'money'): कुछ दूध 'some milk', कुछ पैसा 'some money'.

उसकी जेब में कुछ पैसा था ।	There was some money in his pocket.
कुछ दाल लीजिए न?	Take some daal, won't you?

g) कुछ is also an *adverb*, qualifying an adjective: कुछ महँगा 'rather expensive' (compare बहुत महँगा 'very expensive', and काफ़ी महँगा 'quite expensive'):

यह कपड़ा कुछ मोटा है ।	This cloth is rather coarse.
यह कुरता कुछ लंबा है ।	This kurta is a bit long.

h) कोई before a *number* means 'about, approximately': कोई दस लोग 'about ten people':

डिब्बे में कोई दस मोती पड़े थे ।	There were some ten pearls lying in the box.
शहर में कोई आठ-नौ होटल हैं ।	There are some eight or nine hotels in the town.

In this usage, कोई does not change to oblique किसी – hence कोई पाँच मिनट में 'in about five minutes'.

i) कोई and कुछ feature in several useful phrases:

हर कोई	everyone
कोई न कोई	someone or other
कोई और, और कोई	someone else
सब कुछ	everything
कुछ न कुछ	something or other
कुछ और, और कुछ	something else, some more

> **!** Don't confuse किसी (oblique of कोई 'someone' etc.) with किस (oblique of कौन 'who? – see 3.4).

7.3 चाहिए 'is wanted/ needed'

The word चाहिए means 'is wanted, is needed'. The *thing wanted* becomes the grammatical subject; the person doing the wanting is in the oblique with को. This is a मुझको type of construction (see 6.5).

दादी को नया चश्मा चाहिए ।	Grandma needs new glasses.
आपको क्या चाहिए ?	What do you want/ need?
हमें रोटी चाहिए, चावल नहीं ।	We want roti (bread), not rice.

For the past, simply add था / थी / थे / थीं to चाहिए. This auxiliary agrees with the subject, i.e. the thing wanted:

हमें दो साइकिलें चाहिए थीं ।	We needed two bicycles.
मुझे इसी रंग का कपड़ा चाहिए था ।	I needed cloth of *this* colour.

Some speakers nasalize the -ए ending in the plural: मुझे पाँच कमरे चाहिएँ 'I need five rooms'.

> **!** दादी को चश्मे की ज़रूरत है (literally 'to Grandma is a need of glasses') is an alternative way of saying 'Grandma needs glasses'; ज़रूरत is a feminine noun meaning 'need'. Compare ज़रूर 'of course', and ज़रूरी 'necessary, urgent'.

◗ 7b   Who works where?

खन्ना जी	प्रकाश, इन सब कमरों में कौन कौन काम करता है ?
प्रकाश	सर, पहले और दूसरे कमरों में दफ़्तर के बड़े बाबू काम करते हैं ।
खन्ना जी	और यह तीसरा कमरा किसका है ?
प्रकाश	अभी तीसरे और चौथे कमरों में कोई नहीं है सर ।
खन्ना जी	तो आपका कमरा कौनसा है ? पाँचवाँ ? छठा ?
प्रकाश	अभी मैं छोटू के कमरे में काम करता हूँ । [*मन में सोचता है* – *"मुझे अलग कमरा चाहिए !"*]
खन्ना जी	तीसरा कमरा ख़ाली है, उसे लेना । आपको और कोई चीज़ चाहिए ?
प्रकाश	जी सर, उस कमरे में नया पंखा चाहिए । बहुत ज़रूरी है – पुराना पंखा काम नहीं करता ।
खन्ना जी	गरमी का मौसम मार्च से पहले नहीं शुरू होता । पंखा बाद में लेना ।
प्रकाश	जी सर ।

कौन कौन	which various people?	चाहिए	(is) needed
पहला	first	और कोई	any other
दूसरा	second	जी	yes
बाबू^m	clerk	ज़रूरी	necessary, urgent
तीसरा	third	गरमी ^f	heat; summer
चौथा	fourth	मार्च^m	March
पाँचवाँ	fifth	शुरू होना	to begin
छठा	sixth	बाद में	later on
अलग	separate, different		

Khanna ji Prakash, who works in all these rooms?

Prakash Sir, in the first and second rooms the senior clerks of the office work.

Khanna ji And whose is this third room?

Prakash There's nobody in the third and fourth rooms yet sir.

Khanna ji So which is you room? The fifth? The sixth?

Prakash At the moment I work in Ramdas's room. [*Thinks to himself: 'I need a separate room!'*]

Khanna ji The third room's vacant – take it. Do you need anything else?

Prakash Yes sir, a new fan's needed in that room. It's very urgent – the old fan doesn't work.

Khanna ji The hot weather doesn't start before March. Get a fan later on.

Prakash Yes sir.

> **!** पंखा बाद में लेना – the infinitive verb लेना is here used as a 'deferred' command, i.e. one which will be acted on at some point in the future. See 5.2.

Grammar
7.4 Ordinal numbers

पहला	first	छठा	sixth
दूसरा	second	सातवाँ	seventh
तीसरा	third	आठवाँ	eighth
चौथा	fourth	नवाँ	ninth
पाँचवाँ	fifth	दसवाँ	tenth

Thereafter, simply add -वाँ to the cardinal number (Appendix 1): बारहवाँ, बीसवाँ 'twelfth, twentieth'. The ordinal numbers inflect like other adjectives, but with nasal endings -वीं, -वें; thus पाँचवीं सड़क के दसवें मकान में 'in the tenth house of the fifth road'.

Written Hindi sometimes borrows Sanskrit ordinal numbers (प्रथम 'first', द्वितीय 'second', तृतीय 'third', चतुर्थ 'fourth', पंचम 'fifth', etc.) for formal effect – rather as English can use Roman numerals in such set contexts as 'World War II' – द्वितीय महायुद्ध.

7.5 Aggregatives

Forms such as दोनों 'both, the two' indicate the total or *aggregate* number of items in a group. दोनों itself is irregular; other aggregatives simply add -ओं to the number:

तीनों बच्चे	all three children
चारों तरफ़	(on) all four sides, all around

Aggregatives can also refer to multiples of a number:

दर्जनों छात्र	dozens of students	(दर्जन	a dozen)
सैकड़ों विद्यार्थी	hundreds of students	(सैकड़ा	a hundred)
हज़ारों रुपये	thousands of rupees	(हज़ार	thousand)
लाखों औरतें	lakhs of women	(लाख	hundred thousand)
करोड़ों बच्चे	crores of children	(करोड़	ten million)

7.6 Conjunct verbs

As you have already seen, many verbs are formed by simply combining करना 'to do' with a noun or adjective.

शुरू करना	to begin	ख़त्म करना	to finish
बंद करना	to shut	साफ़ करना	to clean

These verbs are 'transitive' – that is, they can take a direct object: काम शुरू करना 'to begin work'; कमरा साफ़ करना 'to clean a room'. Many such verbs have 'intransitive' counterparts, i.e. verbs whose action is intrinsic and has no direct object: 'we start work' is transitive, with 'work' as object of 'we start', while 'work starts early today' is intransitive, with 'work' itself as subject. The distinction is not too clear in English, because the same verb often does duty for both transitive and intransitive; but in Hindi, transitive verbs using करना have intransitive equivalents using होना.

हमारी क्लास नौ बजे शुरू होती है ।	Our class begins at nine o'clock.
दरवाज़े रात को बन्द होते हैं ।	The doors are closed at night.
छुट्टियाँ अक्सर शनिवार को शुरू होती हैं ।	The holidays usually start on a Saturday.

EXERCISE 7a.1 Translate.

1 Father used to work in some office and used to get home late.
2 Some 12 students are sitting on the floor; we need some more chairs.
3 On Saturdays we used to meet some friends.
4 We don't like this cold food – we want some rice and daal.
5 Isn't there any cheap hotel here? The Taj is rather expensive!
6 'Give this money to someone else.' 'Yes, but to whom?'
7 We needed the car keys but there was nobody in the house.
8 In the evening, Grandma used to read the Ramayan and we used to watch old films.

EXERCISE 7a.2 Write ten चाहिए sentences on the model मुझे कुछ नए कपड़े चाहिए, pairing items as you like from the list.

1	I need	a good dictionary
2	you need	about ten chairs
3	they needed	a beautiful pearl
4	who (?) needs	some money
5	my friend needs	thousands of rupees
6	these students needed	today's newspapers
7	that other man needs	some hot water
8	those girls need	some more time
9	someone needed	a cigarette
10	nobody needs	a new house

EXERCISE 7a.3 Rewrite your ten sentences on the model मुझे कुछ नए कपड़ों की ज़रूरत है.

EXERCISE 7b.1 Rewrite the following sentences in the past tense, then translate them.

१   अरुण अपने बड़े भाई प्रकाश के साथ रहता है; वह किताबें लिखता है ।

२   खन्ना साहिब कहते हैं कि उनके दफ़्तर में दर्जनों लोग हैं लेकिन कोई ठीक से काम नहीं करता है ।

३   दादी जी नहीं जानती हैं कि उनके पिताजी किस कालेज में पढ़ाते थे ।

४   अध्यापक जी कहते हैं कि "कोई" और "कुछ" का फ़र्क समझना बहुत ज़रूरी है ।

५   छात्र अपने अध्यापक से हज़ारों मुश्किल सवाल पूछता है ।

६   क्या किसी को मालूम है कि संगीता का दोस्त सुहास कहाँ रहता है ?

७   किसको मालूम है कि ऋषि और राज की उम्र में कितना फ़र्क है ?

८   दादी जी सोचती हैं कि हिन्दुस्तान स्वर्ग के समान है । वे अपने बचपन के सपने बहुत देखती हैं ।

९   मालूम होता है कि प्रताप अभी दिल्ली में नहीं है शायद अपने पिताजी के यहाँ है ।

१०   कुछ विद्यार्थियों के ख़याल में आठवाँ और दसवाँ सवाल सबसे मुश्किल हैं ।

EXERCISE 7b.2 Translate.

IN THE HOTEL

Boy	Come, sir. What would you like?
Khanna	I want some hot food and coffee.
Boy	Sir, the kitchen closes early on Sunday. There isn't any hot food. [leave 'any' untranslated]
Khanna	All right, give me some fruit. And clean my room tomorrow morning; it's very dirty.
Boy	Sir, tomorrow is my holiday. Please tell (कहना) someone else.
Khanna	But I need the coffee right away. Bring it and close the door.
Boy	Sir, the electricity (बिजली f) is off (बंद) at the moment. Please have ('drink') some cold water.
Khanna	This hotel is useless (बेकार); and you're useless too. I'm off.

Vocabulary

अलग separate, different	औरत ^f woman
आठ eight	करोड़ ^m ten million
उर्दू ^f Urdu	कानपुर ^m Kanpur
और कोई any other	किसी oblique of कोई

कुछ some; somewhat; something;	compartment
कुछ और something else, some	तरफ़ f side, direction
more; कुछ न कुछ something or	तीसरा third
other	तृतीय third, IIIrd
के नज़दीक near	दर्जन f a dozen
के समान like, equal to	दूर distant, far, away
कोई anyone, someone; some, any,	दूसरा second
about; कोई और someone else;	देर f delay, a while
कोई न कोई someone or other;	द्वितीय second, IInd
कोई नहीं no one	नवाँ ninth
कौन कौन which various people	पंचम fifth, Vth
खड़ा standing, waiting	पढ़ाना to teach
ख़त्म finished; ख़त्म करना to finish	पहला first
ख़ास special, particular	पाँचवाँ fifth
गरमी f heat; summer	प्रथम first, Ist
चतुर्थ fourth, IVth	फ़र्क m difference, separation
चावल m rice	बाद में later on
चाहिए (is) needed	बाबू m clerk
चौथा fourth	बिजली f electricity
छठा sixth	बेकार useless
छुट्टी f holiday; free time	बैठा seated, sitting
ज़मीन f ground; land	महायुद्ध m great war
ज़रूरत f need	मार्च m March
ज़रूरी urgent, necessary	मुसलमान m Muslim
जवाब देना to reply	मोती m pearl
जी yes	रंग m colour
जेब f pocket	रोटी f bread; food
ठीक से properly; exactly	लाख m hundred thousand
डाक्टर m doctor	वजह f reason, cause
डिब्बा m box; railway	शनिवार m Saturday

शाम ^f evening	सैर ^f walk, trip; सैर करना to go for
शुरू करना, होना to begin	a walk, trip
सपना ^m dream; सपना देखना to	स्वर्ग ^m heaven
dream	हज़ार ^m thousand
सब कुछ everything	हर each, every; हर कोई everyone
सिनेमा ^m cinema	होटल ^m hotel; cafe
सैकड़ा ^m a hundred	

8 | WHAT IS ARUN DOING IN LUCKNOW?

अरुण लखनऊ में क्या कर रहे हैं ?

In this unit you will learn how to

- talk about things that are happening now
- describe ownership and possession – 'to have'
- use a range of adverbs
- use dates

8a   Arun in Lucknow

रफ़ीक़	अरुण, मेरे दिली दोस्त ! तुम यहाँ लखनऊ की तंग गलियों में क्या कर रहे हो ?
अरुण	एक मित्र के साथ कुछ काम कर रहा हूँ; हमारी एक पुस्तक निकल रही है ।
रफ़ीक़	तो क्या तुम आजकल लखनऊ में ठहर रहे हो ?
अरुण	नहीं नहीं, अभी तो दिल्ली में अपने भाई के यहाँ रह रहा हूँ ।
रफ़ीक़	तुम्हारा अपना मकान नहीं है, दिल्ली में ?

अरुण	नहीं है; पर मैं अभी सोच रहा था कि मुझे नया घर चाहिए । प्रकाश के तीन बच्चे हैं; वे मुझे बहुत तंग करते हैं ।
रफ़ीक़	हाँ, तुम तो परेशान दिख रहे हो । अभी तुम्हें कोई ख़ास तकलीफ़ है ?
अरुण	थोड़ी-सी थकान है, और कुछ नहीं ।
रफ़ीक़	तो मेरे साथ चाय पियो । चलो, राम साहब के यहाँ चलते हैं ।
अरुण	नहीं, मुझे देर हो रही है – विलंब हो रहा है; देखो, मेरे मित्र प्रेम अभी आ रहे हैं ।

दिली	'of the heart', intimate	तंग करना	to hassle, harass
तंग	narrow	दिखना	to appear, seem
गली^f	lane	तकलीफ़^f	trouble, distress
पुस्तक^f	book	थोड़ा-सा	a little
निकलना	to come/go out	थकान^f	tiredness
आजकल	nowadays	देर^f, विलंब^m	delay

Rafiq	Arun, my dear friend! What are you doing here in the narrow lanes of Lucknow?
Arun	I'm doing some work with a friend; a book of ours is coming out.
Rafiq	So are you staying in Lucknow nowadays?
Arun	No no, at the moment I'm living at my brother's place in Delhi.
Rafiq	You don't have your own house in Delhi?
Arun	I don't, but I was just thinking that I need a new home. Prakash has three children; they harrass me a lot.
Rafiq	Yes, you are looking hassled. Do you have any particular trouble just now?
Arun	A little tiredness, nothing else.
Rafiq	Then have tea with me. Come, we're off to Ram Sahib's.
Arun	No, I'm getting late – getting delayed; look, my friend Prem is just coming.

Grammar

8.1 The continuous tenses

Continuous tenses describe actions that are going on at the time: they are '-ing' tenses. The tense is made up of three elements: the verb stem (बोल from बोलना), plus रहा/ रही/ रहे which gives the 'continuous' sense, plus the auxiliary verb (हूँ, है, था etc.).

	MASCULINE	FEMININE	
Present	मैं बोल रहा हूँ	बोल रही हूँ	I am speaking
	तू बोल रहा है	बोल रही है	you are speaking
	यह, वह बोल रहा है	बोल रही है	he, it, she is speaking
	हम बोल रहे हैं	बोल रही हैं	we are speaking
	तुम बोल रहे हो	बोल रही हो	you are speaking
	आप बोल रहे हैं	बोल रही हैं	you are speaking
	ये, वे बोल रहे हैं	बोल रही हैं	they are speaking
Past	मैं बोल रहा था	बोल रही थी	I was speaking
	तू बोल रहा था	बोल रही थी	you were speaking
	यह, वह बोल रहा था	बोल रही थी	he, it, she was speaking
	हम बोल रहे थे	बोल रही थीं	we were speaking
	तुम बोल रहे थे	बोल रही थीं	you were speaking
	आप बोल रहे थे	बोल रही थीं	you were speaking
	ये, वे बोल रहे थे	बोल रही थीं	they were speaking

हम लोग हिन्दी सीख रहे हैं ।	We are learning Hindi.
वह अपने भाई के बारे में पूछ रही है ।	She's asking about her brother.
तुम कौनसी कहानी पढ़ रही हो ?	Which story are you reading?
हम आज का प्रोग्राम बना रहे हैं ।	We're making a plan for today.
मैं अभी घर नहीं जा रहा हूँ ।	I'm not going home just yet.
मैं सोमवार को घर आ रही हूँ ।	I'm coming home on Monday.
क्या आप खाना तैयार कर रहे हैं ?	Are you preparing food?
तुम ग़लत नंबर मिला रहे थे !	You were ringing the wrong number!

The continuous tense is used for identification on the phone:

आप कौन बोल रही हैं ?	Who is that speaking? ('Who are you speaking?')
मैं उषा बोल रही हूँ ।	This is Usha speaking. ('I Usha am speaking')

8.2   Expressions for 'to have'

Hindi has no verb 'to have'. Instead, it uses the verb होना 'to be' in three different constructions, using the postpositions को, के पास and का/की/के respectively.

+ को   Already seen in 4.4 — 'to have a cold' etc:

पिंकी को ज़ुकाम है ।	Pinkie has a cold.
संगीता को बुख़ार था ।	Sangeeta had a fever.

+ के पास   For the possession of things, 'portable' items, time, money and so on; also for servants (!):

राज के पास बहुत खिलौने हैं ।	Raj has lots of toys.
हमारे पास समय नहीं है ।	We don't have time.
उनके पास बहुत पैसा था ।	They had lots of money.
खन्ना के पास ड्राइवर है ।	Khanna has a driver.
मेरे पास कुछ भी नहीं है ।	I have nothing at all.

+ का/ की/ के   For relatives, houses, parts of the body:

राम के दो भाई हैं ।	Ram has two brothers.
कृष्ण का एक घर है ।	Krishna has one house.
शिव की तीन आंखें हैं ।	Shiva has three eyes.
प्रकाश के तीन बच्चे हैं ।	Prakash has three children.
मेरे पिता का एक अस्पताल है ।	My father owns a hospital.

Remember that some possessive pronouns – e.g. मेरा, तुम्हारा – don't contain का. Compare:

अक्षय के पाँच बच्चे हैं ।	Akshay has five children.
मेरे पाँच बच्चे हैं ।	I have five children.
शिव की तीन आँखें हैं ।	Shiva has three eyes.
मेरी सिर्फ़ एक आँख है ।	I have only one eye.

In referring to relatives, some speakers use के (rather than का or की) regardless of number and gender:

बंटी के आठ लड़कियाँ हैं ।	Bunty has eight daughters.
लक्ष्मी के एक लड़का है ।	Lakshmi has one son.

8b   Khanna Sahib's coming to dinner!

प्रकाश	प्यारी, आज रात को खन्ना साहब यहाँ आ रहे हैं ।
कमला	हे भगवान ! क्या उनका सारा परिवार भी आ रहा है ?
प्रकाश	हाँ । पर उनका सिर्फ़ एक बेटा है – हरीश । वह अठारह साल का है ।
कमला	क्या खन्ना की छोटी बहिन नहीं आ रही है ? क्या नाम है उसका – पिंकी ?
प्रकाश	नहीं । वह तो अलग रहती है; दूसरे लोग ऊपर रहते हैं, वह नीचे रहती है ।
कमला	ख़ैर, तुम जल्दी से कुछ सब्ज़ी लाना । हमारे पास कुछ भी नहीं है ।
प्रकाश	गोश्त भी चाहिए न ? खन्नाजी और उनकी पत्नी दोनों गोश्त खाते हैं ।
कमला	उनकी पत्नी का कोई नाम नहीं है ?
प्रकाश	मुझे क्या मालूम । खन्नाजी उन्हें हमेशा "हरीश की माँ" कहते हैं ।
कमला	ख़ैर, तुम अभी बाज़ार जाओ । सारे दिन ऐश करते हो ! जाओ न !
प्रकशा	हाँ हाँ, जा रहा हूँ । मेरा सिर क्यों खा रही हो ? ऋषि, तू साथ चल ।

हे	Oh !	सब्ज़ी ^f	vegetable(s)
भगवान ^m	God	के पास	in (our) possession
अठारह	eighteen	ऐश ^m	wanton luxury; ऐश करना
अलग	separately		to live a life of pleasure
ऊपर	above; upstairs	सिर ^m	head; सिर खाना to pester
नीचे	below; downstairs	साथ	along, with, in company

Prakash	Darling, tonight Khanna Sahib is coming here.
Kamala	Oh God! Is the whole family coming too?
Prakash	Yes. But he has just one son – Harish. He is 18.
Kamala	Isn't Khanna's younger sister coming? What's her name – Pinkie?
Prakash	No. She lives separately; the others live upstairs, she lives downstairs.
Kamala	Well anyway, fetch (buy, get) some vegetables quickly. We don't have anything at all.
Prakash	We need meat too, don't we? Khanna ji and his wife both eat meat.
Kamala	Doesn't his wife have a name?
Prakash	How do I know? Khanna ji always calls her 'Harish's mother'.
Kamala	Well anyway, you go to the market right now. You laze around all day! Go, won't you?

Prakash   Yes, yes, I'm going. Why are you pestering me ? Rishi, you come along too.

Grammar

8.3   Some adverbial phrases

Up to this point, you have seen that the oblique case (3.2) only occurs before a postposition. An exception to this rule is with adverbial phrases such as उस दिन '[on] that day'. One may imagine that को has been dropped from such a phrase. Here are some more:

अगले महीने	next month	तीसरे पहर	in the afternoon
इस तरफ़	in this direction	दूसरे दिन	the next day
दाहिने / बायें	to the right/ left	उन दिनों	in those days
सवेरे	in the early morning	सारे दिन	all day
पिछले साल	last year	किस समय	at what time

Similarly, the destination of a 'motion' verb is usually oblique: कलकत्ते जाना 'to go to Calcutta'; उस शहर जाना, 'to go to that city'.

मैं अपने गाँव जा रहा हूँ ।	I'm going to my village.
वे लोग आगरे जा रहे हैं ।	They're going to Agra.

The postpositions से and पर also form adverbial phrases. से can be dropped where indicated by brackets:

बस से	by bus	ठीक तरह (से)	properly
हाथ से	by hand	ठीक से	properly, precisely
देर से	late	ज़ोर से	forcefully, loudly
अच्छी तरह (से)	well	ध्यान से	attentively
बुरी तरह (से)	badly	———	
किस तरह (से)	how?	ठीक समय पर	punctually
सावधानी से	carefully	आम तौर पर/ से	usually
जल्दी (से)	quickly	ख़ास तौर पर/ से	specially

The second part of a compound postposition (e.g. बाहर from के बाहर) can comprise an adverb:

PHRASE WITH POSTPOSITION		PHRASE WITH ADVERB	
घर के बाहर	outside the house	बाहर जाओ	go outside

कमरे के अंदर	inside the room	अंदर आओ	come inside
मेरे साथ	with me	तुम भी साथ चलो	you come along too
अलमारी के ऊपर	on top of the cupboard	ऊपर देखो	look up
कपड़े के नीचे	under the cloth	वह नीचे रहती है	she lives downstairs
दुकान के सामने	opposite the shop	वह सामने रहती है	she lives opposite
दुकान के नज़दीक	near the shop	वह नज़दीक रहता था	he lived nearby
कल के बाद	after tomorrow	दस साल बाद	ten years later

Some adverbs ending in -ए form pairs with similar adjectives:

ADJECTIVE		ADVERB	
कैसा	of what kind?	कैसे	how?
सीधा	straight	सीधे	straight
दाहिना, बायाँ	right, left	दाहिने, बायें	to the right, left

The Hindi equivalents of 'this evening, this morning' are आज शाम, आज सुबह; the pronouns यह, इस are *not* used here.

8.4   What's today's date?   आज की तारीख़ क्या है ?

Dates use ordinal numbers for the first two days of the month (पहली, दूसरी 'first, second', both agreeing with feminine तारीख़ 'date'); and with cardinal numbers (तीन, चार etc.) thereafter:

पहली जनवरी	the 1st of January	तीन मार्च	the 3rd of March
दूसरी मई को	on the 2nd of May	दस जून को	on the 10th of June

Years are expressed with the word सन् 'year'. No word for 'and' stands between the hundreds and the tens: thus १९४७ is सन् उन्नीस सौ सैंतालीस '(the year) nineteen hundred [and] forty-seven'.

आज पाँच जुलाई सन् उन्नीस सौ निन्यानवे है । Today is the 5th of July 1999.

(See the appendixes for more on dates and numbers.)

8.5 Word order

A typical sentence word order is: subject, adverb, indirect object + को, direct object, verb:

SUBJECT	ADVERB	IND.OBJ.+ को	DIR.OBJ.	VERB
केशव	रोज़	हम को	फल	भेजता है ।

Keshav sends us fruit every day.

Variations on this neutral word order will emphasise a particular component:

केशव रोज़ फल हम को भेजता है ।   Keshav sends *us* fruit every day.

केशव फल हम को रोज़ भेजता है ।   Keshav sends us fruit *every day*.

So much depends on the style and context of what's being said that rules are not easily given for word order; but these last examples show that the position just before the verb often bears emphasis.

A word or phrase whose meaning is already implicit in a sentence may be thrown in as an afterthought at the end. Sentences from Dialogue 8B might have appeared as follows:

उनका सारा परिवार भी आ रहा है क्या ?   (the sentence is *implicitly* a question)

तो क्या छोटी बहिन नहीं आ रही है उनकी ?   ('possession' is clear from the context)

8.6 Some colloquial usages, and pronunciation reminders

By now, you are well used to the pronouns यह, वह as singular, and ये, वे as plural. But out there in the real world, this clearcut distinction of number is not always honoured: यह and वह can both appear as plurals, even though this is not a standard grammatical use. Likewise, many people's pronunciation of यह will convince you that they're actually saying ये. Remember also that वह is usually pronounced as if spelt वो – and a few Hindi-speakers (perhaps influenced by Urdu, where *vo* is the standard form for both singular and plural) even adopt this form in writing.

Another common 'infringement' of the grammatical rules involves inconsistency in honorific levels. It's not unusual to hear someone saying आप बैठो, anomalously pairing the तुम imperative with the pronoun आप. This is perhaps felt to be a comfortable compromise between the two levels: give your addressee the benefit of the doubt by calling him or her आप, then go for a friendlier tone by switching down to the तुम imperative.

The 'royal we' is very common in Hindi: some people hardly ever use मैं, preferring हम across the board. But it has a colloquial ring, and there's nothing 'royal' about it at all. Some women use the *masculine* first person plural when referring to themselves.

A quite different effect is heard as a heated argument escalates and speakers drop progressively from high (आप) to low (तू) honorific levels! Remember that तू (and even तुम) can sound offensively blunt out of context; Hindi has a nice idiomatic verb, तू-तू मैं-मैं करना, 'to call names, trade insults'.

Hindi is spoken across a wide geographical area; its speakers include many for whom it is not a first language, and it is often heavily influenced by the grammar and vocabulary of dialects or neighbouring languages. Like most spoken languages, then, Hindi has rich internal variety. This makes Hindi-speakers very tolerant of grammatical deviance; but a non-Indian *accent* may prove much more of a block to understanding. So it's timely now to revise some pronunciation points. Many learners of Hindi need in particular to remember the following distinctions:

- between dental and retroflex consonants: दाल / डाल
- between non-aspirates and aspirates: सात / साथ
- between single and double consonants: बचा / बच्चा
- between short and long vowels: कम / काम

Also, remember the 'purity' of the vowels, particularly ए and ओ (से and सो do *not* rhyme with 'say' and 'so').

The glossary at the end of the book provides excellent pronunciation practice: read whole sequences of headwords aloud, or ask a Hindi-speaker to do so for you and repeat them afterwards. Also, practise distinguishing clearly between the two members of 'minimal pairs' (pairs of words that are identical except for one distinguishing feature) such as the following:

जाना	to go	जानना	to know
दिली	of the heart	दिल्ली	Delhi
दल	political party	दाल	daal
दाल	daal	डाल	branch
पल	moment	फल	fruit
मोटी	fat (f)	मोती	pearl
मोर	peacock	मोड़	turn, bend
सात	seven	साथ	(in) company
ताली	clapping	थाली	tray, plate of food
कम	less	काम	work
में	in	मैं	I
है	is	हैं	are

EXERCISE 8a.1 Change imperfective verbs into continuous verbs. Then translate.

१   प्रताप बहुत ध्यान से हिन्दी पढ़ता है ।

२   मैं तो अच्छा पैसा कमाता हूँ ।

३   क्या तुम गाड़ी चलाते हो ?

४   संगीता और उसका छोटा भाई सिनेमा जाते हैं ।

५   प्रताप अपने दोस्तों के साथ गोश्त खाता है ।

EXERCISE 8a.2 Translate.

1   He is preparing different food for you.
2   Tell her that she was dialling the wrong number.
3   He's coming to Delhi with his relatives tomorrow.
4   How many sisters do you have? I have two sisters.
5   All three doctors are working at that same hospital.
6   He used to dream of me but now he is dreaming of you.
7   Why are you not giving an answer to my question, Sangeeta?
8   We were talking to your neighbours about you.

EXERCISE 8a.3 Pratap phones Mohan – from Kathmandu! Supply Mohan's responses:

प्रताप	नमस्ते मोहन ! मैं प्रताप बोल रहा हूँ – नेपाल से ! क्या हाल है ?
मोहन	....
प्रताप	मैं यहाँ कुछ दोस्तों के साथ नेपाल की सैर कर रहा हूँ ।
मोहन	....
प्रताप	नहीं, ऋषि और राज घर पर हैं, अपनी बहिन के साथ ।
मोहन	....
प्रताप	अभी तो हम लोग काठमांडु में एक होटल में ठहर रहे हैं । बहुत महँगा है ।
मोहन	....
प्रताप	पर यहाँ तो हमारा कोई दोस्त है नहीं – हम किसी को भी नहीं जानते नेपाल में ।
मोहन	....
प्रताप	अच्छा, तो मुझे अपने रिश्तेदारों का पता दीजिए, मैं उन्हें अभी फ़ोन करता हूँ !

EXERCISE 8b.1 Translate, using *postpositions* in the first column and related *adverbs* in the second, as in the model.

I live near Calcutta.	I live nearby.
मैं कलकत्ते के पास रहता हूँ ।	मैं पास रहता हूँ ।

1	Sit outside the house.	Sit outside.
2	Look behind the chair.	Look back.
3	We're standing opposite the door.	The shop is opposite.
4	Come towards me.	Come this way.
5	Don't sleep under the tree.	Sleep downstairs.
6	Both brothers are with me.	You come along too.
7	Put it on top of the cupboard.	You go upstairs.
8	We live near the cycle shop.	They live nearby.

EXERCISE 8b.2 Answer the following questions.

१　आपका जन्मदिन कब है ?
२　आज की तारीख़ क्या है ?
३　कल कौनसा दिन था ?
४　क्या आपके बच्चे हैं ?
५　आपके कितने भाई और बहिनें हैं ? उनकी कितनी उम्र है ?

६   क्या आपके पास बहुत पैसा है ? क्या आपको और पैसा चाहिए ? क्यों ?

७   क्या आपका अपना घर है ? या आप दूसरे लोगों के घर में रहते हैं / रहती हैं ?

८   क्या आपको ज़ुकाम या बुख़ार है ? आपकी तबियत कैसी है ?

९   आपके ख़याल में क्या प्रताप संगीता से डरता है ?

१०   तीन घंटे पहले आप क्या कर रहे थे / कर रही थीं ?

Vocabulary

अंदर	inside, within	ज़ोर ^{m}	force, strength
अगला	next	डाल ^{f}	branch (of tree)
अठारह	eighteen	तंग	narrow; तंग करना to harass
अलग	separately	तकलीफ़ ^{f}	trouble, distress
अस्पताल ^{m}	hospital	तरह ^{f}	way, manner
आँख ^{f}	eye	तारीख़ ^{m}	date
आगरा ^{m}	Agra	ताली ^{f}	clapping
आजकल	nowadays	तू-तू मैं-मैं करना	to call names
आम	ordinary; आम तौर पर usually	तैयार करना	to prepare
ऊपर	above; up; upstairs	थकान ^{f}	tiredness
ऐश ^{m}	luxury; ऐश करना to live a life of pleasure	थाली ^{f}	platter
		थोड़ा-सा	a little
कमाना	to earn	दल ^{m}	political party
कलकत्ता ^{m}	Calcutta	दाहिना	right (opp. of left)
कहानी ^{f}	story	दिखना	to appear, seem
काठमांडु ^{m}	Kathmandu	दिली	'of the heart', intimate
के पास	in (our) possession	देर ^{f}	delay; a while
ग़लत	wrong, incorrect	नंबर ^{m}	number
गली ^{f}	lane	नज़दीक	near, nearby
घंटा ^{m}	hour	निकलना	to come/go out, emerge
चलाना	to drive	निन्यानवे	ninety-nine
जन्मदिन ^{m}	birthday	नीचे	below, down, downstairs
जून ^{m}	June	नेपाल ^{m}	Nepal

पल ^m moment

पहर ^m part of the day

पिछला last, previous

पुस्तक ^f book

पूरा full, complete

प्रोग्राम ^m programme, plan

फ़रवरी ^f February

बनाना to make

बाद (में) later

बायाँ left (opp. of right)

भगवान ^m God

भेजना to send

मई ^f May

महीना ^m month

मिलाना to dial, phone

मोड़ ^m turn, bend

मोर ^m peacock

विलंब ^m delay

सन् ^m year (of calendar or era)

सब्ज़ी ^f vegetable(s)

सवेरा ^m early morning

साथ along, with, in company

सावधानी ^f care

सिर ^m head; सिर खाना to pester

सीधा straight, straightforward; सीधे straight; to the right

सैंतालीस forty-seven

हाथ ^m hand

हे Oh !

9 | IN THE FUTURE
भविष्य में

In this unit you will learn how to
- use the future tense
- express assumptions – 'I suppose'
- talk about quantity
- use verbal nouns – *'speaking* is easy'

9a   Dinner at home, or the cinema with Pinkie?

पिंकी	संगीता, आज रात को तुम मेरे साथ सिनेमा चलोगी ?
संगीता	मुश्किल है । तुम्हारा सारा परिवार तो हमारे यहाँ आ रहा है ।
पिंकी	तो तुम घर पर बैठी रहोगी ? मेरे घर के लोग तुम्हें अच्छी तरह बोर करेंगे ।
संगीता	ठीक है, आऊँगी । पर अगर ऋषि या राज माँ को बताता है तो...
पिंकी	वे किसी को क्यों बताएँगे । चुप रहेंगे । भोले-से लड़के हैं, दोनों ।
संगीता	बात यह है कि... माँ को नहीं मालूम कि मैं बाहर जा रही हूँ ।
पिंकी	अगर तुम मेरे साथ सिनेमा जाओगी तो उनका क्या नुक़सान होगा ?
संगीता	माँ कहती हैं... मेरा मतलब है... उन्हें मालूम है कि तुम्हारा भतीजा मेरी उम्र का है ।

पिंकी　　　हरीश तो हमारे साथ थोड़े आएगा ! वह तो तुम्हारे माँ-बाप की दावत में
　　　　　　जा रहा होगा ।

संगीता　　फिर मुश्किल शायद कम होगी । पर माँ को क्या बताऊँगी ?

बोर करना	to bore	नुक़सान ^m	harm
अगर	if	भतीजा ^m	nephew
भोला	innocent, guileless; भोला-सा	थोड़े	scarcely
	quite innocent	दावत ^f	(invitation to) a dinner

बोर करना to bore
अगर if
भोला innocent, guileless; भोला-सा quite innocent
नुक़सान ^m harm
भतीजा ^m nephew
थोड़े scarcely
दावत ^f (invitation to) a dinner

Pinkie　　Sangeeta, will you come with me to the cinema tonight?

Sangeeta　It's difficult. Your whole family is coming to our place.

Pinkie　　So you'll stay sitting at home? My relatives will bore you thoroughly.

Sangeeta　All right, I'll come. But if Rishi or Raj tells Mother, then...

Pinkie　　Why would they tell anyone. They'll keep quiet. They're quite innocent boys, both of them.

Sangeeta　The thing is that... Mother doesn't know that I'm going out.

Pinkie　　What's the harm to her if you go to the cinema with me?

Sangeeta　Mother says... I mean... she knows your nephew is my age.

Pinkie　　Harish will hardly be coming with us! He'll be going to your parents' dinner party.

Sangeeta　Then maybe it'll be less difficult. But what will I tell Mother?

Grammar

9.1　The future tense

The future tense is one of the easiest. It consists of a single word, with no auxiliary (unlike the English!).

मैं बोलूँगा	बोलूँगी	I will speak
तू बोलेगा	बोलेगी	you will speak
यह, वह बोलेगा	बोलेगी	he, it, she will speak
हम बोलेंगे	बोलेंगी	we will speak
तुम बोलोगे	बोलोगी	you will speak
आप बोलेंगे	बोलेंगी	you will speak
ये, वे बोलेंगे	बोलेंगी	they will speak

The masculine endings are just -ऊँगा for मैं, -एगा for all the other singulars; -ओगे for तुम, and -एँगे for all the other plurals. Feminines follow suit, with -ई as the final vowel. The bad news is that the three very common verbs होना, लेना, देना are irregular:

मैं हूँगा, हूँगी	लूँगा, लूँगी	दूँगा, दूँगी
तू होगा, होगी	लेगा, लेगी	देगा, देगी
यह / वह होगा, होगी	लेगा, लेगी	देगा, देगी
हम होंगे, होंगी	लेंगे, लेंगी	देंगे, देंगी
तुम होगे, होगी	लोगे, लोगी	दोगे, दोगी
आप होंगे, होंगी	लेंगे, लेंगी	देंगे, देंगी
ये / वे होंगे, होंगी	लेंगे, लेंगी	देंगे, देंगी

शर्मा जी तुमको फ़ोन करेंगे ।	Sharma ji will phone you.
मैं कभी वाराणसी आऊँगा ।	I'll come to Varanasi sometime.
माँ शराब नहीं ख़रीदेंगी ।	Mother won't buy alcohol.
वह इससे ज़्यादा नहीं लेगी ।	She won't take more than this.
प्रताप तो ध्यान नहीं देगा !	Pratap won't pay attention!
पंडित जी गाना गाएँगे ।	Pandit ji will sing a song.

Verbs whose stems end in ऊ or ई shorten these in the future tense: छूना > छुएगा, पीना > पिएगा.

9.2 Future tense in the auxiliary verb

The future of the auxiliary verb होना can be used within tenses such as the continuous. Compare the following three continuous tenses:

वह जा रहा है ।	He is going.	(present auxiliary है)
वह जा रहा था ।	He was going.	(past auxiliary था)
वह जा रहा होगा ।	He will be going.	(future auxiliary होगा)

These sentences are in the present continuous, past continuous and future continuous respectively. Some more examples of the future continuous:

प्रताप अगले हफ़्ते तक दिल्ली लौट रहा होगा ।	Pratap will be returning to Delhi by next week.

अरुण की किताब थोड़े दिनों में निकल रही होगी ।	Arun's book will be coming out in a few days.
आज शाम को कमला खाना तैयार कर रही होगी ।	Kamala will be preparing food this evening.

A similar construction applies with imperfective tenses, e.g. वह जाता होगा 'he will be going (habitually)'; but such usages mostly have a special implication, as described in the next section.

9.3 'Presumptive' uses of the future

The English sentence 'That man will be our neighbour' is ambiguous: it can indicate real future time (tomorrow, next week), or it can be an assumption about the present (presumably he's our neighbour). This usage is common in Hindi, both with the simple future, होगा (as in the first example below), and with the future as auxiliary (as in the remaining examples):

वह आदमी हमारा पड़ोसी होगा ।	That man will/must be our neighbour.
बच्चे सो रहे होंगे ।	The kids will/must be sleeping.
दूसरे लोग अभी आ रहे होंगे ।	The others will/must be on their way just now.
आप उर्दू समझते होंगे ?	Presumably you understand Urdu?
शर्माजी संस्कृत जानते होंगे ।	Sharmaji will/must know Sanskrit.
वे गाड़ी का इंतज़ाम कर रहे होंगे ।	They will/must be making arrangements for a car.

 ## 9b   Arun and his co-author

अरुण	प्रेम, हमारी पुस्तक छपने को तैयार है । ग्यारह सौ प्रतियाँ छप रही हैं, वाराणसी में ।
प्रेम	तो दिल्ली लौटने से पहले आप उन्हें पिक-अप करने वाराणसी जाएँगे ?
अरुण	अभी मेरे लिए उधर जाना कठिन होगा । हम उन्हें डाक से मँगवाएँगे ।
प्रेम	बुक के डिस्ट्रिब्यूशन और पब्लिसिटी का क्या होगा ?

अरुण	सारी व्यवस्था यहीं हो रही है; इसीलिए मैं लखनऊ में दस दिन और रुक रहा हूँ ।
प्रेम	आप सोचते हैं किताब ख़ूब बिकेगी? अच्छा-ख़ासा पैसा हाथ आएगा ?
अरुण	पैसा कहाँ से हाथ आएगा, प्रेम ? अधिक से अधिक चार सौ प्रतियाँ बिकेंगी ।
प्रेम	पर मेरे ख़याल से तो लोग किताब को पसंद करेंगे । "वर्थ रीडिंग" है – पढ़ने-लायक़ है !
अरुण	है तो सही; परंतु आपके कहने से कुछ नहीं होगा । यदि जनता ख़रीदेगी, तो देखेंगे !

NB: Prem's English words are not given in the glossary.

छपना	to be printed	अच्छा-ख़ासा	really good
ग्यारह	eleven	हाथ आना	to come to hand
कठिन	hard, difficult	अधिक से अधिक	at the most
डाक़ f	mail, post	लायक़	worth (doing)
मँगवाना	to order, send for	पसंद करना	to like, approve
व्यवस्था f	arrangement(s)	सही	true, correct
रुकना	to stop, stay on	परंतु	but
बिकना	to be sold	जनता f	public, the people

Arun	Prem, our book's ready for printing. 1100 copies are being printed, in Varanasi.
Prem	So will you go to Varanasi to pick them up before returning to Delhi?
Arun	It'll be hard for me to go there just now. We'll send for them by post.
Prem	What will happen about the distribution and publicity of the book?
Arun	All the organising's happening here; that's why I'm stopping in Lucknow ten days more.
Prem	D'you think the book will sell well? We'll make loads of money?
Arun	How ('from where') will we make money, Prem. At the most 400 copies will sell.
Prem	But in *my* opinion people will like the book; it's 'worth reading' – worth reading!

Arun   It is indeed; but your saying it won't effect anything. If the
                 public buys, then we'll see!

🔊 Grammar
9.4   The emphatic ही

The word ही emphasises or restricts the word or phrase that
precedes it: मैं ही 'I myself' or 'only I'; बहुत ही अच्छा 'very good
indeed'. Often ही can be translated as 'only'; elsewhere the
translation depends on context.

मैं हिन्दी ही बोलूँगा ।	I shall speak Hindi only.
हमारा एक ही मकान है ।	We have only one house.

In many ways, ही operates like भी (2.3): it qualifies the word or
phrase *immediately preceding it*, and not being a postposition it
needs no change of case.

मैं सोमवार को ही आऊँगी ।	I'll come on Monday itself.
मैं ही सोमवार को आऊँगी ।	I'll come on Monday myself.

Some pronouns coalesce with ही, giving special forms:

मुझ	+	ही	=	मुझी		उस	+	ही	=	उसी
तुझ	+	ही	=	तुझी		हम	+	ही	=	हमीं
यह	+	ही	=	यही		तुम	+	ही	=	तुम्हीं
वह	+	ही	=	वही		इन	+	ही	=	इन्हीं
इस	+	ही	=	इसी		उन	+	ही	=	उन्हीं

> ❗ वही / उसी 'that very one' also means 'the same': वही आदमी 'the
> same man', उसी दिन 'that same day'.

Some adverbs also coalesce with ही:

यहाँ	+	ही	=	यहीं	right here
वहाँ	+	ही	=	वहीं	right there
अब	+	ही	=	अभी	right now
सब	+	ही	=	सभी	all, absolutely all

असली हिन्दी हमीं बोलते हैं ।	It is we who speak the real Hindi.
वही गुंडा मुझसे भी पैसा माँग रहा था ।	The same lout was demanding money from me too.
हम यहीं रहेंगे, हिलेंगे ही नहीं !	We'll stay right here, we won't even move!
डाक्टर साहब, अभी आइएगा ।	Doctor, please come at once.

> ❗ Look carefully: यहीं and वहीं are different from यही and वही !
> And notice also the difference in emphasis between इस लिए
> 'so, therefore' and इसी लिए 'for this reason', *that's why*.

हम यहीं रहते हैं ।	We live right here.
मैं भी यही सोचता हूँ ।	I too think the same thing.
हम वहीं जाएँगे ।	We'll go right there.
हम वही करेंगे ।	We'll do just that.

9.5 Some expressions of quantity

The word बहुत is both adjective (बहुत लोग 'many people') and adverb (बहुत बड़ा 'very big'). This can lead to ambiguities: बहुत अच्छी किताबें could theoretically mean either 'many good books' or 'very good books'. To remove this ambiguity and specify the former sense, the suffix -सा/-सी/-से can be added to the adjective:

बहुत अच्छी किताबें	very good books
	(adverb बहुत qualifies अच्छी)
बहुत-सी अच्छी किताबें	many good books
	(adjective बहुत-सी qualifies किताबें)

In a more general usage, -सा modifies or lightens the meaning of the word it's suffixed to, giving an '-ish' sense: लाल-सी रोशनी 'reddish light'; महँगे-से कपड़े 'quite expensive clothes'. Like English 'quite', its emphasis is rather ambiguous: sometimes it seems to enhance the sense of the adjective, sometimes to tone it down.

ज़्यादा and अधिक 'much, many, more' and कम 'little, few, less' are , like बहुत, both adverbs and adjectives. The sense 'too much' is expressed by बहुत ज़्यादा/अधिक, and 'too little' by बहुत कम, although the sense of 'excess' is not as specific as in these English expressions.

गरमियों में (बहुत) ज़्यादा लोग मसूरी आते हैं ।	In the summer (too) many people come to Mussoorie.
दाल में नमक बहुत ज़्यादा है ।	There's too much/a lot of salt in the daal.
वह छात्र बहुत कम काम करता है ।	That student does very little work.

Some more everyday phrases:

कम से कम at least	ज़्यादा से ज़्यादा at most
थोड़ा-बहुत a certain amount	अधिक से अधिक at most

काफ़ी quite (काफ़ी दूर, काफ़ी अच्छा); enough (काफ़ी पैसा, काफ़ी खाना)

9.6   The infinitive as verbal noun: जाना 'to go, going'

The infinitive – बोलना 'to speak' – can be used as a noun, also meaning 'speaking'.

सिग्रेट पीना मना है ।	Smoking is prohibited.
हिन्दी समझना आसान है ।	To understand Hindi is easy.
होना या न होना ।	To be or not to be.

Like any other masculine noun, this verbal noun inflects in the oblique case before a postposition: जाने से पहले, करने के बाद 'before going, after doing'. Hindi uses पर like English 'on' in पहुँचने पर 'on arriving'.

घर पहुँचने पर हमें फ़ोन करना ।	On arriving home, phone us.
मेरे जाने के बाद तुम क्या करोगे ?	What will you do after my going?
पत्र लिखने में क्या फ़ायदा है ?	What's the point in writing a letter?
चिल्लाने की (कोई) ज़रूरत नहीं है !	There's no need to shout!

The oblique infinitive expresses purpose: हम अँग्रेज़ी पढ़ाने अमरीका जा रहे हैं 'We are going to America to teach English'. The oblique infinitive may stand alone, or be followed by के लिए or को:

मैं खाना खाने किसी होटल जाऊँगी ।	I'll go to some hotel to eat.

| वह कुछ ख़रीदने (के लिए) बाज़ार जा रहा है । | He's going to the market (in order) to buy something. |
| गाड़ी ठीक करने को कोई मिस्तरी भेजो । | Send some mechanic to fix the car. |

The idiomatic English use of 'going to' as meaning 'about to' is reflected in Hindi also: मैं गाना गाने जा रहा हूँ 'I'm going to sing a song'.

> **!** Why is there no को after मिस्तरी 'mechanic', when in 5.4 we saw that a person as direct object takes को? Because the person here is not individualised – it's not a particular mechanic but कोई मिस्तरी, *any* mechanic. (मिस्तरी, incidentally, is from Portuguese 'mestre'.)

The oblique infinitive + (के) योग्य or (के) लायक़ means 'worth doing':

| "टीच योरसेल्फ़ हिन्दी" पढ़ने लायक़ है; | *Teach Yourself Hindi* is worth reading; |
| हाँ, और उसका कैसेट सुनने योग्य है । | Yes, and its cassette is worth listening to. |

In 6.1 we saw the usage मुझे हिन्दी आती है 'I know Hindi'. Similarly, आना is used with an infinitive verb as subject, meaning 'to know how to...'. Being sentence subject, the infinitive is in the direct case:

मुझे तैरना आता है ।	I am able to swim, can swim.
तुम्हें गाड़ी चलाना नहीं आता है ?	You can't drive a car?
उन्हें पढ़ना तो आता है पर लिखना नहीं आता ।	They can read but they can't write.

EXERCISE 9a.1 Translate.

1   The others will arrive by tomorrow morning.
2   Some day I will tell you the full story.
3   I know that he will not reply to my letters.
4   Your father must be earning good money these days.

5   They will be thinking that she must be living a life of luxury.

6   My sister will be driving my car today.

✔ **EXERCISE 9a.2** Answer the questions on Dialogue 8b:

१   क्या कमला को ख़ुशी है कि आज रात को कुछ मेहमान आ रहे हैं ? आपको कैसे
       मालूम है ?

२   क्या पिंकी अपने बड़े भाई के परिवार के साथ रहती है ?

३   खाना तैयार करने के लिए घर में किन चीज़ों की ज़रूरत है ?

४   प्रकाश को क्यों नहीं मालूम है कि श्रीमती खन्ना का पहला नाम क्या है ?

५   क्या कमला के ख़याल से उसका पति बहुत मेहनती आदमी है ? ऐसा कौन
       सोचता है ?

✔ **EXERCISE 9a.3** Answer the questions on Dialogue 9a.

१   आज शाम को प्रताप और कमला के यहाँ कौन नहीं आ रहा होगा, और क्यों ?

२   संगीता किस चीज़ से डरती है ?

३   संगीता के भाइयों के बारे में पिंकी का क्या ख़याल है ?

४   आपके ख़याल में हरीश के बारे में कमला क्या सोचती होगी ?

५   हरीश सिनेमा क्यों नहीं जाएगा ?

✔ **EXERCISE 9b.1** Translate Pratap's letter from a friend in Canada.

प्रिय प्रताप,
तुम कैसे हो ? दिल्ली में सब ठीक चल रहा है ? मैं बहुत देर के बाद यह ख़त लिख रही हूँ ।
तुम जानते होगे कि मैं भी हिन्दी सीखने के लिए भारत आने का प्रोग्राम बना रही हूँ । मुझे
आशा है कि बहुत ध्यान से पढ़ने के बाद मैं भी तुम्हारी तरह अच्छी हिन्दी सीखूँगी । कम से
कम यही तो इरादा है । हिन्दी समझना एक बात है लेकिन रवानी से बोलना दूसरी बात !
मेरी सहेली राजेश्वरी को जानते हो न ? उसकी बहिन उषा वाराणसी में रहती है । मैं उसी
के साथ ठहरूँगी । उसका घर कालेज से काफ़ी दूर है; कालेज तो रामनगर में है, महाराजा के
महल के नज़दीक, और उषा का घर बनारस हिन्दू विश्वविद्यालय (बी० एच० यू०) के अन्दर
है । बी० एच० यू० के आस-पास बहुत-से विद्यार्थी रहते होंगे । वे रिक्शे से कालेज जाते होंगे;
मैं भी उन्हीं के साथ जाऊँगी । पिताजी कहते हैं कि मेरा अकेले जाना ठीक न होगा क्योंकि
वाराणसी के नौजवान बहुत गुंडागर्दी मचाते हैं और लड़कियों को तंग करते हैं । इसको
"ईव-टीज़िंग" कहते हैं, न ?

कहने की ज़रूरत नहीं कि मैं भारत हवाई जहाज़ से आऊँगी । दिल्ली पहुँचने पर तुम को फ़ोन करूँगी । दिल्ली में दो-तीन दिन ठहरने के बाद मैं रेलगाड़ी से बनारस जाऊँगी । उषा मुझसे मिलने स्टेशन आएगी । गाड़ी उधर बहुत सवेरे पहुँचती है । "उषा काल" को उषा के दर्शन ! मैं उषा को नहीं जानती; उसे कैसे पहचानूँगी, समझ में नहीं आता । शायद राजेश्वरी के पास उसका कोई पुराना फ़ोटो होगा । उषा का पति विश्वविद्यालय में इतिहास का प्राध्यापक है । राजेश्वरी का कहना है कि पति-पत्नी में बहुत झगड़ा होता है । तीन बच्चे भी हैं, छोटे-बड़े । ऐसे घर में मेहमान बनना कैसा होगा, मालूम नहीं ! ख़ैर, अगर तुम्हारे पास समय होगा, तो तुम भी कभी बनारस ज़रूर आना । दिल्ली पहुँचने पर तुम्हें फ़ोन करूँगी । अपना ध्यान रखना ।

तुम्हारी गीता

EXERCISE 9b.2 Translate.

1   Will there be any special difficulty (मुश्किल f) in learning Urdu?
2   Next month our students will be going to Lucknow to study Hindi.
3   Your brother must know (use आना, 6.1) quite good Hindi by now.
4   My friends' father will come to meet me at Varanasi station.
5   There are lots of places worth seeing near Delhi.
6   We will go with you to Mussoorie to see the mountains.

EXERCISE 9b.3 Fill the gaps with the direct or oblique form of the given infinitive verb, then translate.

१ संस्कृत... आसान नहीं है; लेकिन इसे... में बहुत फ़ायदा है । (पढ़ना to study)
२ मैं फ़िल्म... जा रहा हूँ; तुम भी चलो – फ़िल्म... लायक़ होगी ।   (देखना to see)
३ क्या गाड़ी... आपको पसंद है ? मुझे तो गाड़ी... नहीं आता । (चलाना to drive)
४ क्या सिग्रेट... ग़लत है ? हाँ ज़रूर, और... में फ़ायदा भी क्या है ? (पीना to smoke)
५ क्या तुम तबला... यहाँ आते हो ? हाँ, मुझे तबला... बहुत पसंद है । (बजाना to play)

Vocabulary

अकेले	alone	अमरीका ^m	America
अगर	if	असली	real
अच्छा-ख़ासा	really good	आसान	easy
अधिक	much, many, more; अधिक	इंतज़ाम ^m	arrangement(s),
से अधिक	at the most		organisation

इतिहास ^m history

इरादा ^m intention

ईव-टीज़िंग ^f 'Eve-teasing' – sexual harrassment of girls & women

उषा ^f dawn

कठिन hard, difficult

कभी sometime

कम से कम at least

कमाना to earn

काल ^m time, period of day

के आस-पास around, in vicinity of

ख़रीदना to purchase, buy

गरमियाँ ^{f.pl} summer

ग़लत wrong

गाना^{1 m} song

गाना² to sing

गुंडा ^m lout, hooligan; गुंडागर्दी ^f hooliganism

ग्यारह eleven

चिल्लाना to shout

छपना to be printed

जनता ^f public, the people

ज़्यादा से ज़्यादा at the most

ठीक करना to put right, fix

डाक ^f mail, post

तबला ^m tabla (drum)

तैरना to swim

थोड़ा-बहुत a certain amount

थोड़े scarcely, by no means

दर्शन ^m vision (of), audience or auspicious meeting (with)

दावत ^f (invitation to) a dinner

ध्यान देना to pay attention

नमक ^m salt

नुक़सान ^m harm

नौजवान ^m youth, young man

पत्र ^m letter

परंतु but

पसंद करना to like, approve

पहचानना to recognise

पहुँचना to arrive

प्राध्यापक ^m lecturer

फ़ायदा ^m profit, advantage, point

फ़ोन करना to phone

बजाना to play (music)

बनारस ^m Banaras, Varanasi

बिकना to be sold

बी० एच० यू० ^m BHU (Banaras Hindu University)

बोर करना to bore

भतीजा ^m nephew

भविष्य ^m future

भोला innocent, guileless, simple

मँगवाना to order, send for

मचाना to create (noise etc.)

मना prohibited

मसूरी ^f Mussoorie

महाराजा ^m maharaja

(से) मिलना	to meet	विश्वविद्यालय ^m	university

(से) मिलना   to meet

मिस्तरी ^m   mechanic, artisan

यहीं   right here, in this very place

रवानी ^f   fluency

रुकना   to stop, stay on

रेलगाड़ी ^f   train

रोशनी ^f   light

लायक़   worth (doing)

लौटना   to return

वहीं   right there, in that very place

विश्वविद्यालय ^m   university

व्यवस्था ^f   arrangement(s)

समझ ^f   understanding; समझ में
 आना to enter the understanding,
 be understood

सही   true, correct

हवाई जहाज़ ^m   aeroplane

हाथ आना   to come to hand

हिलना   to move, stir

ही   only (emphatic)

10 | WHAT SHOULD I SAY?
मैं क्या बोलूँ ?

In this unit you will learn how to

- express doubts and possibilities
- make suggestions
- give gentle commands
- use conditionals: 'if...'

10a   Chotu leaves a message for Prakash

छोटू	हेलो, मैं छोटू बोल रहा हूँ । क्या प्रकाश जी हैं ? मैं उनका चपरासी हूँ ।
कमला	नहीं छोटू, बाहर हैं । आधे घंटे में आएँगे । मैं उन्हें कोई मेसेज दूँ ?
छोटू	जी, आप उन्हें यह बताएँ कि खन्ना साहब उनसे बात करना चाहते हैं ।
कमला	कोई ज़रूरी बात है ? आख़िर हम तो आज रात को ही उनसे मिल रहे हैं ।
छोटू	शायद इसी बारे में खन्ना जी का कोई निवेदन हो ।
कमला	और तुमसे मेरा यह निवेदन है, छोटू, कि तुम अपनी बात ख़त्म करो । मेरे पास समय नहीं है ।

छोटू	मैडम, बहुत ज़रूरी है कि प्रकाश जी ख़ुद खन्ना साहब से बात करें ।
कमला	बताऊँगी उनको । तुम खन्ना साहब से कहो कि यहाँ आठ बजे आएँ ।

चपरासी ^m	peon, orderly	आख़िर	after all
आधा ^m	half	बारे में	about, concerning
मेसेज ^m	'message'	निवेदन ^m	request
चाहना	to want, wish	ख़ुद	oneself (himself)

Chotu	Hello, this is Chotu here. Is Prakash ji there? I'm his peon.
Kamala	No Chotu, he's out. He'll come in half an hour. Should I give him some message?
Chotu	Yes, please tell him (this,) that Khanna Sahib wants to talk to him.
Kamala	Is it something urgent? After all we're meeting him just tonight.
Chotu	Perhaps that's what Khanna ji might have some request about.
Kamala	And my request to you, Chotu, is that you finish what you have to say. I have no time.
Chotu	Madam, it's very important that Prakash ji phone Khanna Sahib himself.
Kamala	I'll tell him. You tell Khanna Sahib that they should come here at eight.

Grammar

10.1 The subjunctive

The subjunctive is a 'mood' or form of the verb whose action is uncertain, speculative, desired, or suggested: 'I may speak, might speak, should speak' etc. To form the Hindi subjunctive, simply take the future verb, e.g. बोलूँगा, and remove the -गा/ -गी/ -गे ending, leaving बोलूँ. Masculine and feminine forms are identical; and all plural forms except तुम are identical, ending in -एँ.

मैं बोलूँ	I may speak	हम बोलें	we may speak
तू बोले	you may speak	तुम बोलो	you may speak
—		आप बोलें	you may speak
यह, वह बोले	he, she, it may speak	ये, वे बोलें	they may speak

मैं कुछ बोलूँ ?	May/should I say something?
हम भी चलें ?	May/should we go too?
आप यहीं रहें ।	You should stay right here. Please stay right here.

This last example shows how the 'suggestive' implication of the second-person subjunctive (तुम रहो, आप रहें) can also be interpreted as a mild command. Indeed the तुम form of the subjunctive – रहो, बोलो, जाओ – is identical with the imperative. The negative for subjunctives is न. Some more examples:

अपने जूते यहाँ उतारें / उतारिए ।	Please take your shoes off here.
अपना पता यहाँ लिखें / लिखिए ।	Please write your address here.
मंदिर के अंदर फ़ोटो न खींचो ।	Don't take photos inside the temple.
आप से निवेदन है कि आप बैठे रहें ।	You are requested to remain seated.

This last sentence means literally 'there is a request of you that you remain seated'. This is a common formula: an opening clause indicates the existence of a hope, wish, expectation, possibility, request, etc., while the second clause (introduced by कि 'that') spells out the detail of that wish etc. with a subjunctive verb:

मुझे आशा थी कि वह पत्र लिखे ।	I hoped he/she might write a letter.
हमें उम्मीद है कि इलाज लंबा न हो ।	We hope the treatment won't be long.
छोटू से कहो कि वह चाय लाए ।	Tell Chotu to bring tea ('that he should bring tea').
संभव है कि ट्रेन देर से पहुँचे ।	It's possible that the train may arrive late.
असंभव है कि वे ऐसी भूल करें ।	It's impossible that they would make such a mistake.
बहुत ज़रूरी है कि तुम कल रात तक लौटो ।	It's vital that you return by tomorrow evening.

By now you'll be getting a feel for the uncertain, speculative, 'maybe' senses of the subjunctive. Equivalent sentences in the future tense show a more clearcut expectation, a more confident hope:

मुझे विश्वास था कि वह पत्र लिखेगा ।	I was confident that he would write a letter.
हमें यक़ीन है कि इलाज लंबा नहीं होगा ।	We are sure that the treatment won't be long.

10.2 The subjunctive in the auxiliary verb

As with the future tense (9.2), the subjunctive of the auxiliary verb होना can appear within tenses such as the continuous and the imperfective. Compare the following:

राज सो रहा होगा ।	Raj will/must be sleeping.
राज सो रहा हो ।	Raj may be sleeping.
उषा यहाँ रहती होगी ।	Usha will/must be living here.
उषा वाराणसी में रहती हो ।	Usha may be living in Varanasi.

10.3 The verb चाहना

चाहना means 'to want, to wish'. It is used with a direct infinitive verb as follows:

पिताजी घर जाना चाहते हैं ।	Father wants to go home.
मैं उर्दू भी सीखना चाहता हूँ ।	I want to learn Urdu too.
उर्वशी मुझसे मिलना नहीं चाहती ।	Urvashi doesn't want to meet me.

This construction only applies when the subject of the 'wanting' and the subject of the 'doing' are *one and the same* – 'Father' in the first example. But if Father wants *someone else* to do something, the change of subject calls for a more complex construction: 'Father wishes that I should go home', with the second verb in the subjunctive.

पिताजी चाहते हैं कि मैं घर जाऊँ ।	Father wants me to go home.
उर्वशी चाहती है कि मैं दूर रहूँ ।	Urvashi wants me to keep away.

चाहना also means 'to like, love, be fond of':

सब लोग तुम्हें बहुत चाहते हैं ।   Everyone's very fond of you.

मजनूँ लैला को बहुत चाहता था ।   Majnu loved Laila very much.

> **!** Don't confuse these uses of चाहना with the quite separate
> चाहिए construction (7.3).

10b Sangeeta's dilemma

संगीता	ऋषि, अगर मैं आज रात को पिंकी से मिलने जाऊँ तो तुम अम्माँ को नहीं बताओगे न ?
ऋषि	तुम बाहर जा रही हो ? पर अम्माँ चाहती हैं कि तुम यहीं घर पर ही रहो।
संगीता	हाँ, मालूम है । पर घर में तो बड़ी बोरियत होगी । तुम्हीं बताओ – रहूँ कि जाऊँ ?
ऋषि	मामला कुछ टेढ़ा है ! मैं पिताजी से पूछूँ कि उनका क्या ख़याल है ? तुम उनकी सलाह लो ।
संगीता	हाँ पूछो न, देखें पिताजी क्या कहते हैं । पर अगर वे सो रहे हों तो उन्हें मत जगाना ।
ऋषि	थोड़ी देर पहले तो बाहर जानेवाले थे । अम्माँ कह रही थीं कि पिताजी सब्ज़ी लाएँ ।
कमला	[*दूर से*] ऋषि ! ओ ऋषि ! राज से कहो कि वह दूधवाले को बुलाए ।
ऋषि	[*संगीता से*] राज तो दूध पीनेवाला बच्चा है ही – दूधवाले को क्यों नहीं बुलाएगा !

बोरियत ^f	boredom	मामला ^m	matter, affair
कि	or	टेढ़ा	twisted, complex

Sangeeta	Rishi, if I go to meet Pinkie tonight you won't tell Mum will you?
Rishi	You're going out? But Mum wants you to stay here.
Sangeeta	Yes I know. But it will be very boring at home. You tell me – should I stay or go?
Rishi	It's a rather tricky matter! Should I ask Father what he thinks? Take his advice.

Sangeeta	Yes, ask won't you, let's see what Father says. But if he's sleeping don't wake him.
Rishi	A little while ago he was about to go out. Mum was saying that he should get vegetables.
Kamala	[*from a distance*] Rishi! Oh Rishi! Tell Raj to call the milkman.
Rishi	[*to Sangeeta*] Raj *is* a milk-drinking kid – why wouldn't he call the milkman!

Grammar

10.4 Conditional sentences (1)

You've already seen some conditional sentences, for example in Dialogue 9a. There are two clauses: an 'if' clause beginning अगर, and a 'then' clause beginning तो.

In 'if' sentences referring to future events, the verb choice for the अगर clause is between imperfective, subjunctive and future, usually with a future verb in the तो clause. The perceived likelihood of the condition being fulfilled varies accordingly:

अगर पानी पड़ता है तो हम अंदर रहेंगे ।	If it rains, we'll stay inside. (*imperfective*: neutral forecast)
अगर पानी पड़ेगा तो हम अंदर रहेंगे ।	If it rains, we'll stay inside. (*future*: rain likely)
अगर पानी पड़े तो हम अंदर रहेंगे ।	Should it rain, we'll stay inside. (*subjunctive*: rain less likely)

The following examples show imperatives in the तो clause; यदि 'if' is a Sanskritic synonym for अगर.

यदि जाना चाहते हो तो अभी जाओ ।	If you wish to go, go now.
अगर तू ख़ाली हो तो मेरे साथ चल ।	If you're free, come with me.

Tenses such as the continuous may also appear in an अगर clause:

अगर वह सो रही हो तो उसे जगाना ।	Wake her if she's sleeping.
अगर राम आ रहा है तो मैं भी आऊँगा ।	If Ram's coming I'll come too.

In English, 'then' is optional in an 'if' sentence ('if she comes [then] I'll tell her'); but in Hindi अगर can be dropped, while तो is essential.

| दादी कहती हैं, (अगर) पानी पड़े तो बाहर मत जाना । | Grandma says, if it rains, don't go out. |

10.5 The suffix -वाला

The suffix वाला / वाली / वाले relates a person to the noun it adjoins: दूधवाला 'milkman', दिल्लीवाली 'woman from Delhi', गाँववाले 'villagers'. The initial noun may be in the oblique: रिक्शेवाला 'rickshaw driver'.

पुलिसवाले को नाराज़ मत करना ।	Don't displease the policeman.
कुछ पैसेवाले तो बड़े कंजूस होते हैं ।	Some rich folk are very mean.
हिन्दीवालों को अपनी भाषा पर गर्व है ।	Hindi-speakers are proud of their language.

Suffixed to an adverb, वाला forms an adjective – ऊपरवाला कमरा 'upstairs room', पासवाली दुकान 'nearby shop'; or a noun – ऊपरवाला 'God' (the one up above).

मुझे बीचवाली तस्वीर पसंद है ।	I like the middle picture.
सब कुछ ऊपरवाले के हाथ में है ।	Everything's in God's hand(s).
कौनसी गाड़ी हमारी है ? यह-वाली ।	Which car is ours? This one.

Suffixed to an oblique infinitive verb, वाला refers to that verb's action, either as noun (हिन्दी बोलनेवाला 'Hindi-speaker', शहर के रहनेवाले 'townspeople') or adjective (आनेवाला कल 'tomorrow', आनेवाले हफ़्ते में 'in the coming week').

सिग्रेट पीनेवालो, बाहर बैठो !	Cigarette smokers, sit outside!
मुझे झूठ बोलनेवाले बच्चों से नफ़रत है !	I hate children who tell lies!
आप कहाँ के रहनेवाले हैं ?	Where are you from?

The same construction can mean 'about to...' – जानेवाला 'about to go'.

दुकान बंद होनेवाली है ।	The shop's about to close.
हम अभी फ़ोन करनेवाले थे ।	We were just about to phone.
वह अभी जानेवाली थी ।	She was just about to go.

EXERCISE 10a.1 Fill the gap with a subjunctive, using the verb indicated. Then translate.

१   क्या मैं भी तुम्हारे साथ … , या यहीं घर पर … ?   (जाना; रहना)

२   अगर मौसम ख़राब न… तो शायद वे लोग शाम तक गाँव… ।   (होना; पहुँचना)

३   उचित है कि वह तुम्हारे आने से पहले घर को ख़ाली… ।   (करना)

४   ज़रूरी नहीं है कि हम किसी की सलाह… या किसी की बात… ।   (लेना; सुनना)

५   उससे कहो कि वह आज रात तक जवाब… और अपनी ज़िम्मेदारी न… ।   (देना; भूलना)

६   आपसे निवेदन है कि आप इलाज के पैसे अभी… ।   (देना)

EXERCISE 10a.2 Transpose imperative to चाहना + subjunctive on the pattern shown. Then translate the new sentence.

आप अभी घर जाइए । →   मैं चाहता हूँ कि आप अभी घर जाएँ ।

                          I want you to go home right now.

१   आप तुरंत जवाब दीजिए ।   (मैं चाहता हूँ कि…)

२   तुम चुप रहो ।   (मैं चाहता हूँ कि…)

३   गाय को न मारो ।   (मैं चाहता हूँ कि…)

४   सीढ़ियों पर न बैठो ।   (मैं चाहता हूँ कि…)

५   मेरा हाथ पकड़ !   (मैं चाहता हूँ कि…)

६   आज की संस्कृत की क्लास पढ़ाइए ।   (मैं चाहता हूँ कि…)

EXERCISE 10a.3 Complete the sentence with an appropriate clause. Then translate.

१   अगर आप ख़ाली हों तो ....

२   यदि आपको असुविधा न हो तो अवश्य ....

३   अगर तुम उनसे मिलना चाहती हो तो ....

४   यदि यह काम सचमुच बहुत ही कठिन है तो ....

५   अगर पुलिस आएगी तो ....

६   .... तो आप किसी दोस्त की सलाह लें ।

७   .... तो वह तुम पर ज़रूर गुस्से होगा ।

८   .... तो आप अभी भारत न जाएँ ।

९   .... तो बहुत बुरा होगा ।

१०   .... तो मैं भी तुम्हारे साथ जाऊँगी ।

EXERCISE 10b.1 Translate Kamala's note to Prakash.

प्रकाश – खन्ना जी चाहते हैं कि तुम उन्हें फ़ोन करो । भूलो मत – शायद आज रात के बारे में कोई ज़रूरी बात हो । मैं अभी सब्ज़ीवाले के पास जा रही हूँ । मेरे कहने पर भी तुम सब्ज़ी नहीं लाते हो – भूलने में तो माहिर हो । उसके बाद थोड़ी देर के लिए सुरेश से मिलने जाऊँगी । गाड़ी तो तुम्हारे पास है इसलिए मैं बाज़ार आटो से जाऊँगी । दुकानों से चावल वग़ैरह चाहिए – तुम लाना । नए काँटे, चम्मच, छुरियाँ भी चाहिए । सब चीज़ों की लिस्ट सोनेवाले कमरे की मेज़ पर पड़ी है । अब की बार किसी चीज़ को मत भूलना । सारी चीज़ें तुम मार्केट-वाली दुकान से लेना; गली-वाली दुकान पर मत जाना, वहाँ तो दाम बहुत ऊँचे होते हैं । तुमसे क्या कहूँ ? तुम तो किसी चीज़ की सही क़ीमत भी नहीं जानते ! ठीक से ख़रीदारी करना भी नहीं आता तुम्हें ।

मैं तो डेढ़ घंटे में आऊँगी । अगर तुम पहले घर लौटोगे (मतलब – इससे पहले कि मैं लौटूँ) तो बैठनेवाले कमरे को साफ़ करो । नहीं तो बाद में करना; पर करना तो सही । मैं बार-बार तुम्हारी माँ से कहती हूँ कि वे सफ़ाई के काम में हाथ बँटाएँ मगर मेरी बात कौन सुनता है । तुम्हारी माँ तो दिन भर मक्खियाँ मारती हैं । पता नहीं इस घर में सब लोग इतने कामचोर क्यों होते हैं । काम करनेवाली मैं ही हूँ । समझ में नहीं आ रहा कि मैं इतना लंबा नोट क्यों लिख रही हूँ । मेरे पास वक़्त भी कहाँ है ? जल्दी में हूँ, मुझे देर हो रही है । क०

EXERCISE 10b.2 Answer the questions on Kamala's note.

१	आपके ख़याल से कमला क्यों नाराज़ है ?

२	क्या खन्ना जी चाहते थे कि प्रकाश उन्हें वापस फ़ोन करे ?

३	आज इतनी ख़रीदारी क्यों हो रही है ?

४	सब्ज़ी ख़रीदने के बाद कमला किससे मिलने जाएगी ?

५	अगर प्रकाश जल्दी घर वापस आए तो वह क्या करे ?

६	कौनसी दुकान गली-वाली दुकान से ज़्यादा सस्ती है ?

७	प्रकाश को कैसे पता चलेगा कि घर में किन चीज़ों की ज़रूरत है ?

८	कमला क्यों चाहती है कि दादी जी घर की सफ़ाई करें ?

९	कमला की बातें कौन सुनता है ?

१०	क्या कमला सोचती है कि दादी जी घर में बहुत मदद देती हैं ?

EXERCISE 10b.3 Translate.

1   Kamala wants Prakash to do some shopping for tonight's dinner.
2   Nobody knows why everything in the nearby shop is so expensive.
3   It's possible that Pratap may return from Nepal by tonight.
4   For some reason, even Sangeeta wants Pratap to come home soon.
5   If Pratap's train is late, someone might go to meet him at the station.
6   If Pratap brings something for Sangeeta, what will she say?

Vocabulary

अब की बार this time	गाय ^f cow
अवश्य certainly	गुस्से angry
असंभव impossible	चपरासी ^m peon, orderly
आख़िर after all	चम्मच ^m spoon
आटो ^m auto-rickshaw	चाहना to want, wish, be fond of
आधा ^m half	छुरी ^f knife
इतना so (as in 'so big'), so much	ज़िम्मेदारी ^f responsibility
इलाज ^m treatment, cure	झूठ ^m lie
उचित proper, appropriate	टेढ़ा twisted, complex
उतारना to take down, take off	डेढ़ one and a half
उम्मीद ^f hope	तुरंत immediately
ऊँचा high	दाम ^m price
कंजूस miserly, mean	नहीं तो otherwise
काँटा ^m fork	निवेदन ^m request
कामचोर work-shy, lazy	नोट ^m note
कि or	पकड़ना to catch, grab, hold
ख़रीदारी ^f buying, shopping	पड़ना to fall
ख़ाली करना to vacate	पता ^m address; **पता नहीं** don't
खींचना to draw; take (photo)	know, no idea; **पता होना** to
ख़ुद oneself	know, be aware
गर्व ^m pride	पानी पड़ना to rain

पुलिस ^f (used in singular) police

बार ^f time, occasion; बार बार time and again

बारे में about, concerning

बोरियत ^f boredom

भारी heavy

भूल ^f mistake; भूल करना to make a mistake

भूलना to forget, err

मंदिर ^m temple

मक्खी ^f fly; मक्खियाँ मारना to 'kill flies', laze about

मगर but

मदद ^f help; मदद देना to help

मामला ^m matter, affair

माहिर expert, skilled

यक़ीन ^m confidence, faith

यदि if

रिक्शा ^m rickshaw

लिस्ट ^f list

वक़्त ^m time

वापस back; वापस आना to come back

विश्वास ^m belief, confidence

संभव possible

सफ़ाई ^f cleaning

सलाह ^f advice

सीढ़ी ^f stair, staircase

हफ़्ता ^m week

हाथ बँटाना to lend a hand

11 | PRATAP HAS COME BACK

प्रताप वापस आया है

In this unit you will learn how to
- describe past events
- distinguish regular actions from one-off events

11a Pratap rejoins his Hindi class

शर्मा जी	अरे प्रताप ! तुम तो बहुत दिनों के बाद क्लास में आए हो ! क्या तुम बाहर गए थे ?
प्रताप	जी हाँ, मैं काठमांडू गया था । माफ़ कीजिएगा । अभी कल रात को ही दिल्ली लौटा ।
शर्मा जी	माफ़ी माँगने की कोई ज़रूरत नहीं है; पर तुम नेपाल में क्या कर रहे थे ?
प्रताप	मैं कुछ दोस्तों के साथ ट्रेकिंग करने गया था, पर आख़िर में हम काठमांडू में ही रहे ।
शर्मा जी	क्यों ? क्या हुआ ? कोई दुर्घटना तो नहीं हुई ?
प्रताप	जी नहीं; मेरे पिताजी मुझसे मिलने नेपाल आए थे, इसलिए मैं उनके साथ उनके कुछ दोस्तों से मिलने गया ।
शर्मा जी	अब मैं समझा । तो सुनो प्रताप, नेपाल में तुम कुछ हिन्दी बोले ?
प्रताप	जी हाँ, उधर बहुत-से लोग हिन्दी बोलते हैं । मैं अपनी हिन्दी नहीं भूला हूँ !
शमा जी	और क्या तुम्हारे पिताजी भी तुम्हारे साथ दिल्ली वापस आए हैं ?
प्रताप	जी हाँ, हम साथ साथ आए । वे तो डिफ़ेंस कालोनी में किसी दोस्त से मिलना चाहते हैं ।

माफ़ करना	to forgive, excuse	**आख़िर में**	in the end
माफ़ी f	forgiveness	**दुर्घटना** f	accident
ट्रेकिंग f	'trekking'	**साथ साथ**	together

Sharma ji	Oh Pratap! You've come to class after a long time! Did you go away?
Pratap	Yes, I'd gone to Kathmandu. I'm sorry. I returned to Delhi just yesterday night.
Sharma ji	There's no need to apologise; but what were you doing in Nepal?
Pratap	I'd gone to do some trekking with some friends, but in the end we stayed in Kathmandu.
Sharma ji	Why? What happened? There wasn't an accident was there?
Pratap	No, my father had come to meet me, so I went with him to see some friends of his.
Sharma ji	Now I understand. So listen Pratap, did you speak some Hindi in Nepal?
Pratap	Yes, lots of people speak Hindi there. I haven't forgotten my Hindi!
Sharma ji	And has your father come back to Delhi with you too?
Pratap	Yes, we came together. He wants to meet some friend in Defence Colony.

Grammar
11.1 Transitivity

Intransitive verbs are those which do not take a direct object: they describe a change of state (e.g. a motion or movement) – 'He arrived'; 'We'll go to India'; 'She got up' – rather than an action done *to* something. (In English we can't say 'He arrived the house' or 'We'll go India', because these verbs are intransitive.)

A transitive verb is one that *can* take a direct object – it describes an action done to something: 'I drank the water'; 'Sweep the floor!'; 'We'll write a letter'. Such verbs are still transitive even when there's no object expressed: 'I drank'; 'Sweep!'; 'We'll write'.

In the perfective tenses – 'I spoke, have spoken, had spoken' – most *intransitive* verbs in Hindi take a construction in which the verb agrees with the subject, as in other tenses met earlier; these are introduced in 11.2 below. (लाना 'to bring', though transitive, shares this construction.) But most *transitive* verbs follow a quite distinctive construction, introduced in 11.3. The two constructions are then brought together in 11.4. Each section has its own dialogue.

11.2 Perfective tenses – intransitive verbs

The perfective tenses refer to *completed* actions: 'I rose, I have risen, I had risen'. The participle consists of stem + -आ, -ए, -ई, ईं; thus उठा, उठे, उठी, उठीं.

The Hindi equivalents of the auxiliary 'have' and 'had' in these tenses are हूँ and था respectively: मैं उठा हूँ, मैं उठा था. The tense मैं उठा था 'I had risen', can also refer to a relatively remote past, with the sense 'I rose [some time ago]'.

	MASCULINE	FEMININE	
मैं	उठा, उठा हूँ, उठा था	उठी, उठी हूँ, उठी थी	I rose, have risen, had risen
तू	उठा, उठा है, उठा था	उठी, उठी है, उठी थी	you rose, have risen, had risen
यह/वह	उठा, उठा है, उठा था	उठी, उठी है, उठी थी	he/it/she rose, has risen, had risen
हम	उठे, उठे हैं, उठे थे	उठीं, उठी हैं, उठी थीं	we rose, have risen, had risen
तुम	उठे, उठे हो, उठे थे	उठीं, उठी हो, उठी थीं	you rose, have risen, had risen
आप	उठे, उठे हैं, उठे थे	उठीं, उठी हैं, उठी थीं	you rose, have risen, had risen
ये/वे	उठे, उठे हैं, उठे थे	उठीं, उठी हैं, उठी थीं	they rose, have risen, had risen

Verbs whose stems end in a vowel (e.g. आ- from आना 'to come') insert a य between the stem and the masculine singular participle ending (giving आया), and optionally elsewhere:

आना –   आया, आई, आईं, आए   (optionally आयी, आयीं, आये)

(The verbs जाना and होना have irregular perfectives:

जाना –	गया, गए, गई, गईं	(optionally गये, गयी, गयीं)
होना –	हुआ, हुए, हुई, हुईं	

> ❗ हुआ means 'happened' and describes an *action*; था means 'was' and describes a *state*.

This construction *only applies with intransitive verbs*, such as घूमना 'to roam, tour'; ठहरना 'to stay, wait'; चलना 'to move'; निकलना 'to emerge'; पड़ना 'to fall, befall'; पहुँचना 'to arrive'; बजना 'to resound, chime'; भूलना 'to forget'; मिलना 'to meet'; रहना 'to stay, remain'; रोना 'to weep'; लौटना 'to return'; होना 'to occur'; and, as noted earlier, लाना 'to bring'.

क्या हुआ ?	What happened?
माली लौटा ।	The gardener returned.
लड़कियाँ कल पहुँचीं ।	The girls arrived yesterday.
लड़के ख़ूब रोये ।	The boys cried a lot.
क्या तुम मेरी दवा भी लाए ?	Did you bring my medicine too?
कुछ नहीं हुआ है ।	Nothing has happened.
क्या पिताजी लौटे हैं ?	Has Father returned?
तुम घर पहुँचे हो ।	You have reached home.
मैं भी कई बार रोया हूँ ।	I too have cried several times.
ऋषि आपकी दवा लाया है ।	Rishi has brought your medicine.
क्या कोई दुर्घटना हुई थी ?	Had some accident happened?
हम लोग दस बजे तक लौटे थे ।	We had returned by 10 o'clock.
माताजी परसों पहुँची थीं ।	Mother had arrived the day before yesterday.
दोनों औरतें रोई थीं ।	Both women had cried.
वह उसे कल ही लाया था ।	He'd brought it *yesterday*.

11b   What Pratap did in Nepal

शर्मा जी	तो यह बताओ प्रताप, नेपाल में तुमने नेपाली भाषा सीखी ?
प्रताप	मैंने कोई बीस-पच्चीस शब्द सीखे, इससे ज़्यादा नहीं ।
शर्मा जी	और क्या तुमने कुछ ख़रीदा ? कोई उपहार या भेंट ?
प्रताप	जी हाँ, मैंने कुछ तिब्बती ज़ेवर ख़रीदे, और दो चाँदी की मूर्तियाँ भी ख़रीदीं ।
शर्मा जी	काठमांडू में तुमने कुछ फ़ोटो खींचे ?
प्रताप	फ़ोटो खींचने का इरादा तो था, पर नेपाल पहुँचने पर मैंने अपना कैमरा बेचा ! मजबूरी थी ।
शर्मा जी	तुमने ऐसा क्यों किया ? पैसे की इतनी भारी आवश्यकता थी क्या ?
प्रताप	हाँ, क्योंकि पिताजी ने मुझसे चार हज़ार रुपए उधार लिए थे, कुछ तोहफ़े ख़रीदने के लिए ।

नेपाली	Nepali	कैमरा m	camera
बीस	twenty	बेचना	to sell
पच्चीस	twenty-five	मजबूरी f	compulsion
शब्द m	word	आवश्यकता f	necessity
उपहार m	present, gift	रुपया m	rupee; money
भेंट f	gift, presentation	उधार m	loan; **उधार लेना** to
तिब्बती	Tibetan		borrow
ज़ेवर m	(item of) jewellery	तोहफ़ा m	a present
फ़ोटो m	photograph		

Sharma ji	So tell me Pratap, did you learn the Nepali language in Nepal?
Pratap	I learnt some 20 or 25 words, not more than this.
Sharma ji	And did you buy anything? Some present or gift?
Pratap	Yes, I bought some Tibetan jewellery, and I also bought two silver images.
Sharma ji	Did you take some photos in Kathmandu?
Pratap	I intended to take pictures, but I sold my camera on arriving in Nepal. I had no choice.
Sharma ji	Why did you do such a thing? Did you need money so badly?
Pratap	Yes, because Father had borrowed 4000 rupees from me, to buy some presents.

🔊 Grammar

11.3 Perfective tenses – transitive verbs

The perfective tenses of transitive verbs have a unique construction, still based on a participle comprising stem + -आ, -ए, -ई, -ईं. The following example uses the transitive verb लिखना ' to write':

लड़के ने पाँच चिट्ठियाँ लिखीं ।   The boy wrote five letters.

For the English subject 'the boy', Hindi has लड़के ने, in which the 'agentive' postposition ने is an untranslatable word indicating the agent or 'doer' of the action. The verb लिखीं agrees with the चिट्ठियाँ 'letters' – feminine plural. See how the verb agreement changes through the following sequence:

लड़के ने एक चिट्ठी लिखी । The boy wrote one letter.
                     (लिखी agrees with चिट्ठी fem. singular)
लड़के ने दो चिट्ठियाँ लिखीं। The boy wrote two letters.
                     (लिखीं agrees with चिट्ठियाँ fem. plural)
लड़के ने एक पत्र लिखा ।   The boy wrote one letter.
                     (लिखा agrees with पत्र masc. singular)
लड़के ने पाँच पत्र लिखे । The boy wrote five letters.
                     (लिखे agrees with पत्र masc. plural)

Agreement also applies to the *auxiliary* verb (e.g. in सुना है, सुना था):

राम ने दस प्याले ख़रीदे हैं ।   Ram has bought ten cups.
                     (ख़रीदे हैं agrees with प्याले masc. plural)
लड़की ने कई गीत गाए हैं ।   The girl has sung several songs.
                     (गाए हैं agrees with गीत masc. plural)
चोरों ने खिड़की तोड़ी थी ।   The thieves had broken a window.
                     (तोड़ी थी = खिड़की fem. singular)
तुमने चिट्ठियाँ कहाँ रखी हैं ? Where have you put the letters?
                     (रखी हैं agrees with चिट्ठियाँ fem. plural)
मैंने कई किताबें पढ़ी थीं ।   I had read several books.
                     (पढ़ी थीं agrees with किताबें fem. plural)

If no direct object is expressed, or if the direct object takes the postposition को, the verb is invariably in the masculine singular:

लड़की ने ध्यान से सुना ।	The girl listened carefully. (no object expressed)
लड़की ने दोनों गीतों को सुना ।	The girl listened to both the songs.
लड़कियों ने चिट्ठी को पढ़ा था ।	The girls had read the letter.

> **!** Not sure when to use को with a direct object? See 5.4.

A few verbs that normally follow the intransitive construction (11.2) switch to the transitive construction when a direct object is expressed. Examples include समझना 'to understand':

हम समझे ।	We understood. (no object expressed)
हमने तुम्हारी बात नहीं समझी ।	We didn't understand your point.

> **!** In the Glossary, verbs that take the ने construction are marked with a capital 'N' (करना[N]); verbs that *sometimes* take it are marked with a lower-case 'n' (समझना[n]); verbs that *never* take it are unmarked (आना). This is an important aid, because transitivity is not a completely reliable indicator of which verbs take ने.

Some common verbs have irregular perfective participles:

करना	किया	किए	की	कीं
लेना	लिया	लिए	ली	लीं
देना	दिया	दिए	दी	दीं
पीना	पिया	पिए	पी	पीं

There's one more thing to learn for this rather demanding construction – a special set of pronouns used with ने, some of which differ from the usual oblique pronouns (3.4):

मैं	मैंने	हम	हमने	कौन	किसने (singular)
तू	तूने	तुम	तुमने	कौन	किन्होंने (plural)
यह	इसने	ये	इन्होंने	कोई	किसीने
वह	उसने	वे	उन्होंने		
		आप	आपने		

11c　Pratap phones home

प्रताप	हलो माँ, मैं प्रताप बोल रहा हूँ ।
अनीता	प्रताप ! तुमने कई हफ़्तों से फोन नहीं किया, फ़ैक्स नहीं भेजा ! क्या हुआ ?
प्रताप	मैं नेपाल में घूमने गया था । वहाँ से मैं आपके लिए कुछ सुन्दर चीज़ें लाया हूँ माँ !
अनीता	हाँ, लाए होंगे, और तुम्हें ख़ूब मज़ा भी आया होगा ! पर तुम्हारी हिन्दी की पढ़ाई... ?
प्रताप	अभी क्लास में ग्यारहवाँ पाठ चल रहा है । मेरे नेपाल जाने से पहले हम तीसरा पाठ कर रहे थे ।
अनीता	तो तुम बहुत पीछे छूटे होंगे । या तुमने नेपाल में भी अपना पढ़ाई जारी रखी ?
प्रताप	जारी तो रखी, लेकिन ज़्यादा काम नहीं किया क्योंकि मैंने पिताजी के साथ कई दिन गुज़ारे ।
अनीता	अच्छा, वह भी वहाँ आया था ! मैंने सोचा था कि वह लखनऊ में होगा, अपने घर में ।

फ़ैक्सm	fax	**पीछे**	behind
घूमना	to travel for pleasure, tour	**छूटना**	to be left, fall back
मज़ाm	fun, pleasure, enjoyment	**जारी**	current, continuing; **जारी**
पढ़ाईf	studies, studying	**रखना**	to maintain
पाठm	lesson, chapter	**गुज़ारना**	to spend (time)

Pratap	Hello Mum, this is Pratap speaking.
Anita	Pratap! You haven't phoned or sent a fax for several weeks. What happened?
Pratap	I went travelling in Nepal. I've brought some lovely things for you from there, Mum!
Anita	Yes, you must have, and you must have had a great time too! But your Hindi studies...?
Pratap	Just now the eleventh lesson's going on; before I went to Nepal we were doing the third lesson.
Anita	Then you must have fallen far behind. Or did you keep your studies going in Nepal too?
Pratap	Yes I did, but I didn't do a lot of work because I spent several days with Father.
Anita	Oh, he came there too! I'd thought he must be in Lucknow, at his home.

Grammar

11.4 More on perfective verbs

Dialogue 11c uses perfective tenses of both transitive and intransitive verbs. It includes examples of the perfective with a future-tense auxiliary (होगा), yielding the sense 'will have done, must have done' etc. (see 9.2. and 9.3 for parallels in the imperfective and continuous tenses). The auxiliary may also appear in the subjunctive (हो), giving the sense 'may have done' etc. Here then is the full set of perfective possibilities:

उन्होंने फ़ैक्स भेजा ।	They sent a fax.
उन्होंने फ़ैक्स भेजा है ।	They have sent a fax.
उन्होंने फ़ैक्स भेजा था ।	They had sent a fax.
उन्होंने फ़ैक्स भेजा होगा ।	They will/must have sent a fax.
उन्होंने फ़ैक्स भेजा हो ।	They may have sent a fax.

Finally, here are some more examples of perfective tenses. Make sure you understand the agreement of each verb. When you've done this, you have mastered a really essential construction.

नई किताब सन् २००० तक निकली होगी । The new book will have come out by 2000.

मुमकिन है कि दादाजी न पहुँचे हों ।	It's possible that Grandpa may not have arrived.
दोनों लड़कियाँ ऊपरवाले कमरे में सोईं ।	Both girls slept in the upstairs room.
उसने उनके मीठे शब्दों को सुना ।	He/she listened to their sweet words.
हमने उन्हें भूत की कहानी सुनाई थी ।	We had told them a ghost story.
रात को हमें नींद नहीं आई ।	We didn't sleep at night. ('sleep didn't come')
हमने एक अच्छी-सी फ़िल्म देखी ।	We saw quite a good film.
धोबी ने हमारे सारे कपड़े धोए हैं ।	The dhobi has washed all our clothes.
मेरी कुरसी किसने ली ? किसी लड़के ने ।	Who took my chair? Some boy.
गीता अपना सामान लाई है ।	Gita has brought her luggage.
संगीता ने कमरा ख़ाली पाया ।	Sangeeta found the room empty.

> ⚠ Remember that the verb लाना 'to bring', though transitive, does *not* take the ने construction.

✔ EXERCISE 11a.1 Translate.

१　लड़कियाँ कल सुबह बनारस पहुँचीं । / पहुँची हैं , पहुँची थीं, पहुँची होंगी, पहुँची हों
२　आज वे देर तक सोईं ।　/ सोई हैं, सोई थीं, सोई होंगी, सोई हों
३　वे तीन बार गंगा देखने घाट पर गईं ।　/ गई हैं, गई थीं, गई होंगी, गई हों
४　दोपहर को वे कुछ दोस्तों से मिलीं ।　/ मिली हैं, मिली थीं, मिली होंगी, मिली हों
५　उन्हें बहुत आनंद आया ।　/ आया है, आया था, आया होगा, आया हो

✔ EXERCISE 11a.2 Translate.

1　My sons went to India.　/ have been, had been, will have been, may have been

2　They toured (घूमना) for two weeks.　/ have toured, had toured, will have toured, may have toured

3   They stayed in cheap hotels. / have stayed, had stayed, must have stayed, may have stayed

4   They spoke (बोलना) a little Hindi. /have spoken, had spoken, must have spoken, may have spoken

5   They had quite a good time. /have had, had had, must have had, may have had

EXERCISE 11b.1 Translate.

१   पापा ने पेट की दवा ख़रीदी । / ख़रीदी है, ख़रीदी थी, ख़रीदी होगी, ख़रीदी हो

२   उन्होंने सही क़ीमत दी । / दी है, दी थी, दी होगी, दी हो

३   दुकानदार ने ज़्यादा माँगा । / माँगा है, माँगा था, माँगा होगा, माँगा हो

४   पापा ने शिकायत की । / की है, की थी, की होगी, की हो

५   माँ ने तमाशे को देखा । / देखा है, देखा था, देखा होगा, देखा हो

EXERCISE 11b.2 Translate.

1   The dhobi washed both saris. / has washed, had washed, will have washed, may have washed

2   He only gave one sari back. / has given, had given, will have given, may have given

3   His wife wore (पहनना) the other. / has worn, had worn, will have worn, may have worn

4   We saw her at someone's wedding. / have seen, had seen, will have seen, may have seen

5   They apologised. / have apologised, had apologised, will have apologised, may have apologised

EXERCISE 11c.1 Add को to the direct object. Then translate.

MODEL: उसने खिड़की खोली । → उसने खिड़की को खोला ।
       He/she opened the window.

१   दुकानदार ने पापा की शिकायत सुनी थी ।

२   पर उसने पापा की बातें नहीं मानीं ।

३   माँ ने दुकानदार की बाँह पकड़ी ।

४   पापा ने अपने पैसे वापस लिए होंगे क्योंकि ...

५   ... दुकानदार ने अपनी भारी-सी लाठी उठाई ।

EXERCISE 11c.2 Remove को from the direct object. Then translate.

MODEL: उसने दोनों किताबों को पढ़ा । → उसने दोनों किताबें पढ़ीं ।
He/she read both books.

१ मैंने अपने सारे कपड़ों को उतारा ।

२ डाक्टर ने अपनी सिग्रेट को ख़त्म किया और उँगलियों को गिलास में धोया ।

३ फिर उन्होंने दराज़ में से अपनी किताब को निकाला ...

४ ...और अपने चश्मे को नाक पर सीधा किया ।

५ तब उन्होंने अपनी आँखों को बंद किया और दो प्रसिद्ध फ़िल्मी गीतों को सुनाया ।

EXERCISE 11c.3 Write (or make up) a diary entry for any recent day.

(Say what time you got up, what you had for breakfast, where you went, whom you met, etc. Pay careful attention to which verbs take the ने construction and which do not.)

Vocabulary

आख़िर में in the end, after all	गीत ^m song
आनंद ^m joy, enjoyment; आनंद आना to feel enjoyment	गुज़ारना to spend (time)
	घाट ^m (steps at) riverbank
आवश्यकता ^f necessity	घूमना to tour, roam
उँगली ^f finger	चोर ^m thief
उठाना to pick up	छूटना to be left, fall back
उधार ^m loan; उधार लेना to borrow	जारी current, continuing; जारी रखना to maintain
उपहार ^m present, gift	ज़ेवर ^m (piece of) jewellery
कब when?	ट्रेकिंग ^f 'trekking'
क़ीमत ^f price, value, cost	तमाशा ^m spectacle, show
कैमरा ^m camera	तिब्बती Tibetan
खोलना to open	तोड़ना to break
गंगा ^f Ganges	तोहफ़ा ^m a present
गिलास ^m tumbler (glass or metal)	दवा ^f medicine

दादा ^m paternal grandfather

दुकानदार ^m shopkeeper

दुर्घटना ^f accident

देर तक until late

दोपहर ^f noon, afternoon

नाक ^f nose

नींद ^f sleep; नींद आना to feel
   sleepy

पच्चीस twenty-five

पढ़ाई ^f studies, studying

परसों the day before yesterday;
   the day after tomorrow

पहनना to put on, wear

पाठ ^m lesson, chapter

पाना to find, obtain

पीछे behind

पेट ^m stomach

प्याला ^m cup

प्रसिद्ध famous

फ़िल्म ^f film

फ़िल्मी film-related, film-style

फ़ैक्स ^m fax

फ़ोटो ^m photograph

बजना to resound, chime

बाँह ^f (upper) arm

बीस twenty

बेचना to sell

भूत ^m ghost

भेंट ^f gift, presentation

मजबूरी ^f compulsion

मज़ा ^m fun, pleasure, enjoyment;
   मज़ा आना to enjoy, have fun

मानना to accept, believe

माफ़ करना to forgive, excuse

माफ़ी ^f forgiveness; माफ़ी माँगना
   to apologise

माली ^m gardener

मीठा sweet

मुमकिन possible

रोना to weep, cry

लाठी ^f lathi, stick

वापस लेना to take back

शब्द ^m word

शिकायत ^f complaint; शिकायत
   करना to complain

साथ साथ together

सुनाना to relate, tell, recite

12 | ASK HIM AND TELL ME
उनसे पूछकर मुझे बता दो

In this unit you will learn how to
- link verbs in sequence
- tell the time in detail
- talk about ability to do things
- express nuance in verb actions

12a Khanna phones Prakash

खन्ना प्रकाश, मैं खन्ना बोल रहा हूँ । यह बताइए – आज रात के डिनर में आपकी बेटी रहेगी ?

प्रकाश अभी "गृह मंत्री" से पूछकर बताऊँगा । कृपा करके एक मिनट होल्ड कीजिएगा सर । [*आवाज़ धीमी करके*] कमला, खन्ना साहब पूछ रहे हैं कि क्या संगीता होगी आज रात को ?

कमला [*ऊँची आवाज़ में*] ऐसा क्यों पूछ रहे हैं ? संगीता से उन्हें क्या लेना-देना !

प्रकाश पता नहीं खन्ना साहब के मन में क्या बात होगी । अभी पूछकर बताऊँगा ।

कमला हाँ पूछो तो सही – पर उनसे इतनी ज़्यादा जी-हुज़ूरी मत करना !

प्रकाश वे मेरे मालिक हैं कि नहीं ? तुम चाहती हो कि मैं पानी में रहकर मगर से वैर करूँ ? [*आवाज़ मीठी करके*] खन्ना साहब, कोई ख़ास बात थी ?

खन्ना हमारा बेटा हरीश है न ? हम ज़रा सोच रहे थे... ख़ैर, कोई बात नहीं !

डिनर ^m dinner	धीमा low, faint
गृह मंत्री ^{m,f} Home Minister (wife)	लेना-देना ^m dealings, connection
कृपा करके kindly, please	जी-हुज़ूरी ^f sycophancy, flattery
मिनट ^m minute	कि or
होल्ड करना to hold (phone line)	मगर ^m crocodile
आवाज़ ^f voice, sound	वैर ^m hostility

Khanna	Prakash, it's Khanna speaking. Tell me this – will your daughter be at tonight's dinner?
Prakash	I'll just ask the 'Home Minister' and tell you. Kindly hold a moment sir. [*lowering his voice*] Kamala, Khanna Sahib's asking if Sangeeta will be there tonight.
Kamala	[*in a high voice*] Why is he asking such a thing? What business does he have with Sangeeta!
Prakash	I don't know what must be in Khanna Sahib's mind. I'll just ask and tell you.
Kamala	Yes, do ask – but don't be such a yes-man to him!
Prakash	Is he my boss or not? Do you want me to antagonise the crocodile while living in the water? [*sweetening his voice*] Khanna Sahib, was there anything in particular?
Khanna	You know our son Harish? We were just thinking... Well anyway, never mind!

> **!** वे मेरे मालिक हैं कि नहीं ? Note this use of कि for 'or' between a simple pair of alternatives. चाय लेंगे कि काफ़ी ?

Grammar

12.1 जाकर 'having gone, after going'

जाकर (verb stem + कर) means literally 'having gone' or 'after going'. It's often used for the first of two verbs describing a sequence of events, where English might use two main verbs linked by 'and'– 'She opened the door and came in'. खोलकर means 'having opened' or 'after opening' – दरवाज़ा खोलकर वह कमरे में आई. This form is called the 'conjunctive particle' or the 'absolutive' – technical names for a beautifully simple grammatical device!

उधर बैठकर आराम करो ।	Sit over there and rest.
हम अपने दोस्तों से मिलकर गपशप करते थे ।	We used to meet our friends and chat.
काफ़ी पीकर मैंने सीग्रेट भी पी ।	After drinking coffee I had a cigarette too.
वह टैक्सी बुलाकर सीधे घर गई ।	She called a taxi and went straight home.

Colloquially, -कर can be replaced by -के, giving जाके, खोलके etc. Note that करना has करके *only*.

हाथ धोके खा !	Wash your hands before eating!
मैं उन्हें फ़ोन करके बताऊँगा ।	I'll phone them and tell them.
सड़क को पार करके बायें मुड़ना ।	After crossing the road turn left.

The conjunctive particle is independent of the main verb: it has no impact on the surrounding grammar. In the first example below, बैठना is intransitive, but the main verb is खाना, which is transitive and takes ने; in the second example, बनाना is transitive, but the main verb is लाना, which does *not* take ने.

| उसने फ़र्श पर बैठकर आम खाया । | He/she sat on the floor and ate a mango. |
| छोटू चाय बनाके लाया । | Chotu made tea and brought it. |

Thus the conjunctive particle phrase is a bit like a parenthesis, insulated from the main clause: उसने (फ़र्श पर बैठकर) आम खाया; छोटू चाय (बनाके) लाया.

> **!** The subject of the conjunctive particle is usually the same as the subject of the main verb.

Some conjunctive particles function as adverbs:

उसने हँसकर कहा, "तुम पागल हो!" ।	He/she said laughingly, 'You're crazy!'
माली दौड़कर पहुँचा ।	The gardener arrived running.
मेहरबानी करके / कृपा करके	kindly, please

The following phrases are also based on conjunctive particles:

| को छोड़कर | apart from, except for | (से) होकर | via |
| जान-बूझकर | deliberately | भूलकर भी | even by mistake |

मुझको छोड़कर कोई नहीं बोला ।	Nobody spoke apart from me.
गाड़ी आगरे से होकर ग्वालियर जाती है ।	The train goes via Agra to Gwalior.
तुम हमें जान-बूझकर चिढ़ाती हो !	You irritate us on purpose!
वहाँ भूलकर भी न जाना !	Don't even *think* of going there!

12.2 What's the time?

Telling the time involves the following vocabulary:

बजना	to chime, resound	डेढ़	one and a half
पौन, पौना	three-quarters	ढाई	two and a half
सवा	one and a quarter	साढ़े	plus a half (with three and upwards)

कितने बजे हैं? / क्या बजा है ? / क्या टाइम हुआ ? What's the time?				
पौन बजा है It's... 12.45	एक बजा है 1 o'clock	सवा बजा है 1 .15	डेढ़ बजा है 1.30	पौने दो बजे हैं 1.45
दो बजे हैं It's...2 o'clock	सवा दो बजे हैं 2.15	ढाई बजे हैं 2.30	पौने तीन बजे हैं 2.45	साढ़े तीन बजे हैं 3.30

Saying 'at' a particular time involves the oblique form बजे (used adverbially – see 8.3):

एक बजे आओ ।	Come at one o'clock.
हम लोग डेढ़ बजे पहुँचेंगे ।	We'll arrive at 1.30.

Minutes *before* and *after* the hour are expressed by बजने में and बजकर respectively. बजना also features in other tenses and expressions:

सात बजने में दस मिनट हैं ।	It's ten to seven.
आठ बजकर बीस मिनट हैं ।	It's twenty past eight.
गाड़ी पहुँची सात बजने में दस मिनट पर ।	The train arrived at ten to seven.
भारत में रात के नौ बज रहे हैं ।	It's just nine at night in India. (nine is striking)
सुबह के दस बजनेवाले हैं ।	It's nearly ten in the morning. (ten's about to strike)
ठीक ग्यारह बजने पर गाड़ी छूटेगी ।	The train will depart at eleven on the dot.

Traditional Indian timekeeping divided the day into eight three-hour 'watches' called पहर (Sanskrit प्रहर). The word survives in the following expressions:

दोपहर	noon, early afternoon
तीसरे पहर	in the afternoon
आठों पहर	all day long (आठों 'all eight' – see 7.5)

12b   Dinner preparations

कमला	ओ अरुण, ज़रा प्रताप के कमरे में जाकर एक कुरसी ले आना । उधर रख देना ।
अरुण	जी, अवश्य, तुरंत ला दूँगा । कोई विशेष कुरसी चाहिए ?
कमला	कोई भी लाओ । तब सुरेश को फ़ोन करके उनसे पूछना कि क्या वे भी डिनर में आ सकते हैं ।
अरुण	उन्हें बुलाने की आवश्यकता नहीं है भाभीजी, यदि उन्हें अवकाश हो तो आ ही जाएँगे ।
कमला	और तुम भी रहोगे, अरुण ? तुमसे मिलकर खन्ना जी ख़ुश हो जाएँगे ।
अरुण	खेद की बात है कि मैं नहीं रुक सकता । अपने प्रकाशक के यहाँ भोजन करने जा रहा हूँ ।
कमला	तो तुम खन्ना साहब से मिलना नहीं चाहते ? बाद में पछताओगे !
अरुण	मैं तो उनसे मिल चुका हूँ । एक मित्र के विवाह में हमारी भेंट हुई थी । अद्भुत आदमी हैं ।

विशेष	particular	भोजन ^m	food

विशेष   particular   भोजन ^m   food
सकना   to be able   भोजन करना   to dine, eat
आवश्यकता ^f   necessity   चुकना   to have already done
भाभी ^f   elder brother's wife विवाह ^m   marriage
अवकाश ^m   leisure, free time   भेंट ^f   meeting, encounter
खेद ^m   regret   अद्भुत   remarkable
प्रकाशक ^m   publisher

Kamala	Oh Arun, just go into Pratap's room and bring a chair. Put it over there.
Arun	Yes of course, I'll fetch it immediately. Do you require any particular chair?
Kamala	Bring any one. Then phone Suresh and ask him if he can come to the dinner too.
Arun	It's not necessary to invite him, sister-in-law; if he's at leisure he's sure to turn up.
Kamala	And will you stay too, Arun? Khanna ji will be pleased to meet you.
Arun	Regrettably I cannot stay. I'm going to dine at my publisher's.
Kamala	So you don't want to meet Khanna ji? You'll regret it later!
Arun	I've met him already. We met at a friend's wedding. He's a remarkable man.

Grammar
12.3 सकना, पाना, चुकना

These three verbs are used with the stem of a preceding verb (खाना 'to eat' in our example) to give the senses shown:

खा सकना	to be able to eat
खा पाना	to manage to eat
खा चुकना	to have already eaten, finished eating

वह खा सकती है ।	She can eat.
क्या तुम कल आ सकते हो ?	Can you come tomorrow?
वह तेरे साथ नहीं जा सकेगी ।	She won't be able to go with you.

मैं पूरे सेब को नहीं खा पाया ।	I couldn't eat the whole apple.
तुम उसकी हिन्दी समझ पाओगे ?	You'll manage to understand his Hindi?
"ढ़" को ठीक से बोल पाना मुश्किल है ।	It's difficult to manage to say '*ṛha*' correctly.

हम खाना खा चुके हैं ।	We have already eaten.
धोबी कपड़े धो चुका होगा ।	The dhobi will have finished washing the clothes.
चाय पी चुके हो? हाँ, पी चुका हूँ ।	Had your tea? Yes, finished it.

As some of the examples show, these constructions *don't* take ने.

क्या संगीता ने वह काम ख़त्म किया है ?	Has Sangeeta finished that work? (ने with करना)
नहीं, वह उसे ख़त्म नहीं कर पाई ।	No, she didn't manage to finish it. (no ने with कर पाना)

And चुकना is rarely used in the negative.

क्या संगीता नाश्ता कर चुकी है ?	Has Sangeeta already had breakfast?
नहीं, उसने नाश्ता नहीं किया है ।	No, she hasn't had breakfast. (चुकना dropped in negative)

> **!** The verb stem cannot be left out in this usage: सकना / पाना / चुकना do not stand alone.

12.4 Compound verbs (1)

'Compound verbs' operate like सकना: verb stem + auxiliary verb. In a compound verb, the auxiliary loses its own primary meaning, but lends a certain shade of meaning to the main verb. For example, while बैठना means 'to sit', बैठ जाना means 'to sit down'.

The nuance they express is often very subtle and their function is best absorbed gradually from examples, though their grammatical structure is easy enough.

The ने construction applies only when both the main verb and the auxiliary verb are ने verbs. Three auxiliaries are introduced here: जाना, लेना, देना; others follow in 17.3.

जाना gives a sense of completeness, finality, or change of state.

आना	to come	आ जाना	to arrive
खाना	to eat	खा जाना	to eat up
पीना	to drink	पी जाना	to drink up
बैठना	to sit	बैठ जाना	to sit down
समझना	to understand	समझ जाना	to realise
सोना	to sleep	सो जाना	to go to sleep
होना	to be	हो जाना	to become

सीता रामायण को अंत तक सुन गई ।	Sita listened to the Ramayan right to the end.
छोटू आधी बोतल पी गया था ।	Chotu had consumed half the bottle.
पुलिस साढ़े दस बजे आ गई ।	The police turned up at half past ten.
दुकानें सात बजे बंद हो जाती हैं ।	The shops close (become closed) at seven o'clock.
तुम मेरी तकलीफ़ समझ गए होगे ।	You must have realised my distress.

With a few verbs that can be either intransitive or transitive (बदलना to change, खोना to lose/ be lost), using जाना as auxiliary specifies *intransitive* usage.

| उनका नंबर बदल गया होगा । | Their number must have changed. |
| मोती खो गए । | The pearls got lost. |

लेना suggests that the benefit of an action flows *towards* the doer		**देना** suggests that the benefit of an action flows *away from* the doer	
कविता पढ़ लो ।	Read the poem to yourself.	कविता पढ़ दो ।	Read the poem out.
यह पता लिख लो ।	Take a note of this address.	वह पता लिख दो ।	Write out that address.
थैला रख लो ।	Keep the bag.	थैला रख दो ।	Put the bag down.

The 'benefit-towards-the-doer' implication of लेना may imply a sense of achievement – मैंने सारा काम कर लिया है 'I've done all the work' (and it's a relief to have finished it!).

The following examples show how compounds can colour meaning. Being concerned with the *manner* in which a thing happens or is done, they're mostly used with completed actions and imperatives – much less with negated verbs, conjunctive particles (12.1), continuous tenses (8), or statements that are hypothetical or speculative. This is because an event that hasn't taken place at all cannot have taken place in a particular manner, and compound verbs express *manner* above all.

मैं थोड़ी उर्दू भी बोल लेता हूँ ।	I (can) also speak a little Urdu.
रेडियो पर समाचार सुन लें ?	Shall we have a listen to the news on the radio?
मेरी जेब में से चाबी ले लो ।	Take the key from my pocket.
अपना पैसा रख लो, भैया ।	Keep your money, brother.
हमने नई गाड़ी ख़रीद ली है ।	We have bought a new car.
पत्र पढ़के इसे पापा को दे दो ।	Read the letter and give it to Father.
मिठाइयाँ बच्चों में बाँट दीजिए ।	Distribute the sweets among the children.

माँ ने हमें सारी कहानी सुना दी ।	Mother related the whole story to us.
मैंने तेरा सामान रिक्शे पर रख दिया ।	I put your luggage onto the rickshaw.
हमने पुरानी गाड़ी को बेच दिया है ।	We have sold the old car.

12.5 Verbs in combination

These work similarly to compound verbs (12.4), the difference being that here, each of the two verbs adds its own meaning to the overall expression. आना or जाना are the usual auxiliaries, and hence the ने construction is not involved.

लौट आना	to come back	लौट जाना	to go back
ले आना	to bring	ले जाना	to take away
निकल आना	to come out	निकल जाना	to go out

Slightly different to these is चला जाना 'to go one's way': चला is a participle, not a stem, and must agree with the subject – लक्ष्मी चली गई 'Lakshmi went away'. चला आना 'to come up, approach' is also found.

हम होली से पहले भारत लौट जाएँगे ।	We'll go back to India before Holi.
इस बदमाश को ले जाओ ।	Take this rogue away.
मुझे यहाँ खड़ा देखकर वह चली गई ।	Seeing me standing here she went away.

EXERCISE 12a.1 Make single sentences of the following pairs, using a conjunctive particle. Then translate.

MODEL: वह कमरे में आया । उसने चाय पी । > उसने कमरे में आकर चाय पी ।
                He/she came into the room and had tea.

१   संगीता घर गई । उसने किसी दोस्त को फोन किया ।

२   ऋषि ने अपनी किताब खोली । उसने दो-तीन कहानियाँ पढ़ीं ।

३   कमला ने अपना काम ख़त्म किया । वह तुरंत बाहर गई ।

४   हम छोटू के यहाँ जाएँगे । हम खाना बनाएँगे ।

५   खन्ना जी डिब्बे में आए । उन्होंने ऊपरवाली बर्थ पर अपना सामान रखा ।

EXERCISE 12a.2 Replace the 'infinitive + के बाद' with a conjunctive particle. Then translate.

MODEL: घर जाने के बाद हम रेडियो सुनेंगे । > घर जाकर हम रेडियो सुनेंगे ।
          After going/when we go home we'll listen to the radio.

१   आज सुबह नहाने के बाद तूने साबुन को कहाँ रखा ?

२   परीक्षा देने के बाद प्रताप और उसके साथी कम से कम दो हफ़्ते तक आराम करेंगे ।

३   अपनी डिगरी पास करने के बाद तुम क्या करना चाहते हो ?

४   लन्दन वापस आने के बाद उसने भारत के बारे में कई पुस्तकें लिखीं ।

५   शाम को दफ़्तर से लौटने के बाद प्रकाश कभी कभी बाज़ार में सैर करते हैं ।

EXERCISE 12b.1   Translate.

1   What's the time? It's half past seven. I've already had breakfast.

2   I usually arrive at half-past eight, but today I couldn't come until a quarter to nine.

3   I have lunch (दोपहर का खाना) between 1.30 and 2.30.

4   Will the students come at exactly eleven o' clock? No, they'll turn up by a quarter past.

5   By a quarter to one in the morning I managed to finish my studies.

EXERCISE 12b.2   Complete the replies, using the compound verb given in brackets:

१   आप हिन्दी बोलते हैं ? हाँ, ... (बोल लेना)

२   क्या उसने काम ख़त्म कर लिया है ? नहीं, ... (कर सकना)

३   क्या बच्चे सो रहे हैं ? हाँ, वे तो हमेशा सात बजे... (सो जाना)

४   क्या संगीता ने खाना खा लिया है ? हाँ, वह आधे से ज़्यादा ... (खा चुकना)

५   दुकान अभी बंद नहीं हुई ? क्यों ? वह तो चार बजे ... (बंद हो जाना)

Vocabulary

अंत ^m end

अद्भुत remarkable

अवकाश ^m leisure, free time

आठों पहर all day long

आम ^m mango

आराम करना to rest

आवाज़ ^f voice, sound

आवश्यकता ^f necessity

कविता ^f poem; poetry

कि or

कृपा ^f kindness, grace; कृपा करके kindly, please

खेद ^m regret

खोना to lose

गृह मंत्री ^{m, f} Home Minister

ग्वालियर ^m Gwalior

चला आना to come back; चला जाना to go one's way

चिढ़ाना to irritate, tease

चुकना (after verb stem) to have already done

(को) छोड़कर apart from, except for

जान-बूझकर deliberately

जी-हुज़ूरी ^f sycophancy, flattery

टैक्सी ^f taxi

डिगरी ^f degree

डिनर ^m dinner

ढाई two and a half

तीसरे पहर in the afternoon

दौड़ना to run

धीमा low, faint

नहाना to bathe, wash

नाश्ता ^m breakfast

पछताना to regret, repent

परीक्षा ^f examination; परीक्षा देना to take (sit) an exam

पाना (after verb stem) to manage to

पार करना to cross

पास करना to pass (exam etc.)

पौन, पौना three-quarters

प्रकाशक ^m publisher

बदमाश ^m villain, rogue

बदलना to change

बर्थ ^m berth

बाँटना to divide

बोतल ^f bottle

भाभी ^f elder brother's wife

भूलकर भी even by mistake

भेंट ^f meeting, encounter

भोजन ^m food; भोजन करना to dine

मगर ^m crocodile

मिठाई ^f sweet, sweet dish

मिनट ^m minute

मुड़ना to turn

मेहरबानी करके kindly, please

रेडियो ^m radio

ले आना to bring; ले जाना to take away

लेना-देना ^m dealings, connection
विवाह ^m marriage
विशेष particular
वैर ^m hostility
सकना (after verb stem) to be able
समाचार ^m news
सवा one and a quarter, plus a
  quarter
साढ़े plus a half

सात seven
साथी ^m companion, friend
साबुन ^m soap
सेब ^m apple
(से) होकर via
होली ^f Holi, springtime festival
  of colours
होल्ड करना to hold (phone line)

13 | THOSE WHO KNOW
जो जानते हैं

In this unit you will learn how to

- use relative clauses: 'the day when...', 'the one who...'
- express compulsion: 'I should, must...'
- talk about availability: 'to get'

13a   Pratap practises his Hindi with Rishi

ऋषि	जब तुम नेपाल से लौटे तब तुम्हारी माँ ने क्या कहा फोन पर ?
प्रताप	उन्होंने कहा कि आगे चलकर मुझे बहुत मेहनत करनी पड़ेगी ।
ऋषि	जब तक तुम हमारे यहाँ रहोगे तब तक तुम्हें हिन्दी ही बोलनी चाहिए ।
प्रताप	हाँ, जब से भारत आया हूँ तब से मैं हिन्दी ही बोल रहा हूँ ।
ऋषि	और जैसे ही तुम लन्दन लौटोगे वैसे ही अपनी हिन्दी को भूल जाओगे !
प्रताप	नहीं, जब तक मैं हिन्दी ठीक से नहीं सीखूँगा तब तक मुझे अपनी पढ़ाई को जारी रखना है ।
ऋषि	लंदन वापस जाकर तुमको कुछ हिन्दी-बोलनेवाले दोस्तों से मिलकर बात करनी चाहिए ।
प्रताप	यही करूँगा । और आज तो "जब"-वाले वाक्यों का अच्छा अभ्यास हुआ है !

जब... तब when... then	**जब से... तब से** since the time
आगे later, ahead; **आगे चलकर** in	when... since then
future, from now on	**जैसे ही... वैसे ही** as soon as ... then
मेहनत f hard work	**जब तक नहीं... तब तक** until... until
जब तक... तब तक for as long as...	then
for that long	**अभ्यास** m practice
चाहिए should, ought to	

Rishi	What did your mother say on the phone when you returned from Nepal?
Pratap	She said that from now on I'd have to work very hard.
Rishi	As long as you stay with us you should speak only Hindi.
Pratap	Yes, since I came ('have come') to India I've been speaking only Hindi.
Rishi	And as soon as you go back to London you'll forget your Hindi!
Pratap	No, until I learn Hindi properly I must keep my studies going.
Rishi	After going back to London you should meet some Hindi-speaking friends and talk.
Pratap	I'll do just that ('this'). And today I've had good practice of '*jab*'-type sentences!

Grammar

13.1 जब... तब, 'when... then' (Relative clauses 1)

Hindi has several 'relative-correlative' constructions – structures for building sentences such as 'When the train comes, I'll go' or 'The person who wrote this is a fool', in which two adjacent statements are related to one another as paired clauses.

We deal first with relative-correlative expressions for time: जब... तब 'when... then'; further structures come in 13.3 and 14.4-7. Relative pronouns and adverbs all begin with a 'ज-', whereas interrogatives such as कब 'when?' begin with a 'क-'. (By contrast, English 'w' words such as 'when' are both relative and interrogative.)

The Hindi construction uses a balanced pair of clauses: '*When* the train comes, *then* I will go'. जब 'when' introduces the relative clause, and तब 'then' introduces the correlative clause.

जब गाड़ी आएगी तब मैं जाऊँगा ।	When the train comes I'll go.
जब घंटी बजती है तब हम काम ख़त्म करते हैं ।	When the bell rings we stop work.
जब मैं कहूँगा तब आना ।	Come when I tell you. ('When I say, come then.')

तब is often replaced by तो, because the correlative is often a *consequence* of the relative:

जब कुत्ता भौंकता है तो छोटू डर जाता है ।	When the dog barks Chotu gets scared.
जब बारिश होती है तो मैं बाहर नहीं जाता ।	When it rains I don't go out.

Among emphatic forms are जब भी 'whenever', and तभी 'at that very time, instantly'. Other relative-correlative pairs are:

जब से 'since (the time) when...' तब से 'since then':

जब से तू आई है तब से मैंने काम ही नहीं किया है ।	Since you came I haven't worked at all.
जब से मैंने छाता ख़रीद लिया तब से पानी नहीं पड़ा ।	Since I bought myself an umbrella it hasn't rained.

जब तक 'as long as, by the time that...' तब तक 'by then':

जब तक वह रहेगा तब तक मैं ख़ुश रहूँगी ।	As long as he stays I'll remain happy.
जब तक मैं पहुँचा तब तक वह जा चुकी थी ।	By the time I arrived she had already gone.

जब तक... न/ नहीं 'until...' तब तक 'until then':

जब तक मैं न कहूँ तब तक तुम यहीं रहोगे ।	You'll stay right here until I say ('as long as I don't say').
जब तक वे नहीं खाएँगे तब तक मैं भी भूखा रहूँगा ।	Until they eat I too will go hungry.

ज्योंही / जैसे ही 'as soon as...' त्योंही / वैसे ही 'at that moment, then'

ज्योंही मैंने घंटी बजाई त्योंही बस चल दी ।	As soon as I rang the bell, the bus set off.
जैसे ही वह बैठ गया वैसे ही बत्ती बंद हो गई ।	As soon as he sat down the light went out.

In both English and Hindi, the clause order can be reversed ('I haven't worked at all since you came', etc.); but it's best to stick to the जब... तब order until the construction becomes fully clear. The reversing of clauses is looked at in 14.8.

13.2 Infinitive + चाहिए, 'should, ought'

The sense 'should, ought' is expressed with the infinite verb + चाहिए. चाहिए means 'is wanted/needed' (and is an old form of the passive). The person under compulsion takes को. In past contexts, the auxiliary था is added.

मुझको अंदर जाना चाहिए ।	I should go inside.
हमको चलना चाहिए ।	We should set off.
तुमको भी आना चाहिए था ।	You should have come too.

If there's a direct object, the infinitive (and any auxiliary) agrees with it:

उनको हिन्दी सीखनी चाहिए ।	They should learn Hindi. (हिन्दी fem. singular)
हमको ये काम ख़त्म करने चाहिए ।	We should finish these jobs. (ये काम masc. plural)
तुम्हें दो चिट्ठियाँ लिखनी चाहिए थीं ।	You should have written two letters. (दो चिट्ठियाँ fem. plural)

But if the direct object takes को, then the verb stays in the -ना form, with auxiliary also invariable as था. (This may remind you of a similar rule relating to the ने construction – see 11.3.)

तुम्हें इस किताब को पढ़ना चाहिए ।	You should read this book.
उन्हें बच्चों को नहीं मारना चाहिए ।	They shouldn't hit the children.
हमें घंटी को बजाना चाहिए था ।	We should have rung the bell.

With intransitive verbs such as होना and रहना, the infinitive can agree with a subject (without को being involved):

आम पक्के होने चाहिए ।	The mangoes should be ripe.
चाय गरम रहनी चाहिए ।	The tea should remain hot.

This usage without को usually involves inanimate objects; they are not under the 'moral' or pragmatic kind of compulsion that rests on a *person* (with को... चाहिए), as the following pair of sentences shows:

| मौसम अच्छा होना चाहिए । | The weather should be good. (no को; no moral implication) |
| बच्चों को चुप रहना चाहिए । | Children should keep quiet. (with को and moral implication) |

> **!** Unsure when to use को with a direct object? See 5.4.

Notice the difference in meaning between (a) चाहिए with a noun, 'is wanted/needed' (7.3) and (b) चाहिए with a verb, 'should/ought'. Different again is the straightforward meaning of चाहना as 'to want', which can be used either (c) with a noun or (d) with an infinitive verb in the direct case (e.g. पीना). Here's the full set.

(a)	मुझे चाय चाहिए ।	I want/need tea.
(b)	मुझे चाय पीनी चाहिए ।	I should drink tea.
(c)	मैं बियर चाहता हूँ ।	I want beer.
(d)	मैं बियर पीना चाहता हूँ ।	I want to drink beer.

13.3 Infinitive + होना / पड़ना, 'I am to, must'

The infinitive verb + होना or पड़ना is used in a parallel construction to that of चाहिए, with the same rules of agreement, but meaning 'have to' rather than 'should'.

Using होना gives a relatively mild sense of 'compulsion', as in describing tasks that are to be done *as a matter of course*:

आज मुझे दिल्ली जाना है;	Today I have to go to Delhi;
तुमको भी आना होगा ।	you'll have to come too.
वहाँ जाकर हमें कुछ चीज़ें ख़रीदनी हैं...	When we go there we have to buy some things...
और उन चीज़ों को घर लाना होगा ।	and we'll have to bring those things home.

These sentences could be translated 'I am to... you are to', etc. – it's a sense of programmed events rather than forced compulsion. Again, the sense can be of simple intention:

तुम्हें हाथ धोने हैं ?	Like to wash your hands?
कल हमें आराम करना था ।	Yesterday we were to rest.

Using पड़ना implies an *external* compulsion – one that's beyond the control of the individual. In the perfective (पड़ा), such compulsion is often *unplanned* or *unwelcome*:

बारिश की वजह से हमें छाता ख़रीदना पड़ा ।	Because of the rain we had to buy an umbrella.
गाड़ी छूट चुकी थी इसलिए उन्हें बस पकड़नी पड़ी ।	The train had already left so they had to catch a bus.
धोबी बीमार था इसलिए हमें गंदे कपड़े पहनने पड़े ।	The dhobi was ill so we had to wear dirty clothes.

Here, incidentally, we see an almost literal sense of पड़ना as 'to fall':

ख़त का जवाब मुझे देना पड़ा ।	It fell to me to answer the letter.

The imperfective (पड़ता है / पड़ता था) indicates *habitual* or *regular* compulsion:

हमें हर हफ़्ते इलाहाबाद जाना पड़ता है ।	We have to go to Allahabad every week.
हमें गुरु जी के लिए खाना बनाना पड़ता था ।	We used to have to cook for guru ji.
उन दिनों हमें सब कुछ हाथ से करना पड़ता था ।	In those days we had to do everything by hand.

The future (पड़ेगा) is parallel to होगा, but with stronger compulsion:

हमें दो टैक्सियाँ लेनी पड़ेंगी ।	We will have to get two taxis.
उन्हें बहुत काम करना पड़ेगा ।	They'll have to do a lot of work.
कलकत्ते जा रहे हो ? तुम्हें बँगला सीखनी पड़ेगी !	Going to Calcutta? You'll have to learn Bengali!

तुमको जाना चाहिए । You should go. (*moral* compulsion)

तुमको जाना है । You are to go. (*neutral* compulsion)

तुमको जाना पड़ेगा । You will have to go. (strong *external* compulsion)

13b At the dinner

खन्ना जी	[*धीमी आवाज़ में*] जो लड़का कोने में बैठा है, वह तुम्हारा कौन लगता है राज ?
राज	अंकल, वह हमारा रिश्तेदार नहीं है । वह लन्दन से आया है, हिन्दी सीखने के लिए ।
सुरेश	जिन लोगों को असली हिन्दी सीखनी हो, उन्हें दिल्ली में नहीं रहना चाहिए ।
कमला	ऐसा क्यों कहते हैं सुरेश ? कौनसी ऐसी बात है जो दिल्ली में नहीं मिलती है?
सुरेश	इधर हमारे पंजाबी भाइयों ने हमारी हिन्दी भाषा को बरबाद कर दिया है ।
प्रकाश	[*खन्ना की ओर नज़र डालकर*] अरे नहीं, बिलकुल नहीं ! हिन्दी को पंजाबियों की बहुत बड़ी देन है !
ऋषि	हाँ, सही बात है; और हिन्दी और पंजाबी बहुत मिलती-जुलती हैं अंकल !
खन्ना जी	जो चीज़ें मिलती-जुलती हैं, उनमें भी अनबन हो सकती है ऋषि ।
कमला	हाँ ऋषि, तुम राज से मिलते हो, पर लड़ने में तुम्हें देर नहीं लगती ! [*सब हँसते हैं*]

कोना ^m corner	डालना to throw
लगना to be related, attached; to be expended (of time)	देन ^f contribution, gift
इधर recently, latterly	मिलना-जुलना to resemble
बरबाद करना to ruin	अनबन ^f discord
नज़र ^f glance, look	लड़ना to fight, quarrel

Khanna ji	[*In a low voice*] What relation to you is that boy who's sitting in the corner, Raj?
Raj	Uncle, he's not a relative of ours. He's come from London to learn Hindi.
Suresh	People who want to learn the real Hindi shouldn't stay in Delhi.
Kamala	Why do you say that Suresh? What is there that one can't get in Delhi?
Suresh	Our Panjabi 'brothers' have ruined our Hindi language of late.
Prakash	[*throwing a glance at Khanna*] Oh no, not at all! The Panjabis have [made] a huge contribution to Hindi.
Rishi	Yes, it's true; and Hindi and Panjabi are very much alike, uncle!
Khanna ji	Even things that are alike can have discord between them Rishi.
Kamala	Yes Rishi, you look like Raj, but it doesn't take long for you to fight! [*all laugh*]

> इधर applies to both *time* ('recently') and *space* ('over here').

 ## Grammar

13.4 जो... वह – 'the one who ...' (Relative clauses 2)

जो means '(the one) who/which'. It is both singular and plural.

जो आदमी बाहर खड़ा है	the man who is standing outside
जो बोलता है	he who speaks
जो खिलौने मैंने तुझे दिए	the toys I gave you

Such relative clauses are paired with correlative clauses, on the pattern of जब... तब (13.1); the correlative here is वह / वे. The जो clause defines an item about which something *further* is said in the correlative clause.

जो आदमी बाहर खड़ा है वह विदेशी है ।	The man who is standing outside is a foreigner.
जो बोलता है वह नहीं जानता ।	He who speaks, does not know.
जो खिलौने मैंने तुझे दिए बे कहाँ हैं ?	Where are the toys I gave you?

Many such Hindi sentences are ordered quite differently from their English equivalents. 'Where are the toys I gave you?' becomes 'the toys that I gave you, where are they?' in the Hindi clause order. (Possible variations are discussed in 14.8.)

जो has the oblique forms जिस, जिसने (singular), and जिन, जिन्होंने (plural); these sit in parallel to उस, उसने and किस, किसने etc.

जिस बूढ़े ने हमारा घर ख़रीदा वह मर गया है ।	The old man who bought our house has died.
जिनको अपने दोस्तों से लड़ना हो उनकी क़िस्मत बुरी है ।	Those who have to fight their friends are unfortunate.
जिस दिन उनकी शादी हुई उसी दिन मेरा तलाक़ हो गया ।	The very day they married I got divorced.

In जिस बूढ़े ने हमारा घर ख़रीदा वह मर गया है, the relative is oblique (जिस बूढ़े) because of the postposition ने; but the correlative is direct (वह) because it's the subject of the verb मर गया है. Thus the relative and correlative pronouns match the grammar *of their respective clauses*. Test this principle in the following examples:

जो किताब मेज़ पर पड़ी है उसे पढ़ लेना ।	Read the book that's lying on the table.
जिसने यह लिखा था वह मूर्ख होगा ।	The person who wrote this must be a fool.
जो लोग 'खन्ना' कहलाते हैं वे पंजाबी होते हैं ।	People who are called 'Khanna' are Panjabis.
जिन दोस्तों को हमने बुलाया था वे नहीं आ सकते ।	The friends we invited cannot come.

| जो फ़िल्म मैंने देखी, उसका हीरो बहुत बदसूरत है । | The hero of the film I saw is very ugly. |
| जिस जवान लड़की से तुमने बातें कीं वह कौन है ? | Who is the young girl you talked to? |

जो कोई means 'anyone, whoever'; जो भी, 'whoever, anyone at all, whichever', is more emphatic. जो कुछ is 'whatever':

| आपके पास जो कुछ हो, उसे दे देना । | Give whatever you have. |
| गुरु जो भी बोलता है उसे उसका शिष्य लिख लेता है । | Whatever the guru says, his disciple takes down. |

When relating to a subject that's hypothetical or indefinite in some way, such pronouns often take a subjunctive verb.

| जो कोई सोचता हो कि हिन्दी आसान है उसका विचार ग़लत है । | Anyone who may think Hindi is easy has the wrong idea. |

Occasionally one sees the old correlative pronoun सो – especially in aphorisms and old saws:

| जो हो सो हो । | What is to be will be. |

13.5 मिलना 'to be available' ('to get')

मिलना means 'to be received, obtained, found', and it's the usual way of expressing 'to get'. The item received ('your fax' in the first example) is the grammatical subject, and the receiver takes को.

माँ को तुम्हारा फ़ैक्स मिला ।	Mum received your fax.
बेचारे छोटू को क्या मिलेगा ?	What will poor Chotu get?
इस होटल में कमरा मिल जाएगा ।	[You'll] get a room in this hotel.

The last example shows how मिलना can mean 'to be available' without necessarily specifying the receiver.

The same मिलना construction using को can also mean 'to meet' when an encounter between people is *unplanned*:

| कल हम को सीता मिली । | Yesterday we met Sita (by chance). |

But when 'We met Sita' refers to a *planned* encounter, 'we' becomes the subject, and Sita takes से.

कल हम सीता से मिले ।　　　Yesterday we met Sita (intentionally).

मिलना also means 'to resemble'; in such senses it can link with जुलना 'to be joined' to form मिलना-जुलना. And finally: मिलकर or मिल-जुलकर ('having met and joined') has the idiomatic sense 'together'.

उषा तुमसे बहुत मिलती-जुलती है ।　　Usha looks very much like you.

हम सब मिल-जुलकर यह काम करेंगे ।　　We'll all do this work together.

13.6 लगना 'how does it strike you?' (do you like?)

लगना means 'to be attached, applied, stuck': टिकट लिफ़ाफ़े पर लगी थी 'the stamp was affixed to the envelope'. It also means 'to strike' in describing an experience or reaction; the experiencer takes को.

दिल्ली आपको कैसी लगती है ?　　How do you like Delhi (how does Delhi strike you)?

यह शहर मुझे बहुत अच्छा लगता है ।　　I like this city very much.

यहाँ मेरा मन / दिल लगता है ।　　I feel at home here.

डाकू को दो गोलियाँ लगीं ।　　The bandit was hit by two bullets.

हमारे जवानों को चोट लगी ।　　Our soldiers got injured.

हमें डर लग रहा है ।　　We're feeling afraid.

तुम्हें ठंड / गरमी लग रही होगी ।　　You must be feeling cold / hot.

मुझे प्यास / भूख लगी है ।　　I'm feeling thirsty / hungry.

उन्हें बहुत बुरा लगा ।　　They felt very bad, aggrieved.

लगना also means 'to seem, appear'; and 'to catch' (of fire or illness).

तेरी कहानी थोड़ी अजीब लगती है ।　　Your story seems a little odd.

यह वाक्य ठीक नहीं लगता ।　　This sentence doesn't seem right.

ऊपरवाले कमरे में आग लग गई ।　　Fire broke out in the upstairs room.

बेचारे को ज़ुकाम लग गया है ।　　The poor fellow's caught a cold.

लगना also means 'to be taken, be expended (of time)'. The action that's done takes an infinitive + में, and the unit of time (minutes, days) is the subject: 'in making tea five minutes are taken':

चाय बनाने में पाँच मिनट लगते हैं ।	Making tea takes five minutes.
घर पहुँचने में एक घंटा लगेगा ।	It will take one hour to get home.
उसका ख़त पढ़ने में मुझे २५ मिनट लगे ।	It took me 25 minutes to read his letter.

This sense of 'being expended' also applies to money:

गाड़ी को ठीक करने में रु० ५०० लगेंगे ।	It'll cost Rs. 500 to fix the car.

Finally, लगना can indicate a blood relationship: अरुण संगीता का चाचा लगता है, 'Arun is Sangeeta's uncle' ('is related to Sangeeta as uncle').

EXERCISE 13a.1 Complete the replies using a चाहिए construction. Then translate the replies.

MODEL: क्या मैं भी लखनऊ जाऊँ ?   हाँ, आपको जाना चाहिए ।
       Yes, you should go.

१ क्या हम चाय तैयार कर दें ?   हाँ, हमको...
२ बच्चों को कौन खाना खिलाएगा ?   पापा को ही...
३ क्या मेरी सहेली हिन्दुस्तानी कपड़े पहने ?   जी नहीं, उसको...
४ क्या मुझे ताज होटल में कमरा मिल जाएगा ?   हाँ, तुम्हें...
५ परीक्षाओं के बाद हम थोड़ा आराम करें ?   हाँ, हमें...
६ मैं उसकी जेब से थोड़ा पैसा लूँ ?   नहीं, तुमको...

EXERCISE 13a.2 Replace चाहिए constructions with पड़ना in the future tense; then translate the new version.

१ तुझे मेरी सहेली की सलाह लेनी चाहिए ।
२ मुझे रोज़ पढ़ाई का काम करना चाहिए ।
३ माँ कहती हैं कि मुझे हर हफ़्ते उन्हें चिट्ठी लिखनी चाहिए ।
४ अगर चोरी का डर है तो हमें एक ताला ख़रीदना चाहिए ।
५ अगर चावल न मिले तो तुम्हें रोटी खानी चाहिए ।
६ हमें कम से कम दो भाषाएँ सीखनी चाहिए ।

EXERCISE 13a.3 Complete the sentences with an appropriate clause. Then translate.

१   जैसे ही वह कमरे में आया ....

२   जब तक मुझे उधार का पैसा नहीं मिलेगा ....

३   जब आपको फ़ुरसत हो ....

४   ज्योंही मुझे महसूस हुआ कि उसे यह जगह अच्छी नहीं लगती ....

५   .... तब हम अवश्य मिलेंगे ।

६   .... तब तक वह तुम्हें माफ़ नहीं करेगा ।

७   .... तब से मुझे उसकी एक भी चिट्ठी नहीं मिली ।

८   .... तभी हम तुम्हें तुम्हारा पैसा वापस देंगे ।

EXERCISE 13b.1 Translate. (Begin by establishing a जो clause – 'the shop which I showed you, in it...'; 'the books which you need, them you will find', etc.)

1   You can get foreign clothes in the shop that I showed you.
2   You will find the books you need on that table.
3   Did you get the letter that I sent you?
4   Those who get the chance should meet again next year.
5   The children we saw yesterday are my friend's children.
6   The man who looks like my brother is my uncle.
7   The lock we bought in Khan Market is quite strong.
8   You should learn the sentences you wrote yesterday.
9   People who smoke should stay outside.

EXERCISE 13b.2 Answer the questions on Dialogues 13a (1-4) and 13b (5-8):

१   प्रताप की माँ ने उससे कब कहा कि उसको मेहनत करनी पड़ेगी ?

२   जब से प्रताप भारत आया है तब से वह क्या कर रहा है ?

३   जब प्रताप लन्दन जाएगा तब उसे किन लोगों से मिलना चाहिए ?

४   आज प्रताप को ऋषि से बात करने से क्या फ़ायदा मिला ?

५   जो लड़का कोने में बैठा है, उसके बारे में कौन पूछ रहा है ?

६   क्या सुरेश संगीता का भाई लगता है ?

७   जिस दिन यह डिनर हुआ, उस दिन अरुण को कहाँ जाना था ?   (12b देखें)

८   अंत में कमला विषय को क्यों बदलना चाहती है ?

EXERCISE 13b.3 Write six sentences of advice to travellers in India, using चाहिए constructions (13.2); then rewrite them substituting subjunctive verbs (10.1).

MODEL: आप को इलाहाबाद ज़रूर जाना चाहिए । >   आप इलाहाबाद ज़रूर जाएँ ।

Vocabulary

अजीब strange, odd	जब तक... तब तक for as long as...
अनबन f discord	for that long
अभ्यास m practice	जब तक नहीं... तब तक until... until
आग f fire	then
आगे later, ahead; आगे चलकर in	जब से... तब से since the time
future, from now on	when... since then
इधर recently, latterly	जवान adj/ m young, youthful;
इलाहाबाद m Allahabad	soldier
कहलाना to be called, named	जैसे ही... वैसे ही as soon as ... then
क़िस्मत f fate	जो who/which, the one
की वजह से because of	who/which
कोना m corner	जो कुछ whatever
गुरु m teacher, guru	जो कोई whoever
गोली f bullet	जो भी whoever, whatever
घंटी f bell	टिकट m/ f ticket; stamp
चल देना to set off	ठंड f cold
चाहिए (with infinitive) should	डर m fear
चोट f hurt, injury	डाकू m dacoit, bandit
चोट लगना to get hurt	डालना to throw
चोरी f theft, robbery	तलाक़ m divorce; तलाक़ होना to
छाता m umbrella	become divorced
जगह f place	ताला m lock
जब... तब when.. then	दिल लगना to feel at home

देन ^f contribution, gift

नज़र ^f glance, look

पक्का ripe

प्यास ^f thirst; प्यास लगना thirst to strike – to feel thirsty

फ़ुरसत ^f leisure, free time

बँगला ^f Bengali (language)

बत्ती ^f light, lamp

बदसूरत ugly

बरबाद करना to ruin

बारिश ^f rain; बारिश होना to rain

बियर ^m beer

बेचारा ^{adj/ m} poor, wretched, helpless; poor fellow

भूख ^f hunger; भूख लगना hunger to strike – to feel hungry

भूखा hungry

भौंकना to bark

मन लगना to feel at home

मरना to die

मिलना to be available; to resemble; मिलना-जुलना to resemble; मिल-जुलकर together, jointly

मूर्ख ^m fool

मेहनत ^f hard work

रोज़ every day, daily

लगना to strike; to appeal; to seem; to catch (of fire, illness); to be related, attached; to be expended (of time, money)

लड़ना to fight, quarrel

लिफ़ाफ़ा ^m envelope

वाक्य ^m sentence

विचार ^m thought, idea, opinion

विषय ^m subject

शादी ^f marriage, wedding; X की शादी Y से होना X to marry Y

शिष्य ^m disciple

सो he, she, it (archaic)

हीरो ^m 'hero', male film-star

14 | THIS WAS BOUGHT IN KATHMANDU

यह तो काठमांडु में ख़रीदा गया

In this unit you will learn how to
- use the passive: 'this was bought'
- use 'to begin' and 'to allow'
- use the remaining relative constructions

14a   Sangeeta gets touchy

सुरेश	तुम्हें ये नेपाली ज़ेवर कहाँ से मिले, संगीता ? बहुत बढ़िया हैं ।
संगीता	ये तो काठमांडु से ही लाए गए थे, अंकल ! इधर सब लोग इस तरह के ज़ेवर पहनने लगे हैं ।
सुरेश	अच्छे लगते हैं । अच्छा एक बात बताओ — कल की दावत में हरीश क्यों नहीं आया ?
संगीता	पता नहीं । उसे बुलाया तो गया था । शायद उसके पिता ने उसे आने नहीं दिया ।
सुरेश	पर मुझे तो बताया गया था कि खन्ना साहब चाहते थे कि तुम दोनों...
संगीता	रहने दो, अंकल ! ये ऊल-जलूल बातें हैं ! दूरदर्शन पर ख़बरें देखी जाएँ ?

सुरेश	अरे, बड़ों से ऐसी बातें की जाती हैं ?
संगीता	माफ़ कीजिए, अंकल, मुझसे गुस्ताख़ी हो गई – पर मुझसे तो हरीश का चेहरा देखा नहीं जाता ।
कमला	[*अन्दर आकर*] क्यों सुरेश, आपको क्या हो गया? बहुत नाराज़ लग रहे हैं !
सुरेश	हाँ, मैं अभी तुम्हारी बेटी से हरीश के बारे में कुछ पूछने लगा था कि वह तू-तू मैं-मैं करने लगी !

बढ़िया	(inv.) nice, of good quality	दूरदर्शन ^m	television; Door-
लगना	(with obl. infinitive) to start, to begin to		darshan (national TV network)
		ख़बर^f	news
देना	(with obl. infinitive) to allow to, let	गुस्ताख़ी^f	rudeness, impertinence
		चेहरा ^m	face, features
ऊल-जलूल	silly, pointless	कि	when (suddenly)

Suresh	Where did you get this Nepali jewellery, Sangeeta? It's really nice.
Sangeeta	It was brought from Kathmandu itself, Uncle! Recently everyone's started wearing this kind of jewellery.
Suresh	It looks good. Now tell me one thing – why didn't Harish come to last night's dinner?
Sangeeta	No idea. He *was* invited. Maybe his father didn't let him come.
Suresh	But I'd been told that Khanna Sahib wanted you two to...
Sangeeta	Let it be, uncle! This is silly talk! Shall we watch the TV news?
Suresh	What, is that how one talks to one's elders?
Sangeeta	Sorry, uncle, I was rude – but I can't stand Harish's face.
Kamala	[*coming in*] Why Suresh, what's happened to you? You're looking very cross!
Suresh	Yes, I'd just started asking your daughter something about Harish when she suddenly started being abusive!

Grammar
14.1 बोला जाना 'to be spoken' – the passive

The active verb 'to speak' is बोलना; the passive verb 'to be spoken' is बोला जाना. Thus the Hindi passive consists of *perfective* participle (e.g. बोला, लिखा, बनाया) +the auxiliary verb जाना. Both parts agree with the subject.

हिन्दी कई प्रदेशों में बोली जाती है ।	Hindi is spoken in many states.
यह कपड़ा जयपुर में बनाया जाता है ।	This cloth is made in Jaipur.
बहुत-से ऐसे पत्र लिखे जाते हैं ।	Many such letters are written.

The passive can be used with any tense, and with compound verbs (12.4).

संस्कृत प्राचीन काल में बोली जाती थी ।	Sanskrit was spoken in ancient times.
यह लेख जून में लिखा गया ।	This article was written in June.
दो नए पुल बनाए जाएँगे ।	Two new bridges will be built.
भूखों को खाना दिया जा रहा है ।	The hungry are being fed.
चाय अभी लाई जाए ।	Tea should be brought *now*.
बिजली बन्द कर दी गई थी ।	The electricity had been cut off.

> **!** बिजली बन्द कर दी गई थी – a complex verb phrase!
>
> बन्द 'closed'
> बन्द करना 'to close'
> बन्द कर देना compound verb
> बन्द कर दिया जाना passive infinitive
> बन्द कर दिया गया था remote past (11.2)
> बन्द कर दी गई थी agreement with fem. subject बिजली

Adding को to the subject makes the passive verb revert to masculine singular:

सड़कें साफ़ की गईं > सड़कों को साफ़ किया गया ।	The roads were cleaned.
किताब पढ़ी गई > किताब को पढ़ा गया ।	The book was read.

This process is similar to that in both ने (11.3) and चाहिए (13.2):

मैंने किताब पढ़ी > मैंने किताब को पढ़ा ।	I read the book.
हमें किताब पढ़नी चाहिए > हमें किताब को पढ़ना चाहिए ।	We should read the book.

Some more passive examples with को –

मच्छरों को मारा गया ।	The mosquitoes were killed.
उनको इसके बारे में बताया जाएगा ।	They will be told about this.
हमें पाकिस्तान भेजा जा रहा है ।	We're being sent to Pakistan.
बिजली को बन्द कर दिया गया था ।	The electricity had been cut off.

What is the passive *for*? A passive verb tends to focus attention on the *action done* rather than the 'doer' or 'agent' of the action, who is often not mentioned at all. When mentioned, the agent takes the postposition से or, in a more formal style, के द्वारा.

यह काम किसी और से किया जाए ।	This work should be done by someone else.
ताज महल शाहजहाँ के द्वारा बनाया गया था ।	The Taj Mahal was built by Shah Jahan.

Even some intransitive verbs can be used in the passive: बैठा जाए ? 'Shall we sit?' (lit. 'shall it be sat [by us]?'). In this construction, the perfective participle for जाना is जाया, not गया.

बाज़ार जाया जाए ?	Shall we go to the market?
चला जाए ?	Shall we be off?

The passive with से (not के द्वारा) can imply inability or unwillingness to do something:

यह खाना मुझसे खाया नहीं जाता ।	I can't (bear to) eat this food.
इतनी गरमी में हमसे सोया नहीं गया ।	We couldn't sleep in such heat.
मुझसे न रहा गया ।	I couldn't contain myself.

> Participle + जाना gives a *passive* verb, e.g. बोला जाना 'to be spoken'; but stem + जाना gives a *compound* verb, e.g. बोल जाना 'to speak out' (12.4).

14.2 Transitivity and the passive

The concept of transitivity, met in 11.1, needs revisiting here. Hindi makes a greater distinction between transitive and intransitive verbs than English does, as the following example of active (not passive) verbs shows:

INTRANSITIVE	TRANSITIVE
टूटना to break	तोड़ना to break
बोतल टूटती है ।	वह बोतल को तोड़ता है ।
The bottle breaks.	He breaks the bottle.

The English verb 'to break' covers both what happens to the bottle (an intransitive action) and what the person does to the bottle (a transitive action); but Hindi has two separate verbs. Sometimes the only way an intransitive action can be expressed in English is with a passive verb: 'this cloth *is made* in Jaipur' – it would be odd to say 'this cloth comes into being in Jaipur', an intransitive equivalent. Hindi, on the other hand, can express similar meanings through the transitive verb बनाना used in the passive (like 'is made') and the intransitive verb बनना used in the active (like 'comes into being'):

यह कपड़ा जयपुर में बनाया जाता है ।	This cloth is made in Jaipur.
यह कपड़ा जयपुर में बनता है ।	This cloth is made in Jaipur.

The same applies with many other such pairs, such as transitive बेचना 'to sell' and intransitive बिकना 'to be sold':

यहाँ किताबें बेची जाती हैं ।	Books are sold here.
यहाँ किताबें बिकती हैं ।	Books are sold here.

The former sentence (passive transitive बेचा जाना) focuses attention on the *act of selling*, while the latter (active intransitive बिकना) focuses on a more general sense of books being available. Such nuances depend greatly on the context of the sentence.

इधर मकान बनाए जाएँगे / बनेंगे ।	Houses will be built here.
कपड़े नदी में धोए जाते हैं / धुलते हैं ।	Clothes are washed in the river.
काम शुरू किया गया / शुरू हुआ ।	Work was begun/ began.

14.3 पानी पड़ने लगा 'it began raining' – to begin to

The oblique infinitive + लगना means 'to begin to'. लगना does *not* take ने; and it's only rarely used in the negative.

बारिश होने लगी ।	It began to rain.
बच्चे तालियाँ बजाने लगे ।	The children began to clap.
माँ मेरा नाम चिल्लाने लगीं ।	Mother began calling my name.
हमें प्यास लगने लगी ।	We began feeling thirsty.
मुझे महसूस होने लगा कि यह पाठ तो कभी ख़त्म नहीं होगा ।	It began to feel to me that this chapter would never end.

Another way to express 'to begin to' is with a *direct* infinitive + शुरू करना, e.g. लिखना शुरू करना 'to begin to write'. This often implies a greater sense of planned action or deliberate purpose than the लगना usage, and so isn't normally used with spontaneous, unplanned sensations like thirst, or natural actions like rain falling.

पिछले साल मैंने लिखना शुरू किया ।	Last year I took up writing.
हम उर्दू सीखना शुरू करेंगे ।	We'll start learning Urdu.

> **!** लगना as 'to begin' takes *oblique* infinitive: but शुरू करना takes *direct* infinitive.

14.4 मुझे जाने दो ! 'let me go!' – to allow

The oblique infinitive + देना means 'to allow to, to let'. देना *does* take ने, and the perfective verb agrees with a direct object (unless marked with को) – see agreement with गाड़ी in the first example:

चाचाजी ने मुझे अपनी गाड़ी चलाने दी ।	Uncle let me drive his car.
पिताजी ने बच्चे को मिठाइयाँ खाने दीं ।	Father let the child eat the sweets.
बिल्ली को मक्खन न खाने देना ।	Don't let the cat eat the butter.
अरे, रहने दो ! बारिश होने दो !	Oh, let it be! Let it rain!

14b Arun's book

प्रकाश	तुम्हारी किताब की क्या ख़बर है अरुण ? ख़ूब बिक रही होगी ?
अरुण	जितनी प्रतियाँ बिकनी चाहिए उतनी नहीं बिकी हैं । बहुत निराशा हुई ।
प्रकाश	तो जिस तरह की किताबें आम लोगों को पसंद हैं, उस तरह की क्यों नहीं लिखते ?

अरुण	नहीं साहब, ऐसा घटिया साहित्य मुझसे लिखा नहीं जाएगा !
प्रकाश	तब तो तुम्हें सफल लेखक बनने के सपने को भूलना होगा ।
अरुण	आपके विचार में, आर्थिक सफलता प्राप्त करने से ही कोई व्यक्ति सफल हो जाता है क्या ?
प्रकाश	मेरे ख़याल से तुम्हें प्रेम की कहानियाँ लिखनी चाहिए, तब पढ़नेवाले ख़ुश हो जाएँगे ।
अरुण	जैसी कहानियाँ तुम्हें पसंद हैं, वैसी कहानियाँ जनता के मन को भ्रष्ट कर देती हैं, प्रकाश ।
प्रकाश	किताब पढ़ने से किसका मन कभी भ्रष्ट हो गया ? सभी तरह का साहित्य चलता है, लेखक महोदय !

जितना... उतना	as much as...	सफलता [f]	success
निराशा [f]	disappointment, despair	प्राप्त करना	to obtain, attain
घटिया (inv.)	inferior, low grade	व्यक्ति [m]	person, individual
साहित्य [m]	literature	प्रेम [m]	love
सफल	successful	भ्रष्ट	corrupted; भ्रष्ट करना to corrupt
लेखक [m]	writer	महोदय	gentleman; sir
आर्थिक	financial		

Prakash	What's the news of your book, Arun? Must be selling well?
Arun	Not as many copies have sold as should have done. I'm very disappointed.
Prakash	Then why don't you write the kind of books that ordinary people like?
Arun	No sir, I couldn't bring myself to write such inferior literature!
Prakash	Then you'd better forget the dream of becoming a successful writer.
Arun	In your opinion, does an individual become succesful merely by acquiring financial success?
Prakash	In my opinion you should write love stories, then the readers will be happy.
Arun	Stories of the kind you like corrupt the mind of the public, Prakash.
Prakash	Whose mind ever got corrupted by reading a book? Every kind of literature has its place, Mr Writer sir!

ऋ Grammar

14.5 जितना... उतना 'as much as' (Relative clauses 3)

Our third foray into relative-correlative constructions deals with
जितना... उतना 'as much... that much':

जितना तुमको चाहिए, उतना लो ।	Take as much as you want.
उनकी जितनी ज़मीन है उतनी ही हमारी भी है ।	We have just as much land as they do.
जितने लोग हिन्दी बोलते हैं, उतने बँगला नहीं बोलते।	Not as many people speak Bengali as speak Hindi.
जितनी अच्छी पुरानी फ़िल्में थीं उतनी अच्छी नई फ़िल्में नहीं हैं ।	The new films aren't as good as the old films were.
भारत की जितनी आबादी है उतनी पाकिस्तान की नहीं है ।	Pakistan's population is not as big as India's.

14.6 जैसा... वैसा 'as... so' (Relative clauses 4)

This relative-correlative pair describes likeness of *kind* and *manner*.
Firstly, they are adjectival (describing a *thing*):

जैसा बाप वैसा बेटा ।	Like father, like son.
जैसी दाल हमें चाहिए वैसी यहाँ नहीं मिलती ।	The kind of daal we need isn't available here.
जैसा महीन काम वह करता है वैसा और कोई नहीं कर पाता ।	Nobody else can achieve the delicate work that he does.

Secondly, they are adverbial (describing an *action*):

जैसा तुम चाहो वैसा ही करो ।	Do just you like.
देवनागरी जैसी लिखी जाती वैसी ही पढ़ी भी जाती है ।	Devanagari is read just as it's written.

जिस तरह का... उस तरह का is an alternative for the adjectival type:

जिस तरह के लोग उस इलाक़े में रहते हैं, उस तरह के लोग चोरी नहीं करते !	People of the kind who live in that area don't steal!

And similarly जिस तरह (से)... उस तरह (से) is an alternative for the adverbial type:

जिस तरह से तू भूतों से डरता है उसी तरह से मैं तुझसे डरता हूँ ।	I fear you just as you fear ghosts.

14.7 जहाँ... वहाँ 'where... there' (Relative clauses 5)

Our final relative-correlative context relates to *place*; and जहाँ भी means 'wherever'.

जहाँ मैं रहता हूँ वहाँ कोई उर्दू नहीं जानता ।	Where I live nobody knows Urdu.
जहाँ नदी या तालाब हो वहाँ आबादी भी होगी ।	Where there's a river or a pond there will also be habitation.
वह हीरो जहाँ भी जाता है वहाँ भीड़ लगती है ।	Wherever that film-star goes a crowd gathers.
जहाँ फूल है वहाँ काँटा भी होगा ।	Where there's a flower there will also be a thorn.

जिधर... उधर 'whither... thither' is a close parallel to जहाँ... वहाँ (and relates to इधर 'here, over here', उधर 'there, over there', and किधर 'whereabouts?'):

जिधर से तू आया है, उधर वापस जा !	Go back where you came from!

14.8 Clause reversal (Relative clauses 6)

Relative-correlative constructions were introduced in 13.1, 13.4, and 14.4-6. Revise those sections before continuing.

The relative-correlative sentences seen so far have had the relative clause first and the correlative clause second. Hindi, like English, also uses other patterns. The two clauses may often be reversed, as is shown in the following pairs of sentences, prefaced by relevant section numbers (possible variations in the English are not shown):

13.1 जब तक बिजली नहीं आएगी तब तक हमें ठंडे पानी से नहाना पड़ेगा ।

हमें तब तक ठंडे पानी से नहाना पड़ेगा जब तक बिजली नहीं आएगी ।

We'll have to bathe in cold water until the electricity comes.

13.4 जिस लड़के ने यह प्याला तोड़ दिया उसको बुलाओ ।
उस लड़के को बुलाओ जिसने यह प्याला तोड़ दिया ।
Call the boy who broke this cup.

14.4 जितना खाना बन चुका हो उतना खिला दो ।
उतना खाना खिला दो जितना बन चुका हो ।
Serve however much food is already prepared.

14.5 जैसा मौक़ा आज मिला है वैसा दुबारा नहीं मिलेगा ।
वैसा मौक़ा दुबारा नहीं मिलेगा जैसा आज मिला है ।
An opportunity such has arisen today won't come again.

14.6 जहाँ हमारी पहली मुलाक़ात हुई थी हम वहीं चलें ।
हम वहीं चलें जहाँ हमारी पहली मुलाक़ात हुई थी ।
Let's go to the place where we first met.

Some relative clauses use mixed pairs of pronouns rather than the formal relative-correlative pairs introduced earlier:

14.4 जितने लोग पार्टी में आए थे, सभी शादी-शुदा थे । However many people (all the people who) had come to the party, all of them were married.

14.6 जिस तरह का खाना हमें चाहिए था, वह तो नहीं मिलेगा ।
We won't get the kind of food we wanted.

A relative clause may be used as a parenthesis within a sentence, or as an afterthought:

प्रताप (जो लन्दन से है) कई महीनों से हमारे यहाँ रह रहा है ।
Pratap (who is from London) has been staying at our place for several months.

अनीता हर हफ़्ते फ़ोन करती है – जो प्रताप को कुछ बुरा लगता होगा ।
Anita phones every week – which must rather annoy Pratap.

Some speakers add कि to a relative pronoun such as जो; this does not affect meaning.

कुछ बोलनेवाले तो "जो" के बाद "कि" भी जोड़ देते हैं, जो कि वाक्य के अर्थ में कोई परिवर्तन नहीं लाता है ।

Some speakers add 'कि' after 'जो', which does not bring any alteration to the meaning of the sentence.

EXERCISE 14a.1 Rewrite the following in the passive, omitting any reference to an 'agent'. Then translate the passive version.

MODEL: हमने ये समोसे कल रात बनाए थे । → ये समोसे कल रात बनाए गए ।

These samosas were made last night.

१   तमिल तो दक्षिण भारत में बोलते हैं ।

२   हम सारी तैयारियाँ ६ बजे तक करेंगे ।

३   यह चिट्ठी मैं हवाई डाक से भेजूँगा ।

४   इस विश्वविद्यालय में कुछ लोग संस्कृत भी पढ़ते हैं ।

५   मंदिर में फोटो नहीं खींचना चाहिए ।

६   हमें ज़िन्दगी को थोड़ा और सरल बनाना चाहिए ।

EXERCISE 14a.2 Translate.

1   The newest houses were built just last year.
2   All the letters had been put in one big envelope.
3   It was said in the newspaper that the thieves had been caught.
4   Several strange books have been written about Indian languages.
5   Sangeeta began thinking that Sunday would never come.
6   It started to rain, so Kamala didn't let Raj go out.
7   When the children began to feel hungry I let them eat.
8   We were told that the guests had begun to arrive.
9   Don't let anyone come in until I tell you.
10   In future, people who don't work will not be given any money.

EXERCISE 14a.3 Write a brief third-person account, in Hindi, of Dialogue 14a.

EXERCISE 14b.1 Complete the sentence with an appropriate clause. Then translate.

१   मेरे जितने दोस्त हैं, ...

२   तुम जितने ध्यान से पढ़ोगे, ...

३   जितनी अच्छी यह नई किताब है, ...

४   जहाँ हम लोग रहते हैं, ...

५   .... जहाँ बहुत कम लोग जाते हों ।

६   .... वहाँ अमीर लोगों की आबादी ज़रूर होगी ।

७   .... उतने ही हमारे पास भी हैं ।

८   .... उतना बड़ा लखनऊ नहीं है ।

EXERCISE 14b.2 Translate the following extract from Pratap's letter to his mother.

कल मुझे कमला और प्रकाश कुमार के डिनर में बुलाया गया । बहुत ही शानदार डिनर था । हमें जितना खाना खिलाया गया, उतना मैंने कभी नहीं खाया है ! जब कमला जी मुझे तीसरी बार और खाना देने लगीं तो मैं "बस! बस!" कहने लगा, पर उन्होंने ध्यान नहीं दिया । गोश्त, सब्ज़ी, दाल, रोटी, चावल, चटनी – इतना ज़्यादा खाना तैयार किया गया था कि मैं बता नहीं सकता ! जैसा हिन्दुस्तानी खाना लन्दन में मिलता है, वैसा नहीं था; यहाँ तो हर चीज़ एकदम ताज़ी थी, और जितनी ताज़ी थी, उतनी ही स्वादिष्ट ! मिठाई तो किसी दुकान से लाई गई थी, पर मिठाई को छोड़कर हर चीज़ घर में ही बनाई गई थी । खाना बनाने में तो कमला जी माहिर हैं ।

लेकिन तुम अपने मन में पूछ रही होगी, डिनर में कौन कौन आया था ? मैं बताता हूँ । अपनी पढ़ाई की वजह से मैं तो देर से पहुँचा । मेरे पहुँचने पर मुझे कमरे के एक कोने में बिठाया गया । खन्ना जी को सबों के बीच में बिठाया गया, और उनकी बग़ल में उनकी पत्नी, जो मुझे बहुत अच्छी लगीं । उनके लड़के को भी बुलाया गया था, पर किसी वजह से वह नहीं आया । संगीता अपनी सहेली पिंकी (खन्ना जी की छोटी बहिन) के साथ फ़िल्म देखने गई थी; वे लोग फ़िल्म के ख़त्म होने पर क़रीब ग्यारह बजे घर आ गईं और जितना खाना बचा था, खा लिया । (फ़िल्म थी "हम आपके हैं कौन", जो कई साल पहले बनाई गई थी; संगीता तो उसे कम से कम चार-पाँच बार देख चुकी होगी, उसे फिर से क्यों देखना चाहती थी, मेरी समझ में नहीं आता ।) सुरेश भी आए थे; कमला जी ने उन्हें अपने पास बिठा लिया । अरुण तो किसी दोस्त से मिलने गए थे इसलिए वे तो "अनुपस्थित" थे । उन्हें इस प्रकार के शब्द बहुत पसंद हैं – अपनी बोली में वे इतने संस्कृत के शब्द लाद देते हैं कि मुझसे तो उनकी आधी बातें समझी नहीं जातीं ।

डिनर के दौरान हिन्दी के बारे में बहुत-सी दिलचस्प बातें कही गईं । सुरेश ने कहा कि दिल्ली की हिन्दी भ्रष्ट हो गई है, पंजाबी ज़बान के कारण । (शर्माजी भी क्लास में कह रहे थे कि पंजाबी लोग ज़्यादातर "मैंने जाना है" कहते हैं, जो कि ग़लत प्रयोग है – "मुझे जाना है" ही सही है ।) पर जब सुरेश ने यह बात कही तो प्रकाश जी ने ऐसे आँखें दिखाईं कि सुरेश बेचारे चुप हो गए । बात यह है न, कि खन्ना जी ख़ुद पंजाबी हैं; और उनके सामने प्रकाश एकदम दब जाते हैं – भीगी बिल्ली की तरह ! अंत में कमला जी ने विषय बदलकर ऋषि और राज के बारे में कोई मज़ाक़ किया तो सब लोग हँसने लगे । पर बाद में कमला जी ने सुरेश को ख़ूब डाँटा होगा !

श्रीमती खन्ना बहुत अच्छी महिला हैं । भाषाओं के बारे में बहुत जानती भी हैं । जब मैंने उनसे पूछा कि "राजस्थान" में "थ" क्यों है जब कि "पाकिस्तान" में "त" ही है तो उन्होंने यह कहकर बात को समझा दिया कि "स्थान" तो संस्कृत का शब्द है जब कि "स्तान" फ़ारसी का है । दोनों शब्दों का वही अर्थ है – "जगह" । तो शब्दों के भी परिवार होते हैं ! पर कुमार परिवार की तरह नहीं । बिलकुल नहीं !

Vocabulary

अनुपस्थित absent	(के) द्वारा by, by means of
अमीर rich, wealthy	के बीच में in the middle of
अर्थ ^{m} meaning	ख़बर ^{f} news; information
आँखें दिखाना to look angrily	गुस्ताख़ी ^{f} rudeness, impertinence
आबादी ^{f} population, settlement	घटिया (inv.) inferior, lowgrade
आर्थिक financial	चटनी ^{f} chutney
इलाक़ा ^{m} area	चेहरा ^{m} face, features
ऊल-जलूल silly, pointless	चोरी करना to steal
क़रीब about, roughly	जब कि while
काँटा ^{m} thorn; fork	ज़बान ^{f} language, tongue
कारण ^{m} reason, cause	जहाँ... वहाँ where... there
कि when suddenly	जितना... उतना as much as...
किधर where? whither?	जिधर... उधर whither... thither
की बग़ल में next to	जैसा... वैसा as... so
के कारण because of	जोड़ना to add

डाँटना to scold	बिठाना to make sit
तमिल ^f Tamil	बिल्ली ^f cat
ताज़ा fresh	बोली ^f speech, dialect
तालाब ^m pond	भीगा wet; भीगी बिल्ली ^f 'wet cat',
तालियाँ बजाना to clap	timid creature
दक्षिण ^m south	भ्रष्ट corrupted; भ्रष्ट करना to corrupt
दबना to yield, cower	मक्खन ^m butter
दिलचस्प interesting	मच्छर ^m mosquito
दुबारा again, a second time	मज़ाक़ ^m joke
दूरदर्शन ^m television; Door-	महसूस होना to be felt,
darshan (national TV network)	experienced
देना (with obl.inf.) to allow to, let	महिला ^f lady
धुलना to be washed	महीन fine, delicate
नदी ^f river	महोदय ^m gentleman, sir
निराशा ^f disappointment, despair	मुलाक़ात ^f meeting, encounter
परिवर्तन ^m alteration	मौक़ा ^m chance, opportunity
पाकिस्तान ^m Pakistan	राजस्थान ^m Rajasthan
पुल ^m bridge	लगना (with obl. inf.) to begin to
प्रकार ^m manner, way, type, kind	लादना to load
प्रदेश ^m state, province	लेख ^m article (written)
प्रयोग ^m use, usage	लेखक ^m writer
प्राचीन ancient	व्यक्ति ^m person, individual
प्राप्त करना to obtain, attain	शादी-शुदा (inv.) married
प्रेम ^m love	शानदार magnificent
फ़ारसी ^f Persian	सफल successful
फूल ^m flower	सफलता ^f success
बचा saved, left	साहित्य ^m literature
बढ़िया (inv.) nice, of good quality	स्वादिष्ट tasty
बस enough! that's all!	हवाई डाक़ ^f airmail

15 | GO ON LEARNING HINDI!

हिन्दी सीखते जाओ !

In this unit you will learn how to

- use new ways of describing habitual actions
- use reflexive pronouns – 'I myself'

15a Pratap's 'new peacock'

दादी जी	तुम कब से हिन्दी सीख रहे हो प्रताप ?
प्रताप	मैं तीन साल से सीख रहा हूँ । शुरू में मैं एक ईवनिंग क्लास में सीखा करता था ।
दादी जी	तुमने किससे सीखी ? तुम्हारा उच्चारण तो बहुत साफ़ है ।
प्रताप	हमारे लन्दन-वाले अध्यापक यू० पी० से थे । वे कहते थे कि हिन्दी बोलते जाओ, बोलते जाओ...
दादी जी	और तुम्हें हमारी हिन्दी भाषा पसंद है बेटे ?
प्रताप	जिस दिन मैंने हिन्दी सीखना शुरू किया, उसी दिन से मेरे जीवन में एक नया मोर आया ।

दादी जी	[*ख़ूब हँसकर*] अरे "मोर" नहीं बेटे, "मोड़" ! "एक नया मोड़" !
प्रताप	[*झेंपकर*] माफ़ कीजिए दादीजी, ऐसी उच्चारण की ग़लतियाँ मुझसे हमेशा हुआ करती हैं !
दादी जी	कोई बात नहीं, हिन्दी सीखते जाओ, सीखते जाओ ! जीते रहो, बेटे ।

कब से	since when?	जीवन ^m	life
शुरू ^m	beginning	झेंपना	to be embarrassed
ईवनिंग क्लास ^f	'evening class'	ग़लती ^f	mistake
यू० पी० ^m	UP (Uttar Pradesh)	जीते रहो	bless you ('stay living')

Dadi ji	Since when have you been learning Hindi, Pratap?
Pratap	I've been learning for three years. In the beginning I used to study in an evening class.
Dadi ji	Whom did you learn from? Your pronunciation is very clear.
Pratap	Our London teacher was from UP. He used to say 'Go on talking Hindi, go on talking…'.
Dadi ji	And you like our Hindi language, child?
Pratap	From the very day I began learning Hindi, my life took a new peacock.
Dadi ji	[*laughing loudly*] Oh, not *mor* ['peacock'] child, *moṛ*! ['turn'] ! 'A new turn'!
Pratap	[*abashed*] Sorry Dadi ji, I'm always making these mistakes in pronunciation!
Dadi ji	Never mind, go on learning Hindi, go on learning! Bless you, son.

Grammar
15.1 करता रहना/जाना 'to go on doing'

An imperfective participle + रहना means 'to keep on doing': वह काम करती रही 'she went on working'. The participle agrees with the subject.

हम लोग रात भर काम करते रहे ।	We went on working all night.
वह शराबी है न? शराब पीता रहेगा ।	He's a drunk isn't he? He'll go on drinking.
अगर दिन भर पढ़ते रहोगे तो थक जाओगे ।	If you go on reading all day you'll get tired.

An imperfective participle + जाना also means 'to keep on doing', but suggests a *progressive* action, as if heading for some kind of culmination: किराया बढ़ता गया 'the rent went on increasing'.

भिखारी चपातियाँ खाता जा रहा है ।	The beggar is going on eating chapatties.
यात्री रिक्शे पर सामान लादता गया ।	The traveller went on loading stuff onto the rickshaw.
सलमान साहब उपन्यास लिखते जाएँगे ।	Salman Sahib will go on writing novels.

15.2 किया करना 'to do habitually'

A perfective participle + करना means 'to do something habitually': वह सोमवार को फ़िल्में देखा करती है 'she makes a habit of seeing films on Mondays'. The participle is invariable in -आ (masculine singular).

वह हमें गालियाँ दिया करती है ।	She's forever calling us names.
हर हफ़्ते मुझे एक पत्र लिखा करो ।	Write me a letter every week.
ब्राह्मण गंगा में स्नान किया करते हैं ।	Brahmins bathe in the Ganges.
गुरु जी पेड़ के नीचे बैठकर पढ़ाया करते थे ।	Guru ji used to teach sitting under a tree.

The construction can even be used with intransitive verbs like होना (using the participle हुआ), जाना (using the participle जाया) and आना:

१ अगस्त को एक आम छुट्टी हुआ करती थी ।	There used to be a public holiday on 1 August.
हम लोग समुद्र के किनारे जाया करते थे ।	We used to go to the seaside.
मैं विश्वविद्यालय पैदल जाया करती हूँ ।	I go to the university on foot.
कभी कभी हमारे यहाँ आया करो, न ?	Come to our place from time to time, won't you?

15.3 से revisited

The postposition से has such a variety of uses that it's worth bringing them together here. We've already seen the following:

from	मैं दिल्ली से आ रही हूँ ।	I'm coming from Delhi.
by	मैं ट्रेन से आऊँगी ।	I'll come by train.
with	मैंने अपने पैसे से टिकट ख़रीदा ।	I bought a ticket with my own money.
than	राजधानी दूसरी गाड़ियों से महँगी है ।	The Rajdhani is more expensive than other trains.
because of, with	यात्री ठंड से काँपने लगे ।	The passengers began shivering with cold.

> **!** For 'in company with', use के साथ (not से): हम आपके साथ चलेंगे 'We'll go with you'.

Added to a noun, से forms an adverb, on the same pattern as the English 'with difficulty':

मुश्किल से	with difficulty
आसानी से	easily, with ease
आराम से	comfortably
ख़ुशी से	happily
देर से	late

A more formal style of adverb is based on the noun रूप 'form':

औपचारिक रूप से	formally
अनौपचारिक रूप से	informally
व्यक्तिगत रूप से	individually

Several common verbs take से –

इनकार करना	वह लड़की मेरे यहाँ आने से इनकार कर रही है !
to refuse	That girl is refusing to come to my place!
कहना	मैंने उससे कहा कि दूसरे लोग भी होंगे ।
to say	I told her that others would be there too.
डरना	वह मेरी माँ से डरती होगी ।
to fear	She must be afraid of my mother.

नफ़रत करना	या शायद वह मुझसे नफ़रत करती है ।
to hate	Or perhaps she hates me.
नाराज़ होना	मुमकिन है कि वह मुझसे नाराज़ हो ।
to be displeased	It's possible that she's angry with me.
पूछना	मैं उसकी सहेली से उसके बारे में पूछूँ ?
to ask, enquire	Should I ask her friend about her?
प्यार करना / होना	मैं उससे प्यार करता हूँ, मगर उसको मुझसे प्यार नहीं है !
to love	I love her, but she has no love for me!
बातें करना	इसके बारे में किससे बातें करूँ ?
to converse	Who can I talk to about this?
मिलना	मेरे दोस्त तो मुझसे मिलना भी नहीं चाहते ।
to meet	My friends don't even want to meet me.
माँगना	तो किससे मदद माँगूँ ?
to demand, ask for	So whom should I ask for help?
लड़ना	उसका बड़ा भाई मुझसे लड़ना चाहता है ।
to fight	Her elder brother wants to fight me.
शादी करना	प्यारी, क्या तू मुझसे शादी करेगी ?
to marry	Beloved, will you marry me?
शिकायत करना	हे भगवान, वह मेरी पत्नी से शिकायत करने गई है ।
to complain	O God, she's gone to complain to my wife.

 Such verbs stand *without* से if the sense of connection is implicit rather than explicit: हम उनसे मिलेंगे 'We'll meet them', but फिर मिलेंगे '[We'll] meet again', 'See [you] later'.

से also means 'since': कब से ? कल से 'Since when? Since yesterday'. Describing a situation which still exists in the present, a present-tense verb is used:

हम लोग सोमवार से यहाँ हैं ।   We've been here since Monday.

तुम कब से लखनऊ में रह रहे हो ?	Since when have you been living in Lucknow?
हम लोग चार साल से सितार सीख रहे हैं ।	We've been learning the sitar for four years.

15b Harish at his father's office

हरीश छोटू, एक मज़ाक़ सुनोगे ? दो शराबी आधीरात को आपस में बातें कर रहे हैं । पहला शराबी दूसरे शराबी से पूछता है, "भैया, रात को सूरज क्यों नहीं निकलता है ?" । दूसरा शराबी क्या जवाब देता है, जानते हो ?

छोटू [*जंभाई लेकर*] आप बताइए तो देखेंगे ।

हरीश दूसरा शराबी कहता है, "निकलता तो है, लेकिन इतने घने अँधेरे में दिखाई नहीं देता !" ।

छोटू [*बत्तीसी दिखाकर*] वाह ! वाह ! कितना बढ़िया मज़ाक़ है ! "इतने घने अँधेरे में दिखाई नहीं देता" । वाह !

हरीश अच्छा छोटू, पिताजी भी दिखाई नहीं दे रहे हैं । बाहर गए हैं क्या?

छोटू हाँ, खन्ना जी अचानक किसी से मिलने गए हैं । परेशान-से लग रहे थे ।

हरीश क्या पिता जी ख़ुद गाड़ी चला रहे थे ?

छोटू जी नहीं । खन्ना-जी जैसे बड़े लोग गाड़ी स्वयं क्यों चलाएँगे ! उनके पास ड्राइवर तो है ।

हरीश पिता जी का कहना था कि आज सिवाय चौकीदार के, सब लोग छुट्टी पर होंगे ।

छोटू पर हमारे जैसे ग़रीब आदमियों को छुट्टी कब मिलती है भैया ? इधर तो हमारी हालत बहुत ख़राब है ।

हरीश अगर तुम तरक़्क़ी करना चाहते हो तो पिताजी से ख़ुद बात कर लो । वे अपने आप तो कुछ नहीं करेंगे तुम्हारे लिए।

छोटू मैं उनसे कुछ कहना चाहता था, मगर मारे डर के मैं कुछ कह नहीं पाया ।

हरीश अरे छोटू, डरपोक मत बनो तुम !

आधीरात ^f	midnight	जंभाई ^f	yawn; जंभाई लेना to yawn
आपस में	between themselves	घना	thick, dense
सूरज ^m	sun	अँधेरा ^m	darkness

बत्तीसी ^f set of 32 – the teeth;	चौकीदार ^m watchman
बत्तीसी दिखाना to grin broadly	जैसा like, such as
दिखाई देना to be visible, appear	ग़रीब poor
अचानक suddenly, unexpectedly	हालत ^f state, condition
-सा -like, -ish	तरक़्क़ी ^f progress, advancement
स्वयं oneself	अपने आप of one's own accord
ड्राइवर ^m driver	के मारे on account of, through
के सिवाय apart from	डरपोक timid

Harish	Chotu, will you listen to a joke? Two drunks are talking together at midnight. The first drunk asks the second drunk, 'Brother, why doesn't the sun come out at night?' Do you know what the second drunk replies?
Chotu	[*yawning*] You tell me and we'll see.
Harish	The second drunk says, 'It *does* come out, but it's not visible in such deep darkness!'
Chotu	[*grinning broadly*] Wah! Wonderful! What a fine joke! 'It's not visible in such deep darkness.' Wonderful!
Harish	OK Chotu, Father's not to be seen anywhere either. Has he gone out?
Chotu	Yes, Khanna ji has suddenly gone out to meet someone. He was looking a bit worried.
Harish	Was Father driving the car himself?
Chotu	No. Important people like Khanna ji don't drive themselves! He has a driver after all.
Harish	Father was saying that everyone except the watchman would be on holiday today.
Chotu	But when do poor people like us get a holiday, brother? We're in a very bad state here.
Harish	If you want to make progress (be promoted), talk to Father yourself. He won't do anything of his own accord.
Chotu	I wanted to say something to him, but I was afraid to speak.
Harish	Oh Chotu, don't be a wimp!

 'I wanted to...': such past contexts take चाहना in the imperfective (चाहता था), because they describe an ongoing state of mind rather than a specific action.

Grammar

15.4 जैसा 'like'

जैसा is a postposition meaning 'like'. Like the possessive का (5.3), it agrees adjectivally with a subject noun or pronoun, while also putting a preceding noun or pronoun into the oblique:

मुझ जैसे लोग काम नहीं करते ।	People like me don't work.
तेरे हाथ किसी कोमल फूल जैसे हैं ।	Your hands are like some soft flower.

An alternative structure is based on a possessive pronoun – उनके जैसे 'like them', हमारे जैसे 'like us'.

मेरे जैसे आदमी के बारे में कौन परवाह करता है ?	Who cares about a man like me?
छोटू के जैसे मूर्ख मत बनो ।	Don't be a fool like Chotu.

The adverb जैसे (कि) means 'as, just as'; and with a subjunctive verb, 'as though'.

जैसे तुम्हें बताया जा चुका है, नल का पानी पीने लायक़ नहीं है ।	As you've already been told, the tap water isn't drinkable.
वह हँसने लगी जैसे कि पागल हो ।	She started laughing as though she were mad.

15.5 -सा '-ish, -like'

-सा/-सी/-से is suffixed to adjectives to moderate their sense a little:

मेरा गोरा-सा चेहरा और लाल-सी नाक	my palish face and reddish nose
तेरे भोले-से सवाल	your rather innocent questions

As in English 'rather', -सा can emphasise a quality while ostensibly moderating it:

छोटी-सी चिड़िया	a tiny little bird
बहुत-से नेता	lots of leaders (politicians)

-सा can also be suffixed to a noun+ possessive:

नेता का-सा घमंड	arrogance like a politician's
बंदर की-सी पूंछ	a tail like a monkey's

It can also be suffixed to various parts of the verb:

औरत बैठ-सी गई ।	The woman kind of sat down.
सपने में मैं उड़-सा रहा था ।	In the dream I was as if flying.

It takes a regular oblique case when required:

उस घने-से जंगल में	in that quite dense jungle
ठंडे से पानी में	in the coldish water

-सा is also an element of the word कौनसा 'which'; similarly, कोई-सा means 'any one (out of a range of choices)':

कोई-सी किताब ले लो ।	Take any book.
कौनसी लूँ ?	Which one should I take?

And finally, एक-सा means 'similar':

एक-सी चीज़ें	similar things
हमारे घर एक-से हैं ।	Our houses are similar.

15.6 Inverted postpositions

Some compound postpositions may optionally be inverted without affecting the sense.

के बिना	पैसे के बिना, बिना पैसे के	without money
के बजाय	फल के बजाय, बजाय फल के	instead of fruit
के मारे	डर के मारे, मारे डर के	on account of fear
के सिवा	आपके सिवा, सिवा आपके	apart from you

15.7 Reflexive pronouns

ख़ुद means 'myself', 'yourself' etc., depending on the subject; आप and स्वयं (pronounced *svayam*) are more formal equivalents.

वह ख़ुद गाड़ी नहीं चलाता ।	He doesn't drive the car himself.
मैंने यह फ़ोटो ख़ुद खींचा ।	I took this photo myself.
पंडित जी स्वयं ही आएँगे ।	Pandit ji will come in person.

Oblique cases usually involve अपने को or अपने आप को –

अमित अपने को बड़ा आदमी समझता है ।	Amit considers himself a big shot.
डाकू अपने आप को मारने लगा ।	The bandit began beating himself.

अपने आप also means 'of one's own accord'; आपस में means 'between themselves, among themselves'.

पहिया अपने आप घूमने लगा ।	The wheel began turning of its own accord.
लड़के आपस में फुसफुसाने लगे ।	The boys began whispering amongst themselves.

EXERCISE 15a.1 Fill the gaps in the 'imperfective + रहना / जाना' constructions. Then translate.

१   हम दिन भर काम करते .... ।

२   बेचारी छात्रा दस दिन तक पढ़ती .... ।

३   आप ध्यान से काम .... रहिए, तभी सफल होंगे ।

४   सरकार की शक्ति बढ़ती .... , यहाँ तक कि हमें देश को छोड़ना पड़ा ।

५   बादल और भी घने होते .... , फिर दस दिन तक बर्फ़ गिरती .... ।

EXERCISE 15a.2 Rewrite using the 'perfective + करना' construction. Then translate.

१   पिताजी एक मशहूर सरकारी अख़बार चलाते थे ।

२   वह बदमाश अपने बच्चों को मारता है ।

३   सच है कि किसी ज़माने में हमारे भी कई नौकर होते थे ।

४   शाम को दादीजी हमेशा मंदिर जाती हैं ।

५   हमारे पड़ोसी हमें अक्सर धोखा देते हैं ।

EXERCISE 15a.3 Complete the sentence using an appropriate clause. Then translate.

१   जैसा आपने कहा था, वैसा ही ....

२   जैसी फ़िल्में आजकल बन रही हैं, ...

३   जिस तरह की नौकरी मैं करती हूँ ....

४   .... उस तरह के मकान पुराने शहर में नहीं मिलते ।

५   .... वैसा मौक़ा तुम्हें दुबारा नहीं मिलनेवाला है ।

✓ EXERCISE 15b.1 Translate.

1   People like him don't get a job easily.
2   As dozens of people had already told me, the man had gone mad.
3   He slept as though he had not slept for several weeks.
4   We have been living in this country since 1947.
5   Since the accident happened he has not driven the car.
6   You should complain to the doctor if the medicine doesn't work.
7   I wanted to talk to the boss but I was too afraid to say anything.
8   You'll have to fetch the newspapers yourself today because the paper boy is sick.

✓ EXERCISE 15b.2 Answer the questions on Dialogues 15a and 15b.

१   प्रताप कितने साल से हिन्दी पढ़ रहा है ? और आप ? आपने हिन्दी सीखना कब शुरू किया ?

२   जो आदमी प्रताप को लंदन में हिन्दी पढ़ाया करता था, वह कहाँ से था ?

३   क्या प्रताप कभी कभी उच्चारण की गलतियाँ किया करता है ? कोई उदाहरण दीजिए ।

४   क्या प्रताप के पास असल में कोई मोर है ?

५   क्या दादी जी सोचती हैं कि प्रताप को अपनी हिन्दी की पढ़ाई को छोड़ देना चाहिए ?

६   छोटू को कैसे मालूम है कि खन्ना जी स्वयं गाड़ी नहीं चला रहे हैं ?

७   हरीश क्यों सोचता है कि आज शायद उसके पिताजी गाड़ी चला रहे होंगे ?

८   किन लोगों की हालत ख़राब है ? आपके ख़याल से उनके पास किस तरह की समस्याएँ होंगी?

९   अगर छोटू को तरक़्क़ी करनी हो तो उसे क्या करना चाहिए ?

१०   आपके ख़याल से क्या खन्ना जी छोटू के बारे में परवाह करते हैं ?

EXERCISE 15b.3 Write (or make up) a diary entry describing a recent day in your life.

Vocabulary

अँधेरा m	darkness	के सिवा, सिवाय	apart from
अगस्त m	August	ग़रीब	poor
अचानक	suddenly, unexpectedly	ग़लती f	mistake
अनौपचारिक रूप से	informally	गाली f	abuse, swearing; गाली देना to abuse, swear at
अपने आप	of one's own accord, oneself	गोरा adj/m	pale, fair; white person
असल में	really, in reality	घना	dense, thick
आधीरात m	midnight	घमंड m	pride, arrogance
आपस में	between/among themselves	चपाती f	chapati
		चौकीदार m	watchman
आसानी से	easily	जंगल m	jungle, scrub
(से) इनकार करना	to refuse (to)	जँभाई f	yawn; जंभाई लेना to yawn
उड़ना	to fly	ज़माना m	period, age, time
उदाहरण m	example	जीते रहो	bless you ('stay living')
उपन्यास m	novel	जीना	to live, be alive
औपचारिक रूप से	formally	जीवन m	life
कब से	since when	जैसा	like, such as
कभी कभी	sometimes	जैसे कि	as if, as though
काँपना	to shiver, tremble	झेंपना	to be embarrassed
किनारा m	edge, shore	ट्रेन f	train
किराया m	rent, fare	डरपोक	timid
के बजाय	instead of	ड्राइवर m	driver
के बिना	without	तरक़्क़ी f	progress, advancement
के मारे	on account of, through	थकना	to be tired

दिखाई देना   to be visible, appear

देर से   late

देश ^m   country

धोखा ^m   trick, deceipt; धोखा देना
  to trick, deceive

नल ^m   pipe, tap

नेता ^m   leader, politician

नौकरी ^f   job, employment, service

पंडित ^m   pandit

परवाह करना   to care

पहिया ^m   wheel

पूँछ ^f   tail

पैदल   on foot, walking

फुसफुसाना   to whisper

बंदर ^m   monkey

बढ़ना   to increase, grow

बत्तीसी ^f   set of 32 – the teeth;
  बत्तीसी दिखाना to grin broadly

बर्फ़ ^f   snow, ice

बादल ^m   cloud

ब्राह्मण ^m   Brahmin

भिखारी ^m   beggar

मशहूर   famous

यात्री ^m   traveller, passenger

यू० पी० ^m   UP (Uttar Pradesh)

राजधानी ^f   'the capital' – name of
  some Delhi express trains

रात भर   all night

व्यक्तिगत रूप से   personally

शक्ति ^f   power

शराबी ^m   drunkard

शुरू ^m   beginning

सच   true

समस्या ^f   problem

समुद्र ^m   sea, ocean

सरकार ^f   government; सरकारी
  governmental

-सा   -like, -ish

सितार ^m   sitar

सूरज ^m   sun

स्नान करना   to bathe (esp. ritually)

स्वयं   oneself

हालत ^f   state, condition

16 HE WAS PRAISING YOU
वह तुम्हारी तारीफ़ कर रहा था

In this unit you will learn how to

- use conjunct verbs
- use emphasis through repetition of words
- use echo words and 'either/or' choices

16a Chotu misses his chance

छोटू	साहब, आपका बेटा हरीश जो है न, वह बड़ा होनहार लड़का लगता है।
खन्ना	वह तुम्हारी भी बहुत तारीफ़ कर रहा था। उल्लू कहीं का !
छोटू	उसकी शादी कब हो जाएगी सर ? अगले महीने वह २० साल का होनेवाला है।
खन्ना	अरे तुमने उसकी उम्र भी मालूम कर ली है ?
छोटू	जिस महीने हरीश का जन्म हुआ, उसी महीने मेरे पिताजी का देहान्त हो गया। इस लिए...
खन्ना	अच्छा, इसी लिए तुम्हें ये सारी बातें याद रहती हैं।

छोटू	हाँ साहब । खन्ना जी, कल जो है, मैंने आपसे एक बात कहने की कोशिश की थी मगर...
खन्ना	तंग मत किया करो छोटू । अभी मुझे एक ज़रूरी मीटिंग का इंतज़ाम करना है ।

तारीफ़ ^f praise; की तारीफ़ करना to praise   इस लिए so

उल्लू ^m 'owl' – stupid person   इसी लिए that's why

कहीं का (derogative) complete, utter   याद रहना to be remembered

मालूम करना to find out, ascertain   की कोशिश करना to try

देहान्त ^m death; का देहान्त होना to die   मीटिंग ^f meeting

इंतज़ाम ^m arrangement; का इंतज़ाम करना to arrange

Chotu	Sahib, you know your son Harish – he seems a very promising boy.
Khanna	He was praising you a lot too. Silly fool!
Chotu	When will he get married sir? He's about to turn 20 next month.
Khanna	What, you've even found out his age?
Chotu	The very month Harish was born, my father died. So...
Khanna	Oh I see, *that's* why you remember all these things.
Chotu	Yes sahib. Khanna ji, yesterday, you know, I tried to say something to you but...
Khanna	Don't always be bothering (me) Chotu. Right now I've got to arrange an important meeting.

जो है underlines an item for special focus, establishing a subject before going into details: लखनऊ की यह तहज़ीब जो है, वह तो सारी दुनिया में मशहूर है 'This Lucknow culture – it's famous the world over.'

Grammar
16.1 Conjunct verbs with करना / होना

FIRST TYPE. Conjunct verbs of the first type were introduced in 7.6: they're based on adjective + करना (साफ़ करना to clean, to 'make clean') or noun + करना (शुरू करना to start, to 'make a start').

Intransitive equivalents take होना instead of करना. We may call the noun component a 'base noun'.

छोटू को अपनी साइकिल ठीक करनी है ।	Chotu has to fix his bike.
दुकानदार दाम को कम करनेवाला नहीं है ।	The shopkeeper isn't about to lower the price.
कार्यक्रम ५ बजे शुरू हुआ / होगा ।	The programme began/ will begin at 5 o'clock.

SECOND TYPE. In the second type, the base noun is 'possessed' by the verb's object, using का/की/के; thus मैं राम की मदद करूँगा 'I'll help Ram' (literally 'I'll do Ram's help'; मदद is 'possessed' by राम). Try making up examples of your own based on the following:

With *masculine* base nouns:

का इंतज़ाम करना	to arrange
का इंतज़ार करना	to wait for
का इस्तेमाल करना	to use
का पीछा करना	to follow

With *feminine* base nouns:

की तलाश करना	to look for
की देखभाल करना	to look after
की निंदा करना	to blame, speak ill of
की तारीफ़ करना	to praise

In the passive, the subject of a conjunct verb is the base noun itself:

नए घर की तलाश की जाएगी ।	A new house will be sought. (तलाश subject)
पुलिस का इंतज़ार किया जाए ।	(We'd) better wait for the police. (इंतज़ार subject)

Similarly, a conjunct verb in a ने construction agrees with its own base noun:

राम ने बच्चों की देखभाल की ।	Ram looked after the children. (की agrees with देखभाल)

उमा ने कंप्यूटर का इस्तेमाल किया ।	Uma used a computer.
	(किया agrees with इस्तेमाल)
मैंने दूसरी ट्रेन का इंतज़ार किया ।	I waited for the next train.
	(किया agrees with इंतज़ार)

The conjunct verb की कोशिश करना 'to try' often follows an infinitive verb, which must be in the oblique because of the की postposition: समझने की कोशिश करो 'try to understand'.

मैंने फ़ोन करने की कोशिश की ।	I tried to telephone.
समय पर आने की कोशिश करो ।	Try to come on time.
उन्होंने अन्दर आने की कोशिश की ।	They tried to come in.

> **!** Practise substituting other verbs for फ़ोन करना in the first of these examples; this is an extremely useful formula.

A few verbs of the second type can drop their possessive का/की/के, thus becoming first-type verbs: तलाश करना 'to search for'. Just occasionally, a base noun even sprouts a -ना ending and thus generates a verb: किसी को तलाशना 'to search for someone'.

कोई नया घर तलाश करें ।	Let's look for some new house.
मैं तुझे दस साल तक तलाशता रहा ।	I went on searching for you for ten years.

Intransitive conjunct verbs are very common in describing events and processes. Remember that the subject of the verb is the event itself – जन्म[m] 'birth', शादी[f] 'marriage', etc.:

पिताजी का जन्म सन् १९१५ में हुआ था ।	Father was born in 1915.
	(जन्म[m] 'birth')
छोटू की शादी अभी नहीं हुई ।	Chotu isn't married yet.
	(शादी[f] 'marriage')
अनीता का तलाक़ कब हुआ ? ।	When did Anita get divorced?
	(तलाक़[m] 'divorce')
ओम का देहान्त हो गया है ।	Om has passed away.
	(देहान्त[m] 'demise')

नई इमारत का उद्घाटन हुआ ।   The new building was opened.

(उद्घाटन [m] 'inauguration')

16.2 Other conjunct verbs

करना and होना are the most common makers of conjunct verbs, but they're not the only ones. For example, the range of possibilities having याद 'memory' as base noun includes:

याद करना	to remember, learn by memory;
	to think of, summon (e.g. an employee)
याद होना	to be remembered
याद आना	to be recalled, come to mind, be missed
याद दिलाना	to remind
याद रखना	to keep in mind, not to forget
याद रहना	to remain remembered

पाठ १६ को ठीक से याद करो ।	Learn lesson 16 properly.
खन्ना जी तुम्हें याद कर रहे हैं ।	Khanna ji wants you to go to him ('is remembering you').
मुझे तेरा चेहरा याद है ।	I remember your face.
मुझे अभी याद आया है कि श्रीमती खन्ना का नाम उमा है ।	I just remembered that Mrs Khanna's name is Uma.
उन्हें कल शाम की याद दिला दो ।	Remind them about tomorrow evening.
जो मैंने तुम्हें बताया, उसे याद रखना ।	Bear in mind what I told you.
प्यारे, तुम सदा याद रहोगे ।	Beloved, I'll always remember you.

The meaning of most conjunct verbs can be deduced easily enough, but some are quite idiomatic. For example, दिखाई देना/पड़ना means 'to be/become visible, to be seen' and its partner सुनाई देना/पड़ना means 'to be/become audible, to be heard'. Neither takes the ने construction!

गली में एक पुरानी गाड़ी दिखाई पड़ी ।　An old car came into view in the alley.

रात को खाँसने की आवाज़ सुनाई देती थी ।　At night the sound of coughing could be heard.

16b Khanna's anxiety about Harish

उमा क्या हुआ मेरे पति-देव? आज तो तुम कहीं ज़्यादा परेशान लग रहे हो ।

खन्ना कहीं हरीश की शादी का इंतज़ाम हो जाए तो... बस, यही चिंता है ।

उमा इसमें चिंता-विंता की क्या बात है ? तुम्हें नहीं मालूम कि उसे संगीता कुमार से प्यार है ?

खन्ना प्यार-व्यार तो हो सकता है, पर ज़रा सोचो, कहीं प्यार से ही शादी बनती है किसी की ?

उमा अरे तुम्हारा सोचने का ढंग तो बिलकुल बूढ़ों का जैसा है ।

खन्ना ज़िंदगी में अहम चीज़ है पैसा । संगीता के पास क्या है ? न पैसा न पेशा ।

उमा दुनिया में तरह तरह के लोग हैं; सबों की अपनी अपनी जगह होती है ।

खन्ना मगर गुज़ारे के साधन भी होने चाहिए – चाहे कोई काम करे चाहे चोरी !

पति-देव ^m 'respected husband'		न... न neither... nor	
कहीं ज़्यादा particularly		पेशा ^m profession	
चिंता ^f anxiety, concern		दुनिया ^f world	
चिंता-विंता ^f anxiety etc.		तरह तरह का of various kinds	
प्यार-वार ^m love and all that		गुज़ारा ^m livelihood, subsistence	
ढंग ^m way, manner		साधन ^m means	
ज़िंदगी ^f life		चाहे...चाहे whether... or	
अहम important			

Uma What's up, my dear husband? You're looking particularly worried today.

Khanna If Harish's marriage could just be fixed somehow... that's all I'm worried about.

Uma What's there to worry about? Don't you know he loves Sangeeta Kumar?

Khanna	There may be love and all that, but just think, does love alone make anyone's marriage?
Uma	Oh really, your way of thinking is just like the old folks'.
Khanna	The important thing in life is money. What does Sangeeta have? Neither money nor profession.
Uma	There are many kinds of people in the world; everyone has (his or) her own place.
Khanna	But there should be a means of livelihood too – whether one works or steals!

तुम्हारा सोचने का ढंग – here तुम्हारा agrees with ढंग, not with सोचने.

Grammar

16.3 कहीं 'somewhere'

कहीं means 'anywhere' or 'somewhere', कहीं और 'somewhere else', कहीं नहीं 'nowhere', सब कहीं 'everywhere', कहीं भी 'anywhere at all', कहीं न कहीं 'somewhere or other'. A versatile little word! Less literal senses include:

somehow, by some means:

कहीं पैसे मिल जाएँ तो समस्या हल हो जाएगी ।
If somehow we get the money, the problem will be solved.

considerably, very much:

दूसरा मकान कहीं ज़्यादा महँगा था ।
The other house was much dearer.

let it not be that, lest (+ न + subjunctive):

मैं डर रहा था कि कहीं मेरी पत्नी न आ जाए ।
I was afraid lest my wife turn up.

is it possible that ? (rhetorical question):

कहीं कोई इनसान अपने बच्चे को मारेगा ?
Would a human being ever beat his own child?

कहीं का ('of somewhere', hence 'of dubious origin') sharpens the edge of an insult or derogatory label:

बदमाश कहीं का !
Wretched scoundrel!

16.4 Repetition of words

Repeating a word may indicate distribution ('one rupee each') or separation ('sit separately'):

हरेक लड़के को एक एक रुपया दो ।	Give each boy one rupee.
तुम दोनों अलग अलग बैठो ।	You two sit separately from each other.
हरेक प्रयोग के तीन तीन उदाहरण हैं ।	There are three examples of each usage.

Or it may indicate variety and diversity:

हमने तरह तरह के जानवर देखे ।	We saw various different kinds of animals.
भारत में आम कहाँ कहाँ मिलते हैं ?	Where in India can you get mangoes?
शादी में तुम्हें कौन कौन मिला ?	Which various people did you meet at the wedding?

Repetition of an adjective or adverb lends it emphasis:

हमें साफ़ साफ़ बताओ ।	Tell us plainly.
बहुत बहुत धन्यवाद ।	Thank you very much indeed.
बड़ी बड़ी आँखें	great big eyes
गरम गरम चाय	piping hot tea

16.5 Echo words

An 'echo word' echoes another word and generalises its sense. Thus चाय-वाय means 'tea etc., tea or something similar', as in चाय-वाय पियो 'Have some tea or something', in which -वाय echoes चाय. Echo words usually begin with व-, but not always; they can be formed quite creatively, often with a dismissive or disdainful sense.

हमें कोई पेंसिल-बेंसिल दो ।	Give us a pencil or something.
हमें किसी तरह की माला-वाला नहीं चाहिए ।	We don't want any kind of garland or anything.
मुझे किसी मीटिंग-शीटिंग में नहीं जाना है ।	I won't go to any meeting or anything of the kind.

Some echo pairings are an established part of Hindi vocabulary:

गप	gossip	गप-शप	chit-chat, tittle-tattle
ठीक	all right	ठीक-ठाक	fine, in good shape
भीड़	crowd	भीड़-भाड़	hustle and bustle

A further type consists of two words of similar meaning:

नौकर-चाकर	servants, etc.	(both words mean ' servant')
मिलना-जुलना	to mix, associate	(both words mean 'to join')
जान-बूझकर	deliberately	('knowing and understanding')

16.6 या तो… या; न… न; चाहे… चाहे

'Either… or' is या (तो)… या.

सिग्रेट को या तो पी लो या मुझे पीने दो ।	Either smoke the cigarette yourself or let me smoke it.
कसूर या तो तेरा है या मेरा ।	The fault is either yours or mine.

'Neither… nor' is न… न.

छोटू न आलसी है न बेवक़ूफ़ ।	Chotu is neither lazy nor stupid.
हम न प्याज़ खाते हैं न लहसुन ।	We eat neither onions nor garlic.

'Whether… or' is चाहे… चाहे / या.

खाना चाहे अच्छा हो चाहे ख़राब	whether the food's good or bad
चाहे मर्द हो या औरत	whether man or woman

चाहे alone means 'no matter whether'; and the formula चाहे… क्यों न हो means 'no matter how/what'.

चाहे जो भी हो, तुम्हें नदी को पार करना होगा ।

No matter what happens, you'll have to cross the river.

चाहे वह कितना बड़ा आदमी क्यों न हो, मैं उससे नहीं मिलूँगा ।

No matter how important a man he may be, I won't meet him.

यह समस्या कितनी ही कठिन क्यों न हो, उसका हल निकाला ही जाएगा ।

No matter how hard this problem may be, it shall be solved.

EXERCISE 16a.1 Answer the questions as fully as possible.

१   क्या आपको साइकिल ठीक करना आता है ?

२   आप सुबह को कितने बजे अपना पढ़ाई का काम शुरू करते / करती हैं ?

३   आप किस तरह की फ़िल्में पसंद करते / करती हैं ?

४   जब आप निबंध वग़ैरह लिखते / लिखती हैं तो क्या आप कंप्यूटर का इस्तेमाल
     करते / करती हैं ?

५   क्या आपने कभी हिन्दी में ई-मेल (ई-पत्र) भेजने की कोशिश की है ?

६   क्या आपकी शादी हो गई है ?

७   क्या आज शाम को किसी दोस्त या सहेली से आपकी मुलाक़ात होगी ?

८   जिस कमरे में आप अभी बैठे / बैठी हैं, वहाँ क्या क्या दिखाई दे रहा है ?

९   आप हिन्दी के नए शब्दों को कैसे याद करते / करती हैं ?

१०   क्या आपको याद है कि आज से ठीक एक साल पहले आप क्या कर रहे थे / कर
     रही थीं ?

EXERCISE 16a.2 Translate.

1   We've been told that we'll have to wait for the other passengers.

2   The luggage has been loaded on the train but nobody has made any
     arrangements for our food.

3   It seems that some passenger has passed away.

4   Please follow those other passengers; we'll look after your children.

5   I tried to phone a friend but the phone wasn't working.

6   They can't use the computer today because there's no electricity.

7   Don't blame the people who work here, it's not their fault.

8   I married the man I met at the station.

EXERCISE 16a.3 Write a third-person account of Dialogues 15b
and 16a.

EXERCISE 16b.1 Complete the sentence with an appropriate
clause. Then translate.

१   जहाँ मैं पैदा हुआ, ...

२   जहाँ जंगली जानवर रहते हैं, ...

३   जहाँ भी तुम बैठना चाहते हो, ...

४   .... मेरी शादी वहीं हुई थी ।

५   .... वहाँ बिजली का इस्तेमाल नहीं किया जाता है ।

६   .... तब तक उनके पिता का देहान्त हो चुका था ।

EXERCISE 16b.2 Translate, bringing out the meaning of any repeated words and echo words.

१   भारत में तुम कहाँ कहाँ घूमे और क्या क्या देखा ?

२   बचपन में उसके तरह तरह के अनुभव रहे होंगे ।

३   सब लोग अपने अपने विचारों में डूब गए थे ।

४   गरम गरम चाय पीकर हम सभी अपने अपने कमरे में चले गए ।

५   कुलियों को बीस बीस रुपये देना ।

६   कहो राजू, ठीक-ठाक हो ?   कुछ चाय-वाय लोगे ?

८   मैं किसी मीटिंग-शीटिंग में जाकर अपना समय क्यों गँवाऊँ ?

EXERCISE 16b.3 Translate.

1   We should give them ten rupees each, so that they can get some tea or something.

2   Whom [which various people] did you encounter in Pakistan?

3   Remember that you shouldn't have any food or anything in such dirty places.

4   You should all take one tablet every day after eating your food.

5   I have neither money nor time, so you'll have to look after the guests yourself.

Vocabulary

अनुभव ^m	experience	इनसान ^m	human being, person
अहम	important	इमारत ^f	building
आलसी	lazy	इस लिए	so
इंतज़ाम ^m	arrangement; का इंतज़ाम करना to arrange	इसी लिए	that's why
		इस्तेमाल ^m	use; का इस्तेमाल करना to use
इंतज़ार ^m	wait, waiting; का इंतज़ार करना to wait for	ई-पत्र ^m	e-mail

ई-मेल ^m e-mail

उदाहरण ^m example

उद्घाटन ^m inauguration

उल्लू ^m 'owl' – stupid person

कंप्यूटर ^m computer

कम करना to reduce

कसूर ^m fault, error

कहीं somewhere; somehow; कहीं और somewhere else; कहीं का downright, utter (see 16.3); कहीं ज़्यादा particularly; कहीं न कहीं somewhere or other; कहीं नहीं nowhere; कहीं भी anywhere at all

कार्यक्रम ^m programme

कुली ^m porter

कोशिश ^f attempt; की कोशिश करना to try

खाँसना to cough

गँवाना to waste, squander

गप ^f, गपशप ^f gossip

गुज़ारा ^m livelihood, subsistence

चाहे... चाहे whether... or

चिंता ^f anxiety

जंगली wild

जन्म ^m birth; का जन्म होना to be born

जानवर ^m animal

ज़िंदगी ^f life

डूबना to be immersed, drown

ढंग ^m way, manner

तरह तरह का of various kinds

तलाश ^f search; की तलाश करना to search for

तलाशना to search for

तहज़ीब ^f refinement, culture

तारीफ़ ^f praise; की तारीफ़ करना to praise

दुनिया ^f world

देखभाल ^f supervision, care; की देखभाल करना to take care of

देहान्त ^m death, demise; का देहान्त होना to die

न... न neither... nor

निंदा ^f blame, speaking ill; की निंदा करना to blame

निकालना to extract, bring out

निबंध ^m essay

नौकर-चाकर ^m servants etc.

पति-देव ^m 'respected husband'

(का) पीछा करना to follow

पेंसिल ^f pencil

पेशा ^m profession

प्याज़ ^m onion

प्रयोग ^m use, usage; का प्रयोग करना to use

बेवकूफ़ stupid

मदद ^f help; की मदद करना to help

मर्द ^m man, male

माला ^f garland

मालूम करना to ascertain

मीटिंग^f meeting

या तो... या   either... or

याद^f   memory; **याद आना** to be recalled, come to mind, be missed; **याद करना** to remember, learn by memory; to think of, summon (e.g. an employee); **याद दिलाना** to remind; **याद रखना** to keep in mind, not to forget; **याद रहना /होना** to be remembered

लहसुन^m   garlic

सदा   always, ever

सवारी^f   rider, passenger

साधन^m   means

सुनाई देना/पड़ना   to be heard, be audible

हरेक   each, every

हल^m solution; **हल होना** to be solved

17 | IF YOU WEREN'T SO STUBBORN...

अगर तुम इतनी ज़िद्दी न होतीं...

In this unit you will learn how to

- use a fuller range of conditional sentences
- express the sense 'although...'
- express nuance through new compound verbs
- distinguish formal and informal styles of vocabulary

 ### 17a Sangeeta angers Prakash

प्रकाश	संगीता बेटी, अगर मैं तुम्हारी शादी की बातचीत शुरू करता तो तुम्हें कैसा लगता ?
संगीता	अगर बातचीत खन्ना से होती तो मैं भाग जाती यहाँ से । मुझे हरीश से सख़्त नफ़रत है !
प्रकाश	तुम इतनी ज़िद्दी न होतीं तो बात बन जाती । हरीश का नाम मैंने कब लिया था ?
संगीता	अगर हरीश नहीं है तो कौन है पापा, जिसे तुम मेरा "जीवन-साथी" बनाना चाहते हो ?

प्रकाश	कल मैंने प्रताप की माँ को लंदन में फ़ोन किया था । वे कहती हैं कि प्रताप राज़ी हो जाएगा ।
संगीता	प्रताप ! वह तो इतना बदसूरत है और... अरे पापा, मज़ाक मत करना !
प्रकाश	हालाँकि प्रताप सुंदर तो नहीं है, फिर भी वह बड़ा होनहार लड़का है ।
संगीता	होनहार मेरा सिर !
प्रकाश	ऐसी बातें मुझसे क्यों सुनी जाएँगी – और अपनी बेटी के मुँह से !

बातचीत ^f	conversation; negotiation over marriage	का नाम लेना	to mention
भागना	to run away, flee	राज़ी	agreeable, content
ज़िद्दी	obstinate, stubborn	हालाँकि	although
बात बनना	an aim to be achieved, to go well	फिर भी	even so
		मेरा सिर	'my foot!'
		मुँह ^m	mouth, face

Prakash	Sangeeta (my) daughter, how would it be if I began marriage negotiations for you ?
Sangeeta	If the negotiations were with Khanna I'd run away from here. I detest Harish.
Prakash	If you weren't so stubborn we'd get somewhere. When did I mention Harish?
Sangeeta	If it's not Harish, who is that you want to make my 'life partner', Papa?
Prakash	Yesterday I phoned Pratap's mother in London. She says that Pratap would agree.
Sangeeta	Pratap! He's so ugly, and... oh Papa, don't joke!
Prakash	Although Pratap isn't handsome, he's a promising boy.
Sangeeta	Promising, my foot!
Prakash	Why should I listen to such things – and from my own daughter!

Grammar

17.1 Conditional sentences (2)

In 10.4 we saw how conditional sentences can use an imperfective, subjunctive or future verb in the अगर clause. Another possibility is a *perfective* verb, such as आया, मिला, or हुआ; thus अगर राम आया तो क्या तुम उससे मिलोगी? 'If Ram comes, will you meet him?' Using the perfective makes the अगर clause a given, a supposition – 'supposing Ram came...'.

अगर कुछ गरम पानी बाक़ी रहा तो मैं भी नहा लूँगा ।	If there's any hot water left I'll bathe too.
अगर तुम्हें छात्रवृत्ति मिली तो भारत जाओ ।	If you get the scholarship, go to India.
यदि मेरी योजना सफल हुई तो आपका भी लाभ होगा ।	If my plan succeeds you'll benefit too.

A condition that remains unfulfilled or hypothetical (e.g. 'if I were rich') uses the imperfective participle *without* auxiliary (e.g. होता, *without* था) in both clauses; the femine plural is nasalised. This construction is so unambiguously conditional that the अगर/यदि is often dropped.

(यदि) तुम मुझे बुलाते तो मैं ज़रूर आता ।	If you called me I would certainly come.
(अगर) मैं कवि होता तो तेरे बारे में कविता लिखता ।	If I were a poet I'd write poetry about you.
(अगर) सीता जी विदेश जातीं तो ज़्यादा पैसे कमातीं ।	If Sita ji went abroad she'd earn more.

The time frame here is unspecific: the first example could also mean 'If you had called me I would certainly have come'. When a specifically *past* time frame is needed, unfulfilled conditions can take a perfective participle + होता (e.g. बुलाया होता) in the अगर clause; the तो clause usually has an imperfective participle alone (आता).

(अगर) तुम १० बजे आए होते तो उनसे बात कर पाते ।	If you'd come at 10 o'clock you'd have been able to talk to them.
(अगर) टिकट मिली होती तो हम भी तुम्हारे साथ आते ।	If we'd received the ticket we would have come with you too.
(अगर) वह ध्यान से पढ़ी होती तो उसे डिगरी मिल जाती ।	If she'd studied attentively she would have got the degree.

Other tenses, such as the continuous, may also appear in an अगर clause:

अगर वह सो रही होती तो उसे जगाना ठीक नहीं होता ।	It wouldn't have been right to wake her if she'd been asleep.

Because they tell of situations which no longer have the potential to be fulfilled, such sentences are sometimes called 'counter-to-fact', 'contrafactuals', or 'impossible conditions'.

17.2 हालाँकि 'Although'

'Although' sentences have two clauses, the first introduced by हालाँकि 'although', the second by फिर भी or तो भी 'even so'.

हालाँकि वह ग़रीब है, फिर भी वह काफ़ी ख़ुश लगता है ।
Although he's poor, he seems quite happy.

हालाँकि उसकी हालत ख़राब है, फिर भी वह ठीक हो जाएगा ।
Although his condition is bad, he'll get better.

हालाँकि उसे बुलाया गया था, फिर भी वह नहीं आई ।
Although she was called, she didn't come.

हालाँकि मज़दूरों ने हड़ताल कर दी, फिर भी मालिक पर कोई असर नहीं पड़ा ।
Although the workers went on strike, it had no effect on the boss.

Formal Hindi uses the Sanskritic यद्यपि... तथापि.

यद्यपि संतोष की पुस्तक शीघ्र ही प्रकाशित हुई, तथापि वे प्रकाशक से संतुष्ट नहीं हैं ।
Although Santosh's book was published very quickly, he is not satisfied with the publisher.

यद्यपि उनकी स्थिति गंभीर है, तथापि वे सुधर जाएँगे ।
Although their situation is grave, they will improve.

17b Sangeeta angers Kamala

कमला	बेटी तुम अपने बाप को बहुत नाराज़ कर बैठीं । तुम्हारी बातें सुनकर उनसे रहा नहीं गया ।
संगीता	मैंने बस इतना कहा कि न हरीश से शादी करूँगी न प्रताप से, तो पिताजी बिगड़ उठे ।
कमला	लेकिन संगू, किसी से तो शादी करनी ही होगी तुम्हें !

संगीता	क्यों माँ ? जिस तरह तुम फँस गईं, उसी तरह मुझे भी फँस जाना है क्या ?
कमला	तुमसे कौन बात करे । कोई अच्छी-सी बात भी कहे तो तुम लड़ने लगती हो ।
सुरेश	[*कमरे में आकर*] यह क्या महाभारत मच रहा है ?
संगीता	अंकल मैंने माँ से कितनी दफ़ा कह रखा है कि शादी नहीं करूँगी मगर वे तो मानतीं नहीं ।
कमला	सुरेश, यह लड़की मेरे सारे सपने तोड़ डालना चाहती है !
सुरेश	ओ कमला, किसके सभी सपने पूरे होते हैं ?

बिगड़ना	to go wrong, get angry	मचना	to break out, be caused
फँसना	to be stuck, caught, snared	दफ़ा ^f	time, occasion
महाभारत ^m	India's mythical epic war		

Kamala	Daughter, you've gone and made your father very angry. He was beside himself at what you said.
Sangeeta	All I said was that I won't marry either Harish or Pratap, and Father went mad.
Kamala	But Sangoo, you'll have to marry someone!
Sangeeta	Why Mum? Must I get trapped the same way you did?
Kamala	Who could talk to you. Even if someone talks nicely to you, you start fighting.
Suresh	[*coming into the room*] What's this Mahabharata breaking out?
Sangeeta	Uncle, I've told Mum so many times that I won't marry, but she won't accept (it).
Kamala	Suresh, this girl wants to shatter all my dreams.
Suresh	O Kamala, who has all their dreams fulfilled?

Grammar
17.3 Compound verbs (2)

Compound verbs using the auxiliaries जाना, लेना and देना were introduced in 12.4. It is now time to look at some more auxiliaries. Remember that ने constructions apply only when main verb and auxiliary *both* take ने.

डालना indicates that an action is done vigorously, decisively, violently, or recklessly:

गुंडों ने मेरे कुरते को फाड़ डाला ।	The ruffians tore my kurta apart.
दंगे के दिन उन्होंने तीन आदमियों को मार डाला ।	On the day of the riot they killed three men.
दवा पीने से तबियत ठीक हो जाएगी – पी डालो !	Taking the medicine will make you better – drink it down!

बैठना implies that an action was done foolishly or stubbornly:

ओहो ! छोटू क्या कर बैठा है ?	Oho! What's Chotu gone and done?
जो भी मन में आया, उमा वही कह बैठी ।	Uma blurted out whatever came into her mind.
उस दिन हम सचमुच ग़लती कर बैठे ।	That day we really blundered.

पड़ना adds a sense of suddenness or change of state. Its literal sense 'to fall' sometimes shows through in a sense of *downward* movement:

ज्योंही गाड़ी रुकी त्योंही हम उतर पड़े ।	We got down as soon as the train stopped.
मैं रो पड़ा मगर तू हँस पड़ी ।	I burst into tears but you burst out laughing.
अचानक ऐसा हुआ कि तीन अजनबी डिब्बे में घुस पड़े ।	Suddenly it happened that three strangers burst into the compartment.

उठना suggests the inception of an action or feeling. Its literal sense 'to rise' sometimes shows through in a sense of *upward* movement:

हड़ताल की ख़बर सुनकर पिताजी बिगड़ उठे ।	Hearing news of the strike Father lost his temper.
लकड़ियों का ढेर जल उठा ।	The pile of logs burst into flames.
जब तुम बाँसुरी बजाने लगे तो बूढ़े नाच उठे ।	When you began playing the flute the old men broke into a dance.

रखना – the basic sense of 'to keep, maintain' can imply a firmness of action, or one whose results or implications might last over time:

सुनो, चाबी मैंने पुलिस को दे रखी है – उनसे लेकर दरवाज़ा खोल लेना ।	Listen, I've given the key to the police; get (it) from them and open the door.
हमने उसको साफ़ कह रखा है कि हम नहीं जाएँगे, मगर वह मानता ही नहीं ।	We've told him clearly that we won't go, but he just won't accept (it).
हमने एक अच्छा-सा घर देख रखा है ।	We've seen, got our eye on, a pretty good house.

17.4 The vocabulary of Hindi

Like all languages, Hindi inherits vocabulary from a variety of sources. This contributes to its flexibility and richness. Different contexts need different styles of vocabulary: formal Hindi uses many Sanskrit loanwords, whereas colloquial Hindi admits a freer mix of words from Sanskrit, Persian, English and Portuguese. (Some Persian loanwords come from Arabic and Turkish.) The name 'Hindi' is itself Persian. It's important to be aware of these different 'registers' in order to be able to hit the right tone: heavily Sanskritised Hindi, for example, may sound comically over-formal in everyday speech, just as saying 'One desires a residence in relative proximity to the terminus' would sound odd when telling someone that you wanted a house quite near the station. Yet some speakers (like Arun in dialogue 12b) do favour a Sanskritised style, even in conversation.

The main stylistic choice, then, is between a formal-sounding word (usually Sanskritic) and an informal, colloquial synonym (often Persian). Here are some common synonyms or near-synonyms.

PERSO-ARABIC	SANSKRIT	
अख़बार ^m	समाचार-पत्र ^m	newspaper
अगर	यदि	if
अफ़सोस ^m	खेद ^m	regret
आख़िर ^m	अन्त ^m	end

PERSO–ARABIC	SANSKRIT	
आम	साधारण	ordinary
उम्मीद ^f	आशा ^f	hope
किताब ^f	पुस्तक ^f	book
ख़त ^m	पत्र ^m	letter
ख़त्म	समाप्त	finished
ख़बर ^f	समाचार ^f	news
खाना ^m	भोजन ^m	food
ख़ास	विशेष	special
ख़ूबसूरत	सुन्दर	beautiful
गोश्त ^m	माँस ^m	meat
ज़बान ^f	भाषा ^f	language
ज़रूर	अवश्य	of course, certainly
ज़रूरत ^f	आवश्यकता ^f	need, necessity
जवाब ^m	उत्तर ^m	reply
ज़्यादा	अधिक	more
तकलीफ़ ^f	कष्ट ^m	trouble
दोस्त ^m	मित्र ^m	friend
नामुमकिन	असंभव	impossible
फ़र्क़ ^m	भेद ^m, अंतर ^m	difference
फ़ायदा ^m	लाभ ^m	profit, advantage
फ़ुरसत ^f	अवकाश ^m	leisure time
मुमकिन	संभव	possible
मुलाक़ात ^f	भेंट ^f	meeting
मुश्किल	कठिन	difficult
मुसाफ़िर ^m	यात्री ^m	traveller
मेहरबानी ^f	कृपा ^f	kindness
लेकिन, मगर	परंतु, किंतु	but
वक़्त ^m	समय ^f	time
वजह ^f	कारण ^m	reason, cause
शादी ^f	विवाह ^m	marriage

PERSO-ARABIC	SANSKRIT	
शुक्रिया	धन्यवाद	thank you
शुरू ^m	आरंभ ^m	beginning
सफ़र ^m	यात्रा ^f	journey
सवाल ^m	प्रश्न ^m	question
साल ^m	वर्ष ^m	year
हफ़्ता ^m	सप्ताह ^m	week

English words are also used very commonly in Hindi – as favoured by Prem in dialogue 9b. In cities like Delhi and Bombay, words such as क़लम, घड़ी, प्याला, बायाँ, दाहिना are losing ground to their English equivalents – पेन, वॉच, कप, लेफ़्ट, राइट. Helped by the rapid expansion of satellite television, Hindi is now absorbing English words faster than ever. The influence of English even extends into Hindi idiom (e.g. दूसरे शब्दों में 'in other words') and, occasionally, syntax; but such matters are beyond the scope of this book. The positive side of this is that learners of Hindi can feel free to use an English word for which they don't know the Hindi – इसमें कोई "प्रॉब्लम" नहीं है!

 Recognising source languages: only Sanskrit loanwords contain ज्ञ, ण, ष, क्ष, : (*avagraha*); only words inherited from Persian contain क़, ख़, ग़.

The facility of basing innumerable verbs on करना greatly aids the take-up of loanwords, and even such unexpected items as की लुक-आफ़्टर करना 'to look after' (with feminine gender following देखभाल) are not uncommon in informal speech.

Some words which seem familiar from English are far from being loanwords: the intransitive verb कटना 'to be cut' and its transitive equivalent काटना 'to cut' derive from Sanskrit – evidence of the ancient links between Indo-European languages. By the same token, English has borrowed numerous words from Hindi: words such as लूटना, ठग and खाट are not derived from 'to loot', 'thug' 'cot', but are the *sources* of these English words.

Although many English words are widely understood in India, this comprehension depends on their following *Indian* pronunciation.

The phonetic nature of the Devanagari script prepares the learner for this, as Hindi spellings reflect Indian pronunciations of English words.

Some Hindi-speakers find initial conjuncts such as the 'sk' in स्कूल easier to pronounce if an initial vowel is added: forms such as इस्कूल, इस्टेशन are sometimes heard (but are rare in writing).

EXERCISE 17a.1 Translate.

1 If you had gone by plane you would have arrived by now.
2 Although I tried to stop them, they did not pay attention to my advice.
3 If Delhi weren't so far from here I'd come to see you straightaway.
4 If I'd known how bad his state was I wouldn't have told him the truth.
5 If the hero weren't so popular, nobody would come to see such a film.
6 Although she knew my grandfather well, she suggested we invite him.
7 If you'd told me how serious the problem was I would not have wasted my time.
8 Although I said that this was not my fault, he still complained.

EXERCISE 17a.2 Rewrite, using a हालांकि construction. Then translate the new version.

१   कोशिश करने पर भी मैं काम को पूरा नहीं कर पाया ।

२   मैं रात भर तलाश करती रही, पर वह पुराना पत्र नहीं मिला ।

३   मैंने रस्सी को काटने की बहुत कोशिश की मगर वह कटी नहीं ।

४   हमारे शिकायत करने पर भी कोई परवाह नहीं करता ।

EXERCISE 17a.3 Write a new Dialogue 16a (between Chotu and Khanna ji) as Chotu would have liked it to go.

EXERCISE 17b.1 Answer the questions on Dialogues 16b (1-4) and 17a (5-8).

१   खन्ना जी को किस बात की चिंता है ?

२   क्या उमा भी इस बात के बारे में परेशान है ? इसका कारण क्या है ?

३   खन्ना जी क्यों सोचते हैं कि हरीश को संगीता से शादी नहीं करनी चाहिए ?

४   शादी के मामले में आप किनके विचारों से सहमत हैं – खन्ना के या उमा के ? क्यों ?

५   क्या संगीता हरीश से इतना प्यार करती है जितना हरीश उससे करता है ?

६   प्रकाश क्यों कहता है कि संगीता ज़िद्दी है ?

७   क्या प्रकाश अनीता से बात कर चुका है ? क्या उनकी बातचीत रूबरू हुई थी ?

८   अगर आप प्रताप की जगह होते/ होतीं, तो क्या आप संगीता की गुस्ताख़ी को माफ़
      करते / करतीं?   क्यों/ क्यों नहीं?

✔ EXERCISE 17b.2 Rewrite the following, using compound verbs as
indicated; then translate.

१   एक साल के अन्दर मैंने पूरे सात लेख लिखे । [+ डालना]

२   उसने जो पैसे बड़ी मेहनत करके कमाये थे, सब को गँवाया है । [+ देना]

३   अरे, तुम किस तरह की पागल बातें बोले ? [+ बैठना]

४   मेरे बेटे ने गुस्से में अपने सबसे क़ीमती कपड़ों को फाड़ा । [+ डालना]

५   समाचार को सुनकर छोटू हँसा [+ उठना] लेकिन दूसरे लोग रोए । [+ पड़ना]

६   पुलिस ने कहा [+ रखना] है कि बेचारा खिड़की से गिरा था । [+ पड़ना]

७   जैसे ही दूसरे लोग आए [+ जाना], हमने काम आरंभ किया । [+ देना]

८   जिसने हमारे दोस्त को मारा [+ डालना], उससे हम रूबरू बात करें । [+ लेना]

✔ EXERCISE 17b.3 Write five Hindi sentences using Perso-Arabic
vocabulary from the list in 17.4, then rewrite them in a more formal
register using synonyms from the Sanskrit list.

Vocabulary

अंतर ^m difference	उत्तर ^m reply
अजनबी ^m stranger	उबलना to boil, rage
असर ^m effect, impact; असर पड़ना	ओहो oho! oh no!
to have an effect	कटना to be cut
आख़िर ^m end	कवि ^m poet
आरंभ ^m beginning	कष्ट ^m trouble, distress
उतरना to get down, alight	काटना to cut

किंतु but

क़ीमती costly, valuable

ख़बर ^f news

खाट ^f bedstead, 'cot'

गंभीर serious, profound

गुस्सा ^m anger; angry

घड़ी ^f wristwatch

घुसना to enter (forcibly, or uninvited)

छात्रवृत्ति ^f scholarship

जलना to burn

ज़िद्दी obstinate, stubborn

ठग ^m swindler, robber

ढीला loose

ढेर ^m pile, heap

तथापि nevertheless, even so

दंगा ^m riot

दफ़ा ^f time, occasion

दिमाग़ ^m mind, brain

नाचना to dance

(का) नाम लेना to mention

नामुमकिन impossible

निहायत extremely

प्रकाशित published

प्रश्न ^m question

फँसना to be stuck, caught, snared

फाड़ना to tear

फिर भी even so

बरदाश्त करना to tolerate, endure

बाँसुरी ^f bamboo flute

बाक़ी remaining, left

बात बनना an aim to be achieved, to go well

बातचीत ^f conversation, negotiation

बिगड़ना to go wrong, get angry

भागना to run away, flee

भेद ^m difference

मचना to break out, be caused

मज़दूर ^m worker, labourer

महाभारत ^m India's mythical epic war

माँस ^m meat

मुँह ^m mouth, face

मुसाफ़िर ^m traveller

मेरा सिर 'my foot!'

यद्यपि although

यात्रा ^f journey, travel

योजना ^f plan, scheme

रस्सी ^f string, cord

राज़ी agreeable, content

रूबरू face to face

रोकना to stop

लकड़ी ^f wood; stick

लाभ ^m profit, advantage

लूटना to loot, steal, pillage

लोकप्रिय popular

वर्ष ^m year

वापस मिलना to be got back

शीघ्र soon, quickly

शूटिंग ^f	'shooting', filming	साधारण	ordinary
संतुष्ट	satisfied	सुझाव ^m	suggestion; **सुझाव देना** to
संतोष ^m	satisfaction		make a suggestion
सप्ताह ^m	week	सुधरना	to improve, be put right
सफ़र ^m	journey, travel	हड़ताल ^f	strike, lockout; **हड़ताल**
समाचार-पत्र ^m	newspaper	**करना**	to strike
समाप्त	finished, concluded	हालाँकि	although
सहमत	in agreement		

18 | A LOVE THAT WON'T BE STOPPED

ऐसा प्यार जो रोके भी नहीं रुकता

In this unit you will learn how to
- use participles for several new functions
- distinguish transitive and intransitive verbs
- use causative verbs – to 'get something done'

18a   Sangeeta confides in Suresh

सुरेश	तुम हाथों में सिर थामे क्यों बैठी हो संगीता ? तुम्हें क्या तकलीफ़ है ?
संगीता	माँ की ज़िद सुनते सुनते मैं तंग आ गई हूँ अंकल । वे किसी छुटभैये से मेरी शादी करने पर तुली हुई हैं । और बिना मेरी राय पूछे !
सुरेश	ज़ाहिर है कि तुम्हारा दिल किसी और से लगा हुआ है । मैंने अभी तुम्हें किसी आदमी से बातें करते हुए सुना है फ़ोन पर । कौन था ?
संगीता	वही था जिससे मुझे प्यार है । या तो उसी से शादी करूँगी, या करूँगी ही नहीं – दुनिया चाहे माने या न माने !
सुरेश	वह अधेड़ उम्र का शख़्स तो नहीं है, जिसे मैंने परसों-नरसों प्रताप के साथ बग़ीचे में टहलता हुआ देखा ? वह सुहास ?
संगीता	हाँ, वही । और मैं तो जी ही नहीं सकती उसके बिना । वह अभी यहाँ आ रहा है, मुझसे मिलने । उसके आते ही हम दोनों साथ भाग निकलेंगे ।
सुरेश	अरे तुम क्या पागल इरादा बना बैठी हो ? किसी अजनबी से इस तरह इश्क़ लड़ाते हुए तुम्हें शर्म नहीं आती ?
संगीता	इसमें शर्म की क्या बात है ? अगर सुहास अजनबी भी होता तो भी मैं उससे प्यार करती । लेकिन जिसके बेटे को इस घर में रहते कोई आठ महीने हुए हैं, उसे अजनबी कैसे कहा जा सकता है ?
सुरेश	इसी घर में ? तुम्हारा कहने का मतलब.... प्रताप ? संगू, तुम क्या कह रही हो ?
संगीता	[ठंडी साँस भरकर] हाँ, सुहास प्रताप का पिता है ।

सुरेश	अब बात समझ में आ रही है कुछ कुछ ! जो नेपाली ज़ेवर तुम पहने हुए थीं उस दिन, वे सुहास के दिए हुए थे, न कि प्रताप के ! मगर... मगर... जिसकी शादी किसी और से हो चुकी है उससे तुम कैसे शादी करोगी, संगू ?
संगीता	सुहास शादी-शुदा नहीं है, तलाक़-शुदा है । अनीता को छोड़े हुए उसे पूरे चार साल हो गए हैं ।
सुरेश	तो क्या तुम्हारे बेचारे माँ-बाप को इन सारी प्रेम-कहानियों की कुछ ख़बर है ?
संगीता	[उठकर, *बाहर देखती हुई*] घर छोड़ते वक़्त मैं उन्हें सब कुछ समझा दूँगी । सब कुछ समझा दूँगी... [*बाहर से रुकती हुई टैक्सी की आवाज़ सुनाई देती है*]

थामना	to hold, support	नरसों	three days ago/ahead
ज़िद f	obstinacy	टहलना	to stroll
तंग आना	to be fed up	इश्क़ m	romantic love; **इश्क़ लड़ाना** to have an affair
छुटभैया m	a nobody, someone of no importance		
X की शादी Y से करना	to marry X to Y	शर्म f	shame; **शर्म आना** to feel ashamed
तुलना	to be determined (to, **पर**)	साँस f	sigh; **ठंडी साँस भरना** to heave a deep sigh
राय f	opinion		
ज़ाहिर	clear, evident	न कि	and not
अधेड़	middle aged	तलाक़-शुदा	divorced
शख़्स m	individual, fellow	समझाना	to explain

Suresh	Why are you sitting holding your head in your hands, Sangeeta? What's your trouble?
Sangeeta	I'm fed up listening constantly to Mum's obstinacy, Uncle. She's determined to marry me to some nobody. And without asking my opinion!
Suresh	It's clear that you're in love with someone else. I just heard you talking to some man on the phone. Who was it?
Sangeeta	It was the person I'm in love with. I'll either marry him, or won't marry at all – whether the world accepts it or not!
Suresh	It's not that middle-aged fellow I saw strolling in the garden with Pratap two or three days ago? That Suhas?

Sangeeta	Yes, him. And I cannot *live* without him. He's just coming here to meet me. As soon as he arrives we'll elope together.
Suresh	Oh no, what mad scheme have you gone and made up? Aren't you ashamed, carrying on with some stranger like this?
Sangeeta	What's shameful about it? Even if Suhas were a stranger I'd still love him. But how can someone whose son has been living in this house for some eight months be called a stranger?
Suresh	In this house? You mean to say... Pratap? Sangoo, what are you saying?
Sangeeta	[*heaving a deep sigh*] Yes, Suhas is Pratap's father.
Suresh	Now I'm beginning to understand the thing a little! That Nepali jewellery you were wearing that day was given by Suhas, not by Pratap! But... but... how will you marry someone who's already married to someone else, Sangoo?
Sangeeta	Suhas isn't married, he's divorced. It's a full four years since he left Anita.
Suresh	So are your poor parents aware of all these love stories at all?
Sangeeta	[*getting up, looking out*] As I leave home I'll explain everything to them. I'll explain everything... [*the sound of a stopping taxi is heard from outside*]

Grammar
18.1 Participles

In English, participles like 'passing, passed' can either be part of a main verb ('the days are passing, the days have passed'), or can have a subsidiary role to the main verb, acting adverbially ('the days seem short in passing' or adjectivally 'I remember passed days'). A similar process applies in Hindi, using the imperfective and perfective participles (बीतता, बीता) in a number of constructions.

Sometimes the participle may take the auxiliary हुआ, whose slight effect is to confirm the *ongoing* quality of an imperfective (बीतता हुआ 'passing'), or the *completed* quality of a perfective (बीता हुआ 'passed').

Adding हुआ can resolve ambiguity. The basic sentence खिलौना टूटा था can mean either 'the toy was broken' (a state) or 'the toy had broken' (a past action). The former sense is specified by adding हुआ (खिलौना टूटा हुआ था), and the latter sense is specified by using a compound verb (खिलौना टूट गया था).

Used as an adjective, the participle (+ auxiliary) agrees with the noun it qualifies:

IMPERFECTIVE		PERFECTIVE	
बीतते (हुए) दिन	passing days	बीते (हुए) दिन	passed days
जलती (हुई) कार	a burning car	जली (हुई) कार	a burned car
हँसते (हुए) लड़के	laughing boys	फटी (हुई) किताबें	torn books

पुलिस ने भागते हुए चोर को पकड़ा ।	The police caught the absconding thief.
माँ ने रोती हुई लड़की को गोद में उठा लिया ।	Mother took up the crying girl into her lap.
वह रेडियो सुनता हुआ आदमी कौन है ?	Who is that man listening to the radio?
हमने कोई लड़की सड़क पर बैठी हुई देखी ।	We saw some girl sitting ('seated') on the road.
पलंग पर कुछ कपड़े पड़े हुए थे ।	There were some clothes lying ('fallen') on the bed.
वह रेशम की बनी हुई साड़ी सबसे सुन्दर है ।	That sari made of silk is the loveliest.

The perfective participle usages just shown describe a *state* that results from a previous *action*: the girl *had sat down* on the road (action) and consequently was now 'sitting' there (state); the clothes *had fallen* onto the bed (action) and consequently were now 'lying' there (state).

Used as an adverb, the participle (+ auxiliary) has an invariable -ए ending:

चिड़िया आकाश में उड़ते हुए दिखाई दी ।	The bird appeared flying in the sky.
हमने भूत को चलते-फिरते देखा ।	We saw the ghost wandering about.

मैंने उन्हें आपकी तारीफ़ करते सुना है ।	I have heard them praising you.
माँ अपना सामान पकड़े हुए खड़ी थीं ।	Mother was standing holding her luggage.
धोबी इस्तरी को लिए हुए आया था ।	The dhobi had come bringing ('taking') the iron.
वह सलवार क़मीज़ पहने हुए थी ।	She was wearing a salwar-qamiz.

> **!** खड़ा 'standing' is an adjective rather than a verb participle; but it behaves just like बैठा 'sitting, seated', पड़ा 'lying, fallen', लेटा 'lying, reclined' etc. Like these participles, it can take an auxiliary – खड़ा हुआ (like बैठा हुआ and पड़ा हुआ).

Participle constructions based on these principles are many and various. Here are some of the most important ones:

a) A participle is repeated (without हुआ) when an action is repeated over time:

दिन भर खेलते खेलते बच्चे थक गए ।	Playing all day the children got tired.
इंतज़ार करते करते वह बेचैन हो रही थी ।	Waiting constantly she was becoming restless.
बस्ती में घूमते घूमते हम ऊब गए ।	We got bored wandering around the settlement.

Or when an action runs in parallel to that of the main verb:

टी०वी० को देखते देखते मैं इस्तरी कर रहा था ।	While watching TV, I was doing the ironing.
गाड़ी की मरम्मत करते करते मिस्तरी गाना गाता रहा ।	While repairing the car the mechanic went on singing.
हिन्दी सीखते सीखते हम हँसी-मज़ाक भी कम नहीं करते ।	While learning Hindi we have plenty of laughs too.

Or to stress that the main-verb action happened *just* as the subsidiary action was done:

> घर पहुँचते पहुँचते मेरे मन में तरह तरह की शंकाएँ पैदा हुईं ।
>
> Arriving home, many kinds of doubts arose in my mind.
>
> निबंध ख़त्म करते करते मुझे महसूस होने लगा कि मैंने ग़लत विषय चुना है ।
>
> As I finished the essay I began to feel that I'd chosen the wrong subject.

b) A repeated imperfective participle in -ए followed by बचना 'to escape, survive' describes a narrow escape:

साइकिल से टकराकर वह गिरते गिरते बचा ।	Colliding with the bicycle, he nearly fell.
पुल से गिरकर वह डूबते डूबते बची ।	Falling from the bridge she narrowly escaped drowning.

c) An imperfective participle in -ए followed by समय or वक़्त means 'at the time of doing':

घर जाते समय हमसे मिलना ।	Meet us on your way home.
मरते वक़्त लोगों को बचपन के दिन याद आते हैं ।	At the time of dying, people remember their childhood days.

d) An imperfective participle in -ए followed by ही means 'immediately on doing', 'as soon as':

होटल पहुँचते ही हमने खाना खा लिया ।	We had our meal as soon as we reached the hotel.
पत्र पाते ही मैंने उत्तर लिख डाला ।	Immediately on receiving the letter I dashed off a reply.

In the two examples above, the main verb and the participle share a single subject. But when two separate entities are involved, the participle may be 'possessed' (using का) by one of them:

ख़त के आते ही मैंने जवाब लिख डाला ।	As soon as the letter came I dashed off a reply.

| आपके स्वीकार करते ही दूसरों को भी बुलाया जाएगा । | As soon as you accept, the others will be invited too. |

e) To indicate the passage of time *since a completed event took place*, the perfective participle is used as follows, with the unit of time as grammatical subject:

| मेरे कुत्ते को मरे हुए सिर्फ़ एक महीना हुआ है । | It's only one month since my dog died. |
| श्रुति को ग्वालियर गए दो हफ़्ते हो गए हैं । | It's two weeks since Shruti went to Gwalior. |

f) To indicate the passage of time *since a current situation began*, the imperfective participle is used as follows:

| मुझे उर्दू सीखते हुए आठ महीने हुए हैं । | I've been learning Urdu for eight months. |
| लंदन में रहते हुए हमें एक साल हुआ है । | We've been living in London for one year. |

g) बिना + perfective participle in -ए (e.g. किए) means 'without doing':

| वह बिना बोले घास काटने लगा । | Without speaking he began to cut the grass. |
| बिना सोचे कुछ मत करना । | Don't do anything without thinking. |

h) Both participles can be 'possessed' like nouns:

मेरा कहा कोई नहीं मानता ।	Nobody accepts what I say ('my utterance').
यह लेख मेरा लिखा हुआ है ।	This article was written by me.
रवि के रहते तू कुछ नहीं कर सकती ।	You can't do anything while Ravi's around.
मेरे जीते जी यह घर बेचा नहीं जाएगा ।	As long as I'm alive this house won't be sold.

i) A pairing of related transitive and intransitive verbs indicates the failure of an attempt (in the intransitive verb) despite someone's trying (in the transitive, 'possessed' by the person making the attempt):

हमारे बचाए वह नहीं बची ।	She didn't survive, despite our trying to save her.
ड्राइवर के रोके भी कार रुक नहीं पाई ।	Despite the driver's trying to stop it the car couldn't stop.
छोटू के उड़ाते भी वह पतंग तो उड़ने का नाम नहीं लेती ।	For all Chotu's attempts, that kite just refuses to fly.

18b   A happy ending

NB: all the quotations in this dialogue are from classic film songs.

[सुहास और संगीता बैठक के एक कोने में सटे हुए बैठे हैं । प्रताप, सुरेश, और कुमार परिवार के सारे सदस्य भी पास बैठे हुए हैं – सिवाय प्रकाश के, जो तेज़ कदमों से बैठक को माप रहा है ।]

प्रकाश   *[झट से ऐनक उतारके]* यह शादी नहीं हो सकती ! मेरे जीते जी यह शादी नहीं होगी !

दादी जी   बेटे, थोड़ी दया से काम लो ! संगू के लिए किसी अच्छे-से लड़के की तलाश

	थी, तो यह सुहास टपक पड़ा ! बड़ा नेक आदमी है, और अच्छे स्वभाव का भी लगता है । इसमें क्या कमी है ? और प्यार जो है...
ऋषि	कमाल है, यहाँ सब लोग फ़िल्मी डॉयलॉग झाड़ने लगे हैं ! [*गाते हुए*] "कभी कभी मेरे दिल में ख़याल आता है... कि जैसे तुझको बनाया गया है मेरे लिए..."
सुरेश	कमला, ज़रा चाय बनवा दो न, सबों के लिए ?
कमला	ऐसे वक़्त में आपको चाय पीने-पिलवाने की कैसे सूझ सकती ?
ऋषि	"... तू सब से पहले सितारों में बस रही थी कहीं... तुझे ज़मीं पे बुलाया गया है मेरे लिए... कभी कभी..."
संगीता	अरे चुप भी करो ऋषि !
सुहास	प्रताप, टैक्सीवाले को कहलवा दो कि वह चला जाए ।
सुरेश	हाँ, टैक्सी को तो बाद में वापस बुलवाया जा सकता है । या आपका यहीं रुकने का इरादा है सुहास ?
कमला	[*सुरेश की बात को काटकर*] सुहास जी, आगे चलकर आप कहाँ रहने की सोच रहे हैं ?
सुहास	कमला जी, मेरा लखनऊ में एक अच्छा-सा घर है । और जैसे ही मेरा लन्दन-वाला घर बिक जाएगा वैसे ही एक नया घर बनवा लूँगा, यहीं दिल्ली में ही आपके इस घर के सामने...
ऋषि	[*एक नया गीत छेड़ते हुए*] "तेरे घर के सामने इक घर बनाऊँगा, तेरे घर के सामने दुनिया बसाऊँगा , तेरे..."
प्रकाश	ऋषि चुप कर । बहुत हो गया । [*सुहास की ओर मुड़कर, त्योरी चढ़ाते हुए*] आपका धंधा क्या है ? आपके गुज़ारे के साधन...?
सुहास	मैं नर्तक हूँ । मेरे लन्दन में रहते समय, जो भारतीय मूल के परिवार वहाँ बस गए हैं, वे मुझसे अपने बच्चों को कथक सिखवाते थे । अब तो मुझे भारत में ही यही काम करने के लिए बुलवाया गया है । श्रावण से स्थायी रूप से इस देश में बसा हुआ हूँ ।
ऋषि	[*फिर से गीत बदलकर*] "सावन का महीना, पवन करे सोर... जियरा रे झूमे ऐसे जैसे बनमा नाचे मोर..."
प्रकाश	[*कमला के कान में फुसफुसाते हुए*] इस साले नचवैये से तुम हमारी इकलौती बेटी की शादी करवाओगी क्या ? हमीं को नाच नचा रहा है यह ! [*सुहास की ओर बढ़ते हुए*] तो सुहास, आपको किसने यहाँ बुलाया है, दिल्ली की छोकरियों को नाच-वाच कराने के लिए ?

सुहास	सरकारी नौकरी है । स्वयं प्रधान मंत्री ने मुझे यह नौकरी दिलवाई थी, यानी उन्होंने ही मुझे सुझाव दिया था कि मैं इस नौकरी के लिए अर्ज़ी दूँ ।
प्रकाश	[*बड़े आश्चर्य से, खुले दिल से मुस्कराते हुए*] अच्छा ! तो नृत्य की दुनिया में आप काफ़ी जाने-पहचाने होंगे । अच्छा-सा वेतन भी मिलता होगा ! [*कमला से, कान में*] संगीता की माँ, बंगाली मार्केट से बढ़िया-सी मिठाई तुरंत मँगवाओ – लड्डू, जलेबियाँ...। [*सुहास से, बड़ी आत्मीयता से*] तो कहिए जनाब, क्या चलेगा ? चाय लेंगे ? नहीं नहीं, चाय का वक़्त निकल गया । बियर लेंगे कि व्हिस्की ?
अरुण	[*अपने आप से*] ऐसा प्रतीत होता है कि हमारी पारिवारिक परिस्थितियों में एक आश्चर्यजनक परिवर्तन शीघ्र ही आनेवाला है ।
सुहास	[*उठ खड़े होकर*] जो भी संगीता लेगी, वही लूँगा । [*संगीता की तरफ़ मुड़ते हुए*] संगू, तुम ही नहीं, तुम्हारे सारे घरवाले भी लाजवाब हैं !

ऋषि और राज	[*हाथ में हाथ मिलाए, नाचते हुए, एक चौथा गीत छेड़कर*] "चौदहवीं का चाँद हो, या आफ़ताब हो; जो भी हो तुम – ख़ुदा की क़सम, लाजवाब हो..." ।
प्रकाश	[*सुहास को गले लगाते हुए*] आओ सुहास बेटे !
सुहास और संगीता	[*एक साथ, प्रकाश से*] पिताजी ! पिताजी !
प्रताप	[*सुहास से*] पिताजी ! तुम्हारे सारे सपने पूरे हो रहे हैं ! ख़ुदा की क़सम, यह तो बड़ा कामयाब दिन निकला !
सुरेश	कामयाब मेरा सिर ! यह डॉयलॉग बहुत लंबा हो रहा है । मैं तो चलता हूँ ।

दादी जी   फ़िल्मी गाने क्या मुझे नहीं आते ? [झूमती हुई, मस्त आवाज़ में गाने
                  लगती हैं] "अच्छा तो हम चलते हैं ! फिर कब मिलोगे ? जब तुम कहोगे
                  ....." [सब लोग हँसते हँसते लोट-पोट हो जाते हैं]

बैठक ^f   sitting room

सदस्य ^m   member

पास   nearby

तेज़   quick, rapid

क़दम ^m   step, pace

मापना   to measure, cover

झट से   suddenly, briskly

ऐनक ^f   spectacles

के जीते जी   during the lifetime of

दया ^f   compassion

स्वभाव ^m   nature, disposition

टपकना   to appear (unexpectedly), drop in

नेक   good, virtuous, decent

कमी ^f   lack, want

कमाल ^m   miracle, wonder

डॉयलॉग ^m   dialogue

झाड़ना   to spout, pour out

बनवाना   to cause to be made

सूझना   to occur to the mind; की [बात] सूझना [an idea] to occur

सितारा ^m   star

बसना   to dwell, settle, inhabit

ज़मीं ^f (usually ज़मीन) ^f   land, earth

पे (=पर)   on, to

चुप करना   to be quiet, shut up

कहलवाना   to send word

बुलवाना   to cause to be called

बात काटना   to interrupt

आगे चलकर   later on, in the future

की [बात] सोचना   to think of doing, intend to do

छेड़ना   to stir up, start up

इक (=एक)   a, one

बसाना   to settle, found

त्योरी ^f   brow; त्योरी चढ़ाना to frown, scowl

धंधा ^m   work, occupation

नर्तक ^m   dancer

मूल ^m   origin

कथक ^m   kathak, a North Indian dance style

सिखवाना   to cause to be taught

श्रावण ^m   Shravan, a monsoon month (July–August)

स्थायी रूप से   permanently

सावन ^m   = श्रावण

पवन ^m   wind

करे   (dialect) = करता/करती है

सोर ^m (=शोर)   noise, tumult (poetic)

जियरा ^m   soul, heart (poetic)

झूमना   to sway (in pleasure); झूमे (dialect) = झूमता है

बन ^m forest, wood, jungle; **बनमा** (dialect) = **बन में**

नाचना to dance; **नाचे** (dialect) = **नाचता है**

कान ^m ear

साला ^{m, adj} wife's brother; term of abuse

नचवैया ^m dancer (derogatory)

इकलौता sole, only (child)

नाच ^m dance; **नाच नचाना** to lead one a fine dance

छोकरी ^f young girl, lass

प्रधान मंत्री ^m prime minister

दिलवाना to cause to be given

यानी that is to say

अर्ज़ी ^f application; **अर्ज़ी देना** to apply

आश्चर्य ^m surprise

खुला open

मुस्कराना to smile

नृत्य ^m dance

जाना-पहचाना recognised, known

वेतन ^m pay, salary

आत्मीयता से cordially

जनाब sir

ह्विस्की ^f whisky

प्रतीत होना to appear, seem

पारिवारिक familial

परिस्थिति(याँ) ^f circumstance(s)

आश्चर्यजनक astonishing

लाजवाब beyond compare

हाथ मिलाना to join hands

चौदहवीं 14th (day of lunar month – full moon day)

आफ़ताब ^m sun

खुदा ^m God; **खुदा की क़सम** by God

क़सम ^f oath

गला ^m throat, neck; **गले लगाना** to embrace

मस्त blithely joyful, delighted

कामयाब successful

लोट-पोट rolling, helpless (with laughter)

[Suhas and Sangeeta are sitting close in a corner of the sitting room. Pratap, Suresh, and all the members of the Kumar family are also sitting nearby – except Prakash, who is pacing rapidly up and down the room.]

Prakash *[whipping his glasses off]* This marriage cannot take place! As long as I'm alive this marriage will not happen!

Dadi ji Son, have a little compassion! We were looking for a suitable boy for Sangoo, and this Suhas turns up! He's a very decent man, and seems kind-hearted. What is there lacking in him? And this thing called love...

Rishi	How amazing, everyone's started spouting film dialogues here. [*singing*] 'At times I fancy in my heart... that just as you were made for me...'
Suresh	Kamala, just get tea made for everybody, won't you?
Kamala	How could you think of drinking and offering tea at such a time?
Rishi	'... You first were dwelling somewhere 'midst the stars... you were called to earth for me...at times...'
Sangeeta	Oh do be quiet, Rishi!
Suhas	Pratap, have word sent to the taxi driver that he should go.
Suresh	Yes, the taxi can be called back later. Or is it your intention to stop here, Suhas?
Kamala	[*interrupting Suresh*] Suhas ji, where are thinking of living in the future?
Suhas	Kamala ji, I have a pretty good house in Lucknow. And as soon as my London house sells I'll get a house built for myself right here in Delhi, opposite this house of yours...
Rishi	[*launching into a new song*] 'Opposite your house I'll build a house, opposite your house I'll found a world, opposite ...'
Prakash	Rishi, shut up. That's quite enough. [*turning towards Suhas, scowling*] What's your trade? Your means of livelihood...?
Suhas	I'm a dancer. While I was living in London, the families of Indian origin who have settled there used to get their children taught kathak by me. Now I've been called to do the same work in India. I've been permanently settled in this country since Shravan.
Rishi	[*changing songs again*] 'In Shravan's month the wind makes moan... my heart's a-sway like peacocks dancing in the wood...'
Prakash	[*whispering in Kamala's ear*] Are you going to marry off our only daughter to this bloody dancer fellow? It's us he's leading a fine dance. [*moving towards Suhas*] So Suhas, who has invited you here to set the young girls of Delhi dancing and prancing?
Suhas	It's a government position. The Prime Minister himself had the job given me, that is to say he himself suggested to me that I apply for it.
Prakash	[*in great surprise, smiling open-heartedly*] Really! So you must be quite well-known in the world of dance ! And you must be

getting a good salary too! [*to Kamala, in her ear*] Sangeeta's mother, have some quality sweets fetched from Bengali Market straightaway – laddus, jalebis... [*to Suhas, very cordially*] Well my dear sir, what'll it be? Will you have tea? No, no, the time for tea has passed – will you have beer, or whisky?

Arun   [*to himself*] It appears that an astonishing transformation is about to occur imminently in our familial circumstances.

Suhas   [*standing up*] I'll have whatever Sangeeta will have. [*turning towards Sangeeta*] Sangoo, not just you, your whole family's beyond compare!

Rishi & Raj [*dancing with hands joined, beginning a fourth song*] 'Are you a waxing moon, or a solar glare; whate'er you are – God's oath! – you are beyond compare...'

Prakash   [*embracing Suhas*] Come Suhas, my son!

Suhas & Sangeeta [*together, to Prakash*] Father! Father!

Pratap   [*to Suhas*] Father! All your dreams are being fulfilled! God's oath, this has turned out to be a very successful day!

Suresh   Successful, my foot! This dialogue is getting very long. Me, I'm leaving.

Dadi ji   [You think that] I can't sing film songs? [*swaying happily, she starts singing in a blithe voice*] 'Well then, I'm leaving. When'll we meet? Whene'er you say...' [*everybody rolls around in helpless laughter*]

> The film lyrics quoted in this dialogue have a poetic register (hence the slightly purple translations): Persian words like आफ़ताब 'sun', dialect forms such as करे (= करता है) and Sanskrit words like पवन 'wind' would be out of place in everyday speech. Arun's speech is, typically, excessively Sanskritised.

Grammar
18.2 Intransitive and transitive verbs

In 14.2 we looked at the operation of intransitive and transitive verbs and saw that Hindi maintains a more crucial difference between the two than English does. For example, the Hindi equivalent of the sentence 'The gardener cut his finger' (माली की उँगली कट गई 'the gardener's finger became cut') will use intransitive

कटना 'to be cut', since using transitive काटना (माली ने अपनी उँगली को काटा, काट दिया) would imply that the cutting was deliberate. In this section, we look at the formal relationships between certain intransitive and transitive verbs.

You will have noticed that transitive verbs are often formed by lengthening the stem of the intransitive:

INTRANSITIVE		TRANSITIVE	
बनना	to be made	बनाना	to make
उठना	to rise	उठाना	to raise
पहुँचना	to arrive	पहुँचाना	to convey
बचना	to escape	बचाना	to save
लगना	to adhere	लगाना	to affix, apply
समझना	to understand	समझाना	to explain

Other transitives are formed by lengthening the non-final syllable:

कटना	to be cut	काटना	to cut
निकलना	to emerge	निकालना	to extract
मरना	to die	मारना	to kill, beat
लदना	to be loaded	लादना	to load

This change is sometimes accompanied by a change to the first syllable. (A semi-vowel, usually ल, is added to a stem ending in a long vowel, as with सोना 'to sleep'.)

ऊ > उ	घूमना	to go round	घुमाना	to make go round
ए > इ	लेटना	to lie down	लिटाना	to lay down
ऐ > इ	बैठना	to sit	बिठाना	to seat
ओ > उ	सोना	to sleep	सुलाना	to make sleep

Other intransitive-transitives pairs are formed by vowel changes as shown here – sometimes with a change of consonant also:

उ > ओ	धुलना	to be washed	धोना	to wash
ऊ > ओ	टूटना	to be broken	तोड़ना	to break
इ > ए	बिकना	to be sold	बेचना	to sell
ई > ए	दीखना	to be visible	देखना	to see

Lengthening of the stem also occurs in the second of two related transitive verbs:

TRANSITIVE 1		TRANSITIVE 2	
खाना	to eat	खिलाना	to serve (food)
बोलना	to speak	बुलाना	to call
देखना	to see	दिखाना	to show
सुनना	to hear	सुनाना	to recite, make hear

Thus some verbs fall into a three-way series: intransitive, plus two successive transitives:

टूटना	to be broken	तोड़ना	to break	तुड़ाना	to have broken
दिखना	to appear	देखना	to see	दिखाना	to show

18.3 Causative verbs

A further extension of the pattern shown in 18.2 is the causative verb, whose stem ends in -वा-. Thus लिखवाना means 'to cause to be written', 'to have written (by somebody)'. That 'somebody', when specified, takes से. Causatives are not always listed independently in dictionaries.

हम घर बनवा रहे हैं ।	We're having a house built.
हमने बच्चों को हिन्दी सिखवाई है ।	We've had Hindi taught to the children.
हमें दर्ज़ी से कुछ कुरते सिलवाने हैं ।	We have to get some kurtas sewn by the tailor.
लखपति ने अपनी कविता का अनुवाद करवाया ।	The millionaire had his poetry translated.
किसी से डाक्टर को बुलवा लो ।	Get someone to call the doctor. (lit. 'Get the doctor called by someone'.)

EXERCISE 18a.1 Answer the questions.

१   इस शहर (या गाँव) में रहते हुए आपको कितने दिन हुए हैं ?

२   जिस कमरे में आप बैठे हुए / बैठी हुई हैं, उसका वर्णन कीजिए ।

३   आज आप कैसे कपड़े पहने हुए हैं ?

४   बिना भारत गए क्या हिन्दी सीखना संभव है ?

५   पैसा जोड़ते जोड़ते जो लोग लाखों रुपये कमाते हैं, उनको क्या कहा जाता है ?

६   इस किताब को छपे हुए कितने साल हुए हैं ?

७   क्या आप नहाते समय गाना गाते / गाती हैं ?   किस तरह का गाना ?

८   क्या इन सवालों के जवाब लिखते लिखते आप थक गए / गई हैं ?

EXERCISE 18a.2 Fill the gaps with the appropriate participle.
Then translate.

१   अपने दोस्तों का इंतज़ार ......[करना]...... हम ऊबने लगे ।

२   फ़र्श पर ......[पड़ना]......कपड़ों को उठाओ और उन्हें उस......[टूटना]...... कुरसी पर
रख दो ।

३   लखनऊ में ......[रहना]......मुझे सात महीने ......[होना]......हैं ।

४   वह ......[गाना]...... लड़की कौन है ?   उसे गाना ......[सीखना]......कितने साल हुए
हैं ?

५   इस स्कूल में ......[पढ़ना]......बच्चे लोग तो काम करने का नाम नहीं लेते ।

६   अंकल के ......[पहुँचना]......ही सारे घरवाले चुप हो गए ।

EXERCISE 18b.1 Translate.

1   If you get thirsty, please have the teaboy called and have yourself
some tea made.

2   If you can't understand the story, get it translated into English by
someone.

3   Pandit ji says we should have the children taught Sanskrit words,
and not Urdu words.

4   Without saying anything she closed the book and put it in the
cupboard.

5   While complaining to the neighbours I was learning Hindi from
them.

6   Watching television I began to realise that many people mix a lot
of English words in their Hindi.

7   The broken toys were lying on the floor.

8   As soon as my friend got home I told her what had happened.

EXERCISE 18b.2 Translate.

आप शायद जानना चाहेंगे कि आगे चलकर कुमार परिवार में क्या क्या हुआ । बहुत लंबी कहानी है; किसी दिन हम इसके बारे में विस्तार से लिखेंगे । फिलहाल मैं आपको बस इतना बताऊँ कि सबों की ज़िन्दगी बड़ी ख़ुशी से बीती (सिवाय बेचारे सुरेश की) । कहने की ज़रूरत नहीं कि संगीता और सुहास की शादी हो गई, और बहुत धूमधाम से; आजकल वे दिल्ली में ही रह रहे हैं, और लखनऊ-वाला घर तो लन्दन से आए हुए कुछ हिन्दी के विद्यार्थियों को किराये पर दे दिया गया है । अगर आप कभी अपने को दिल्ली में पाएँ, तो ख़ाँ मार्केट की किसी दुकान में जाकर आपको संगीता और सुहास ख़रीदारी करते हुए दिखाई देंगे – हमेशा एक साथ, हमेशा मुस्कराते हुए, हमेशा ख़ुश । संगीता को बच्चा भी होनेवाला है । परिवार में एक तकलीफ़ यह हुई कि दादीजी की तबियत कुछ समय के लिए ठीक नहीं रही; दो तीन महीनों तक उनको लेकर बहुत चिंता रही । पर अब तो वे सुधर गई हैं ।

आपको यह जानकर ख़ुशी होगी कि दफ़्तर में प्रकाश की तरक़्क़ी हो रही है, जिसका एक नतीजा यह है कि वह छोटू की मदद भी कर पा रहा है; अभी छोटू गाड़ी चलाना सीख रहा है – वह प्रकाश का ड्राइवर बनेगा । अरुण और प्रेम की दूसरी किताब गरम गरम समोसों की तरह बिक रही है; लगता है कि अंत में उन्होंने प्रकाश की सलाह को स्वीकार कर लिया होगा, क्योंकि उनकी यह दूसरी किताब एक प्रेम कहानी है – "दास्तान दो दिलों की", जिस में संगीता की पूरी कहानी विस्तार से बताई गई है । संभव है कि इसकी फ़िल्म भी बनेगी, बाद में ।

राज और ऋषि के बीच जो वैर था वह धीरे धीरे ख़त्म हो जा रहा है, दोनों में एक दोस्ती-सी बन रही है – हालांकि कभी कभी वह पुराना युद्ध फिर से मच भी जाता है । सुरेश के विषय में क्या कहा जाए; कई कारणों से उसे तो बहुत दु:ख उठाना पड़ा है, और ज़िंदगी से ऊबकर वह शराब कुछ ज़्यादा पीने लगा है । पहले तो वह किसी होटल में काम कर रहा था, पर उसके ज़्यादा पीने की वजह से उसकी नौकरी ख़त्म हो गई है । ख़ुदा जाने, आगे क्या होगा उसका । खन्ना साहब कुछ समय के लिए लन्दन जानेवाले हैं, काम के सिलसिले में, और उमा को भी लन्दन में ही अच्छी-सी नौकरी मिल गई है । हरीश तो अमेरिका के किसी विश्वविद्यालय में बी० ए० करने जाएगा, जबकि पिंकी की शादी एक अँग्रेज़ से होनेवाली है । और प्रताप ? उसकी आगे की कहानी काफ़ी दिलचस्प है (अगर अरुण इस समय यहाँ होता तो कहता कि "अद्भुत है !")। हाँ, प्रताप की ज़िन्दगी में क्या क्या हो जाता है, यह सुनकर आपको आश्चर्य होगा; पर उसकी कहानी तो किसी दूसरी किताब में बताई जाएगी !

EXERCISE 18b.3 Translate.

दोस्तो, आप अभी इस किताब का अठारहवाँ पाठ ख़त्म कर रहे हैं – आपने बहुत मेहनत से काम किया है । रास्ता कुछ लंबा था; आपके साथ चलना मुझे बहुत अच्छा लगा । मुझे आशा है कि भविष्य में आपकी हिन्दी की पढ़ाई जारी रहेगी । यह किताब तो ख़त्म हो रही है, लेकिन पढ़ाई के रास्ते का कोई अंत नहीं है । आपके मन में यह प्रश्न उठ सकता है कि आगे कैसे पढ़ना चाहिए ? मेरा पहला सुझाव यह है कि आप एकाध अच्छे-से शब्दकोश को ज़रूर ख़रीद लें, जिससे कि किताबों और अख़बारों को पढ़ना थोड़ा आसान हो जाएगा । आर० एस० मैकग्रेगर (R.S.McGregor) की "Hindi-English Dictionary", जो आक्सफ़र्ड युनिवर्सिटी प्रेस से प्रकाशित हुई है, बहुत ही अच्छी है; यह शब्दकोश आक्सफ़र्ड से भी छपा है और दिल्ली से भी, इसलिए आसानी से मिलना चाहिए । इसके अलावा हरदेव बाहरी के कई शब्दकोश भी बहुत बढ़िया हैं । इन किताबों को अपने पास रखें । आपको सरल कहानियों को पढ़ने में ज़्यादा मुश्किल नहीं होनी चाहिए । मेरा दूसरा सुझाव यह है कि आप हिन्दी फ़िल्में देखा करें, जिससे कि आपको आम बातचीत को सुनने और समझने का अभ्यास हो जाए । और अगर हो सके तो आप भारत जाने की कोशिश करें – या किसी दूसरे देश में जहाँ हिन्दी भाषा बोली जाती है; तब तो हरेक हिन्दी-बोलनेवाला आपका अध्यापक बन जाएगा, चाहे पंडित हो, चाहे ट्रेन का मुसाफ़िर, चाहे दुकानदार ! जो भी हो, मुझे पूरा विश्वास है कि आपको हिन्दी सीखने और बोलने में बहुत आनंद आएगा । नमस्ते ।

Vocabulary

अधेड़ middle aged	इकलौता sole, only (child)
अनुवाद ^{m} translation	इश्क़ ^{m} romantic love; इश्क़ लड़ाना
अर्ज़ी ^{f} application	to have an affair
आकाश ^{m} sky	इस्तरी ^{f} clothes iron; ironing
आत्मीयता से cordially	उड़ाना to make fly; to indulge
आफ़ताब ^{m} sun, solar glow	ऊबना to be bored
आश्चर्य ^{m} surprise; आश्चर्यजनक	एकाध one or two, a couple (of)
astonishing	कथक ^{m} kathak, a North Indian
इक (=एक) a, one	dance style

क़दम ^m step, pace

कमाल ^m miracle, wonder

कमी ^f lack, want

करे (dialect) = करता/करती है

क़सम ^f oath

कहलवाना to send word

कान ^m ear

ख़ुदा ^m God; ख़ुदा की क़सम by God; ख़ुदा जाने God knows

खुला open

गला ^m throat, neck; गला लगाना to embrace

गिरना to fall

गोद ^f lap, embrace

घास ^f grass

घुमाना to make go round

चुनना to choose

चुप करना to be quiet, shut up

चौदहवीं 14th (day of lunar month – full moon day)

छुटभैया ^m a nobody, someone of no importance

छेड़ना to stir up, start up

छोकरी ^f young girl, lass

जनाब sir

ज़मीं ^f (also ज़मीन ^f) land, earth

जाना-पहचाना recognised, known

ज़ाहिर clear, evident

ज़िद ^f obstinacy

जियरा ^m (poetic) soul, heart

झट से suddenly, briskly

झाड़ना to spout, pour out

झूमना to sway (in pleasure); झूमे (dialect) = झूमता है

टकराना to collide

टपकना to drop in, appear unexpectedly

टहलना to stroll

टूटना to break, be broken

डॉयलॉग ^m dialogue

तंग आना to be fed up

तलाक़-शुदा divorced

तुड़ाना to cause to be broken

तुलना to be determined (to, पर)

तेज़ quick, rapid

थामना to hold, support

दया ^f compassion

दर्ज़ी ^m tailor

दास्तान ^f tale

दिलवाना to cause to be given

दीखना to appear, be visible, seem

दुःख ^m grief, pain, suffering

धंधा ^m work, occupation

धूमधाम ^m pomp, show

न कि and not

नचवैया ^m dancer (derogatory)

नरसों three days ago/ahead

नर्तक ^m dancer

नाच ^m dance; नाच नचाना to lead (someone) a fine dance

नाचना   to dance; नाचे (dialect) =
  नाचता है

नृत्य ᵐ   dance

नेक   good, virtuous, decent

पतंग ᶠ kite (toy)

परिस्थिति(याँ) ᶠ   circumstance(s)

पवन ᵐ   wind

पहुँचाना   to convey, deliver

पारिवारिक   familial

पास   nearby (adverb)

पे (=पर)   on, to

पैदा होना   to be born, produced

प्रतीत होना   to appear, seem

प्रधान मंत्री ᵐ   prime minister

फिरना   to turn, move

फिलहाल   in the meantime

बचना   to escape, survive

बचाना   to rescue, save

बन ᵐ   forest, wood, jungle; बनमा
  (dialect) = बन में

बसना   to dwell, settle, inhabit

बसाना   to settle, found

बस्ती ᶠ   settlement, slum

बात काटना   to interrupt

की [बात] सोचना   to think of
  doing, intend to do

बीतना   to pass (of time)

बेचैन   restless

बैठक ᶠ   sitting room

मरम्मत ᶠ   repair; की मरम्मत करना to

repair, set right

मस्त   blithely joyful, delighted

मापना   to measure, cover

मिलाना   to join (e.g. hands); to mix

मुस्कराना   to smile

मूल ᵐ   origin

यानी   that is to say

राय ᶠ   opinion

रेशम ᵐ   silk

लखपति ᵐ   rich man, 'millionaire'

लगाना   to apply, affix

लदना   to be loaded

लाजवाब   beyond compare

लिटाना   to make lie down

लेटना   to lie, recline

लोट-पोट   rolling, helpless (with
  laughter)

वर्णन ᵐ description; का वर्णन करना
  to describe

विस्तार से   at length, in detail

वेतन ᵐ   pay, salary

शंका ᶠ   doubt, suspicion

शख़्स ᵐ   individual, fellow

शर्म ᶠ shame; शर्म आना to feel
  ashamed

शादी; X की शादी Y से करना to
  marry X to Y

श्रावण ᵐ   Shravan, a monsoon
  month (July–August)

सदस्य ᵐ   member

समझाना   to explain; to talk (someone) round; to console

सलवार क़मीज़ ^f   salwar qameez

साँस ^f sigh; ठंडी साँस भरना to heave a deep sigh

साला ^{m, adj}   wife's brother; term of abuse

सावन ^m = श्रावण, monsoon month (July–August)

सितारा ^m   star

सिलवाना   to cause to be sewn

सिलसिला ^m connection; के सिलसिले में in connection with

सुलाना   to make sleep

सूझना   to occur to the mind

सोर ^m (=शोर ^m)   noise, tumult

स्थायी रूप से   permanently

स्वभाव ^m   nature, disposition

स्वीकार करना   to accept

हँसी-मज़ाक ^m   laughter, fun, joking

हाथ मिलाना   to join hands

ह्विस्की ^f   whisky

APPENDIXES

Appendix 1: Numbers

Try learning the numbers *horizontally* as progressions of tens, as well as *vertically* as progressions of units.

0 शून्य				
1 एक	11 ग्यारह	21 इक्कीस	31 इक्तीस	41 इकतालीस
2 दो	12 बारह	22 बाईस	32 बत्तीस	42 बयालीस
3 तीन	13 तेरह	23 तेईस	33 तैंतीस	43 तैंतालीस
4 चार	14 चौदह	24 चौबीस	34 चौंतीस	44 चवालीस
5 पाँच	15 पंद्रह	25 पच्चीस	35 पैंतीस	45 पैंतालीस
6 छह, छै, छः	16 सोलह	26 छब्बीस	36 छत्तीस	46 छियालीस
7 सात	17 सत्रह	27 सत्ताईस	37 सैंतीस	47 सैंतालीस
8 आठ	18 अठारह	28 अट्ठाईस	38 अड़तीस	48 अड़तालीस
9 नौ	19 उन्नीस	29 उनतीस	39 उनतालीस	49 उनचास
10 दस	20 बीस	30 तीस	40 चालीस	50 पचास

51 इक्यावन	61 इकसठ	71 इकहत्तर	81 इक्यासी	91 इक्यानवे
52 बावन	62 बासठ	72 बहत्तर	82 बयासी	92 बानवे
53 तिरपन	63 तिरसठ	73 तिहत्तर	83 तिरासी	93 तिरानवे
54 चौवन	64 चौंसठ	74 चौहत्तर	84 चौरासी	94 चौरानवे
55 पचपन	65 पैंसठ	75 पचहत्तर	85 पचासी	95 पचानवे
56 छप्पन	66 छियासठ	76 छिहत्तर	86 छियासी	96 छियानवे
57 सत्तावन	67 सरसठ	77 सतहत्तर	87 सत्तासी	97 सत्तानवे
58 अट्ठावन	68 अड़सठ	78 अठहत्तर	88 अट्ठासी	98 अट्ठानवे
59 उनसठ	69 उनहत्तर	79 उन्यासी	89 नवासी	99 निन्यानवे
60 साठ	70 सत्तर	80 अस्सी	90 नब्बे	100 सौ

Numbers featuring 'hundreds' are expressed without the 'and' that appears in English: दो सौ तीन 'two hundred and three'.

Higher numerals are divided by commas to indicate groups of thousands (हज़ार), hundred thousands (लाख, 'lakh'), ten million (करोड़, 'crore'):

100,000 = 1 लाख

100,00,000 = 100 लाख = 1 करोड़ (10,000,000)

२,९२,३०,६३७ दो करोड़ बानवे लाख तीस हज़ार छह सौ सैंतीस (29,230,637)

The term प्रतिशत 'percent' is used before the measured item just like any other 'quantity' word: दस किलो चावल '10 kilos of rice'; दस प्रतिशत लोग '10 percent of the people'.

'Divided by' is बटे 'over' (from बँटना or बटना 'to be divided'), as in address formulae like '17/4 सत्रह बटे चार' ('house 17 in block 4').

Appendix 2: Money and shopping

The rupee (रुपया) consists of 100 paisa (पैसा). Sums of money are quoted in the usual decimal system, preceded by the abbreviation रु० for रुपया; in English this is rendered 'Re.' in the singular, 'Rs' in the plural. Thus रु० ४२.५० is Rs 42.50.

यह कितने का है ?	How much is this?
इसका दाम क्या है ?	What's the price of this?
यह किताब एक सौ साठ रुपये की है ।	This book costs Rs 160.
कुल मिलाकर कितना हुआ ?	How much is that altogether?
डेढ़ सौ रुपये में कितना कपड़ा मिलेगा ?	How much cloth will I get for Rs 150?
केले तुम कैसे दे रहे हो ?	What's the rate for bananas?
बहुत महँगा है, भाव कुछ कम कर देना ।	It's very expensive, bring the rate down a bit.
मेरे पास खुले पैसे नहीं हैं ।	I don't have change.

Appendix 3: The calendar

The western calendar is used for everyday events, but religious and ceremonial events follow the Hindu calendar; this is based on lunar months but solar years, and a 'leap month' (मलमास) added after every 30th month makes up for the discrepancy. Each month is divided into a 'bright' or 'waxing' fortnight (शुक्ल पक्ष) and a 'dark' or 'waning' fortnight (कृष्ण पक्ष or बदी). Although calendars vary, the new year is often celebrated as beginning on the first day of the dark fortnight of the month चैत.

This wheel shows the months in Hindi (outer part of dark circle) and Sanskrit (inner part); all are masculine. English month names ending in -ई are feminine, the rest masculine.

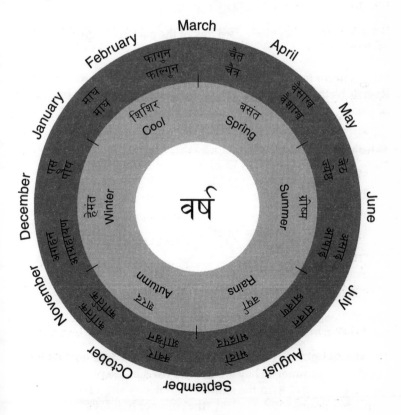

Numerous dating systems other than the western system are used in India. The commonest, विक्रम संवत् ('VS') dates from the era (संवत्) of King Vikramaditya, which began in 57–58 CE. To convert VS to CE, subtract 58 if the VS date falls between the second half of पूस and the first half of फागुन (inclusive); otherwise subtract 57. Vikram dates are usually identified by the word संवत्, while dates in the Christian calendar are preceded by सन् (or ईसवी सन् 'Christian era'); thus संवत् २००४ = ईसवी सन् १९४७.

Examples of dates expressed according to the Vikram calendar are:

माघ शुक्ल पक्ष १२ संवत् २००९   12th day of the bright fortnight of Magh, VS (Vikram Samvat) 2009 (= CE 1952)

आश्विन बदी ३ संवत् १७६८   3rd day of the dark fortnight of Ashwin, VS 1768 (= CE 1711)

Many Hindu festivals are named after the Sanskrit month: राम नवमी, Rama's birthday, is on चैत शुक्ल पक्ष ९ (the ninth day of the bright half of Chait), and जन्माष्टमी, Krishna's birthday, is on भादों कृष्ण पक्ष (the eighth day of the dark half of Bhadon).

The days of the week are:

Monday	सोमवार
Tuesday	मंगलवार
Wednesday	बुधवार
Thursday	गुरुवार, बृहस्पतिवार
Friday	शुक्रवार
Saturday	शनिवार
Sunday	रविवार, इतवार

The 'वार' component, meaning 'day', can be dropped colloquially, leaving सोम, मंगल, बुध etc.

The nouns जाड़ा and सरदी ('cold') are used for 'winter', and गरमी ('heat') for 'summer'. They are usually used in the plural (जाड़ों में 'in the winter, गरमियों में 'in the summer'), but stay singular when used with other nouns (गरमी की छुट्टियाँ 'the summer holidays').

Appendix 4: Kinship terms

The Indian family tree identifies relationships much more precisely than the English equivalent. First cousins are called चचेरा भाई/बहिन (paternal), ममेरा भाई/बहिन (maternal). These are distinguished from सगा भाई / सगी बहिन 'real brother/sister'.

The word साला, 'brother-in-law', doubles as a term of abuse: to call someone साला is to imply carnal knowledge of that person's sister. The word has become so common colloquially that it is even used as adjective. This usage is sometimes extended into adjectival territory, when साला qualifies a noun.

Appendix 5: Body and health

ख़ून ^m, रक्त ^m blood	इलाज ^m treatment, cure
गरदन ^f neck	उलटी ^f (होना, करना) vomiting
गर्भ ^m womb	कब्ज़ ^f constipation
गाल ^m cheek	कमज़ोर weak
घुटना ^m knee	कमज़ोरी ^f weakness
चमड़ी ^f skin	क़ै ^f (आना, होना, करना) vomiting,
छाती ^f, सीना ^m chest	nausea
जीभ ^f tongue	गर्भ ^m होना to be pregnant
जोड़ ^m joint	खाँसी ^f (आना) cough
टाँग ^f leg	चेचक ^f, शीतला ^f smallpox
त्वचा ^f skin	टट्टी ^f (करना) faeces, stool
दाँत ^m tooth	तंदुरुस्त healthy, fit
नाख़ून ^m nail	तंदुरुस्ती ^f, सेहत ^f, स्वास्थ्य ^m health
पसीना ^m (आना) sweat	दर्द ^m (होना, करना) pain
पाँव ^m, पैर ^m foot	दस्त ^m (आना) diarrhoea
पाँव की उँगली ^f toe	पचना to be digested
पीठ ^f back	पेशाब ^m (करना) urine
फेफड़ा ^m lung	बवासीर ^f piles
बाँह ^f arm	मरीज़ ^{m, f}, रोगी ^{m, f} patient
माथा ^m forehead	मलेरिया ^m malaria
शरीर ^m body	सुई ^f (लगाना) injection, 'needle'
हड्डी ^f bone	हैज़ा ^m cholera

उसे गर्भ है ।	She is pregnant.
उसे दस्त आते हैं ।	He/she's got diarrhoea.
मुझे क़ै हो गई ।	I vomited.
कल उसे उलटी हुई ।	He/she vomited yesterday.
उन्हें कब्ज़ है ।	They're constipated.
मुझे खाँसी आती है ।	I have a cough.

मेरा गला ख़राब है ।	I have a sore throat.
उन्हें चोट लगी ।	They got hurt, injured.
मुझे चक्कर आ रहा है ।	I'm feeling dizzy.
हम उसे डाक्टर को दिखाएँगे ।	We'll take him/her to the doctor.
दवा खाओ/पिओ ।	Take/drink the medicine.
मुझे मच्छर/कुत्ते ने काटा है ।	A mosquito/dog has bitten me.
मेरा गला बैठ गया है ।	I am hoarse.
मेरे सिर में दर्द है ।	I have a headache.
मेरे जोड़ दर्द कर रहे हैं ।	My joints are hurting.
उबला पानी पिया करो ।	Always drink boiled water.
शौचालय/टॉयलेट किधर है ?	Where's the loo?

Appendix 6: Letterwriting

प्रिय सुरेश	Dear Suresh
आदरणीय महोदय/महोदया	Dear ('respected') sir/madam
सादर नमस्ते ।	Respectful greeting (opening phrase)
सप्रेम नमस्ते ।	Affectionate greeting (opening phrase)
आप सपरिवार सकुशल होंगे ।	I hope you and your family are well.
तुम्हारा ख़त पढ़कर ख़ुशी हुई ।	I was pleased to read your letter.
आपका १ मई का पत्र मिला ।	I received your letter of 1 May.
प्रकाश की ओर से प्यार ।	Prakash sends his love.
रवि से मेरी नमस्ते कहना ।	Say hello to Ravi.
बच्चों को प्यार ।	Love to the children.
दीवाली की शुभकामनाएँ ।	Best wishes for Diwali.
शेष कुशल है ।	Everything else is all right, auspicious.
पत्र का उत्तर जल्दी दें ।	Reply soon.
आपकी कमला	Yours, Kamala
भवदीय	Yours sincerely (भवदीया fem. writer).
पुनश्च	postscript

Appendix 7: Summary of verb tenses and constructions

References are to the relevant paragraphs.

IMPERFECTIVE	PERFECTIVE	CONTINUOUS
बोलता	बोला	बोल रहा
speaks	spoke	speaking
	वह बोला	
	he spoke	
वह बोलता है 6.1	वह बोला है 11.2	वह बोल रहा है 8.1
he speaks	he has spoken	he is speaking
वह बोलता था 7.1	वह बोला था 11.2	वह बोल रहा था 8.1
he used to speak	he had spoken	he was speaking
वह बोलता होगा 9.2	वह बोला होगा 11.4	वह बोल रहा होगा 9.2
he will/must speak	.... have spoken	.... be speaking
वह बोलता हो 9.3	वह बोला हो 11.4	वह बोल रहा हो 10.2
he may speak, be speaking	.... have spoken	.... be speaking

वह बोलेगी	she will speak 9.1
वह बोले	he/she may speak 10.1
हिन्दी बोली जाती है	Hindi is spoken 14.1
वह बोलती जाती है	she goes on speaking 15.1
वह बोलती रहती है	she continues speaking 15.1
वह बोला करती है	she speaks habitually 15.2
उसे बोलना चाहिए	he/she should speak 13.2
उसे बोलना है	he/she is to speak 13.3
उसे बोलना पड़ता है	he/she has to speak (habitually) 13.3
उसे बोलना पड़ा	he/she had to speak (unexpectedly) 13.3
उसे बोलना पड़ेगा	he/she will *have* to speak 13.3

अगर वह बोले(गी)	if she speaks 10.4
अगर वह बोली	if she spoke, speaks 17.1
अगर वह बोलती	if she spoke, had spoken 17.1
अगर वह बोली होती	if she had spoken 17.1
वह बोल सकती है	she can speak 12.3
वह बोल नहीं पाई	she didn't manage to speak 12.3
उसे बोलना आता है	he/she knows how to speak 9.6
वह बोल चुकी है	she has already spoken 12.3
वह बोलने लगी	she began speaking 14.3
उसने बोलना शुरू किया	he/she began to speak 14.3
उसे बोलने दो	let him/her speak 14.4
वह बोलना चाहती है	she wants to speak 10.3
बोलकर	having spoken 12.1
वह बोलनेवाली है	she is about to speak 10.5
बोल, बोलो, बोलिए(गा), बोलना	speak! 5.2

KEY TO EXERCISES

Pronunciation key

You may like to refer to this key while listening to the sounds and words at the beginning of the cassette.

Vowels

अ *a*	अब *ab*	सब *sab*
आ *ā*	आप *āp*	का *kā*
इ *i*	इस *is*	कि *ki*
ई *ī*	ई-मेल *ī-mel*	की *kī*
उ *u*	उस *us*	पुलिस *pulis*
ऊ *ū*	ऊपर *ūpar*	तू *tū*
ऋ *r̥*	ऋषि *r̥ṣi*	कृपा *kr̥pā*
ए *e*	एक *ek*	के *ke*
ऐ *ai*	ऐसा *aisā*	पैसा *paisā*
ओ *o*	ओर *or*	बोलो *bolo*
औ *au*	और *aur*	चौदह *caudah*

Nasalised vowels

अँ *ã*	हँसी *hãsī*	महँगा *mahãgā*
आँ *ā̃*	हाँ *hā̃*	पाँच *pā̃c*
ईं *ī̃*	ईंट *ī̃ṭ*	आईं *āī̃*
उँ *ũ*	उँगली *ũglī*	मुँह *mũh*
एँ *ẽ*	में *mẽ*	सड़कें *saṛkẽ*
ऐं *aĩ*	मैं *maĩ*	हैं *haĩ*
ओं *õ*	होंठ *hõṭh*	दोस्तों *dostõ*

Consonants

क *ka*	कल *kal*	स्कूल *skūl*	
क़ *qa*	क़ीमत *qīmat*	बाक़ी *bāqī*	
ख *kha*	खाना *khānā*	रखो *rakho*	
ख़ *kha*	ख़याल *khayāl*	सख़्त *sakht*	
ग *ga*	गाना *gānā*	लगा *lagā*	
ग़ *ga*	ग़लत *galat*	बग़ीचा *bagīcā*	
घ *gha*	घर *ghar*	माघ *māgh*	
च *ca*	चाबी *cābī*	चाचा *cācā*	
छ *cha*	छात्र *chātr*	कुछ *kuch*	
ज *ja*	जो *jo*	आज *āj*	
ज़ *za*	ज़रूर *zarūr*	नज़र *nazar*	
झ *jha*	झूठ *jhūṭh*	समझ *samajh*	
ट *ṭa*	टेढ़ा *ṭeṛhā*	मार्केट *mārkeṭ*	
ठ *ṭha*	ठीक *ṭhīk*	पाठ *pāṭh*	
ड *ḍa*	डर *ḍar*	अंडा *aṇḍā*	
ड़ *ṛa*	बड़ी *baṛī*	भीड़ *bhīṛ*	
ढ *ḍha*	ढाई *ḍhāī*	ढंग *ḍhang*	
ढ़ *ṛha*	पढ़ाई *paṛhāī*	डेढ़ *ḍeṛh*	
ण *ṇa*	कारण *kāraṇ*	रामायण *rāmāyaṇ*	
त *ta*	तीन *tīn*	सात *sāt*	
थ *tha*	था *thā*	साथ *sāth*	
द *da*	दो *do*	विदेश *videś*	
ध *dha*	धो *dho*	आधा *ādhā*	
न *na*	नाक *nāk*	निकलना *nikalnā*	
प *pa*	पंजाबी *panjābī*	ऊपर *ūpar*	
फ *pha*	फिर *phir*	सफल *saphal*	
फ़ *fa*	फ़्लैट *flaiṭ*	साफ़ *sāf*	
ब *ba*	बीस *bīs*	अब *āb*	
भ *bha*	भारत *bhārat*	अभी *abhī*	
म *ma*	माँ *mā̃*	धीमा *dhīmā*	

य *ya*	यह *yah*	समय *samay*
र *ra*	रात *rāt*	चार *cār*
ल *la*	लाल *lāl*	कल *kal*
व *va*	वह *vah*	रवि *ravi*
श *śa*	शाबाश *śābāś*	आशा *āśā*
ष *ṣa*	भाषा *bhāṣā*	ऋषि *ṛṣi*
स *sa*	सरल *saral*	दस *das*
ह *ha*	हिन्दी *hindī*	वाह *vāh*

Doubled consonants

अममाँ *ammā̃*, अस्सी *assī*, उत्तर *uttar*, उन्नीस *unnīs*, उम्मीद *ummīd*, उल्लू *ullū*, कुत्ता *kuttā*, गुस्सा *gussā*, चप्पल *cappal*, चम्मच *cammac*, ज़िद्दी *ziddī*, दिल्ली *dillī*, पच्चीस *paccīs*, बत्ती *battī*, रस्सी *rassī*.

1a

१	है	*hai*	That man is Panjabi.
२	हैं	*haĩ*	Are these men Pakistani?
३	है	*hai*	Raj, you're not a good boy.
४	हूँ, हूँ	*hū̃, hū̃*	I'm not German, I'm Russian.
५	हैं, है	*haĩ, hai*	We are not Hindus, but this man is Hindu.
६	हो, हूँ	*ho, hū̃*	Peter, are you English? No, I'm German.
७	हो, हैं	*ho, haĩ*	Are you both English? No, we're American.
८	है, हैं	*hai, haĩ*	Sushila is Gujarati, but Sushil and Ravi are both Panjabi.
९	हैं, हूँ	*haĩ, hū̃*	Are you Pratap? Yes, I'm Pratap.
१०	हैं, हैं	*haĩ, haĩ*	Are those two men German? No, they're English.

1b

Sunday, 15 January

Kamala and Prakash Kumar are very nice people. There are three children – one girl, Sangeeta, and two boys, Rishi and Raj. Sangeeta is very beautiful. Rishi is big [older], Raj is little [younger]. Dadi ji is old but very nice. The house is clean and the garden is very beautiful. My room is quite big. There's one bed, two cupboards (both empty), one small table, two chairs. There isn't a fan, but the room is airy. There is a white Maruti car and two or three old bikes.

2a.1

१   शर्मा जी अध्यापक हैं । *śarmā jī adhyāpak haĩ.*

२   पाँच छात्र और नौ छात्राएँ हैं । *pãc chātr aur nau chātrāẽ haĩ.*

३   जी नहीं, यह काफ़ी महँगी किताब है । *jī nahī̃, yah kāfī mahãgī kitāb hai.*

४   जी नहीं, शब्दकोश बहुत सस्ते हैं । *jī nahī̃, śabdkoś bahut saste haĩ.*

५   रामायण बहुत मोटी किताब है । *rāmāyaṇ bahut moṭī kitāb hai.*

2a.2

Monday 16 January; New Delhi

Everything is OK here. Sharma ji is a good man, but he's quite strict too. We are 14 students. The other students are mostly English, German or American. There are also two Japanese girls. Both are very thin! Delhi is beautiful but the air isn't clean – it's very dirty. The pollution is very bad. But today the weather is all right. How's the weather there?   Pratap

2b.1

१   संगीता लंबी है; ऋषि भी लंबा है । *Sangītā lambī hai; Ṛṣi bhī lambā hai.*

२   अध्यापक सख़्त हैं; वे पागल भी हैं । *adhyāpak sakht haĩ; ve pāgal bhī haĩ.*

३   नया पंखा सस्ता है; और वह अच्छा भी है । *nayā pankhā sastā hai; aur vah acchā bhī hai.*

४   ये जूते गंदे हैं; चप्पलें भी गंदी हैं । *ye jute gande haĩ; cappalẽ bhī gandī haĩ.*

५   वह लड़की मोटी है; वह सुंदर भी है । *vah laṛkī moṭī hai; vah sundar bhī hai.*

६   ये अख़बार अच्छे हैं; ये सस्ते भी हैं । *ye akhbār acche haĩ; ye saste bhī haĩ.*

2b.2

१   ये बच्चे अच्छे नहीं हैं, बीमार हैं । *ye bacce acche nahī̃ haĩ, bīmār haĩ.*

२   हम लंबे नहीं हैं, छोटे हैं । *ham lambe nahī̃ haĩ, choṭe haĩ.*

३   वे किताबें कैसी हैं ? क्या वे अच्छी हैं ? *ve kitābẽ kaisī haĩ? kyā ve acchī haĩ?*

४   वे मेज़ें साफ़ नहीं हैं, बहुत गंदी हैं । *ve mezẽ sāf nahī̃ haĩ, bahut gandī haĩ.*

५   ये नए अख़बार बहुत अच्छे नहीं हैं । *ye nae akhbār bahut acche nahī̃ haĩ.*

६   ये शब्दकोश सस्ते हैं । हाँ, और काफ़ी अच्छे भी हैं । *ye śabdkoś saste haĩ. hã, aur kāfī acche bhī haĩ.*

3a.1

१ प्रताप बिलकुल ठीक है । *Pratāp bilkul ṭhīk hai.*

२ कुमार परिवार में छह लोग हैं – कमला और प्रकाश, दादी जी, संगीता, ऋषि, और राज । *Kumār parivār mẽ chah log haĩ – Kamalā aur Prakāś, Dādī jī, Saṅgītā, Ṛṣi, aur Rāj.*

३ मकान में दस कमरे हैं । एक कमरा छोटा है, दूसरे बड़े हैं । *makān mẽ das kamre haĩ. ek kamrā choṭā hai, dūsre baṛe haĩ.*

४ सारे कमरों में नया सामान है । *sāre kamrõ mẽ nayā sāmān hai.*

५ पंखा मेज़ पर है । वह नया है । *pankhā mez par hai. vah nayā hai.*

६ जी नहीं, दरी भी नई है । वह फ़र्श पर है । *jī nahī̃, darī bhī naī hai. vah farś par hai.*

3a.2 (sample answer)

मेरा कमरा काफ़ी सुन्दर है । कमरा बहुत बड़ा नहीं है, लेकिन हवादार है । यहाँ दो पलंग, एक छोटी मेज़ और कई कुरसियाँ हैं । दीवारों पर अच्छी तस्वीरें हैं, और खिड़कियों पर परदे हैं । ये परदे नए नहीं हैं, काफ़ी पुराने हैं । फ़र्श पर एक छोटी हिन्दुस्तानी दरी है । मेज़ पर दो पंखे हैं; एक बहुत पुराना है लेकिन दूसरा नया है । अलमारियों में बहुत-सारा सामान है; यह मेरा नहीं है !

merā kamrā kāfī sundar hai. kamrā bahut baṛā nahī̃ hai, lekin havādār hai. yahā̃ do palang, ek choṭī mez aur kaī kursiyā̃ haĩ. dīvarõ par acchī tasvīrẽ haĩ, aur khiṛkiyõ par parde haĩ. ye parde nae nahī̃ haĩ, kāfī purāne haĩ. farś par ek choṭī hindustānī darī hai. mez par do pankhe haĩ; ek bahut purānā hai lekin dūsrā nayā hai. almāriyõ mẽ bahut-sārā sāmān hai; yah merā nahī̃ hai !

3b.1

१	यह बड़ा कमरा	इस बड़े कमरे में	लड़के इस बड़े कमरे में हैं ।
२	वे काली कुरसियाँ	उन काली कुरसियों पर	कपड़े उन काली कुरसियों पर हैं ।
३	यह गंदा फ़र्श	इस गंदे फ़र्श पर	इस गंदे फ़र्श पर (एक) दरी है ।
४	ये पुरानी मेज़ें	इन पुरानी मेज़ों पर	किताबें इन पुरानी मेज़ों पर हैं ।
५	वह बड़ा बग़ीचा	उस बड़े बग़ीचे में	उस बड़े बग़ीचे में (एक) गाड़ी है ।
६	ये नए कमरे	इन नए कमरों में	क्या इन नए कमरों में पंखे हैं ?

७	पुराना शहर	पुराने शहर से	वे लड़कियाँ पुराने शहर से हैं ।
८	यह छोटा गाँव	इस छोटे गाँव से	क्या वह लड़का इस छोटे गाँव से है ?
९	यह साफ़ रसोईघर	इस साफ़ रसोईघर में	इस साफ़ रसोईघर में (एक) मेज़ है ।
१०	वे लंबे लड़के	उन लंबे लड़कों से	यह चिट्ठी उन लंबे लड़कों से है ।

1	yah baṛā kamrā	is baṛe kamre mẽ	laṛke is baṛe kamre mẽ haĩ.
2	ve kālī kursiyā̃	un kālī kursiyõ par	kapṛe un kālī kursiyõ par haĩ.
3	yah gandā farś	is gande farś par	is gande farś par (ek) darī hai.
4	ye purānī mezẽ	in purānī mezõ par	kitābẽ in purānī mezõ par haĩ.
5	vah baṛā bagīcā	us baṛe bagīce mẽ	us baṛe bagīce mẽ (ek) gāṛī hai.
6	ye nae kamre	in nae kamrõ mẽ	kyā in nae kamrõ mẽ pankhe haĩ?
7	purānā śahar	purāne śahar se	ve laṛkiyā̃ purāne śahar se haĩ.
8	yah choṭā gā̃v	is choṭe gā̃v se	kyā vah laṛkā is choṭe gā̃v se hai?
9	yah sāf rasoīghar	is sāf rasoīghar mẽ	is sāf rasoīghar mẽ (ek) mez hai.
10	ve lambe laṛke	un lambe laṛkõ se	yah ciṭṭhī un lambe laṛkõ se hai.

3b.2 (sample answer)

ऋषि	माता जी, मेरी नई किताब कहाँ है ?
कमला	शायद उस छोटी मेज़ पर है, बड़े कमरे में ?
ऋषि	नहीं, बड़े कमरे में नहीं है । वहाँ सिर्फ़ मेरा शब्दकोश है ।
कमला	अच्छा । और क्या वह तुम्हारी दराज़ में भी नहीं है ?
ऋषि	नहीं माता जी, मेरी दराज़ में बहुत सामान है, लेकिन किताबें नहीं हैं !
कमला	रसोईघर में एक नई किताब है ।
ऋषि	हाँ, लेकिन वह किताब मेरी नहीं है ।

Ṛṣi	mātā jī, merī naī kitāb kahā̃ hai?
Kamalā	śāyad us choṭī mez par hai, baṛe kamre mẽ?
Ṛṣi	nahī̃, baṛe kamre mẽ nahī̃ hai. vahā̃ sirf merā śabdkoś hai.
Kamalā	acchā. aur kyā vah tumhārī darāz mẽ bhī nahī̃ hai?
Ṛṣi	nahī̃ mātā jī, merī darāz mẽ bahut sāmān hai, lekin kitābẽ nahī̃ haĩ!
Kamalā	rasoīghar mẽ ek naī kitāb hai.
Ṛṣi	hā̃, lekin vah kitāb merī nahī̃ hai.

4a.1

1 Your old fan was stronger than this new fan.
2 Sangeeta is the biggest of the children.

3   Is Rishi less fat than Raj?
4   Is Sangeeta cleverer than Pinkie?
5   Today Pratap is at home but the others are out – perhaps at the market.

4a.2 (ज़्यादा *zyādā* may be replaced with और *aur*, or omitted.)

१   यह आदमी उस लड़की से ज़्यादा लंबा है । *yah ādmī us ādmī se zyādā lambā hai.*

२   क्या तुम्हारी पुरानी गाड़ी इस नई गाड़ी से ज़्यादा अच्छी थी ? *kyā tumhārī purānī gāṛī is naī gāṛī se zyādā acchī hai?*

३   क्या मेरी बहिन मेरे भाई से ज़्यादा मोटी है ? *kyā merī bahin mere bhāī se zyādā moṭī hai?*

४   मैं तुमसे ज़्यादा लंबा/लंबी हूँ लेकिन तुम मुझसे ज़्यादा सुंदर हो । *maĩ tumse zyādā lambā/lambī hũ lekin tum mujhse zyādā sundar ho.*

५   वह हम से ज़्यादा लंबी थी; वह तो सबसे लंबी थी । *vah ham se zyādā lambī thī; vah to sabse lambī thī.*

4b.1

१   पिंकी को मालूम है कि संगीता आज कालेज में नहीं थी । *Pinkī ko mālūm hai ki Saṅgītā āj kālej mē nahī̃ thī.*

२   किसको मालूम नहीं कि सुहास संगीता से बड़ा है ? *kisko mālūm nahī̃ ki Suhās Saṅgītā se baṛā hai?*

३   संगीता को ख़ुशी है कि पिंकी को सुहास पसंद है । *Saṅgītā ko khuśī hai ki Pinkī ko Suhās pasand hai.*

४   प्रताप आज घर पर था; उसको मालूम है कि सुहास कौन है । *Pratāp āj ghar par thā; usko mālūm hai ki Suhās kaun hai.*

५   प्रताप को मालूम है कि संगीता को नई सफ़ेद मारुति पसंद है । *Pratāp ko mālūm hai ki Saṅgītā ko naī safed Māruti pasand hai.*

६   क्या आपको मालूम है कि कमला कल कहाँ थी ? *kyā āpko mālūm hai ki Kamalā kal kahā̃ thī?*

७   हमको अफ़सोस है कि तुम्हारे दोस्त बीमार हैं । *hamko afsos hai ki tumhāre dost bīmār haĩ.*

८   मुझको मालूम नहीं कि वह आदमी कौन है । *mujhko mālūm nahī̃ ki vah ādmī kaun hai.*

4b.2 (sample answers)

१   मेरे कमरे में चार कुरसियाँ हैं । *mere kamre mē cār kursiyā̃ haĩ.*

२   जी नहीं, मेरे पड़ोसी हिन्दुस्तानी नहीं हैं, पाकिस्तानी हैं । *jī nahī̃, mere paṛosī hindustānī nahī̃ haĩ, pākistānī haĩ.*

३ जी हाँ, मेरी किताब मेरी मेज़ पर है । *jī hā̃, merī kitāb merī mez par hai.*

४ हाँ ज़रूर ! मेरे सारे कपड़े बहुत साफ़ हैं ! और तुम्हारे ? *hā̃ zarūr! mere sāre kapṛe bahut sāf haĩ! aur tumhāre?*

५ जी हाँ, मुझको मालूम है कि मेरे पड़ोसी अभी घर पर हैं । *jī hā̃, mujhko mālūm hai ki mere paṛosī abhī ghar par haĩ.*

६ मेरी तबियत ठीक नहीं है । मुझको जुकाम है । *merī tabiyat ṭhīk nahī̃ hai. mujhko zukām hai.*

4b.3 (sample answer)

प्रिय मोहन,

नमस्ते । आप कैसे हैं ? मुझको आशा है कि आप ठीक हैं । यहाँ दिल्ली में तो सब ठीक है । यह शहर मुझको बहुत पसंद है, लेकिन प्रदूषण बहुत ख़राब है । वाराणसी कैसी है ? क्या वहाँ भी प्रदूषण है ? वाराणसी में एक पुराना महल है – क्या आपको मालूम है कि वह कहाँ है ? क्या आप लोग वाराणसी से हैं ? आपके कितने भाई और बहिनें हैं ?

आपका प्रताप

priy Mohan,

namaste. āp kaise haĩ? mujhko āśā hai ki āp ṭhīk haĩ. yahā̃ dillī mē̃ to sab ṭhīk hai. yah śahar mujhko bahut pasand hai, lekin pradūṣaṇ bahut kharāb hai. vārāṇasī kaisī hai? kyā vahā̃ bhī pradūṣaṇ hai? vārāṇasī mē̃ ek purānā mahal hai – kyā āpko mālūm hai ki vah kahā̃ hai? kyā āp log vārāṇasī se haĩ? āpke kitne bhāī aur bahinē̃ haĩ?

āpkā Pratāp

5a.1

१ यहाँ सिग्रेट न पीजिए । *yahā̃ sigreṭ na pījie.*
Please don't smoke here.

२ ज़रा यहाँ ठहरिए । *zarā yahā̃ ṭhaharie.*
Just wait here please.

३ इस कमरे में बैठिए । *is kamre mē̃ baiṭhie.*
Please sit in this room.

४ चाय पीजिए, फल खाइए । *cāy pījie, phal khāie.*
Please have some tea, eat some fruit.

५ मुझे ऋषि के कपड़े दीजिए । *mujhe Ṛṣi ke kapṛe dījie.*
Please give me Rishi's clothes.

६ पानी न पियो; काफ़ी लो । *pānī na piyo; kāfī lo.*
   Don't drink water; take some coffee.

७ आओ । बताओ, क्या हाल है ? *āo. batāo, kyā hāl hai?*
   Come. Tell me, how's things?

८ गाड़ी को इधर लाओ । *gāṛī ko idhar lāo.*
   Bring the car over here.

९ उधर देखो, वह नारा पढ़ो ! *udhar dekho, vah nārā paṛho!*
   Look over there, read that slogan!

१० दरवाज़े को बन्द करो । *darvāze ko band karo.*
   Close the door.

5a.2

१	... कर । *kar*	Don't dirty the blankets.
२	... छू । *chū*	Don't touch the food.
३	... बोल । *bol*	Speak simple Hindi.
४	... लिख । *likh*	Don't write my name in the book.
५	... मार ! *mār*	Don't beat the horse!

5b.1

१ ये मोटे कंबल अलमारी में रखो । *ye moṭe kambal almārī mẽ rakho.*
   Put these thick blankets in the cupboard.

२ यह गरम समोसा खाओ । *yah garam samosā khāo.*
   Eat this hot samosa.

३ वह बड़ी कुरसी इस कमरे में लाइए । *vah baṛī kursī is kamre mẽ lāie.*
   Please bring that big chair into this room.

४ आज का अख़बार पढ़ । *āj kā akhbār paṛh.*
   Read today's newspaper.

५ चाचा जी का दरवाज़ा बन्द करना । *cācā jī kā darvāzā band karnā.*
   Close Uncle's door.

5b.2

१ इन नए खिलौनों को लो । *in nae khilaunõ ko lo.*
   Take these new toys.

२ ऋषि के पुराने कुरते को पहनो । *Ṛṣi ke purāne kurte ko pahno.*
   Wear Rishi's old kurta.

३ गाड़ी की चाबियों को ढूँढ़ो । *gāṛī kī cābiyõ ko ḍhū̃ṛho.*
Find the car keys.

४ इन गंदे कपड़ों को धोना । *in gande kapṛõ ko dhonā.*
Wash these dirty clothes.

५ इस थैले को दराज़ में रखिए । *is thaile ko darāz mẽ rakhie.*
Put this bag in the drawer.

5b.3

१ कमला के देवर का नाम क्या है ?   कमला के देवर का नाम अरुण है । *Kamalā ke devar kā nām kyā hai?   Kamalā ke devar kā nām Aruṇ hai.*

२ क्या ऋषि अभी घर पर है ? जी नहीं, वह अभी खाँ मार्केट में है । *kyā Ṛṣi abhī ghar par hai?   jī nahī̃, vah abhī khā̃ mārkeṭ mẽ hai.*

३ किसको दूध पसंद नहीं है ?   राज को दूध पसंद नहीं है । *kisko dūdh pasand nahī̃ hai?   Rāj ko dūdh pasand nahī̃ hai.*

४ उसको दूध क्यों नहीं पसंद है ?   क्योंकि वह छोटा बच्चा नहीं है । *usko dūdh kyõ nahī̃ pasand hai?   kyõki vah choṭā baccā nahī̃ hai.*

५ कल संगीता के चाचा की चाबियाँ कहाँ थीं ? दरवाज़े की चाबी तो प्रकाश की मेज़ पर पड़ी थी । *kal Saṅgītā ke cācā kī cābiyā̃ kahā̃ thī̃?   darvāze kī cābī to Prakāś kī mez par paṛī thī.*

६ किसको मालूम है कि आज वे चाबियाँ कहाँ हैं ?   ऋषि को मालूम है कि चाबियाँ कहाँ हैं । *kisko mālūm hai ki āj ve cābiyā̃ kahā̃ haĩ?   Ṛṣi ko mālūm hai ki cābiyā̃ kahā̃ haĩ.*

७ क्या आपको मालूम है कि कुमार परिवार का घर कहाँ है ? जी हाँ, मुझको मालूम है कि वह दिल्ली में है । *kyā āpko mālūm hai ki Kumār parivār kā ghar kahā̃ hai?   jī hā̃, mujhko mālūm hai ki vah dillī mẽ hai.*

८ आपके ख़याल में क्या ये सवाल सरल हैं ?   जी हाँ, मेरे ख़याल में तो ये सवाल बहुत सरल हैं ! *āpke khyāl mẽ kyā ye savāl saral haĩ?   jī hā̃, mere khyāl mẽ to ye savāl bahut saral haĩ!*

6a.1 (1-5 are sample answers)

१ मैं लन्दन में रहता/रहती हूँ ।

२ मेरे घर में सिर्फ़ दो लोग रहते हैं । एक कुत्ता भी है ।

३ हिन्दी में "प्रोनंसियेशन" को "उच्चारण" कहते हैं ।

४ मैं चार भाषाएँ बोलता/बोलती हूँ । इनमें से हिन्दी भी एक है ।

५ जी हाँ, लन्दन में मकान बहुत ज़्यादा महँगे होते हैं ।

६ प्रताप अभी प्रकाश और कमला के मकान में रहता है, दिल्ली में ।

७ उस घर में सात लोग रहते हैं ।

८ प्रताप की माँ लन्दन में रहती हैं । उनका नाम अनीता है ।

९ जी नहीं, राज तो काम नहीं करता – वह खेलता है, खाता है, सोता है और शरारत करता है ।

१० संगीता प्रताप को नापसंद करती है (प्रताप के ख़याल से) ।

6a.2

Prakash Kumar works in a big company; his boss's name is Khanna. It seems that Mr Khanna is a big shot; Prakash ji is afraid of him (and perhaps of his (own) wife Kamala as well!). Prakash and Kamala's two sons go to school; and their daughter Sangeeta goes to college. Sangeeta is very clever but she doesn't talk to me much. I think she doesn't like me. Her friend Pinkie comes here often; the two of them chat all day and laugh a lot. Pinkie is Khanna's younger sister; she's older than Sangeeta, but Sangeeta is the more beautiful of the two of them. She is perhaps the most beautiful girl in India!

Dadi ji often asks me what my parents do, who my friends are, and so on. She makes Rishi and Raj laugh a lot – and me too! She's very fond of Raj; she calls him 'Munna' ('little one') or 'my piece-of-the-moon'. Raj doesn't like these names one bit. But he keeps quiet. Everybody loves Dadi ji.

6b.1

1 अपने – Pratap often asks his teacher difficult questions about Hindi.

2 अपने – Dadi tells us about her childhood.

3 उसका; अपनी – Rishi and his brother laugh with their grandmother a lot.

4 तेरी; अपना – Little one, I'm your grandmother; why don't you give me your food to eat?

5   अपना; मेरा – Rishi, you do your work; then give me my food.

6   अपनी; उसकी – Prakash asks his daughter about her friend.

7   अपने; अपनी – Sangeeta tells her father about her friend.

6b.2

मुझे ऋषि कहते हैं । राज मेरा छोटा भाई है; वह थोड़ा पागल है । वह अभी अपने कमरे में नहीं है, वह मेरे कमरे में है । और मैं अपने कमरे में नहीं हूँ, मैं उसके कमरे में हूँ ! उसको नहीं मालूम कि मुझे मालूम है कि वह मेरे कमरे में है । इधर उसके कमरे में कई पुराने अख़बार हैं, लेकिन मैं नहीं जानता कि वे किसके हैं; उसके तो नहीं हैं । राज तो किताबें या अख़बार नहीं पढ़ता । वह अपने दोस्तों के साथ खेलता है पर मुझसे बात नहीं करता । उसके दोस्त मेरे दोस्त नहीं हैं ।

मुझे प्रताप पसंद है । मैं उसके साथ सिनेमा जाता हूँ और हम फ़िल्मों के बारे में बातें करते हैं । मालूम होता है कि वह काफ़ी होशियार है । वह अच्छी हिन्दी बोलता है । उसका उच्चारण भी काफ़ी अच्छा है । वह विदेशी की तरह नहीं बोलता ।

7a.1

१   पिताजी किसी दफ़्तर में काम करते थे और देर से घर पहुँचते थे ।

२   कोई १२ विद्यार्थी फ़र्श पर बैठे हैं; हमें कुछ और कुरसियाँ चाहिए ।

३   शनिवार को हम कुछ दोस्तों से मिलते थे ।

४   हमको यह ठंडा खाना पसंद नहीं – हमें कुछ चावल दाल चाहिए ।

५   क्या यहाँ कोई सस्ता होटल नहीं है? ताज तो कुछ महँगा है !

६   "यह पैसा किसी और को देना !" "हाँ, पर किसको?"

७   हमें गाड़ी की चाबियों की ज़रूरत थी लेकिन घर में कोई नहीं था ।

८   शाम को, दादीजी रामायण पढ़ती थीं और हम लोग पुरानी फ़िल्में देखते थे ।

7a.2 and 7a.3 (sample answers)

१   उन्हें कुछ गरम पानी चाहिए था । उन्हें कुछ गरम पानी की ज़रूरत थी ।

२   मुझे कुछ पैसा चाहिए । मुझे कुछ पैसे की ज़रूरत है ।

३   तुम्हें कुछ और समय चाहिए । तुम्हें कुछ और समय की ज़रूरत है ।

४   मेरे दोस्त को एक अच्छा शब्दकोश चाहिए। मेरे दोस्त को एक अच्छे शब्दकोश की ज़रूरत है ।

५   उन लड़कियों को नया घर चाहिए । उन लड़कियों को नए घर की ज़रूरत है ।

६   किसी को एक सुन्दर मोती चाहिए था । किसी को एक सुन्दर मोती की ज़रूरत थी ।

७   किसको आज के अख़बार चाहिए ?   किसको आज के अख़बारों की ज़रूरत है ?

८   इन विद्यार्थियों को कोई दस कुरसियाँ चाहिए थे । इन विद्यार्थियों को कोई दस कुरसियों की ज़रूरत थी ।

९   सिग्रेट किसी को नहीं चाहिए ।   किसी को सिग्रेट की ज़रूरत नहीं है ।

१० उस दूसरे आदमी को हज़ारों रुपए चाहिए ।   उस दूसरे आदमी को हज़ारों रुपयों की ज़रूरत है ।

7b.1

१   अरुण अपने बड़े भाई प्रकाश के साथ रहता था; वह किताबें लिखता था । Arun lived with his elder brother Prakash; he used to write books.

२   खन्ना साहिब कहते थे कि उनके दफ़्तर में दर्जनों लोग थे लेकिन कोई ठीक से काम नहीं करता था । Khanna Sahib used to say that dozens of people used to work in his office but nobody worked properly.

३   दादी जी नहीं जानती थीं कि उनके पिताजी किस कालेज में पढ़ाते थे । Dadi ji didn't know which college her father used to teach in.

४   अध्यापक जी कहते थे कि "कोई" और "कुछ" का फ़र्क़ समझना बहुत ज़रूरी था । The teacher used to say that it was very important to understand the difference between *koī* and *kuch*.

५   छात्र अपने अध्यापक से हज़ारों मुश्किल सवाल पूछता था । The student used to ask his teacher thousands of difficult questions.

६   क्या किसी को मालूम था कि संगीता का दोस्त सुहास कहाँ रहता था ? Did anyone know where Sangeeta's friend Suhas lived?

७   किसको मालूम था कि ऋषि और राज की उम्र में कितना फ़र्क़ था ? Who knew how much age difference there was between Rishi and Raj?

८   दादी जी सोचती थीं कि हिन्दुस्तान स्वर्ग के समान था । वे अपने बचपन के सपने बहुत देखती थीं । Dadi ji used to think that India was like paradise. She used to dream of her childhood a lot.

९   मालूम होता था कि प्रताप अभी दिल्ली में नहीं था; शायद वह अपने पिताजी के यहाँ था । It seemed that Pratap wasn't still in Delhi; perhaps he was at his father's place.

१० कुछ विद्यार्थियों के ख़याल में आठवाँ और दसवाँ सवाल सबसे मुश्किल थे । In the opinion of some students the eighth and tenth questions were the most difficult.

7b.2   होटल में

लड़का   आइए साहब । आपको क्या चाहिए ?

खन्ना   मुझे कुछ गरम खाना और काफ़ी चाहिए ।

लड़का   सर, रविवार को रसोईघर जल्दी बंद होता है । गरम खाना नहीं है ।

खन्ना   अच्छा, तो मुझे कुछ फल दो । और कल सुबह मेरे कमरे को साफ़ करना; बहुत गंदा है ।

लड़का   सर, कल तो मेरी छुट्टी है । किसी और से कहिएगा ।

खन्ना   पर काफ़ी तो अभी चाहिए । उसे लाओ और दरवाज़ा बंद करो ।

लड़का   सर, अभी तो बिजली बंद है । कुछ ठंडा पानी पीजिए ।

खन्ना   यह होटल बेकार है; तुम भी बेकार हो । मैं चलता हूँ ।

8a.1

१   प्रताप बहुत ध्यान से हिन्दी पढ़ रहा है ।
    Pratap is studying Hindi very attentively.

२   मैं तो अच्छा पैसा कमा रहा हूँ ।
    I, at least, am earning good money.

३   क्या तुम गाड़ी चला रहे हो ?
    Are you driving the car?

४   संगीता और उसका छोटा भाई सिनेमा जा रहे हैं ।
    Sangeeta and her younger brother are going to the cinema.

५   प्रताप अपने दोस्तों के साथ गोश्त खा रहा है ।
    Pratap is eating meat with his friends.

8a.2

१   तुम्हारे लिए वह अलग खाना तैयार कर रहा है ।

२   उसको बताओ कि वह ग़लत नंबर मिला रही थी ।

३   वह कल अपने रिश्तेदारों के साथ दिल्ली आ रहा है ।

४   आपकी कितनी बहिनें हैं? मेरी दो बहिनें हैं ।

५   तीनों डाक्टर उसी अस्पताल पर काम कर रहे हैं ।

६   वह पहले मेरा सपना देखता था पर अब तो वह तुम्हारा सपना देख रहा है ।

७   तुम मेरे सवाल का जवाब क्यों नहीं दे रही हो संगीता ?

८   हम लोग तुम्हारे पड़ोसियों से तुम्हारे बारे में बात कर रहे थे ।

8a.3 (sample answer; only Mohan's lines are given here)

मैं ठीक हूँ । पर आप नेपाल में क्या कर रहे हैं?

क्या ऋषि और राज भी आपके साथ सैर कर रहे हैं ?

आप लोग नेपाल में कहाँ ठहर रहे हैं ?

होटल तो हमेशा महँगे होते हैं । किसी दोस्त के यहाँ ठहरिए ।

मेरे कई रिश्तेदार काठमांडु में रहते हैं । उनसे मिलिए ।

8b.1

१ मकान के बाहर बैठो । बाहर बैठो ।

२ कुरसी के पीछे देखो । पीछे देखो ।

३ हम दरवाज़े के सामने खड़े हैं । दुकान सामने है ।

४ मेरी तरफ़ आओ । इस तरफ़ आओ ।

५ पेड़ के नीचे मत सोना । नीचे सोना ।

६ दोनों भाई मेरे साथ हैं । तुम भी साथ चलो ।

७ उसे अलमारी के ऊपर रखो । तुम ऊपर जाओ ।

८ हम लोग साइकिल की दुकान के पास रहते हैं । वे लोग पास रहते हैं ।

8b.2 (sample answers)

१ मेरा जन्मदिन १५ जनवरी को है ।

२ आज की तारीख़ है रविवार, दस अक्तूबर, सन् उन्नीस सौ निन्यानवे ।

३ कल तो शनिवार था – नौ अक्तूबर ।

४ जी हाँ, मेरे दो बच्चे हैं । दोनों लड़के हैं ।

५ मेरी दो बहिनें हैं; एक छप्पन साल की है, दूसरी बावन या तिरपन साल की । हमारा
कोई भाई नहीं है ।

६ बिलकुल नहीं । मैं अध्यापक हूँ, इसलिए ग़रीब हूँ । मुझे पैसा ज़रूर चाहिए – सब
लोगों की तरह – लेकिन किसी ख़ास काम के लिए नहीं ।

७ मेरा अपना घर है । छोटा है, लेकिन मुझे बहुत पसंद है ।

८ अभी तो मुझे कोई भी तकलीफ़ नहीं है; मेरी तबियत बहुत अच्छी है, शुक्रिया ।

९ मेरे ख़याल से वह संगीता से नहीं डरता; शायद उससे प्यार करता है । पर किसी
वजह से संगीता उससे बात भी नहीं करती ।

१० तीन घंटे पहले मैं … यह किताब पढ़ रहा था !

9a.1

१   दूसरे लोग कल सुबह तक पहुँचेंगे ।

२   किसी दिन मैं आपको पूरी कहानी बताऊँगा/बताऊँगी ।

३   मुझे मालूम है कि वह मेरी चिट्ठियों का जवाब नहीं देगा ।

४   आजकल तुम्हारे पिताजी अच्छा पैसा कमा रहे होंगे ।

५   वे सोच रहे होंगे कि वह ऐश की ज़िन्दगी बिता रहे होंगे/होंगी ।

६   आज मेरी बहिन मेरी गाड़ी चला रही होगी ।

9a.2

१   जी नहीं, कमला को ख़ुशी नहीं है । हमको मालूम है क्योंकि वह कहती है "हे भगवान !" ।

२   जी नहीं, पिंकी का एक अलग घर है ।

३   घर में सब्ज़ी और गोश्त की ज़रूरत है ।

४   क्योंकि खन्ना जी अपनी पत्नी को हमेशा "हरीश की माँ" कहते हैं ।

५   कमला सोचती है कि उसका पति दिन भर ऐश करता है । छोटू ही कहता है कि प्रकाश मेहनती हैं ।

9a.3

१   आज शाम को संगीता और पिंकी दावत में नहीं आएँगी । वे दोनों सिनेमा जा रही हैं ।

२   उसको डर है कि शायद ऋषि या राज माँ को बताएगा कि वह सिनेमा जा रही है ।

३   पिंकी का ख़्याल है कि दोनों लड़के भोले-से हैं; वह सोचती है कि वे चुप रहेंगे, किसी से कुछ नहीं कहेंगे ।

४   कमला सोचती होगी कि शायद हरीश संगीता को तंग करेगा ।

५   क्योंकि वह अपने माँ-बाप के साथ कुमार परिवार की दावत में जा रहा होगा ।

9b.1

Dear Pratap,

How are you? Is everything going OK in Delhi? I'm writing this letter after a long time. You must be aware that I too am planning to come to India to study Hindi. I hope that like you, I'll learn good Hindi, after studying very hard. At least this is the intention. To understand Hindi is one thing but to speak it fluently is something different! You know my friend Rajeshwari don't you? Her sister

Usha lives in Varanasi. It's her I'll stay with. Her house is quite far from the college; the college is in Ramnagar, near the Maharaja's palace, and Usha's house is inside Banaras Hindu University (BHU). Lots of students must be living in the vicinity of BHU. They must go to college by rickshaw; I'll go with them too. Father says that it wouldn't be all right for me to go alone because the Varanasi youths get up to a lot of loutish behaviour and hassle girls. They call this 'Eve-teasing', don't they?

Needless to say, I'll come to India by plane. On reaching Delhi I'll phone you. After staying in Delhi for two or three days I'll go to Banaras by train. Usha will come to meet me at the station. The train gets there very early in the morning. A meeting with 'Usha' [the name means 'dawn'] at dawn! I don't know Usha; how I'll recognise her I've no idea. Maybe Rajeshwari will have some old photo of her. Usha's husband is a history lecturer in the university. Rajeshwari says that the two of them, husband and wife, fight a lot. There are also three kids of various ages. I don't know what it'll be like being a guest in such a household! Anyway, if you have the time, you too be sure to come to Banaras sometime. When I reach Delhi I'll phone you. Take care of yourself.

> Yours, Geeta.

9b.2

१   क्या उर्दू सीखने में कोई ख़ास मुश्किल होगी ?

२   अगले महीने हमारे विद्यार्थी हिन्दी सीखने लखनऊ जा रहे होंगे ।

३   अब तक तुम्हारे भाई को हिन्दी अच्छी तरह आती होगी ।

४   मेरे दोस्तों के पिता जी मुझसे मिलने वाराणसी के स्टेशन आएँगे ।

५   दिल्ली के आस-पास बहुत-सी देखने-लायक़ जगहें हैं ।

६   हम पहाड़ों को देखने आपके साथ मसूरी चलेंगे ।

9b.3

१ पढ़ना	पढ़ने	Studying Sanskrit isn't easy; but there's a lot of advantage in studying it.
२ देखने	देखने	I'm going to see a film; you come too – the film will be worth seeing.
३ चलाना	चलाना	Do you like driving? I can't (don't know how to) drive.

| ८ | पीना | पीने | Is it wrong to smoke? Yes of course, and what's the point in smoking? |
| ५ | बजाने | बजाना | Do you come here to play tabla? Yes, I'm very fond of playing tabla. |

10a.1

१	जाऊँ	रहूँ	Should I go with you, or should I stay right here at home?
२	हो	पहुँचें	If the weather isn't bad, they may reach the village by evening.
३	करे		It's right that he should vacate the house before you come.
४	लें	सुनें	It's not necessary for us to take anyone's advice or listen to what anyone says.
५	दे	भूले	Tell him he should reply by tonight and not forget his responsibility.
६	दें		You are requested to pay for the treatment straightaway.

10a.2

१   कि... आप तुरंत जवाब दें ।   I want you to answer immediately.

२   कि... तुम चुप रहो ।   I want you to keep quiet.

३   कि... तुम गाय को न मारो ।   I don't want you to hit the cow. ('I want you not to...')

४   कि... तुम सीढ़ियों पर न बैठो ।   I don't want you to sit on the stairs. ('I want you not to...')

५   कि... तू मेरा हाथ पकड़े ।   I want you to hold my hand!

६   कि... आप आज की संस्कृत की क्लास पढ़ाएँ ।   I want you to teach today's Sanskrit class.

10a.3   (sample answers)

१   अगर आप ख़ाली हों तो ज़रा इन काग़ज़ों पर नज़र डालिए ।   If you're free, just cast a glance over these papers.

२   यदि आपको असुविधा न हो तो अवश्य हमारे साथ चलें ।   If not inconvenient, certainly come with us.

३ अगर तुम उनसे मिलना चाहती हो तो ८ बजे तक यहाँ आओ । If you want to meet them, come here by 8 o'clock.

४ यदि यह काम सचमुच बहुत ही कठिन हो तो आप किसी से कहें कि वह आपकी मदद करे । If this work is really very hard, ask someone to help you.

५ अगर पुलिस आएगी तो हमें जल्दी ही बताना । If the police come, tell us quickly.

६ अगर आप इसके बारे में परेशान हों तो किसी दोस्त की सलाह लें । If you're worried about this, take advice from some friend.

७ अगर तुम फ़ोटो खींचोगे तो वह तुम पर ज़रूर गुस्से होगा । If you take a photo he'll certainly be angry with you.

८ अगर आपकी तबियत ठीक नहीं है तो आप अभी भारत न जाएँ । If your health isn't good you shouldn't go to India just now.

९ अगर तू मेरी बात नहीं मानती तो बहुत बुरा होगा । It'll be very bad if you don't accept what I say.

१० अगर मुझे फ़ुरसत हो तो मैं भी तुम्हारे साथ जाऊँगा । I'll come with you too if I'm free.

10b.1

Prakash – Khanna ji wants you to phone him. Don't forget – it might be something important about tonight. I'm just going to the vegetable seller. Even when I tell you, you don't bring vegetables – you're expert at forgetting. After that I'll go to see Suresh for a bit. You've got the car so I'll go to the market by auto. We need rice etc. from the shops – you bring it. We also need new forks, spoons and knives. There's a list of everything lying on the table in the bedroom. Don't forget anything this time. Get everything from the shop in the market; don't go to the shop in the lane, the prices there are very high. What can I say to you? You don't even know the proper price for anything! You don't even know how to do the shopping properly.

I'll be back in an hour and a half. If you get home first (I mean – before I do), clean the sitting room. Otherwise do it later; but do it for sure. Time and again I tell your mother that she should lend a hand with the cleaning work, but who listens to me. Your mother just swats flies [idles about] all day. I've no idea why everyone in this house is so work shy. I'm the only one who works. I don't understand why I'm writing such a long note. Do I even have the time? I'm in a hurry, I'm getting late. K.

10b.2

१ मेरे ख़याल से कमला नाराज़ है क्योंकि वह नहीं चाहती कि खन्ना परिवार खाना खाने आए ।

२ हाँ, खन्ना जी चाहते हैं कि प्रकाश उन्हें फ़ोन करें ।

३ ख़रीदारी इसीलिए हो रही है कि बहुत लोग डिनर में आ रहे हैं और घर में खाना नहीं है ।

४ कमला कहती है कि वह अपने दोस्त सुरेश से मिलने जाएगी ।

५ अगर वह पहले घर आए तो वह बैठने-वाले कमरे को साफ़ करे ।

६ बाज़ार-वाली दुकान सस्ती है ।

७ चीज़ों की लिस्ट मेज़ पर पड़ी है ।

८ क्योंकि घर का सारा काम कमला ही करती है ।

९ कमला सोचती है कि उसकी बातें कोई नहीं सुनता । पर प्रकाश तो ज़रूर सुनता है क्योंकि वह कमला से बहुत डरता होगा ।

१० नहीं, वह सोचती है कि दादी जी सिर्फ़ मक्खियाँ मारती हैं ।

10b.3

१ कमला चाहती है कि आज रात के डिनर के लिए प्रकाश कुछ दुकानदारी करे ।

२ किसी को नहीं मालूम है कि पासवाली दुकान में हर चीज़ इतनी महँगी क्यों है ।

३ संभव है कि प्रताप आज रात तक नेपाल से लौटे ।

४ किसी वजह से संगीता भी चाहती है कि प्रताप जल्दी ही घर वापस आए ।

५ अगर प्रताप की गाड़ी देर से पहुँचेगी तो शायद कोई उससे मिलने स्टेशन पर जाएगा ।

६ अगर प्रताप संगीता के लिए कोई चीज़ लाता है तो वह क्या कहेगी ?

11a.1

1 The girls arrived in Banaras yesterday morning. / have arrived, had, will have, may have

2 They slept late last night. / have slept, had, will have, may have

3 They went to the ghat three times to see the Ganges. / have gone, had, will have, may have

4 In the afternoon they met some friends. / have met, had, will have, may have

5 They enjoyed it a lot. / have enjoyed, had, will have, may have

11a.2

१ मेरे लड़के भारत गए । / गए हैं, गए थे, गए होंगे, गए हों

२ वे दो हफ़्ते के लिए घूमे । / घूमे हैं, घूमे थे, घूमे होंगे, घूमे हों

३ वे सस्ते होटलों में रहे । / रहे हैं, रहे थे, रहे होंगे, रहे हों

४ वे थोड़ी हिन्दी बोले । / बोले हैं, बोले थे, बोले होंगे, बोले हों

५ उन्हें काफ़ी मज़ा आया । / आया है, आया था, आया होगा, आया हो

11b.1

1 Papa bought stomach medicine. / has bought, had, will have, may have

2 He paid the correct price. / has paid, had, will have, may have

3 The shopkeeper demanded more. / has demanded, had, will have, may have

4 Papa complained. / has complained, had, will have, may have

5 Ma watched the goings-on. / has watched, had, will have, may have

11b.2

१ धोबी ने दोनों साड़ियाँ धोईं । / धोई हैं, धोई थीं, धोई होंगी, धोई हों

२ उसने एक ही साड़ी वापस दी । / दी है, दी थी, दी होगी, दी हो

३ उसकी पत्नी ने दूसरी पहनी । / पहनी है, पहनी थी, पहनी होगी, पहनी हो

४ हमने उसे किसी की शादी में देखा । / देखा है, देखा था, देखा होगा, देखा हो

५ उन्होंने माफ़ी माँगी । / माँगी है, माँगी थी, माँगी होगी, माँगी हो

11c.1

१ दुकानदार ने पापा की शिकायत को सुना था । The shopkeeper had listened to Papa's complaint.

२ पर उसने पापा की बातों को नहीं माना । But he didn't accept the things Papa said.

३ माँ ने दुकानदार की बाँह को पकड़ा । Ma grabbed the shopkeeper's arm.

४ पापा ने अपने पैसों को वापस लिया होगा क्योंकि... Papa must have taken his money back because...

५ ...दुकानदार ने अपनी भारी-सी लाठी को उठाया । ...the shopkeeper picked up his stout stick.

11c.2

१ मैंने अपने सारे कपड़े उतारे । I took off all my clothes.

२ डाक्टर ने अपनी सिग्रेट ख़त्म की और उँगलियाँ गिलास में धोईं । The doctor finished his cigarette and washed his fingers in a glass.

३ फिर उन्होंने दराज़ में से अपनी किताब निकाली... Then he took his book out from the drawer...

४ ...और अपना चश्मा नाक पर सीधा किया । ... and straightened the specs on his nose.

५ तब उन्होंने अपनी आँखें बंद कीं और दो प्रसिद्ध फ़िल्मी गीत सुनाए । Then he closed his eyes and sang two famous film songs.

11c.3 (sample answer)

आज मैं सात बजे उठा । नाश्ते में मैंने रोटी खाई और चाय पी । आठ बजे मैंने दफ़्तर जाने के लिए बस पकड़ी । काम करने का मन मुझे बिलकुल नहीं था, क्योंकि मुझे बहुत थकान थी । इसलिए मैंने बहुत कम काम किया । कई दोस्तों को फ़ोन किया । उनमें से एक ने कहा कि "शाम को क्यों न मिलें ?" । इसलिए शाम को घर लौटने के बाद मैं उससे मिलने उसके घर गया । हमने उसके यहाँ थोड़ी देर के लिए बातें कीं, फिर एक पासवाले होटल में गए । वहाँ हम ने दाल-रोटी खाई । खाना इतना अच्छा तो नहीं था, पर सस्ता था । फिर ग्यारह बजे मैं घर वापस आया । बस, यही था मेरा दिन का प्रोग्राम ।

12a.1

१ संगीता ने घर जाकर किसी दोस्त को फ़ोन किया । Sangeeta went home and phoned some friend.

२ ऋषि ने अपनी किताब खोलकर दो-तीन कहानियाँ पढ़ीं । Rishi opened his book and read two or three stories.

३ कमला अपना काम ख़त्म करके तुरंत बाहर गई । Immediately after finishing her work Kamala went out.

४ हम छोटू के यहाँ जाकर खाना बनाएँगे । We'll go to Chotu's place and cook.

५ खन्ना जी ने डिब्बे में आकर ऊपरवाले बर्थ पर अपना सामान रखा । Coming into the compartment, Khanna ji put his luggage on the upper berth.

12a.2

१ आज सुबह नहाकर तूने साबुन को कहाँ रखा ? Where did you put the soap after bathing this morning?

२ परीक्षा देकर प्रताप और उसके साथी कम से कम दो हफ़्ते तक आराम करेंगे । After taking the exam, Pratap and his companions will rest for at least two weeks.

३ अपनी डिगरी पास करके तुम क्या करना चाहते हो ? What do you want to do after passing your degree?

४ लन्दन वापस आकर उसने भारत के बारे में कई पुस्तकें लिखीं । Returning to London, he/she wrote several books about India.

५ शाम को दफ़्तर से लौटकर प्रकाश कभी कभी बाज़ार में सैर करता है । Prakash sometimes goes for a stroll in the market after coming home from work in the evening.

12b.1

१ कितने बजे हैं ? साढ़े सात बजे हैं । मैं नाश्ता कर चुका हूँ ।

२ मैं अक्सर साढ़े आठ बजे पहुँचता हूँ, पर आज मैं पौने नौ से पहले नहीं पहुँच पाया ।

३ मैं दोपहर का खाना डेढ़ और ढाई बजे के बीच खा लेता हूँ ।

४ क्या विद्यार्थी ठीक ग्यारह बजे पहुँचेंगे ? नहीं, वे तो सवा ग्यारह तक आ जाएँगे ।

५ सुबह के पौने एक बजे तक मैं अपना पढ़ाई का काम ख़त्म कर पाया ।

12b.2

१ हाँ, बोले लेता हूँ ।

२ नहीं, वह उसे ख़त्म नहीं कर सका ।

३ हाँ, वे तो हमेशा सात बजे सो जाते हैं ।

४ हाँ, वह आधे से ज़्यादा खा चुकी है ।

५ क्यों, वह तो चार बजे बंद हो गई थी ।

13a.1

१   हाँ, हमको चाय तैयार कर देनी चाहिए । Yes, we should prepare tea.

२   पापा को ही बच्चों को खाना खिलाना चाहिए । *Papa* should feed the kids.

३   जी नहीं, उसको हिन्दुस्तानी कपड़े नहीं पहनने चाहिए । No, she shouldn't wear Indian clothes.

४   हाँ, तुम्हें कमरा मिल जाना चाहिए । Yes, you should get a room.

५   हाँ, हमें थोड़ा आराम करना चाहिए । Yes, we should rest a little.

६   नहीं, तुमको उसकी जेब से पैसा नहीं लेना चाहिए । No, you should not take money from his/her pocket.

13a.2

१   तुझे मेरी सहेली की सलाह लेनी पड़ेगी । You will have to take my friend's advice.

२   मुझे रोज़ पढ़ाई का काम करना पड़ेगा । I will have to study everyday.

३   माँ कहती हैं कि मुझे हर हफ़्ते उन्हें चिट्ठी लिखनी पड़ेगी । Mother says I will have to write her a letter every day.

४   अगर चोरी का डर है तो हमें एक ताला ख़रीदना पड़ेगा । If there's a risk of theft we will have to buy a lock.

५   अगर चावल न मिले तो तुम्हें रोटी खानी पड़ेगी । If rice isn't available you will have to eat roti.

६   हमें कम से कम दो भाषाएँ सीखनी पड़ेंगी । We will have to learn at least two languages.

13a.3   (sample answer)

१   जैसे ही वह कमरे में आया वैसे ही बच्ची रो पड़ी । As soon as he came into the room the little girl burst into tears.

२   जब तक मुझे उधार का पैसा नहीं मिलेगा तब तक मुझे यहीं रहना पड़ेगा । Until I get the loan I'll have to stay right here.

३   जब आपको फ़ुरसत हो तो हमारे यहाँ खाना खाने आएँ । When you're free come and eat at our place.

४   ज्योंही मुझे महसूस हुआ कि उसे यह जगह अच्छी नहीं लगती त्योंही मैंने दूसरा घर ढूँढ़ लिया । As soon as I felt that he/she didn't like this place I [looked for and] found a different house.

५ जब तुम दिल्ली में रहने के लिए आओगे तब हम अवश्य मिलेंगे । When you come to live in Delhi we'll definitely meet.

६ जब तक तुम माफ़ी नहीं माँगोगी तब तक वह तुम्हें माफ़ नहीं करेगा । He won't forgive you until you apologise.

७ जब से मैंने उसे अपनी बहिन के बारे में बताया तब से मुझे उसकी एक भी चिट्ठी नहीं मिली । Since I told him/her about my sister I haven't had a single letter from him/her.

८ जब गाड़ी बिकेगी तभी हम तुम्हें तुम्हारा पैसा वापस देंगे । When the car gets sold, we'll return your money.

13b.1

१ जो दुकान मैंने आपको दिखाई थी उसमें विदेशी कपड़े मिलते हैं ।

२ जो किताबें आपको चाहिए, वे उस मेज़ पर मिलेंगी ।

३ जो पत्र मैंने आपको भेजा था, क्या वह मिल गया ?

४ जिन लोगों को मौक़ा मिले उन्हें अगले साल फिर मिलना चाहिए ।

५ जिन बच्चों को हमने कल देखा था वे मेरे दोस्त के बच्चे हैं ।

६ जो आदमी मेरे भाई जैसा लगता है वह असल में मेरा चाचा है ।

७ जा ताला हमने खाँ मार्केट में ख़रीदा, वह काफ़ी मज़बूत है ।

८ जो वाक्य तुमने कल लिखे, तुम्हें उनको सीखना चाहिए ।

९ जो लोग सिग्रेट पीते हैं उनको बाहर ही रहना चाहिए ।

13b.2

१ जब प्रताप की माँ ने उसे फ़ोन किया तभी उसने कहा कि उसे मेहनत करनी पड़ेगी ।

२ जब से प्रताप भारत आया है तब से वह हिन्दी सीख रहा है ।

३ जब प्रताप लन्दन जाएगा तो उसे हिन्दी-बोलनेवाले लोगों से मिलना चाहिए ।

४ उसको "जब"-वाले वाक्यों का अभ्यास करने का मौक़ा मिला ।

५ जो लड़का कोने में बैठा है, उसके बारे में खन्ना जी पूछ रहे हैं ।

६ जी नहीं, सुरेश संगीता का रिश्तेदार तो नहीं है, सिर्फ़ पड़ोसी है ।

७ जिस दिन डिनर हुआ, उस दिन अरुण को अपने प्रकाशक के यहाँ जाना था ।

८ कमला विषय को इसलिए बदलना चाहती है कि उसे डर है कि सुरेश की बातें खन्ना जी को बुरी लगें ।

13b.3 (sample answer)

१ जाने से पहले आपको "वीज़ा" का इंतज़ाम कर लेना चाहिए । जाने से पहले आप "वीज़ा" का इंतज़ाम कर लें ।

२ अगर आपको ट्रेन से सफ़र करना हो तो आपको कई दिन पहले अपना टिकट ख़रीदना चाहिए । ... तो आप कई दिन पहले टिकट ख़रीदें ।

३ आपको नल का पानी नहीं पीना चाहिए । आप नल का पानी न पिएँ ।

४ आपको कोई हिन्दी फ़िल्म ज़रूर देखनी चाहिए ।आप कोई हिन्दी फ़िल्म ज़रूर देखें ।

५ भारत में आपको हिन्दी ही बोलनी चाहिए । भारत में आप हिन्दी ही बोलें ।

६ अगर आपके पास काफ़ी पैसे हैं तो आपको कुछ बढ़िया कपड़े ख़रीदने चाहिए । ... तो आप कुछ बढ़िया कपड़े ख़रीदें ।

14.a.1

१ तमिल तो दक्षिण भारत में बोली जाती है । Tamil is spoken in South India.

२ सारी तैयारियाँ ६ बजे तक की जाएँगी ।   All the arrangements will be made by 6 o'clock.

३ यह चिट्ठी हवाई डाक से भेजी जाएगी । This letter will be sent by airmail.

४ इस विश्वविद्यालय में संस्कृत भी पढ़ी जाती है ।   Sanskrit too is studied in this university.

५ मंदिर में फ़ोटो नहीं खींचा जाना चाहिए ।   Photographs ('a photograph') should not be taken in the temple.

६ ज़िन्दगी को थोड़ा और सरल बनाया जाना चाहिए । Life should be made a little simpler.

14.a.2

१ सबसे नए मकान पिछले साल ही बनाए गए थे ।

२ सारी चिट्ठियों को एक बड़े लिफ़ाफ़े में रखा गया था ।

३ अख़बार में कहा गया था कि चोरों को पकड़ा गया था ।

४ भारतीय भाषाओं के बारे में कई अजीब किताबें लिखी गई हैं ।

५ संगीता सोचने लगी कि रविवार कभी नहीं आएगा ।

६ बारिश होने लगी, इसलिए कमला ने राज को बाहर जाने नहीं दिया ।

७ जब बच्चों को भूख लगने लगी तो मैंने उन्हें खाना खाने दिया ।

८ हमें बताया गया कि मेहमान आने लगे थे ।

९   जब तक मैं तुम्हें न बताऊँ तब तक किसी को अन्दर आने न दो ।

१०   भविष्य में जो लोग काम नहीं करते उन्हें पैसा नहीं दिया जाएगा ।

14.a.3 (sample answer)

जब सुरेश कमरे में आया तो उसने देखा कि संगीता ने कुछ नेपाली ज़ेवर पहने थे । जब उसने उनके बारे में पूछा, तो संगीता ने जवाब दिया कि इन्हें काठमांडु से लाया गया था । फिर सुरेश ने पूछा कि हरीश कल की दावत में क्यों नहीं आया; पर संगीता को मालूम नहीं था । संगीता ने कहा कि शायद हरीश के पिता ने उसे आने नहीं दिया था । सुरेश कहने लगा कि शायद खन्ना साहब चाहते थे... पर संगीता ने सुरेश को अपनी बात को ख़त्म करने नहीं दिया । विषय बदलने के लिए संगीता ने कहा कि दूरदर्शन को देखा जाए । पर उसकी गुस्ताख़ी सुरश को बहुत बुरी लगी थी इसलिए जब कमला कमरे में आई तो सुरेश ने उससे शिकायत की कि तुम्हारी बेटी ने मुझसे बुरी बातें कही हैं ।

14.b.1 (sample answer)

१   मेरे जितने दोस्त हैं, सभी छुट्टी पर गए हैं । All the friends I have, have gone on holiday.

२   तुम जितने ध्यान से पढ़ोगे, उतना सीखोगे । The harder you study the more you'll learn.

३   जितनी अच्छी यह नई किताब है, उतनी अच्छी तुम्हारी किताब नहीं हो सकती । Your book can't be as good as this new book.

४   जहाँ हम लोग रहते हैं, वहाँ कोई शराब की दुकान नहीं है । There's no liquor shop where we live.

५   छुट्टियों में हम वहाँ जाएँ जहाँ बहुत कम लोग जाते हों । On our holidays let's go to a place where very few people go.

६   जहाँ महँगी दुकानें और शानदार होटल हैं वहाँ अमीर लोगों की आबादी ज़रूर होगी । Where there are expensive shops and fancy hotels there are sure to be rich people living.

७   तुम्हारे पास जितने कपड़े हैं उतने ही हमारे पास भी हैं । We have just as many clothes as you do.

८   जितनी बड़ी दिल्ली है उतना बड़ा लखनऊ नहीं है । Lucknow is not as big as Delhi.

14b.2

Yesterday I was invited to Kamala and Prakash Kumar's dinner. It was a very fine dinner. I've never eaten as much as we were given to eat. When Kamala started giving me more for a third time I began saying 'Enough! Enough!' but she took no notice. Meat, vegetables, daal, roti, rice, chutney – so much food had been prepared that I just can't tell you! It wasn't the kind of Indian food you get in London; here everything was completely fresh, and it was as tasty as it was fresh! The sweet dish had been brought from some shop, but apart from the sweet everything had been made at home. Kamala ji is an expert at cooking.

But you must be wondering, who came to the dinner altogether? I'll tell you. I arrived late because of my studying. When I arrived I was sat in a corner of the room. Khanna ji had been sat in the middle, and next to him his wife, whom I thought very nice. Their son had been invited too, but for some reason he didn't come. Sangeeta had gone to see a film with her friend Pinkie (Khanna ji's younger sister); they got home when the film ended at about eleven and they ate whatever food was left. (The film was 'Hum Apke Hain Kaun', which was made several years ago; Sangeeta must have already seen it at least four or five times, and I don't understand why she wanted to see it again.) Suresh also came; Kamala ji sat him near her. Arun had gone to see some friend so he was *'anupasthit'* – absent. He's very fond of such words – he loads his speech with so many Sanskrit words that half of what he says goes right over my head.

Several interesting things about Hindi were said during the dinner. Suresh said that Delhi Hindi has become corrupted, because of Panjabi. (Sharma ji too was saying in class that Panjabis mostly say *'maine jānā hai'* [for 'I have to go'] which is a wrong usage – only *'mujhe jānā hai'* is correct. But when Suresh said this Prakash ji glared at him in such a way that Suresh fell silent, poor fellow. The thing is, you see, that Khanna is himself a Panjabi. And Prakash completely cowers in front of him – like a 'wet cat'! In the end Kamala changed the subject and made some joke about Rishi and Raj, and everyone started laughing. But afterwards Kamala ji must have given Suresh a good scolding!

Mrs Khanna is a very nice lady. She knows a lot about languages too. When I asked her why 'Rajasthan' has a *'th'* while Pakistan only has *'t'* she explained it to me by saying that *'sthān'* is a Sanskrit word while *'stān'* is Persian. Both words have the same meaning – 'place'. So even words have families! But not like the Kumar family. Not at all!

15a.1 (sample answers)

१ हम दिन भर काम करते रहंगे । We'll go on working all day.

२ बेचारी छात्रा दस दिन तक पढ़ती रही । The poor student went on studying for ten days.

३ आप ध्यान से काम करते रहिए, तभी सफल होंगे । Keep working attentively, *then* you'll be successful.

४ सरकार की शक्ति बढ़ती गई, यहाँ तक कि हमें देश को छोड़ना पड़ा । The power of the government kept growing, to the point that we had to leave the country.

५ बादल और भी घने होते गए, फिर दस दिन तक बर्फ़ गिरती रही । The clouds went on thickening , then it kept snowing for ten days.

15a.2

१ पिताजी एक मशहूर सरकारी अख़बार चलाया करते थे । Father used to run a famous government newspaper.

२ वह बदमाश अपने बच्चों को मारा करता है । That scoundrel makes a habit of beating his children.

३ सच है कि किसी ज़माने में हमारे भी कई नौकर हुआ करते थे । It's true that at some time we too used to have several servants.

४ शाम को दादीजी हमेशा मंदिर जाया करती हैं । In the evening Grandmother always goes to the temple.

५ हमारे पड़ोसी हमें अक्सर धोखा दिया करते हैं । Our neighbours regularly trick us.

15a.3

१ जैसा आपने कहा था, वैसा ही हो गया । It happened just as you'd said.

२ जैसी फ़िल्में आजकल बन रही हैं, वैसी फ़िल्में मेरे बचपन में नहीं बनती थीं । The type of films that are being made today weren't made in my childhood.

३ जिस तरह की नौकरी मैं करती हूँ उस तरह की तुम क्यों नहीं करते ? Why don't you do a job like the one I do?

४ जिस तरह के मकान इस इलाक़े में बन रहे हैं उस तरह के मकान पुराने शहर में नहीं मिलते । The kind of houses that are being built in this area aren't to be found in the old city.

५ जैसा मौक़ा तुम्हें आज मिला है वैसा मौक़ा तुम्हें दुबारा नहीं मिलनेवाला है । You're not likely to get another chance like the one you got today.

15b.1

१ उस जैसे लोगों को नौकरी आसानी से नहीं मिलती ।

२ जैसे कि दर्ज़नों लोग मुझे बता चुके थे, वह आदमी पागल हो गया था ।

३ वह इस तरह सोया जैसे वह कई हफ़्तों से सोया न हो ।

४ हम लोग सन् १९४७ से इस देश में रह रहे हैं ।

५ जब से दुर्घटना हुई तबसे उसने गाड़ी नहीं चलाई है ।

६ अगर दवा से कुछ फ़ायदा न हो तो आपको डाक्टर से शिकायत करनी चाहिए ।

७ मैं मालिक से कुछ कहना चाहता था मगर डर के मारे मैं कुछ बोल नहीं पाया ।

८ आज आपको अख़बार ख़ुद लाने पड़ेंगे क्योंकि अख़बार-वाला बीमार है ।

15b.2 (includes sample answers)

१ प्रताप तीन साल से हिन्दी पढ़ रहा है । मैं तो एक साल से पढ़ रहा हूँ । मैंने पिछले साल ही हिन्दी सीखना शुरू किया ।

२ जो आदमी प्रताप को हिन्दी पढ़ाया करता था, वह उत्तर प्रदेश से था ।

३ जी हाँ, वह कभी कभी उच्चारण की गलतियाँ किया करता है; उदाहरण के लिए, जब उसे "मोड़" कहना था उसने "मोर" कहा ।

४ नहीं, उसके पास मोर क्यों होगा !

५ जी नहीं, दादी जी कहती हैं कि प्रताप को हिन्दी सीखनी रहनी चाहिए ।

६ क्योंकि उसको मालूम है कि खन्ना जी के पास ड्राइवर है ।

७ क्योंकि उसके पिताजी ने कहा था कि आज काम करनेवालों की छुट्टी है ।

८ ग़रीब लोगों की हालत ख़राब है; उनको छुट्टी नहीं मिलती, और बहुत मेहनत करने पर भी उन्हें पैसे की कमी रहती है ।

९ छोटू को खन्ना जी से बात करनी चाहिए ।

१० मेरे ख़याल से खन्ना जी छोटू के बारे में परवाह नहीं करते; लेकिन हरीश तो छोटू की मदद करना चाहता है ।

15b.3 (sample answer)

२१ जून १९९९ । शनिवार है । आज कई काम करने थे; कालेज तो नहीं जाना था, लेकिन कालेज का काम बहुत था, और मैं जानता था कि आज नानी जी फ़ोन करेंगी, इसलिए मैंने सोचा कि मुझे बाहर नहीं जाना चाहिए, घर पर रुककर पढ़ाई का काम करूँगा । मगर ऐसा नहीं हुआ । क़रीब दस बजे रवि और रीता ने फ़ोन करके कहा कि हम लोग समुद्र के किनारे जा रहे हैं, तुम भी साथ चलो । मैंने जाने से इनकार तो नहीं किया, बस इतना कहा कि सुनो, एक छोटी-सी समस्या है – शनिवार को मेरी नानी जी अमरीका से फ़ोन किया करती हैं, इसलिए तुम्हारे साथ जाना मुश्किल होगा । फिर रवि गुस्सा होकर कहने लगा कि तुम्हारी नानी के सिवा तुम्हारा कोई नहीं है जिसके बारे में तुम परवाह करते हो ! इसलिए मैंने कहा चलो ठीक है, चलता हूँ तुम्हारे साथ ।

समुद्र के किनारे बहुत भीड़ थी । अच्छी-सी जगह थी लेकिन मेरे लिए तो रवि के गुस्से ने दिन को बरबाद कर दिया था । इतना डरपोक क्यों हूँ मैं ? उसकी बातों पर ध्यान क्यों देता हूँ, जैसे कि वह मेरा बाप हो ! मुझे उसे साफ़ कहना चाहिए था कि आज मुझे बाहर नहीं जाना है; मगर डर के मारे मैं कुछ बोल ही नहीं पाया; और दिन भर मैं नानी जी के फ़ोन के बारे में चिन्ता करता रहा ।

मैं बड़ी देर से घर लौटा । जब मैं कमरे में आया तो फ़ोन पर नानी जी का मेसेज था – "बेटे, आज तुमसे बात नहीं कर पाऊँगी, कुछ दोस्तों के साथ समुद्र के किनारे जा रही हूँ । कल फ़ोन करूँगी । जीते रहो !"

16.a.1 (sample answers)

१   जी हाँ, मुझे साइकिल ठीक करना आता है; मगर साइकल चलाना तो नहीं आता ।

२   आम तौर पर मैं काम साढ़े आठ बजे शुरू करता हूँ; पर जिस दिन मैं देर से उठता हूँ मैं साढ़े नौ से पहले नहीं शुरू करता ।

३   मुझे तो पुरानी फ़िल्में ही पसंद हैं क्योंकि उनके गाने बहुत बढ़िया होते हैं ।

४   जी हाँ, मैं लगभग हर काम के लिए कंप्यूटर का इस्तेमाल करता हूँ !

५   जी हाँ मैं अक्सर हिन्दी में ही ई-मेल भेजा करता हूँ, लेकिन ई-मेल में देवनागरी लिपि का इस्तेमाल करना थोड़ा मुश्किल है ।

६   जी हाँ, मेरी शादी कई साल पहले हुई थी । हमारे तीन बच्चे भी हैं ।

७   जी नहीं, आज तो मुझे किसी से नहीं मिलना है । मुझे अपनी साइकिल को ठीक करना है ।

८   इस कमरे में कई चीज़ें दिखाई दे रही हैं – बहुत सारी किताबें, एक कंप्यूटर, कुछ पुराने अख़बार... और मेज़ पर कई चिट्ठियाँ पड़ी हैं जिनका मुझे जवाब देना चाहिए ।

९   मैं उनको एक काग़ज़ पर लिख लेता हूँ और बार बार उनका सही उच्चारण करने की
    कोशिश करता हूँ ।

१० जी हाँ, एक साल पहले मैं उत्तर प्रदेश के एक छोटे-से गाँव में एक चाय की दुकान पर
    चाय पी रहा था ।

16a.2

१   हमें बताया गया है कि हमें दूसरे यात्रियों का इंतज़ार करना पड़ेगा ।

२   सामान तो ट्रेन पर लाद दिया गया है मगर हमारे खाने का इंतज़ाम किसी ने नहीं
    किया है ।

३   मालूम होता है कि किसी यात्री हा देहान्त हो गया है ।

४   कृपया उन दूसरे यात्रियों का पीछा करें; आपके बच्चों की देखभाल हम लोग करेंगे ।

५   मैंने एक दोस्त को फ़ोन करने की कोशिश की लेकिन फ़ोन काम नहीं कर रहा था ।

६   आज वे कंप्यूटर का इस्तेमाल नहीं कर सकते क्योंकि बिजली नहीं है ।

७   जो लोग यहाँ नौकरी करते हैं, उनकी निंदा न करना, कसूर उनका तो नहीं है ।

८   जिस आदमी से मेरी मुलाक़ात स्टेशन पर हुई, उसी से मैंने शादी कर ली ।

16a.3 (sample answer)

हरीश ने छोटू को एक अच्छा-सा मज़ाक सुनाया, जिसे सुनकर छोटू हँसने लगा । छोटू को
यह भी अच्छा लगा होगा कि उसके मालिक का बेटा उससे इस तरह से बात कर रहा है ।
हरीश छोटू से पूछने लगा कि खन्ना जी कहाँ हैं; और छोटू के जवाब से पता चला कि छोटू
खुश नहीं हैं; वह खन्ना जी से कुछ माँगना चाहता था मगर मारे डर के कुछ बोल न पाया
था । हरीश ने कहा कि किसी से डरने की ज़रूरत नहीं, डरपोक मत बनना ।

बाद में जब खन्ना जी वापस आए तो छोटू ने फिर से उनसे बात करने की कोशिश की ।
शुरू में उसने हरीश की थोड़ी-सी तारीफ़ की, फिर यह पूछा कि हरीश की शादी कब हो
जाएगी । लेकिन इन बातों का खन्ना जी पर कोई असर नहीं पड़ा, और जब छोटू ने खन्ना जी
से अपनी हालत के बारे में कुछ कहना चाहा तो खन्ना जी ने उसकी बात काटकर कहा कि मैं
बड़ी जल्दी में हूँ, मुझे एक मीटिंग का इंतज़ाम करना है । इसलिए फिर से निराशा हुई
बेचारे छोटू को ।

16b.1

१   जहाँ मैं पैदा हुआ, वहाँ पुराने ज़माने में तरह तरह के जंगली जानवर घूमा करते थे ।

    Where I was born, various kinds of wild animals used to roam
    in the olden days.

२   जहाँ जंगली जानवर रहते हैं वहाँ इमारतें नहीं बनाई जानी चाहिए थीं । Build-
    ings should not have been put up where wild animals live.

३   जहाँ भी तुम बैठना चाहते हो, बैठ सकते हो । You can sit wherever you like.

४   जिस गाँव में नानी जी बचपन में रहती थीं मेरी शादी वहीं हुई थी । My
    wedding took place in the very village where my grandmother
    lived in her childhood.

५   गाँव के पुराने इलाक़े में जहाँ गाँधी जी रहा करते थे वहाँ बिजली का इस्तेमाल नहीं
    किया जाता है । In the old area of the village where Gandhi ji used
    to stay, electricity isn't used.

६   जब तक मेरे पड़ोसी घर पहुँचे तब तक उनके पिता का देहान्त हो चुका था । By
    the time my neighbours got home their father had already
    passed away.

16b.2
1   Which different places did you visit in India and what various
    things did you see?
2   In his childhood he must have had many kinds of experience.
3   All the people had become lost ('sunk') in their own thoughts.
4   After having piping hot tea we all went off to our own rooms.
5   Give the porters 20 rupees each.
6   Well Raju, are you in the pink? Like some tea or anything?
7   Why should I waste my time going to some useless meeting?

16b.3
१   हमें उनको दस दस रुपए देने चाहिए जिससे कि वे कुछ चाय-वाय लें ।

२   पाकिस्तान में तुम्हें कौन-कौन मिला ?

३   याद रखो कि ऐसी गंदी जगहों में तुम्हें खाना-वाना नहीं लेना चाहिए ।

४   रोज़ खाना खाने के बाद आप सबों को एक एक गोली खानी चाहिए ।

५   मेरे पास न पैसा है न वक़्त, इसलिए मेहमानों की देखभाल तुम्हें ख़ुद करनी होगी ।

17a.1
१   अगर आप हवाई जहाज़ से गए होते तो अब तक पहुँच जाते ।

२   हालाँकि मैंने उन्हें रोकने की कोशिश की, फिर भी उन्होंने मेरी सलाह पर ध्यान नहीं
    दिया ।

३ अगर दिल्ली यहाँ से इतनी दूर नहीं होती तो मैं तुरंत तुमसे मिलने आता ।

४ अगर मुझे मालूम होता कि उसकी हालत कितनी ख़राब थी तो मैं उसे सच नहीं बताता ।

५ अगर हीरो इतना लोकप्रिय नहीं होता तो ऐसी फ़िल्म देखने कोई भी नहीं आता ।

६ हालाँकि वह मेरे दादा जी को अच्छी तरह जानती थी फिर भी उसने सुझाव दिया कि हम उन्हें बुलाएँ ।

७ अगर तुमने मुझा बताया होता कि समस्या कितनी गंभीर थी तो मैं अपना समय नहीं गँवाता ।

८ हालाँकि मैंने कहा कि कसूर मेरा नहीं है, फिर भी उसने शिकायत की ।

17a.2

१ हालाँकि मैंने बहुत कोशिश की फिर भी मैं काम को पूरा नहीं कर पाया ।
Although I tried a lot, I couldn't complete the work.

२ हालाँकि मैं रात भर तलाश करती रही वह पुराना पत्र नहीं मिला । Although I went on searching all night I didn't find that old letter.

३ हालाँकि मैंने रस्सी को काटने की बहुत कोशिश की, फिर भी वह कटी नहीं ।
Although I tried hard to cut the string it wouldn't cut.

४ हालाँकि हमने शिकायत कर दी फिर भी कोई परवाह नहीं करता ।
Although we complained, nobody cares.

17a.3 (sample answer)

छोटू खन्ना जी, एक बात कहूँ ? अगर आपको फ़ुरसत हो तो...

खन्ना ज़रूर छोटू भैया, ज़रूर, क्या कहना चाहते हो ? तुम्हें किस चीज़ की चिन्ता है ? साफ़ साफ़ कहो !

छोटू सर, मैं अपना काम अच्छी तरह से करता हूँ न? इसलिए मुझे साल में पाँच हफ़्ते की छुट्टी मिलनी चाहिए । और... अगर ज़्यादा पैसा भी मिल जाता तो अच्छा होता ।

खन्ना अरे इतनी-सी बात ? इसका तो इंतज़ाम आज ही किया जाएगा । तुमने पहले क्यों नहीं कहा ?

छोटू सर, मैं आपको तकलीफ़ देना नहीं चाहता था । आप इतने व्यस्त रहते हैं कि...

खन्ना व्यस्त तो हूँ, फिर भी अगर मुझसे बात नहीं करोगे तो किससे करोगे छोटू? हम दोनों साथ साथ काम जो करते हैं, भाइयों के जैसे ।

छोटू खन्ना जी, किन शब्दों में आपसे धन्यवाद कहूँ ?

खन्ना अरे धन्यवाद-बन्यवाद को भूल जाओ । एक बात और – मैं तुमको अपना ड्राइवर बनाने की सोच रहा हूँ । मैं हर तरह से तुम्हारी देखभाल करूँगा, मेरे पुराने दोस्त !

17b.1

१ खन्ना जी को अपने बेटे हरीश की शादी के बारे में चिंता है ।

२ नहीं, उमा परेशान नहीं है । उसको उम्मीद है कि हरीश संगीता से ही शादी करेगा ।

३ खन्ना जी ऐसा सोचते हैं क्योंकि संगीता नौकरी नहीं करती है ।

४ मैं तो उमा से सहमत हूँ क्योंकि जिससे प्यार हो उसी से शादी करनी चाहिए ।

५ नहीं, बिलकुल नहीं । संगीता तो सुहास से ही प्यार करती है, हरीश से नहीं ।

६ क्योंकि शादी के मामले में संगीता अपने माता-पिता की बातें मानने को तैयार नहीं है ।

७ हाँ, प्रकाश अनीता से बात कर चुका है – पर रूबरू नहीं, फ़ोन पर ही ।

८ हाँ, मैं तो संगीता की गुस्ताख़ी को माफ़ कर देता, यह समझकर कि उसकी अपनी ज़िन्दगी है ।

17b.2

१ एक साल के अन्दर मैंने पूरे सात लेख लिख डाले । Within a year I churned out a full seven articles.

२ उसने जो पैसे बड़ी मेहनत करके कमाये थे, सब को गँवा दिया है । He's squandered all the money he earned through hard work.

३ अरे, तुम किस तरह की पागल बातें बोल बैठे ? Oh, what kind of crazy things did you go and say?

४ मेरे बेटे ने गुस्से में अपने सबसे क़ीमती कपड़ों को फाड़ डाला । In anger my son ripped his most expensive clothes to shreds.

५ समाचार को सुनकर छोटू हँस उठा लेकिन दूसरे लोग रो पड़े । On hearing the news Chotu burst out laughing but the others started crying.

६ पुलिस ने कह रखा है कि बेचारा खिड़की से गिर पड़ा था । The police have maintained that the poor fellow had fallen from the window.

७ जैसे ही दूसरे लोग आ गए, हमने काम आरंभ कर दिया । As soon as the other people turned up we began work.

८ जिसने हमारे दोस्त को मार डाला, उससे हम रूबरू बात कर लें । Let's have a face-to-face talk with the person who killed our friend.

17b.3 (sample answers)

१ मेहरबानी करके आप हमारा खाना बनाने की भी तकलीफ़ करें – अगर वक़्त मिले तो ।

२ मुझे उम्मीद है कि इस साल के आख़िर तक यह किताब ख़त्म की जाएगी ।

३ अगर आपको फ़ुरसत हो तो अपने ख़ूबसूरत दोस्त को यह ख़त दे दें । शुक्रिया ।

४ शुरू में मुसाफ़िर को लगा कि सफ़र ज़्यादा मुश्किल होगा लेकिन इसका बहुत फ़ायदा होगा ।

५   सवाल – आम हिन्दी और आम उर्दू में कितना फ़र्क है ? जवाब – कौन कह सकता है
     कि दोनों ज़बानों में कोई ख़ास फ़र्क नहीं है ?

१   कृपा करके आप हमारा भोजन बनाने का भी कष्ट करें – यदि समय मिले तो ।
२   मुझे आशा है कि इस वर्ष के अन्त तक यह पुस्तक समाप्त की जाएगी ।
३   यदि आपको अवकाश हो तो अपने सुंदर मित्र को यह पत्र दे दें । धन्यवाद ।
४   आरंभ में यात्री को लगा कि यात्रा अधिक कठिन होगी किंतु इसका बहुत लाभ होगा ।
५   प्रश्न – "साधारण हिन्दी और साधारण उर्दू में कितना अंतर है ?" उत्तर – "कौन कह
     सकता है कि दोनों भाषाओं में कोई विशेष अंतर नहीं है ?"

18a.1 (sample answers)

१   इस शहर में रहते हुए मुझे कोई बीस साल हुए हैं ।
२   जिस कमरे में मैं बैठा हुआ हूँ, इसमें बहुत सारी किताबें हैं । फ़र्श पर भी किताबों के
     ढेर पड़े हुए हैं । मेज़ पर कुछ लकड़ी के बने हुए खिलौने हैं – एक छोटा-सा हाथी और
     तीन-चार चिड़ियाँ ।
३   आज मैं पुराने कपड़े पहने हुए हूँ क्योंकि मुझे बाहर नहीं जाना है, घर पर ही रहना है ।
४   हाँ, बिना भारत गए हिन्दी सीखी जा सकती है, लेकिन हिन्दी बोलने का पूरा आनंद
     तो भारत में ही आता है ।
५   जो लोग पैसे जोड़ते जोड़ते लाखों रुपए कमाते हैं उनको "लखपति" कहते हैं ।
६   मेरे लिए तो यह सवाल थोड़ा मुश्किल है क्योंकि अभी तक यह किताब छपी ही नहीं है !
७   जी हाँ, नहाते समय मैं अक्सर पुराने फ़िल्मी गाने गाता हूँ – जब घर में अकेला हूँ तो !
८   हाँ, जवाब लिखते लिखते थक तो गया हूँ, लेकिन मुझे मज़ा भी आ रहा है ।

18a.2

१   अपने दोस्तों का इंतज़ार करते करते हम ऊबने लगे । We began to get bored
     waiting for our friends.
२   फ़र्श पर पड़े हुए कपड़ों को उठाओ और उन्हें उस टूटी हुई कुरसी पर रख दो ।
     Pick up the clothes lying on the floor and put them on that
     broken chair.
३   लखनऊ में रहते हुए मुझे सात महीने हुए हैं । I've been living in Lucknow
     for seven months.
४   वह गाती हुई लड़की कौन है ? उसे गाना सीखते कितने साल हुए हैं ? Who is
     that singing girl (that girl who is singing)? How many years
     has she been learning singing?

५ इस स्कूल में पढ़ते हुए बच्चे लोग काम करने का नाम नहीं लेते । The children studying in this school don't even think of working.

६ अंकल के पहुँचते ही सारे घरवाले चुप हो गए । As soon as Uncle arrived the whole family fell silent.

18b.1

१ अगर तुम्हें प्यास लगी तो चायवाले को बुलवाकर चाय बनवा लो ।

२ अगर आप कहानी को नहीं समझ पाते, तो किसी से उसका अँग्रेज़ी में अनुवाद करवा लीजिए ।

३ पंडित जी कहते हैं कि हमें बच्चों को संस्कृत के शब्द सिखवाने चाहिए, न कि उर्दू के ।

४ बिना कुछ कहे मैंने किताब को बंद करके अलमारी में रख दिया ।

५ पड़ोसियों से शिकायत करते समय मैं उनसे हिन्दी सीख रहा था ।

६ टी०वी० देखते देखते मैं समझने लगा कि बहुत-से लोग अपनी हिन्दी में बहुत-से अँग्रेज़ी के शब्द मिला लेते हैं ।

७ टूटे हुए खिलौने फ़र्श पर पड़े हुए थे ।

८ मेरी दोस्त के घर पहुँचते ही मैंने उसे बताया कि क्या हो गया था ।

18b.2

You perhaps might want to know what happened later in the Kumar family. It's a very long story; some day I'll write about it in detail. Meanwhile I'll just tell you that everybody lived very happily (except poor Suresh). No need to say that Sangeeta and Suhas got married, and in fine style; these days they're living in Delhi, and the Lucknow house has been let to some Hindi students who have come from London. If you ever find yourself in Delhi, go into some shop in Khan Market and you'll see Sangeeta and Suhas shopping – always together, always smiling, always happy. Sangeeta is about to have a baby too. One problem in the family has been that Dadi ji's health was poor for some time; for as long as two or three months there was much anxiety about her. But now she's recovered again.

You'll be pleased to know that Prakash is being promoted in the office, one result of which is that he is also able to help Chotu; at the moment Chotu is learning to drive – he'll become Prakash's driver. Arun and Prem's second book is selling like hot cakes; it seems that in the end they must have accepted Prakash's advice, because this second book of theirs is a love story – *A Tale of Two Hearts*, in which

Sangeeta's whole story has been told in detail. It's possible that a film will be made of it too, later on.

The enmity there used to be between Raj and Rishi is gradually coming to an end, and a kind of friendship is forming between them – although from time to time the old warfare breaks out again. What can be said about Suresh? For several reasons he has had to undergo much suffering, and, bored with life, he has started drinking rather heavily. Previously he was working in some hotel, but because of his excessive drinking his job too has come to an end. God knows what will become of him in the future. Khanna Sahib is about to go to London for some time, in connection with work, and Uma has got a good job in London too. Harish will go to do a BA at some American university – while Pinkie is about to marry an Englishman. And Pratap? His continuing story is very interesting (if Arun were here now he'd say it was *adbhut* – 'remarkable'!). You would be astonished to hear what happens in Pratap's life; but his story will be told in some other book!

18b.3

Friends, you are just finishing the 18th chapter of this book – you have worked very hard. The road was a little long; I very much enjoyed walking with you. I hope that your Hindi studies will continue in the future. This book is finishing, but there is no end to the road of studying. The question of how to study further may arise in your mind. My first suggestion is that you be sure to buy yourself one or two good dictionaries, so that reading books and newspapers will become a little easier. R.S. McGregor's *Hindi-English Dictionary*, which is published by the Oxford University Press, is very good indeed; this dictionary is printed from both Oxford and Delhi, and should be readily available. In addition, the several dictionaries by Hardev Bahri are also excellent. Keep these books with you. You shouldn't have too much difficulty reading simple stories.My second suggestion is that you make a habit of watching Hindi films, so that you get practice in hearing and understanding ordinary conversation. And if possible you should try to go to India – or to some other country where Hindi is spoken; then every Hindi-speaker will become your teacher, whether pandit, train passenger, or shopkeeper! Whatever happens, I am confident that you will very much enjoy learning and speaking Hindi. Goodbye.

HINDI–ENGLISH GLOSSARY

Key

inf = infinitive; ^{m} = masculine; ^{f} = feminine; ^{pl} = plural; ^{mf} (e.g. विद्यार्थी^{mf}) = used for both males and females; $^{m/f}$ (e.g. क़लम$^{m/f}$) = used in either gender; inv = invariable noun/adjective in -ā; ^{N} = always uses ने construction in perfective tenses; ^{n} = sometimes uses ने construction in perfective tenses; numbers (1 2 3 etc.) refer to the Unit in which a word first appears.

अ

अंकल ^{m} ankal 5 uncle

अँग्रेज़ ^{m,f} āgrez 1 English person

अंत ^{m} ant 12 end

अंतर ^{m} ant ar 17 difference

अंदर andar 8 inside, within

अँधेरा ^{m} ādherā 15 darkness

अकेला akelā; 4 अकेले (adv.) alone

अकेलापन ^{m} akelāpan 6 loneliness

अक्सर aksar 6 often; usually

अख़बार ^{m} akhbār 2 newspaper

अगर agar 9 if

अगला aglā 8 next

अगस्त ^{m} agast 15 August

अचानक acānak 15 suddenly, unexpectedly

अच्छा acchā 1 good, nice; really? I see!; well, proficiently; अच्छा-ख़ासा really good

अजनबी ^{m} ajnabī 17 stranger

अजीब ajīb 13 strange, odd

अठारह aṭhārah 8 eighteen

अद्भुत adbhut 12 remarkable

अधिक adhik 9 much, many, more; अधिक से अधिक at the most

अधेड़ adheṛ 18 middle-aged

अध्यापक ^{m} adhyāpak 2 teacher

अनबन ^{f} anban 13 discord

अनुपस्थित anupasthit 14 absent

अनुभव ^{m} anubhav 16 experience

अनुवाद ^{m} anuvād 18 translation

अनौपचारिक रूप से anaupcārik rūp se 15 informally

अपना apnā 6 (one's) own; अपने आप of one's own accord, oneself

अफ़सोस ^{m} afsos 4 regret

अब ab 3 now; अब की बार this time

अभी abhī 2 at the moment, right now; still

अभ्यास ^{m} abhyās 13 practice

अमरीकन amrīkan 1 American

अमरीका ^{m} amrīkā 9 America

अमीर *amīr* 14 rich, wealthy

अरे *are* 4 oh! what! hey!

अर्ज़ी f *arzī* 18 application

अर्थ m *arth* 14 meaning

अलग *alag* 7 separate, different; separately

अलमारी f *almārī* 1 cupboard

अवकाश m *avkāś* leisure, free time

अवश्य *avaśy* 10 certainly

असंभव *asambhav* 10 impossible

असर m *asar* 17 effect, impact;

असर पड़ना to have an effect

असल में *asal mē* 15 really, in fact

असली *aslī* 9 real

अस्पताल m *aspatāl* 8 hospital

अहम *aham* 16 important

आ

आँख f *ā̃kh* 8 eye; आँखें दिखाना N to look angrily

आकाश m *ākāś* 18 sky

आख़िर m *ākhir* 18 end; आख़िर (में) in the end, after all

आग f *āg* 13 fire

आगरा m *āgrā* 8 Agra

आगे *āge* 13 later, ahead; आगे चलकर in future, from now on

आज *āj* 2 today

आजकल *ājkal* 8 nowadays

आटो m *āṭo* 10 auto-rickshaw

आठ *āṭh* 7 eight; आठों पहर all day

आत्मीयता से *ātmīytā se* 18 cordially

आदमी m *ādmī* 1 man; person

आधा m *ādhā* 10 half

आधीरात m *ādhīrāt* 15 midnight

आनंद m *ānand* 11 joy, enjoyment; आनंद आना to feel enjoyment

आना *ānā* 5 to come

आप *āp* 1 you (formal)

आपका *āpkā* 3 your, yours

आपस में *āpas mē* 15 between/among themselves

आफ़ताब m *āftāb* 18 sun (poetic)

आबादी f *ābādī* 14 population, settlement

आम¹ m *ām* 12 mango

आम² *ām* 8 ordinary, general; आम तौर पर usually, normally

आरंभ m *ārambh* 17 beginning

आराम m *ārām* 3 rest, comfort; आराम करना N to rest; आराम से comfortably, easily

आर्थिक *ārthik* 14 financial

आलसी *ālsī* 16 lazy

आवश्यकता f *āvaśyaktā* 11 necessity

आवाज़ f *āvāz* 12 voice, sound

आशा f *āśā* 1 hope

आश्चर्य m *āścarya* 18 surprise; आश्चर्यजनक astonishing

आसान *āsān* 9 easy

आसानी से *āsānī se* 15 easily

इ

इंतज़ाम ^m *intazām* 9 arrangement(s), organisation; का इंतज़ाम करना ^N *to arrange*

इंतज़ार ^m *intazār* 16 wait, waiting; का इंतज़ार करना ^N *to wait for*

इकलौता *iklautā* 18 sole, only (child)

इक्कीस *ikkīs* 6 twenty-one

इतना *itnā* 10 so, so much

इतिहास ^m *itihās* 9 history

इधर *idhar* 5 here, over here; recently, latterly

इन *in* 3 oblique of ये *ye*

(से) इनकार करना ^N *(se) inkār karnā* 15 to refuse (to)

इनसान ^m *insān* 16 human being, person

इमारत ^f *imārat* 16 building

इरादा ^m *irādā* 9 intention

इलाक़ा ^m *ilāqā* 14 area

इलाज ^m *ilāj* 10 treatment, cure

इलाहाबाद ^m *ilāhābād* 13 Allahabad

इश्क़ ^m *iśq* 18 romantic love; इश्क़ लड़ाना ^N to have an affair

इस *is* 3 oblique of यह; इस लिए so; इसी लिए *that's* why

इस्तरी ^f *istrī* 18 clothes-iron; ironing

इस्तेमाल ^m *istemāl* 16 use; का इस्तेमाल करना ^N to use

ई

ईंट ^f *īṭ* brick

ई-पत्र ^m *ī-patr* 16 e-mail

ई-मेल ^f *ī-mel* 16 e-mail

ईव-टीज़िंग ^f *īv-ṭīzing* 9 'Eve-teasing' – sexual harassment of girls and women

उ

उँगली ^f *ũglī* 11 finger

उचित *ucit* 10 proper, appropriate

उच्चारण ^m *uccāraṇ* 6 pronunciation

उठना *uṭhnā* 6 to get up, rise

उठाना ^N *uṭhānā* 11 to pick up, lift; to take (तकलीफ़ trouble etc.)

उड़ना *uṛnā* 15 to fly

उड़ाना ^N *uṛānā* 18 to make fly; to squander

उतरना *utarnā* 17 to get down, alight

उतारना ^N *utārnā* 10 to take down/off

उत्तर ^m *uttar* 17 reply

उदाहरण ^m *udāharaṇ* 16 example

उद्घाटन ^m *udghāṭan* 16 inauguration

उधर *udhar* 5 there, over there

उधार ^m *udhār* 11 loan; उधार लेना ^N to borrow

उन *un* 3 oblique of वे *ve*

उन्नीस *unnīs* 6 nineteen

उपन्यास^m *upanyās* 15 novel

उपहार^m *uphār* 11 present, gift

उबलना *ubalnā* 17 to boil; to rage

उम्मीद^f *ummīd* 10 hope

उम्र^f *umr, umar* 4 age

उर्दू^f *urdū* 7 Urdu

उल्लू^m *ullū* 16 'owl' – idiot

उषा^f *uṣā* 9 dawn

उस *us* 3 oblique of वह *vah*

ऊ

ऊँचा *ū̃cā* 10 high

ऊपर *ūpar* 8 above; up; upstairs

ऊबना *ūbnā* 18 to be bored

ऊल-जलूल *ūl-jalūl* 14 silly, pointless

ऋ

ऋषि^m *ṛṣi* 5 sage, seer

ए

एक *ek* 1 one; एक साथ together

एकदम *ekdam* 4 completely

एकाध *ekādh* 18 one or two, a couple (of)

ऐ

ऐनक^f *ainak* 18 spectacles

ऐश^m *aiś* 8 wanton luxury; ऐश करना ^N to live a life of pleasure

ऐसा *aisā* 6 such, thus, like this

ओ

ओ *o* 3 o!

ओहो *oho* 17 oho! oh no!

औ

औपचारिक रूप से *aupcārik rūp se* 15 formally

और *aur* 1 and; more, else, other; और कोई any other

औरत^f *aurat* 7 woman

क, क़

कंजूस *kanjūs* 10 miserly, mean

कंपनी^f *kampanī* 6 company, firm

कंप्यूटर^m *kampyūṭar* 16 computer

कंबल^m *kambal* 5 blanket

कई *kaī* 3 several

कटना *kaṭnā* 17 to be cut

कठिन *kaṭhin* 9 hard, difficult

कथक^m *kathak* 18 kathak, a North Indian dance style

क़दम^m *qadam* 18 step, pace

कपड़ा^m *kapṛā* 3 cloth; garment

कब *kab* 11 when?; कब से since when?

कभी *kabhī* 6 sometime; कभी कभी sometimes; कभी नहीं never

कम *kam* 4 less; little; कम करना ^N to reduce; कम से कम at least

कमरा^m *kamrā* 1 room

कमाना ^N *kamānā* 8 to earn

कमाल ^m *kamāl* 18 miracle, wonder

कमी ^f *kamī* 18 lack, want

करना ^N *karnā* 5 to do

क़रीब *qarīb* 14 near; about, roughly

करोड़ ^m *karoṛ* 7 ten million

कल *kal* 4 yesterday; tomorrow

कलकत्ता ^m *kalkattā* 8 Calcutta

क़लम ^{m / f} *qalam* 3 pen

कवि ^m *kavi* 17 poet

कविता ^f *kavitā* 12 poem; poetry

कष्ट ^m *kaṣṭ* 17 trouble, distress

क़सम ^f *qasam* 18 oath

कसूर ^m *kasūr* 16 fault, error

(से) कहना ^N *kahnā* 5 to say (to); to call

कहलाना *kahlānā* 13 to be called, named

कहाँ *kahā̃* 3 where?

कहानी ^f *kahānī* 8 story

कहीं *kahī̃* 16 somewhere; somehow; कहीं और somewhere else; कहीं का (in insult) complete, utter; कहीं ज़्यादा particularly; कहीं न कहीं somewhere or other; कहीं नहीं nowhere; कहीं भी anywhere at all

काँटा ^m *kā̃ṭā* 10 fork; thorn

काँपना *kā̃pnā* 15 to shiver, tremble

का/की/के *kā/kī/ke* 5 (postposition indicating possession)

काग़ज़ ^m *kāgaz* 2 paper; a piece of paper

काटना ^N *kāṭnā* 17 to cut

काठमांडु ^m *kāṭhmāṇḍu* 8 Kathmandu

कान ^m *kān* 18 ear

कानपुर ^m *Kānpur* 7 Kanpur

काफ़ी ^{1 f} *kāfī* 5 coffee

काफ़ी ² *kāfī* 1 quite, very

काम ^m *kām* 4 work

कामचोर *kamcor* 10 work shy, lazy

कामयाब *kāmyāb* 18 successful

कारण ^m *kāraṇ* 14 reason, cause

कार्यक्रम ^m *kāryakram* 16 programme

काल ^m *kāl* 9 time, age, period

किंतु *kintu* 17 but

कि *ki* 4 (conjunction) that; or; when suddenly

कितना *kitnā* 2 how much/many

किताब ^f *kitāb* 2 book

किधर *kidhar* 14 where? whither?

किन *kin* 3 oblique plural of कौन *kaun* and of क्या *kyā*

किनारा ^m *kinārā* 15 edge, shore

किराया ^m *kirāyā* 15 rent, fare

किस *kis* 3 oblique singular of कौन *kaun* and of क्या *kyā*

किसी *kisī* 7 oblique of कोई *koī*

क़िस्मत ^f *qismat* 13 fate

की तरफ़ *kī taraf* 6 towards

की तरह *kī tarah* 6 like

की बग़ल में *kī bagal mẽ* 14 next to, close by

की वजह से *kī vajah se* 13 because of

क़ीमत ^f *qīmat* 11 price, value, cost; क़ीमती costly, valuable

कुछ *kuch* 7 some; somewhat; something; कुछ और something else, some more; कुछ न कुछ something or other; कुछ नहीं nothing

कुत्ता ^m *kuttā* 5 dog

कुरता ^m *kurtā* 5 kurta, Indian shirt

कुरसी ^f *kursī* 1 chair

कुली ^m *kulī* 16 porter

कृपया *kṛpayā* 2 please

कृपा ^f *kṛpā* 12 kindness, grace; कृपा करके kindly, please

के अंदर *ke andar* 6 inside

के आगे *ke āge* 6 in front of, ahead of

के आस-पास *ke ās-pās* 9 around, in vicinity of

के ऊपर *ke ūpar* 6 on top of

के कारण *ke kāraṇ* 14 because of

के द्वारा *(ke) dvārā* 14 by (means of)

के नज़दीक *ke nazdīk* 7 near

के नीचे *ke nīce* 6 beneath, below

के पहले *ke pahle* 6 before

के पास *ke pās* 6 near; in (one's) possession

के पीछे *ke pīche* 6 behind

के बजाय *ke bajāy* 15 instead of

के बाद *ke bād* 6 after

के बारे में *ke bare mẽ* 6 about, concerning

के बाहर *ke bāhar* 6 outside

के बिना *ke binā* 15 without

के बीच *ke bīc* 14 between; के बीच में in the middle of

के मारे *ke māre* 15 on account of, through

के लिए *ke lie* 6 for

के यहाँ *ke yahã* 6 at the place of

के समान *ke samān* 7 like, equal to

के साथ *ke sāth* 6 with, in company of

के सामने *ke sāmne* 6 facing, opposite

के सिवा, सिवाय *ke sivā, sivāy* 15 apart from

कैमरा ^m *kaimrā* 11 camera

कैसा *kaisā* 2 of what kind, what like, how

को *ko* 3 to, on, at

कोई *koī* 7 anyone, someone; some, about; any; कोई और someone else; कोई न कोई someone or other; कोई नहीं no-one

कोना ^m *konā* 13 corner

कोशिश ^f *kośiś* 16 attempt; की कोशिश करना ^N to try

कौन *kaun* 2 who?; कौन कौन which various people?

कौनसा/सी/से *kaunsā/sī/se* 5 which?

क्या *kyā* 1 what?; question-marker

क्यों *kyõ* 2 why

क्योंकि *kyõki* 2 because

क्लास ^{m / f} *klās* 4 class (in school etc.)

ख, ख़

खड़ा *kharā* 7 standing, waiting

ख़त ^m *khat* 5 letter

ख़त्म *khatm* 7 finished; ख़त्म करना^N to finish

ख़बर ^f *khabar* 14 news, information

ख़याल ^m *khayāl* 5 opinion, thought; (का) ख़याल रखना ^N to take care of

ख़राब *kharāb* 2 bad

ख़रीदना ^N *kharīdnā* 9 to purchase

ख़रीदारी *kharīdārī* 10 buying, shopping

खाँ मार्केट ^m *khā̃ mārket* 5 Khan Market (in Delhi)

खाँसना *khā̃snā* 16 to cough

खाट ^f *khāṭ* 17 bedstead, 'cot'

खाना^{1 m} *khānā* 4 food

खाना^{2 N} *khānā* 5 to eat

ख़ाली *khālī* 1 empty, vacant, free; ख़ाली करना ^N *to vacate*

ख़ास *khās* 7 special, particular

खिड़की ^f *khiṛkī* 1 window

खिलाना ^N *khilānā* 5 to give to eat

खिलौना ^m *khilaunā* 5 toy

खींचना ^N *khī̃cnā* 10 to draw; take (*photograph*)

ख़ुद *khud* 10 oneself

ख़ुदा ^m *khudā* 18 God; ख़ुदा की क़सम by God; ख़ुदा जाने God knows

खुला *khulā* 18 open

ख़ुश *khuś* 2 happy

ख़ुशी ^f *khuśī* 4 happiness, pleasure

ख़ूब *khūb* 6 a lot (of); well

ख़ूबसूरत *khūbsūrat* 4 beautiful

खेद ^m *khed* 12 regret

खेलना ⁿ *khelnā* 6 to play (a game)

ख़ैर *khair* 3 well, anyway

खोना ^N *khonā* 12 to lose

खोलना ^N *kholnā* 11 to open

ग, ग़

गंगा ^f *gangā* 11 Ganges

गंदा *gandā* 2 dirty

गंभीर *gambhīr* 17 serious, profound

गँवाना ^N *gãvānā* 16 to waste, squander

गप ^f, गपशप ^f *gap, gapśap* 6 gossip

गरम *garam* 4 warm, hot

गरमी ^f *garmī* 7 heat; summer; गरमियाँ ^{f.pl} summer

ग़रीब *garīb* 15 poor

गर्व ^m *garv* 10 pride

ग़लत *galat* 8 wrong, incorrect

ग़लती ^f *galtī* 15 mistake

गला ^m *galā* 18 throat, neck; गले लगाना ^N to embrace

गली ^f *galī* 8 lane

गाँव ^m *gām̐v* 3 village

गाड़ी ^f *gāṛī* 1 car; train

गाना^{1 m} *gānā* 9 song

गाना^{2 N} *gānā* 9 to sing

गाय ^f *gāy* 10 cow

गाली ^f *gālī* 15 abuse, swearing; गाली देना ^N to abuse, swear at

गिरना *girnā* 18 to fall

गिलास ^m *gilās* 11 tumbler (glass or metal)

गीत ^m *gīt* 11 song

गुंडा ^m *guṇḍā* 9 lout, hooligan

गुंडागर्दी ^f *guṇḍāgardī* 9 hooliganism

गुजराती *gujarātī* 1 Gujarati

गुज़ारना ^N *guzārnā* 11 to spend (time)

गुज़ारा ^m *guzārā* 16 livelihood, subsistence

गुरु ^m *guru* 13 teacher, guru

गुस्ताख़ी ^f *gustāk̲h̲ī* 14 rudeness, impertinence

गुस्सा ^{m, adj} *gussā* 17 anger; angry

गुस्से *gusse* 10 angry

गृह मंत्री ^{m , f} *gr̥h mantrī* 12 Home Minister

गोद ^f *god* 18 lap

गोरा ^{adj /m} *gorā* 15 fair; white person

गोली ^f *golī* 4 tablet, pill; bullet

गोश्त ^m *gośt* 6 meat

ग्यारह *gyārah* 9 eleven

ग्वालियर ^m *gvāliyar* 12 Gwalior

घ

घंटा ^m *ghaṇṭā* 8 hour

घंटी ^f *ghaṇṭī* 13 bell

घटिया *ghaṭiyā* 14 (inv.) inferior, low grade

घड़ी ^f *ghaṛī* 17 wristwatch

घना *ghanā* 15 dense, thick

घमंड ^m *ghamaṇḍ* 15 pride, arrogance

घर ^m *ghar* 3 house, home; घर पर at home

घाट ^m *ghāṭ* 11 (steps at) riverbank

घास ^f *ghās* 18 grass

घुमाना ^N *ghumānā* 18 to turn, make go round

घुसना *ghusnā* 17 to enter (forcibly, or uninvited)

घूमना *ghūmna* 11 to tour, roam, turn

घोड़ा ^m *ghoṛā* 5 horse

च

चटनी ^f *caṭnī* 14 chutney

चतुर्थ *caturth* 7 fourth, IVth

चपरासी ^m *caprāsī* 10 peon, orderly

चपाती ^f *capātī* 15 chapatti

चप्पल ^f *cappal* 2 sandal

चम्मच ^m *cammac* 10 spoon

चलना *calnā* 5 to move , walk; चल देना to set off; चला आना to come back, come away; चला जाना to go one's way

चलाना ^N *calānā* 8 to drive; to run, manage

चश्मा ^m *caśmā* 3 glasses, specs

चाँद ^m *cā̃d* 6 moon

चाँदी ^f *cā̃dī* 4 silver

चाचा ^m *cācā* 1 (inv.) paternal uncle, father's younger brother

चाबी ^f *cābī* 5 key

चाय ^f *cāy* 4 tea

चार *cār* 3 four

चावल ^m *cāval* 7 rice

चाहना ^N *cāhnā* 10 to want, wish; to be fond of

चाहिए *cāhie* 7 (is) needed; (with infinitive) should, ought to

चाहे... चाहे *cāhe ... cāhe* 16 whether... or

चिंता ^f *cintā* 16 anxiety, concern

चिट्ठी ^f *ciṭṭhī* 2 letter, note, chit

चिड़िया ^f *ciṛiyā* 1 bird

चिढ़ाना ^N *ciṛhānā* 12 to irritate, tease

चिल्लाना ^N *cillānā* 9 to shout

चीज़ ^f *cīz* 3 thing

चुकना *cuknā* 12 (after verb stem) to have already done

चुनना ^N *cunnā* 18 to choose

चुप *cup* 6 silent; चुप करना ^N to be quiet, shut up

चेहरा ^m *cehrā* 14 face, features

चोट ^f *coṭ* 13 hurt, injury; चोट लगना to get hurt

चोर ^m *cor* 11 thief

चोरी ^f *corī* 13 theft, robbery; चोरी करना ^N to steal

चौकीदार ^m *caukīdār* 15 watchman

चौथा *cauthā* 7 fourth

चौदह *caudah* 6 fourteen; चौदहवीं 14th of lunar month, full moon day

छ

छठा *chaṭhā* 7 sixth

छपना *chapnā* 9 to be printed

छह *chah* 3 six

छाता ^m *chātā* 13 umbrella

छात्र ^m *chātr* 2 student

छात्रवृत्ति ^f *chātravṛtti* 17 scholarship

छात्रा ^f *chātrā* 2 female student

छुटभैया ^m *chuṭbhaiyā* 18 a nobody, person of no importance

छुट्टी ^f *chuṭṭī* 7 holiday; free time

छुरी ^f *churī* 10 knife

छूटना *chūṭnā* 11 to depart; to be left, fall back

छूना ^N *chūnā* 5 to touch

छेड़ना ^N *cheṛnā* 18 to stir up, start up

छोकरी ^f *chokrī* 18 young girl, lass

छोटा *choṭā* 1 small, little

छोड़ना ^N *choṛnā* 6 to leave, abandon, give up

(को) छोड़कर *(ko) choṛkar* 12 apart from, except for

ज, ज़

जंगल ^m *jangal* 15 jungle, scrub

जंगली *janglī* 16 wild

जँभाई ^f *jabhāī* 15 yawn; जँभाई लेना^N to yawn

जगह ^f *jagah* 13 place

जगाना ^N *jagānā* 5 to arouse

जनता ^f *jantā* 9 public, the people

जनवरी ^f *janvarī* 1 January

जनाब *janāb* 18 sir

जन्म ^m *janm, janam* 16 birth; का जन्म होना to be born

जन्मदिन ^m *janamdin* 8 birthday

जब 13 when; जब कि while; जब तक... तब तक for as long as... for that long; जब तक नहीं... तब तक until... until then; जब से.. .तब से since the time when... since then

ज़बान ^f *zabān* 14 language, tongue

ज़माना ^m *zamānā* 15 period, age, time

ज़मीन ^f *zamīn* 7 land

ज़रा *zarā* 5 just, a little

ज़रूर *zarūr* 1 of course

ज़रूरत ^f *zarūrat* 7 need

ज़रूरी *zarūrī* 7 necessary, urgent

जर्मन *jarman* 1 German

जलना *jalnā* 17 to burn

जल्दी *jaldī* 5 quickly; soon; early

जवान ^m *javān* 13 young, youthful; soldier

जवाब ^m *javāb* 2 reply, answer; जवाब देना ^N to reply

जहाँ... वहाँ *jahā̃... vahā̃* 14 where... there

जानना *jānnā* 6 to know; जान-बूझकर deliberately, knowingly; जाना-पहचाना recognised, well known

जाना *jānā* 5 to go

जानवर ^m *jānvar* animal

जापानी *jāpānī* 1 Japanese

जारी *jārī* 11 current, continuing; जारी रखना ^N to maintain

ज़ाहिर *zāhir* 18 clear, evident

ज़िंदगी ^f *zindagī* 16 life

जितना... उतना *jitnā... utnā* 14 as much as...

ज़िद ^f *zid* 18 obstinacy

ज़िद्दी *ziddī* 17 obstinate, stubborn

जिधर... उधर *jidhar... udhar* 14 whither...thither

ज़िम्मेदारी *zimmedārī* 10 responsibility

जियरा ^m *jiyrā* 18 soul, heart (poetic)

जी *jī* 1 (respect-marker); yes; जी
नहीं no; जी हाँ yes

जी-हुज़ूरी ^f *jī-huzūrī* 12
sycophancy, flattery

जीना ⁿ *jīna* 15 to live, be alive; के
जीते जी during the lifetime of;
जीते रहो bless you ('stay living')

जीवन ^m *jīvan* 15 life

जुकाम ^m *zukām* 4 a cold

जूता ^m *jūtā* 2 shoe; pair of shoes

जून ^m *jūn* 8 June

जेब ^f *jeb* 7 pocket

ज़ेवर ^m *zevar* 11 (item of) jewellery

जैसा *jaisā* 15 like, such as; जैसा...
वैसा as... so...; जैसे कि as if, as
though; जैसे ही ...वैसे ही as soon as

जो 13 (the one) who/ which; जो
कुछ whatever; जो कोई whoever;
जो भी whoever, whatever

जोड़ना ^N *joṛnā* 14 to add; to save

ज़ोर ^m *zor* 8 force, strength

ज़्यादा *zyādā* 4 much, many, more;
ज़्यादा से ज़्यादा at the most

ज़्यादातर *zyādātar* 2 mostly, most

झ

झगड़ा ^m *jhagṛā* 5 quarrel, row

झट से *jhaṭ se* 18 suddenly, briskly

झाड़ना ^N *jhāṛnā* 18 to spout, pour

झूठ ^m *jhūṭh* 10 lie

झूमना *jhūmnā* 18 to sway

झेंपना *jhēpnā* 15 to be embarrassed

ट

टकराना ⁿ *ṭakrānā* 18 to collide

टपकना *ṭapaknā* 18 to drop in,
appear unexpectedly

टहलना *ṭahalnā* 18 to stroll

टिकट ^{m / f} *ṭikaṭ* 13 ticket; stamp

टुकड़ा ^m *ṭukṛā* 6 piece, bit

टूटना *ṭūṭnā* 18 to break, be broken

टेढ़ा *ṭeṛhā* 10 twisted, complex

टैक्सी ^f *ṭaiksī* 12 taxi

ट्रेकिंग ^f *ṭreking* 11 trekking

ट्रेन ^f *ṭren* 15 train

ठ

ठंड ^f *ṭhaṇḍ* 13 cold

ठंडा *ṭhaṇḍā* 4 cold

ठग ^m *ṭhag* 17 swindler, robber

ठहरना *ṭhaharnā* 5 to stop, wait,
stay

ठीक *ṭhīk* 1 all right; exactly; ठीक
करना ^N to put right, fix; ठीक से
properly; exactly

ड

डर ^m *ḍar* 13 fear

(से) डरना *(se) ḍarnā* 6 to fear

डरपोक *ḍarpok* 15 timid

डाँटना ^N *ḍāṭnā* 14 to scold

डाक ^f *ḍāk* 9 mail, post

डाकघर ^m *ḍākghar* 6 post office

डाकू ^m *ḍākū* 13 dacoit, bandit

डाक्टर ^m *ḍākṭar* 7 doctor

डॉयलॉग ^m *ḍāylāg* 18 dialogue

डाल ^f *ḍāl* 8 branch (of tree)

डालना ^N *ḍālnā* 13 to throw, cast, pour

डिगरी ^f *ḍigrī* 12 degree

डिनर ^m *ḍinar* 12 dinner

डिब्बा ^m *ḍibbā* 7 box; compartment

डूबना *ḍūbnā* 16 to sink, drown

डेढ़ *ḍeṛh* 10 one and a half

ड्राइवर ^m *ḍrāivar* 15 driver

ढ

ढंग ^m *ḍhang* 16 way, manner

ढाई *ḍhāī* 12 two and a half

ढूँढ़ना ^N *ḍhū̃ṛhnā* 5 to look for, find

ढेर ^m *ḍher* 17 pile, heap

त

तंग *tang* 8 narrow; तंग आना to get fed up; तंग करना ^N to harass

तक *tak* 3 up to, as far as; for (in time)

तकलीफ़ ^f *taklīf* 8 trouble, distress

तथापि *tathāpi* 17 nevertheless, even so

तबला ^m *tablā* 9 tabla (drum)

तबियत ^f *tabiyat* 3 health

तमाशा ^m *tamāśā* 11 spectacle, show

तमिल ^f *tamil* 14 Tamil

तरफ़ ^f *taraf* 7 side, direction

तरह ^f *tarah* 8 way, manner; तरह तरह का of various kinds

तलाक़ ^m *talāq* 13 divorce; तलाक़ होना a divorce to happen; तलाक़-शुदा divorced

तलाश ^f *talāś* 16 search; की तलाश करना ^N to search for

तलाशना ^N *talāśnā* 16 to search for

तस्वीर ^f *tasvīr* 3 picture

तहज़ीब ^f *tahzīb* 16 culture, refinement

ताज महल ^m *tāj mahal* 3 Taj Mahal

ताज़ा *tāzā* 14 fresh

तारीख़ ^f *tārīkh* 8 date

तारीफ़ ^f *tārīf* 16 praise; की तारीफ़ करना ^N to praise

ताला ^m *tālā* 13 lock

तालाब ^m *tālāb* 14 pond

ताली ^f *tālī* 8 clapping; तालियाँ बजाना ^N to clap

तिब्बती *tibbatī* 11 Tibetan

तीन *tīn* 1 three

तीसरा *tīsrā* 7 third; तीसरे पहर in the afternoon

तुझ *tujh* 3 oblique of तू *tū*

तुम *tum* 1 you (familiar)

तुम्हारा *tumhārā* 3 your, yours (from तुम)

तुरंत *turant* 10 immediately

तुराना ^N *turānā* 18 to have broken

तुलना *tulnā* 18 to be determined (to, पर)

तू *tū* 1 you (intimate); तू-तू मैं-मैं करना ^N to call names

तृतीय *tr̥tīy* 7 third, IIId

तेज़ *tez* 18 quick, rapid, sharp, bright

तेरा *terā* 6 your, yours (from तू)

तैयार *taiyār* 5 ready; तैयार करना ^N to prepare

तैरना ⁿ *tairnā* 9 to swim

तो *to* 4 so, then; as for; तो सही for sure

तोड़ना ^N *tornā* 11 to break

तोहफ़ा ^m *tohfā* 11 a present

थ

थकना *thaknā* 15 to be tired

थकान ^f *thakān* 8 tiredness

था, थी, थे, थीं *thā, thī, the, thī̃* 4 was, were

थामना ^N *thāmnā* 18 to hold, support

थाली ^f *thālī* 8 platter

थैला ^m *thailā* 5 bag, cloth bag

थोड़ा *thoṛā* 6 a little, a few; थोड़ा-बहुत a certain amount; थोड़ा-सा a little; थोड़े (ही) by no means

द

दंगा ^m *dangā* 17 riot

दक्षिण ^m *dakṣiṇ* 14 south

दफ़ा ^f *dafā* 17 time, occasion

दफ़्तर ^m *daftar* 4 office

दबना *dabnā* 14 to yield, cower

दया ^f *dayā* 18 compassion

दरवाज़ा ^m *darvāzā* 3 door

दराज़ ^f *darāz* 3 drawer

दरी ^f *darī* 3 rug, mat

दर्जन ^f *darjan* 7 a dozen

दर्ज़ी ^m *darzī* 18 tailor

दर्शन ^m *darśan* 9 vision, audience or auspicious meeting

दल ^m *dal* 8 political party

दस *das* 3 ten

दवा ^f *davā* 11 medicine

दादा ^m *dādā* 11 (inv.) paternal grandfather

दादी ^f *dādī* 1 paternal grandmother

दाम *dām* 10 price

दाल ^f *dāl* 4 daal, lentils

दावत ^f *dāvat* 9 (invitation to) a dinner

दास्तान ^f *dāstān* 18 tale (poetic)

दाहिना *dāhinā* 8 right (opp. left)

दिखना *dikhnā* 8 to appear, seem

दिखाई देना/पड़ना *dikhāī denā/paṛnā* 15 to be visible, appear

दिन ^m *din* 6 day; दिन भर all day

दिल ^m *dil* 4 heart; दिल लगना to feel at home; to be in love

दिलचस्प *dilcasp* 14 interesting

दिलवाना [N] *dilvānā* 18 to cause to be given

दिली *dilī* 8 of the heart

दिल्ली [f] *dillī* 2 Delhi

दीखना *dīkhnā* 18 to appear, be visible, seem

दीवार [f] *dīvār* 3 wall

दुःख [m] *duḥkh* 18 grief, pain, suffering

दुकान [f] *dukān* 4 shop

दुकानदार [m] *dukāndār* 11 shopkeeper

दुनिया [f] *duniya* 16 world

दुबला *dublā* 2 thin; दुबला-पतला thin, slight of build

दुबारा *dubārā* 14 again, second time

दुर्घटना [f] *durghaṭnā* 11 accident

दूध [m] *dūdh* 5 milk

दूर *dūr* 7 distant, far, remote

दूरदर्शन [m] *dūrdarśan* 14 television; Doordarshan (Indian TV network)

दूसरा *dūsrā* 1 other, second

देखना [N] *dekhnā* 5 to see, look

देखभाल [f] *dekhbhāl* 16 supervision, care; की देखभाल करना [N] to take care of

देन [f] *den* 13 contribution, gift

देना [N] *denā* 5 to give; (with oblique inf.) to allow to, let

देर [f] *der* 7 delay, a while; देर तक until late; देर से late

देवनागरी [f] *devanāgarī* 6 Devanagari script

देवर [m] *devar* 5 husband's younger brother

देश [m] *deś* 15 country

देहान्त [m] *dehānt* 16 death, demise; का देहान्त होना to die

दो *do* 1 two

दोनों *donõ* 1 both

दोपहर [f] *dopahar* 11 noon, afternoon; दोपहर का खाना [m] lunch

दोस्त [m,f] *dost* 4 friend

दौड़ना *dauṛnā* 12 to run

(के) द्वारा *(ke) dvārā* 14 by, by means of

द्वितीय *dvitīy* 7 second, IInd

ध

धंधा [m] *dhandhā* 18 work, occupation

धन्यवाद *dhanyavād* 2 thank you

धीमा *dhīmā* 12 low, faint

धुलना *dhulnā* 14 to be washed

धूमधाम [m] *dhūmdhām* 18 pomp, show

धोखा [m] *dhokhā* 15 trick, deceipt; धोखा देना [N] to trick, deceive

धोना [N] *dhonā* 5 to wash

धोबी [m] *dhobī* 5 dhobi, washerman

ध्यान ^m *dhyān* 5 attention; ध्यान
देना ^N to pay attention; (का) ध्यान
रखना ^N to take care of, mind;
ध्यान से attentively

न

नंबर ^m *nambar* 8 number

न *na* 2 not; is it not so?; (with
commands) don't; न कि and
not; न... न neither... nor

नज़दीक *nazdīk* 8 near, nearby

नज़र ^f *nazar* 13 glance, look

नचवैया ^m *nacvaiyā* 18 dancer
(derogatory)

नदी ^f *nadī* 14 river

नफ़रत ^f *nafrat* 6 hate, dislike

नमक ^m *namak* 9 salt

नमस्कार *namaskār* 2 hello; goodbye

नमस्ते *namaste* 1 hello; goodbye

नमूना ^m *namūnā* 15 example,
sample, type, specimen

नया (नए, नई) *nayā (nae, naī)* 2 new

नरसों *narsõ* 18 three days
ago/ahead

नर्तक ^m *nartak* 18 dancer

नल ^m *nal* 15 pipe, tap

नवाँ *navā̃* 7 ninth

नहाना *nahānā* 12 to bathe, wash

नहीं *nahī̃* 1 not; नहीं तो otherwise;
not at all, of course not

नाक ^f *nāk* 11 nose

नाचना *nācnā* 17 to dance; नाच
नचाना ^N to lead one a fine dance

नापसंद करना ^N *nāpasand karnā* 6 to
dislike

नाम ^m *nām* 3 name; (का) नाम लेना ^N
to mention; (का) नाम न लेना ^N to
be far from doing something

नामुमकिन *nāmumkin* 17 impossible

नारा *nārā* 5 slogan

नाराज़ *nārāz* 2 angry, displeased

नाश्ता ^m *nāśtā* 12 breakfast

निंदा ^f *nindā* 16 blame, speaking
ill; की निंदा करना ^N to blame

निकलना *nikalnā* 8 to come/ go
out, emerge; to turn out to be

निकालना ^N *nikālnā* 16 to extract,
bring out, discover

निन्यानवे *ninyānve* 8 ninety-nine

निबंध ^m *nibandh* 16 essay

निराशा ^f *nirāśā* 14
disappointment, despair

निवेदन ^m *nivedan* 10 request

निहायत *nihāyat* 17 extremely

नींद ^f *nī̃d* 11 sleep; नींद आना to
feel sleepy

नीचे *nīce* 8 below; down;
downstairs

नुक़सान ^m *nuqsān* 9 harm

नृत्य ^m *nṛtya* 18 dance

नेक *nek* 18 good, virtuous, decent

नेता ^m *netā* 15 leader, politician

नेपाल ^m *nepāl* 8 Nepal

नेपाली *nepālī* 11 Nepali

नोट *noṭ* 10 note, banknote

नौ *nau* 2 nine

नौकर ^m *naukar* 5 servant; नौकर-चाकर ^m servants & domestics

नौकरी ^f *naukarī* 15 job, employment, service

नौजवान ^m *naujavān* 9 youth, young man

प

पंखा ^m *pankhā* 1 fan

पंचम *pancam* 7 fifth, Vth

पंजाबी *panjābī* 1 Panjabi

पंडित ^m *paṇḍit* 15 pandit

पकड़ना ^N *pakaṛnā* 10 to catch, grab, hold

पक्का *pakkā* 13 ripe

पच्चीस *paccīs* 11 twenty-five

पछताना ^N *pachtānā* 12 to regret

पड़ना *paṛnā* 10 to fall, befall

पड़ा *paṛā* 5 lying

पड़ोसी ^m *paṛosī* 4 neighbour

पढ़ना ⁿ *paṛhnā* 5 to read, study

पढ़ाई ^f *paṛhāī* 11 studies, studying

पढ़ाना ^N *paṛhānā* 7 to teach

पतंग ^f *patang* 18 kite (toy)

पतला *patlā* 2 thin

पता ^m *patā* 10 address; पता चलना to come to one's notice; पता नहीं don't know, no idea; पता होना to know, be aware

पति ^m *pati* 3 husband; पति-देव 'respected husband'

पत्थर ^m *patthar* 1 stone

पत्नी ^f *patnī* 3 wife

पत्र ^m *patr* 9 letter

परंतु *parantu* 9 but

पर¹ *par* 2 but

पर² *par* 3 on; at

परदा ^m *pardā* 3 curtain, veil, purdah

परवाह करना ^N *parvāh karnā* 15 to care

परसों *parso* 11 the day before yesterday; the day after tomorrow

परिवर्तन ^m *parivartan* 14 alteration

परिवार ^m *parivār* 3 family

परिस्थिति(याँ) ^f *paristhiti(yā̃)* 18 circumstance(s)

परीक्षा ^f *parīkṣā* 12 examination; परीक्षा देना ^N to sit an exam; (की) परीक्षा लेना ^N to examine (a student)

परेशान *pareśān* 2 troubled, upset

पल ^m *pal* 8 moment

पलंग ^m *palang* 1 bed

पवन ^m *pavan* 18 wind

पसंद *pasand* 4 'liked, pleasing': पसंद करना ^N to like, approve, choose; पसंद होना to appeal, be liked

पहचानना ^N *pahcānnā* 9 to recognise

पहनना ^N *pahannā* 11 to put on, wear

पहर ^m *pahar* 8 'watch', part of day

पहला *pahlā* 7 first

पहले *pahle* 4 previously; first

पहाड़ ^m *pahāṛ* 4 hill, mountain

पहिया ^m *pahiyā* 15 wheel

पहुँचना *pahũcnā* 9 to arrive, reach

पहुँचाना ^N *pahũcānā* 18 to convey, deliver

पाँच *pā̃c* 2 five

पाँचवाँ *pā̃cvā̃* 7 fifth

पाकिस्तान ^m *Pākistān* 14 Pakistan

पाकिस्तानी *pākistānī* 1 Pakistani

पागल *pāgal* 2 mad, crazy

पाठ ^m *pāṭh* 11 lesson, chapter

पान ^m *pān* 5 paan

पाना ^N *pānā* 11 to find, obtain; (after verb stem) to manage to

पानी ^m *pānī* 5 water; पानी पड़ना to rain

पापा ^m *pāpā* 5 (inv.) papa, father

पार करना ^N *pār karnā* 12 to cross

पारिवारिक *pārivārik* 18 familial

पास *pās* 18 nearby (adverb)

पास करना ^N *pās karnā* 12 to pass (exam etc.)

पिछला *pichlā* 8 last, previous

पिता ^m *pitā* 1 (inv.) father

पीछा ^m *pīchā* 16 rear; pursuit; का

पीछा करना ^N to follow

पीछे *pīche* 11 behind

पीना ^N *pīnā* 5 to drink; to smoke

पुराना *purānā* 1 old (of things)

पुल ^m *pul* 14 bridge

पुलिस ^f *pulis* 10 police

पुस्तक ^f *pustak* 8 book

पूँछ ^f *pũch* 15 tail

(से) पूछना ^N *pūchnā* 5 to ask (of)

पूरा *pūrā* 8 full, complete

पेंसिल ^f *pensil* 16 pencil

पे (= पर) *pe* 18 on, to

पेट ^m *peṭ* 11 stomach

पेड़ ^m *peṛ* 5 tree

पेशा ^m *peśā* 16 profession

पैदा होना *paidā honā* 18 to be born, produced

पैसा ^m *paisā* 5 money; paisa (hundredth of a rupee)

पौन, पौना *paun, paunā* 12 three-quarters

प्याज़ ^m *pyāz* 16 onion

प्यार ^m *pyār* 6 love, affection; (को/से) प्यार करना ^N to love

प्यारा *pyārā* 4 dear, lovely; beloved

प्याला ^m *pyālā* 11 cup

प्यास ^f *pyās* 13 thirst; प्यास लगना thirst to strike – to feel thirsty

प्रकाशक ^m *prakāśak* 12 publisher

प्रकाशित *prakāśit* 17 published

प्रति ^f *prati* 1 copy (of book etc.)

प्रतीत होना *pratīt honā* 18 to seem

प्रथम *pratham* 7 first, Ist

प्रदूषण ^m *pradūṣaṇ* 2 pollution

प्रदेश ^m *pradeś* 14 state, province

प्रधान मंत्री ^{m, f} *pradhān mantrī* 18 prime minister

प्रयोग ^m *prayog* 14 use, usage; का प्रयोग करना ^N to use

प्रश्न ^m *praśn, praśan* 17 question

प्राचीन *prācīn* 14 ancient

प्राध्यापक ^m *prādhyāpak* 9 lecturer

प्राप्त करना ^N *prāpt karnā* 14 to obtain, attain

प्रेम ^m *prem* 14 love

प्रसिद्ध *prasiddh* 11 famous

प्रिय *priy* 4 dear

प्रोग्राम ^m *progrām* 8 programme, plan, routine

फ, फ़

फँसना *phãsnā* 17 to be stuck, caught, snared

फ़रवरी ^f *farvarī* 8 February

फ़र्क़ ^m *fark* 7 difference, separation

फ़र्श ^{m / f} *farś* 3 floor

फल ^m *phal* 5 fruit

फाड़ना ^N *phāṛnā* 17 to tear

फायदा ^m *fāydā* 9 profit, advantage

फ़ारसी ^f *fārsī* 14 Persian

फिर *phir* 6 then, so, again; फिर भी even so; फिर से again

फिरना *phirnā* 18 to turn, move

फ़िलहाल *filhāl* 18 in the meantime

फ़िल्म ^f *film* 11 film

फ़िल्मी *filmī* 11 of the films

फ़ुरसत ^f *fursat* 13 leisure, free time

फुसफुसाना *phusphusānā* 15 to whisper

फूल ^m *phūl* 14 flower

फ़ैक्स ^m *faiks* 11 fax

फ़ोटो ^m *foṭo* 11 photograph

फ़ोन करना ^N *fon karnā* 9 to phone

ब

बँगला ^f *bãglā* 13 Bengali (language)

बंद *band* 4 closed, shut; बंद करना ^N to close, shut

बंदर ^m *bandar* 15 monkey

बग़ीचा ^m *bagīcā* 1 garden

बचना *bacnā* 18 to escape, survive

बचपन ^m *bacpan* 6 childhood

बचा *bacā* 14 saved, left

बचाना ^N *bacānā* 18 to rescue, save

बच्चा ^m *baccā* 1 child

बजना *bajnā* 11 to resound, chime

बजाना ^N *bajānā* 9 to play (music)

बजे *baje* 6 o' clock

बड़ा *baṛā* 1 big

बढ़ना *baṛhnā* 15 to increase, grow, advance

बढ़िया *baṛhiyā* 14 (inv.) nice, of good quality

बताना^N *batānā* 5 to tell

बत्ती^f *battī* 13 light, lamp

बत्तीसी^f *battīsī* 15 'set of 32' – full complement of teeth; बत्तीसी दिखाना^N to grin broadly

बदमाश^m *badmāś* 12 villain, rogue

बदलनाⁿ *badalnā* 12 to change

बदसूरत *badsūrat* 13 ugly

बधाई^f *badhāī* 6 congratulation

बन^m *ban* 18 forest, wood, jungle

बनना *bannā* 14 to be, become, be made, act

बनाना^N *banānā* 8 to make

बनारस^m *banāras* 9 Banaras, Varanasi

बरदाश्त करना^N *bardāśt karnā* 17 to tolerate, endure

बरबाद करना^N *barbād karnā* 13 to ruin

बर्फ़^f *barf* 15 snow, ice

बर्थ^{m/f} *barth* 12 berth

बस^{1 f} *bas* 3 bus

बस² *bas* 14 enough! that's all!

बसना *basnā* 18 to settle, inhabit

बसाना^N *basānā* 18 to settle, found

बस्ती^f *bastī* 18 settlement, inhabited area; slum

बहिन^f *bahin* 2 sister

बहुत *bahut* 1 very; बहुत-सारा lots of

बहू *bahu* 1 daughter-in-law

बाँटना^N *bā̃ṭnā* 12 to divide

बाँसुरी^f *bā̃surī* 17 bamboo flute

बाँह^f *bā̃h* 11 (upper) arm

बाक़ी *bāqī* 17 remaining, left

बाज़ार^m *bāzār* 4 market

बात^f *bāt* 2 matter, thing; (से) बात करना^N to talk, converse; बात काटना^N to interrupt; बात बनना to go well, an aim to be achieved

बातचीत^f *bātcīt* 17 conversation, negotiation

बाद (में) *bād (mē̃)* 8 later

बादल^m *bādal* 15 cloud

बाप^m *bāp* 6 father

बाबू^m *bābū* 7 clerk

बायाँ *bāyā̃* 8 left (opp. of right)

बार^f *bār* 10 time, occasion; बार बार time and again

बारह *bārah* 6 twelve

बारिश^f *bāriś* 13 rain; बारिश होना to rain

बारे में *bāre mē̃* 10 about, concerning

बाल-बच्चे^{m p} *bāl-bacce* 4 children, family

बाहर *bāhar* 4 out; outside; away

बिकना *biknā* 9 to be sold

बिगड़ना *bigaṛnā* 17 to go wrong, get angry

बिजली^f *bijlī* 7 electricity

बिठाना^N *biṭhānā* 14 to make sit

बियर^{m/f} *biyar* 13 beer

बिलकुल *bilkul* **2** completely;
  बिलकुल नहीं not at all

बिल्ली ^f *billī* **14** cat

बी० एच० यू० *bī.ec.yū.* **9** BHU
  (Banaras Hindu University)

बीतना *bītnā* **18** to pass (of time)

बीमार *bīmār* **2** ill

बीस *bīs* **11** twenty

बुख़ार ^m *bukhār* **4** fever

बुढ़िया ^f *buṛhiyā* **1** old woman

बुरा *burā* **2** bad

बुलाना ^N *bulānā* **5** to call, invite

बूढ़ा ^{adj/m} *būṛhā* **1** old (of people);
  old man

बेकार *bekār* **7** useless

बेचना ^N *becnā* **11** to sell

बेचारा ^{adj/m} *becārā* **13** poor,
  wretched, helpless; poor fellow

बेचैन *becain* **18** restless

बेटा ^m *beṭā* **2** son, child

बेटी ^f *beṭī* **2** daughter, child

बेवकूफ़ *bavaqūf* **16** stupid

बैठक ^f *baiṭhak* **18** sitting room

बैठना *baiṭhnā* **5** to sit

बैठा *baiṭhā* **7** seated, sitting

बोतल ^f *botal* **12** bottle

बोर करना ^N *bor karnā* **9** to bore

बोरियत ^f *boriyat* **10** boredom

बोलना ⁿ *bolnā* **5** to speak

बोली ^f *bolī* **14** speech, dialect

ब्राह्मण ^m *brāhmaṇ* **15** Brahmin

भ

भगवान ^m *bhagvān* **8** God

भतीजा ^m *bhatījā* **9** nephew

भविष्य ^m *bhaviṣya* **9** future

भाई ^m *bhāī* **2** brother

भागना *bhāgnā* **17** to run away, flee

भाभी ^f *bhābhī* **12** elder brother's wife

भारत ^m *bhārat* **3** India

भारी *bhārī* **10** heavy

भाषा ^f *bhāṣā* **1** language

भिखारी ^m *bhikhārī* **15** beggar

भी *bhī* **2** also, too

भीगा *bhīgā* **14** wet; भीगी बिल्ली ^f
  'drenched cat', timid person

भीड़ ^f *bhīṛ* **3** crowd; भीड़ लगना a
  crowd to gather

भूख ^f *bhūkh* **13** hunger; भूख लगना
  hunger to strike – to feel hungry

भूखा *bhūkhā* **13** hungry

भूत ^m *bhūt* **11** ghost

भूल *bhūl* **10** mistake; भूल करना ^N
  to make a mistake

भूलना *bhūlnā* **10** to forget, err;
  भूलकर भी even by mistake

भेंट ^f *bheṭ* **11** gift, presentation;
  meeting, encounter

भेजना ^N *bhejnā* **8** to send

भेद ^m *bhed* **17** difference

भैया ^m *bhaiyā* **5** (inv.) brother

भोजन ^m *bhojan* **12** food; भोजन
  करना ^N to dine, eat

भोला *bholā* 9 innocent, guileless

भौंकना *bhaŭknā* 13 to bark

भ्रष्ट *bhraṣṭ* 14 corrupted; भ्रष्ट करना[N] to corrupt

म

मँगवाना[N] *māgvānā* 9 to order, send for

मंदिर[m] *mandir* 10 temple

मकान[m] *makān* 1 house

मक्खन[m] *makkhan* 14 butter

मक्खी[f] *makkhī* 10 fly; मक्खियाँ मारना[N] to 'kill flies', laze about

मगर[1] [m] *magar* 12 crocodile

मगर[2] *magar* 10 but

मचना *macnā* 17 to break out, be caused

मचाना[N] *macānā* 9 to create (noise etc.)

मच्छर[m] *macchar* 14 mosquito

मज़दूर[m] *mazdūr* 17 labourer

मज़बूत *mazbūt* 4 strong

मजबूरी[f] *majbūrī* 11 compulsion

मज़ा[m] *mazā* 11 fun, pleasure, enjoyment; मज़ा आना to have fun

मज़ाक़[m] *mazāq* 14 joke

मत *mat* 5 don't (in commands)

मतलब[m] *matlab* 4 meaning

मदद *madad* 10 help; मदद देना[N] *madad denā* to help; की मदद करना[N] to help

मन[m] *man* 6 mind; heart; मन लगना to feel at home

मना *manā* 9 forbidden, prohibited

मरना *marnā* 13 to die

मरम्मत[f] *marammat* 18 repair; की मरम्मत करना[N] to repair, set right

मर्द[m] *mard* 16 man, male

मशहूर *maśhūr* 15 famous

मसूरी[f] *masūrī* 9 Mussoorie

मस्त *mast* 18 joyous, delighted

महँगा *mahāgā* 2 expensive

महल[m] *mahal* 4 palace

महसूस करना[N] *mahsūs karnā* 6 to feel, experience; महसूस होना to be felt, experienced

महाभारत[m] *mahābhārat* 17 India's mythical epic war

महायुद्ध[m] *mahāyuddh* 7 great war

महाराजा[m] *mahārājā* 9 maharaja

महिला[f] *mahilā* 14 lady

महीन *mahīn* 14 fine, delicate

महीना[m] *mahīnā* 8 month

महोदय *mahoday* 14 gentleman; term of address

माँ[f] *mā̃* 4 ma, mother

माँस[m] *mā̃s* 17 meat

माता[f] *mātā* 1 mother

मानना[N] *mānnā* 11 to accept, believe

मानव[m] *mānav* 1 man

मापना *māpnā* 18 to measure, cover

माफ़ करना [N] *māf karnā* 11 to forgive, excuse

माफ़ी [f] *māfī* 11 forgiveness; माफ़ी माँगना [N] to apologise

मामला [m] *māmlā* 10 matter, affair

मारना [N] *mārnā* 5 to beat, hit, kill

मारुति [f] *māruti* 1 Maruti (car make)

मार्च [m] *mārc* 7 March

मालिक [m] *mālik* 6 boss

माला [f] *mālā* 16 garland

माली [m] *mālī* 11 gardener

मालूम *mālūm* 4 known; मालूम नहीं [I] don't know; मालूम करना [N] to ascertain

माहिर *māhir* 10 expert, skilled

मिठाई [f] *miṭhāī* 12 sweet, sweet dish

मित्र [m, f] *mitr* 4 friend

मिनट [m] *minaṭ* 12 minute

(से) मिलना *(se) milnā* 9 to meet; to be available; to resemble; मिलना-जुलना to resemble; मिल-जुलकर together, jointly

मिलाना [N] *milānā* 8 to dial, phone; to join (e.g. hands); to mix

मिस्तरी [m] *mistrī* 9 mechanic, artisan

मीटिंग [f] *mīṭing* 16 *meeting*

मीठा *mīṭhā* 11 sweet

मुँह [m] *mūh* 17 mouth, face

मुझ *mujh* 3 oblique of मैं

मुड़ना *muṛnā* 12 to turn

मुन्ना *munnā* 6 'Munna' – nickname for little boy

मुमकिन *mumkin* 11 possible

मुलाक़ात [f] *mulāqāt* 14 meeting, encounter

मुश्किल [adj /f] *muśkil* 6 difficult; difficulty

मुसलमान [m, f] *musalmān* 7 Muslim

मुसाफ़िर [m] *musāfir* 17 traveller

मुस्कराना *muskarānā* 18 to smile

मूर्ख [m] *mūrkh* 13 fool

मूर्ति [f] *mūrti* 1 statue, image

मूल [m] *mūl* 18 origin

में *mē* 3 in; में से from among, out of

मेज़ [f] *mez* 1 table

मेरा *merā* 3 my, mine; मेरा सिर 'my foot!'

मेहनत [f] *mehnat* 13 hard work

मेहनती *mehnatī* 4 hardworking

मेहमान [m] *mehmān* 6 guest

मेहरबानी [f] *meharbānī* 2 kindness; मेहरबानी करके 12 kindly, please

मैं *maī* 1 I

मैडम [f] *maiḍam* 2 madam

मोटा *moṭā* 2 fat, thick, coarse

मोड़ [m] *moṛ* 8 turn, bend

मोती [m] *motī* 7 pearl

मोर [m] *mor* 8 peacock

मौक़ा [m] *mauqā* 14 chance, opportunity

मौसम [m] *mausam* 2 weather

य

यक़ीन ^m *yaqīn* 10 confidence, faith

यदि *yadi* 10 if

यद्यपि *yadyapi* 17 although

यह *yah* 1 he, she, it, this

यहाँ *yahā̃* 1 here

यहीं *yahī̃* 9 right here, in this very place

या *yā* 2 or; या तो... या either... or

यात्रा ^f *yātrā* 17 journey, travel

यात्री ^m *yātrī* 15 traveller, passenger

याद ^f *yād* 16 memory; याद आना to be recalled, come to mind, be missed; याद करना ^N to remember, memorise; to think of, summon (e.g. an employee); याद दिलाना ^N to remind; याद रखना ^N to keep in mind, not to forget; याद रहना to be remembered; याद होना to be remembered

यानी *yānī* 18 that is to say

यार ^{m, f} *yār* 9 friend (esp. vocative)

यू० पी०^m *yū. pī.* 15 UP, Uttar Pradesh

ये *ye* 1 these, they; he, she (formal)

योजना ^f *yojnā* 17 plan, scheme

र

रंग ^m *rang* colour

रखना ^N *rakhnā* 5 to put; to keep

रवानी ^f *ravānī* 9 fluency

रविवार ^m *ravivār* 1 Sunday

रसोईघर ^m *rasoīghar* 3 kitchen

रस्सी ^f *rassī* 17 string, cord

रहना *rahnā* 5 to stay, remain, live

राजधानी ^f *rājdhānī* 15 capital; name of some Delhi express trains

राजस्थान ^m *Rājasthān* 14 Rajasthan

राजा ^m *rājā* 1 king

राज़ी *rāzī* 17 agreeable, content

रात ^f *rāt* 3 night; रात भर all night

रामायण ^m *rāmāyaṇ* 2 Ramayan (epic poem)

राय ^f *rāy* 18 opinion

रिक्शा ^m *rikśā* 10 rickshaw

रिश्तेदार ^{m, f} *riśtedār* 4 relative

रुकना *ruknā* 9 to stop; to stay on

रुपया ^m *rupayā* 11 rupee; money

रूबरू *rūbarū* 17 face to face

रूसी *rūsī* 1 Russian

रे *re* 3 eh, oh, hey

रेडियो ^m *reḍiyo* 12 radio

रेलगाड़ी ^f *relgāṛī* 9 train

रेशम ^m *reśam* 18 silk

रोकना ^N *roknā* 17 to stop

रोज़ *roz* 13 every day, daily

रोटी ^f *roṭī* 7 bread; food

रोना ⁿ *rona* 11 to weep, cry

रोशनी ^f *rośnī* 9 light

ल

लंदन ^m *landan* 3 London

लंबा *lambā* 2 tall, high

लंबाई ^f *lambāī* 6 height, length

लकड़ी ^f *lakṛī* 17 wood; stick

लखनऊ ^m *lakhnaū* 6 Lucknow

लखपति ^m *lakhpati* 18 rich man, 'millionaire'

लगना *lagnā* 13 to strike; to appeal; to seem; to catch (of illness, fire); to be related, attached; to gather (of crowds); to be expended (of time); (with obl. inf.) to begin to

लगाना ^N *lagānā* 18 to apply, affix

लड़का ^m *laṛkā* 1 boy

लड़की ^f *laṛkī* 1 girl

(से) लड़ना ⁿ *(se) laṛnā* 13 to fight, quarrel

लदना *ladnā* 18 to be loaded

लहसुन ^m *lahsun* 16 garlic

लाख ^m *lākh* 7 hundred thousand

लाजवाब *lājavāb* 18 beyond compare

लाठी ^f *lāṭhī* 11 lathi, stick

लादना ^N *lādnā* 14 to load

लाना *lānā* 5 to bring

लाभ ^m *lābh* 17 profit, advantage

लायक़ *lāyaq* 9 worth (doing)

लाल *lāl* 1 red

लिखना ^N *likhnā* 5 to write

लिटाना ^N *liṭānā* 18 to make lie down

लिपि ^f *lipi* 6 script, alphabet

लिफ़ाफ़ा ^m *lifāfā* 13 envelope

लूटना ^N *lūṭnā* 17 to loot, steal

ले आना *le ānā* 12 to bring

ले जाना *le jānā* 12 to take away

लेकिन *lekin* 1 but

लेटना *leṭnā* 18 to lie, recline

लेख ^m *lekh* 14 article (written)

लेखक ^m *lekhak* 14 writer

लेना ^N *lenā* 5 to take, receive; लेना-देना ^m dealings, connection

लोकप्रिय *lokpriy* 17 popular

लोग ^{m pl} *log* 1 people

लोट-पोट *loṭ-poṭ* 18 rolling, helpless (with laughter)

लौटना *lauṭnā* 9 to return

व

वक़्त ^m *vaqt* 10 time

वग़ैरह *vagairah* 3 and so on, etc.

वजह ^f *vajah* 7 reason, cause

वर्णन ^m *varṇan* 18 description; (का) वर्णन करना ^N to describe

वर्ष ^m *varṣ* 17 year

वह *vah* 1 he, she, it, that

वहाँ *vahā̃* 3 there; वहीं right there, in that very place

वाक्य ^m *vāky* 13 sentence

वापस *vāpas* 10 'back': वापस आना to come back; वापस जाना to go back; वापस मिलना to be got back; वापस लेना ^N to take back

वाराणसी ^f *vārāṇasī* **4** Varanasi, Banaras

-वाला *-vālā* **10** suffix linking following word to preceding noun

वाह *vāh* **6** (expresses admiration or scorn) wonderful!

विचार ^m *vicār* **13** thought, idea, opinion

विदेश ^m *videś* **4** foreign country; abroad

विदेशी ^{m f} *videśī* **6** foreigner

विद्यार्थी ^{m, f} *vidyārthī* **2** student

विलंब ^m *vilamb* **8** delay

विवाह ^m *vivāh* **12** marriage, wedding

विषय ^m *viṣay* **13** subject

विशेष *viśeṣ* **12** particular

विश्वविद्यालय ^m *viśvavidyālay* **9** university

विश्वास ^m *viśvās* **10** belief, confidence

विस्तार से *vistār se* **18** at length, in detail

वे *ve* **1** those, they; he, she (formal)

वेतन ^m *vetan* **18** pay, salary

वैर ^m *vair* **12** hostility

वैसे *vaise* **6** actually, in fact

व्यंग्य ^m *vyangy* **6** sarcasm

व्यक्ति ^m *vyakti* **14** person, individual

व्यक्तिगत रूप से *vyaktigat rūp se* **15** personally

व्यवस्था ^f *vyavasthā* **9** arrangement

श

शंका ^f *śankā* **18** doubt, suspicion

शक्ति ^f *śakti* **15** power

शख़्स ^m *śak͟hs* **18** individual, fellow

शनिवार ^m *śanivār* **7** Saturday

शब्द ^m *śabd* **11** word

शब्दकोश ^m *śabdkoś* **2** dictionary

शराब ^f *śarāb* **6** alcoholic drink

शराबी ^m *śarābī* **15** drunkard

शरारत ^f *śarārat* **6** mischief

शर्म ^f *śarm* **18** shame; शर्म आना to feel ashamed

शहर ^m *śahar* **3** town, city

शादी ^f *śādī* **13** marriage, wedding; उमा की शादी राम से करना ^N to marry Uma to Ram; उमा की शादी राम से होना Uma to marry Ram; शादी-शुदा (inv.) married

शानदार *śāndār* **14** magnificent

शाबाश *śābāś* well done! bravo!

शाम ^f *śām* **7** evening

शायद *śāyad* **3** perhaps

शिकायत ^f *śikāyat* **11** complaint; शिकायत करना ^N to complain; उमा की शिकायत राम से करना ^N to complain about Uma to Ram

शिष्य ^m *śiṣy* **13** disciple

शीघ्र *śīghr* 17 soon, quickly

शुक्रवार *m* *śukravār* 6 Friday

शुक्रिया *śukriyā* 1 thank you

शुद्ध *śuddh* 6 pure, unmixed

शुरू *m* *śurū* 15 beginning; शुरू करना *N* to begin (something) ; शुरू होना (something) to begin

शूटिंग *f* *śūṭing* 17 shooting, filming

शैतान *m* *śaitān* 5 devil

श्रावण *m* *śrāvaṇ* 18 Shravan, a monsoon month (July–August)

श्री *śrī* 2 Mr; Lord (with deity)

श्रीमती *śrīmatī* 2 Mrs

स

संतुष्ट *santuṣṭ* 17 satisfied

संतोष *m* *santoṣ* 17 satisfaction

संभव *sambhav* 10 possible

संस्कृत *f* *sanskṛt* 5 Sanskrit

सकना *saknā* 12 (after verb stem) to be able

सख़्त *sakht* 2 stern, strict, intense

सड़क *f* *saṛak* 3 street, road

सच *sac* 15 true

सचमुच *sacmuc* 5 really

सदस्य *m* *sadasy* 18 member

सदा *sadā* 16 always, ever

सन् *m* *san* 8 year (of calendar, era)

सपना *m* *sapnā* 7 dream; सपना देखना *N* to dream, have a dream

सप्ताह *m* *saptāh* 17 week

सफ़र *m* *safar* 17 journey, travel

सफल *saphal* 14 successful, fruitful

सफलता *f* *saphaltā* 14 success

सफ़ाई *f* *safāī* 10 cleaning

सफ़ेद *safed* 1 white

सब *sab* 2 everything, all; सब कुछ *everything*

सब्ज़ी *f* *sabzī* 8 vegetable(s)

समझ *f* *samajh* 9 understanding; समझ में आना to enter the understanding, be understood

समझना *n* *samajhnā* 6 to understand, consider, reckon

समझाना *N* *samjhānā* 18 to explain; to console

समय *m* *samay* 3 time

समस्या *f* *samasyā* 15 problem

समाचार *m* *samācār* 12 news; समाचार-पत्र *m* newspaper

समाप्त *samāpt* 17 finished, concluded

समुद्र *m* *samudr* 15 sea, ocean

समोसा *m* *samosā* 4 samosa

सर *sar* 2 sir

सरकार *f* *sarkār* 15 government

सरकारी *sarkārī* 15 governmental

सरल *saral* 5 simple

सलवार क़मीज़ *f* *salvār qamīz* 18 salwar qameez

सलाह *f* *salāh* 10 advice

सवा *savā* 12 one and a quarter

सवाल ^m *savāl* 2 question

सवेरा ^m *saverā* 8 early morning

सस्ता *sastā* 2 cheap

सहमत *sahmat* 17 in agreement

सही *sahī* 9 true, correct; तो सही
for sure

सहेली ^f *sahelī* 6 girl's female friend

साँस ^f *sā̃s* 18 sigh; ठंडी साँस भरना ^N
to heave a deep sigh

-सा *-sā* 15 -like, -ish

साइकिल ^f *sāikil* 1 bicycle

साड़ी ^f *sāṛī* 6 sari

साढ़े *sāṛhe* 12 plus a half

सात *sāt* 12 seven

साथ *sāth* 8 along, with, in
company; साथ साथ together

साथी ^{m , f} *sāthī* 12 companion,
friend

साधन ^m *sādhan* 16 means

साधारण *sādhāraṇ* 17 ordinary

साफ़ *sāf* 1 clean, clear; clearly;
साफ़ करना ^N to clean

साबुन ^m *sābun* 12 soap

सामान ^m *sāmān* 3 furniture, things,
luggage

सारा *sārā* 3 all, whole

साल ^m *sāl* 6 year

साला ^{m , adj} *sālā* 18 wife's brother;
term of abuse

सावधानी ^f *sāvdhānī* 8 care

सावन ^m *sāvan* 18 = श्रावण

साहब ^m *sāhab* 2 Mr; sir

साहित्य ^m *sāhity* 14 literature

सिग्रेट ^f *sigreṭ* 5 cigarette

सितार ^m *sitār* 15 sitar

सितारा ^m *sitārā* 18 star

सिनेमा ^m *sinemā* 7 cinema

सिर ^m *sir* 8 head; सिर खाना ^N to
plague, pester

सिर्फ़ *sirf* 1 only

सिलवाना ^N *silvānā* 18 to cause to
be sewn

सिलसिला ^m *silsilā* 18 connection;
के सिलसिले में in connection with

सीखना ^N *sīkhnā* 6 to learn

सीट ^f *sīṭ* 12 seat

सीढ़ी ^f *sīṛhī* 10 stair, step, staircase

सीधा *sīdhā* 8 straight, straightforward; सीधे straight; to the right

सुझाव ^m *sujhāv* 17 suggestion;
सुझाव देना ^N to make a suggestion

सुधरना *sudharnā* 17 to improve,
be put right

सुधारना ^N *sudhārnā* 15 to improve,
put right

सुनना ^N *sunnā* 5 to listen, hear

सुनाई देना/पड़ना *sunāī dena/paṛnā* 16
to be heard, be audible

सुनाना ^N *sunānā* 11 to relate, tell,
recite, sing

सुन्दर *sundar* 1 beautiful

सुबह ^f *subah* 3 morning

सुलाना[N] *sulānā* 18 to make sleep

सूझना *sūjhnā* 18 to occur to the mind

सूरज[m] *sūraj* 15 sun

से *se* 3 by, since, from, with

से पहले *se pahle* 6 before

सेब[m] *seb* 12 apple

सैंतालीस *saintālis* 8 forty-seven

सैकड़ा[m] *saikṛā* 7 a hundred

सैर[f] *sair* 7 walk, trip; सैर करना[N] to go for a walk, trip

सो *so* 13 he, she, it (archaic)

सोचना[N] *socnā* 6 to think; की [बात] सोचना[N] to think of doing

सोना[1][m] *sonā* 4 gold

सोना[2] *sonā* 6 to sleep

सोमवार[m] *somvār* 2 Monday

सोलह *solah* 2 sixteen

सौ *sau* 4 hundred

स्टेशन[m] *sṭeśan* 6 station

स्थायी रूप से *sthāyī rūp se* 18 permanently

स्थिति[f] *sthiti* 15 situation

स्नान *snān* 15 bath, ritual bathing

स्वभाव[m] *svabhāv* 18 nature, disposition

स्वयं *svayam* 15 oneself

स्वर्ग[m] *svarg* 7 heaven

स्वादिष्ट *svādiṣṭ* 14 tasty

स्वीकार करना[N] *svīkār karnā* 18 to accept

ह

हँसना *hãsnā* 6 to laugh

हँसाना[N] *hãsānā* 6 to make laugh

हँसी-मज़ाक[m] *hãsī-mazāk* 18 laughter, fun, joking

हज़ार[m] *hazār* 7 thousand

हड़ताल[f] *haṛtāl* 17 strike, lockout; हड़ताल करना[N] to strike

हफ़्ता[m] *haftā* 10 week

हम *ham* 1 we, us

हमारा *hamārā* 6 our, ours

हमेशा *hameśā* 6 always

हर, हरेक *har* 7 each, every; हर कोई *everyone*

हल[m] *hal* 16 solution; हल होना to be solved

हलो, हेलो *halo, helo* 2 hello

हवा[f] *havā* 2 air

हवाई जहाज़[m] *havāī jahāz* 9 aeroplane

हवाई डाक[f] *havāī ḍāk* 14 airmail

हवादार *havādār* 1 airy

हाँ *hā̃* yes

हाथ[m] *hāth* 8 hand; हाथ आना to come to hand; हाथ बँटाना[N] to lend a hand; हाथ मिलाना to join hands

हाल[m] *hāl* 2 condition, state

हालत[f] *hālat* 15 state, condition

हालाँकि *hālā̃ki* 17 although

हिन्दी[f] *hindī* 2 Hindi

हिन्दुस्तानी *hindustānī* 1 Indian

हिन्दू *hindū* 9 Hindu

हिलना *hilnā* 9 to move, stir

ही *hī* 9 only; (emphatic)

हीरो^m *hīro* 13 'hero', male film-
    star

हूँ *hū̃* 1 am

हे *he* 8 Oh!

है *hai* 1 is

हैं *haĩ* 1 are

होंठ^m *hõṭh* lip

हो *ho* 1 are

होटल^m *hoṭal* 7 hotel; cafe

होनहार *honhār* 6 promising

होना *honā* 5 to be, become,
    happen; (से) होकर via

होली^f *holī* 12 Holi, springtime
    festival of colours

होल्ड करना^N *holḍ karnā* 12 to hold
    (phone line)

होशियार *hośiyār* 4 clever,
    intelligent

ह्विस्की^f *hviskī* 18 whisky

ENGLISH–HINDI GLOSSARY

(For numbers, see Appendix 1)

Key

inf = infinitive; ^{m} = masculine; ^{f} = feminine; ^{pl} = plural; $^{m\,f}$ (e.g. विद्यार्थी$^{m\,f}$) = used for both males and females; $^{m/f}$ (e.g. क़लम$^{m/f}$) = used in either gender; inv = invariable noun/adjective in -$\bar{a}$; ^{N} = always uses ने construction in perfective tenses; ^{n} = sometimes uses ने construction in perfective tenses.

---

a एक, कोई

abandon, to छोड़ना ^{N}

able, to be सकना 12.3

about (approximately) क़रीब, लगभग; (with number) कोई 7.2; (concerning) (के) बारे में

above (के) ऊपर

abroad विदेश

absent अनुपस्थित

abuse, swearing गाली ^{f}; to abuse गाली देना ^{N}

accept, to स्वीकार करना ^{N}; मानना ^{N}

accident दुर्घटना ^{f}

actually वैसे, असल में

add, to जोड़ना ^{N}

address पता ^{m}

advice सलाह ^{f}

aeroplane हवाई जहाज़ ^{m}

affection प्यार ^{m}

affix, to लगाना ^{N}

after के बाद

afraid (of), to be (से) डरना 15.3

afternoon तीसरे पहर

again फिर, फिर से

age (of person) उम्र ^{f}

Agra आगरा ^{m}

agreeable, content राज़ी

agreed, in agreement सहमत

ahead (of) (के) आगे

air हवा ^{f}

airmail हवाई डाक ^{f}

airy हवादार

alcoholic drink शराब ^{f}

alight, to उतरना

all सब, सभी; whole सारा, तमाम; all day दिन भर; all right ठीक

Allahabad इलाहाबाद ^{m}

allow, to: oblique inf. + देना ^{N} 14.4

alone अकेला; (adverb) अकेले

along with साथ

already अभी, अभी से (or use verb stem + चुकना 12.3)

also भी (*follows* word, 2.3)

alteration परिवर्तन ^m

although हालाँकि, यद्यपि 17.2

always हमेशा; as always, हमेशा की तरह

America अमरीका ^m; American अमरीकन

among के बीच; among themselves आपस में; from among में से

ancient प्राचीन

and और

angry गुस्से; displeased नाराज़; to become angry गुस्से होना, बिगड़ना

answer जवाब ^m; to answer जवाब देना ^N

anxiety परेशानी ^f; चिंता ^f

any कोई 7.2; (with uncountable, e.g. 'water') कुछ 7.2

anyone कोई 7.2; anyone at all कोई भी

anywhere (at all) कहीं (भी) 16.3

apart from के सिवा/ सिवाय; (को) छोड़कर

apologise (to), to (से) माफ़ी माँगना ^N 15.3

appear, to दिखना, दीखना, दिखाई देना/पड़ना 15b; to seem मालूम होना 6.1

apple सेब ^m

application अर्ज़ी ^f

appropriate उचित

area, district इलाक़ा ^m

arm, upper arm बाँह ^f

around, in vicinity of के आस-पास

arouse from sleep, to जगाना ^N

arrange, to का इंतज़ाम करना ^N 16.1

arrangement व्यवस्था ^f, इंतज़ाम ^m

arrive, to पहुँचना

arrogance घमंड ^m

article (written) लेख ^m

as if, as though जैसे, मानो (with subjunctive verb; 15.4)

as much as... जितना...उतना 14.5

as soon as जैसे ही 13.1

ask, to पूछना ^N 15.3

at को; at night रात को; (with place, e.g 'at home') पर; at least कम से कम

attempt कोशिश ^f; to attempt की कोशिश करना ^N 16.1

attention ध्यान ^m; to pay attention ध्यान देना ^N

attentively ध्यान से

August अगस्त ^m

auto-rickshaw आटो ^m

available, to be मिलना 13.5

back (in sense 'return') वापस

bad ख़राब, बुरा

bag, cloth bag थैला ^m

Banaras बनारस ^m, वाराणसी ^f

bandit डाकू ^m

bark, to भौंकना

bathe, to नहाना

bathroom बाथरूम ^m

be bored, to ऊबना

be cut, to कटना

be, to होना; बनना

beat, to मारना ^N

beautiful सुन्दर, ख़ूबसूरत

because क्योंकि

because of की वजह से, के कारण

become, to बनना

bedstead पलंग ^m, खाट ^f

beer बियर ^m

before (के/से) पहले

beggar भिखारी ^m

begin to, to oblique inf. + लगना;
   direct inf. + शुरू करना ^N

beginning शुरू ^m, आरंभ ^m

behind (के) पीछे

belief विश्वास ^m

bell घंटी ^f

below (के) नीचे

beneath (के) नीचे

Bengali language बँगला ^f

berth बर्थ ^{m/f}

between के बीच; between
   themselves आपस में

bicycle साइकिल ^f

big बड़ा

bird चिड़िया ^f

birth जन्म ^m

birthday जन्मदिन ^m

black काला

blame, speaking ill निंदा ^f;
   to blame, censure दोष देना ^N,
   की निंदा करना ^N 16.1

blanket कंबल ^m

boil, to उबलना; उबालना ^N

book किताब ^f; पुस्तक ^f

bore, to बोर करना ^N, उबा देना ^N

boredom बोरियत ^f

born, to be पैदा होना; का जन्म होना
   16.1

borrow, to उधार लेना ^N

boss मालिक ^m

both दोनों

bother, harass, to तंग करना ^N

bottle बोतल ^f

box डिब्बा ^m

boy लड़का ^m

Brahmin ब्राह्मण ^m

branch (of tree) डाल ^f

bravo वाह

bread रोटी ^f; (loaf) डबल रोटी ^f

break out (of noise, fight), to मचना

break, be broken, to टूटना

break, to तोड़ना ^N

breakfast नाश्ता ^m; to have
   breakfast, नाश्ता करना ^N

brick ईंट ^f

bridge पुल ^m

bright (intelligent) होशियार, तेज़

bring, to लाना, ले आना

briskly झट से

broken टूटा

brother भाई [m]

brother-in-law (husband's younger brother) देवर [m]; (wife's brother) साला [m]

building इमारत [f]

bullet गोली [f]

burn, to जलना; जलाना [N]

bus बस [f]

but लेकिन, पर, मगर, किंतु, परंतु

butter मक्खन [m]

buy, to ख़रीदना [N]

buying, shopping ख़रीदारी

by से; by means of (के) द्वारा; (in time, e.g. 'by now') तक

cafe होटल [m]

Calcutta कलकत्ता [m]

call (invite), to बुलाना [N]; (give name, to) कहना 6.1; बुलाना [N]

called (named), to be कहलाना

camera कैमरा [m]

can: *see* 'able, to be'

capital city राजधानी [f]

car गाड़ी [f], कार [f]

care सावधानी [f]; to take care of की देखभाल करना [N] 16.1

care, to परवाह करना [N]

cat बिल्ली [f]

catch, to पकड़ना [N]; (of fire, illness) लगना 13.6

cause कारण [m]

certain amount, a थोड़ा-बहुत

certainly ज़रूर, अवश्य

chair कुरसी [f]

chance, opportunity मौक़ा [m]

change, to बदलना [N]

chapatti चपाती [f]

cheap सस्ता

child बच्चा [m]

childhood बचपन [m]

choose, to चुनना [N]

chutney चटनी [f]

cigarette सिग्रेट [f]

cinema सिनेमा [m]

circumstance(s) परिस्थिति(याँ) [f]

city शहर [m]

clapping ताली [f]; to clap तालियाँ बजाना [N]

class (in school etc.) क्लास [m/f]

clean साफ़; to clean साफ़ करना [N], की सफ़ाई करना [N] 16.1

cleaning सफ़ाई [f]

clear साफ़; evident ज़ाहिर, स्पष्ट

clearly साफ़

clerk बाबू [m]

clever (intelligent) होशियार; (cunning) चतुर

closed बंद; to close, बंद करना [N]

cloth कपड़ा [m]

clothing, item of कपड़ा [m]

cloud बादल [m]

coffee काफ़ी [f]

cold ठंड [f]; (adj.) ठंडा; (nose cold) जुकाम [m] 8.2

college कालेज [m]

collide, to टकराना [n]

colour रंग [m]

come, to आना

come out, emerge, to निकलना

comfort आराम [m]; comfortably आराम से

companion साथी [m,f]

company, firm कंपनी [f]

compartment (railway) डिब्बा [m]

compassion दया [f]

complain, to शिकायत करना [N]; to complain to Raj about Ram, राज से राम की शिकायत करना [N] 16.1

complaint शिकायत [f]

completely एकदम, पूरी तरह से, बिलकुल

compulsion मजबूरी [f]

computer कंप्यूटर [m]

concern चिंता [f]

condition, state हाल [m], हालत [f]

confidence यक़ीन [m]; विश्वास [m]

congratulation बधाई [f]

connection सिलसिला [m]; in connection with के सिलसिले में

contribution देन [f]

conversation बातचीत [f]

copy (of book etc.) प्रति [f]

cordially आत्मीयता से

corner कोना [m]

correct सही

corrupt(ed) भ्रष्ट; to corrupt भ्रष्ट करना [N]

cough, to खाँसना

country देश [m]

couple (of), a एकाध (singular)

cow गाय [f]

crazy पागल

create (noise etc.), to मचाना [N]

crocodile मगर [m]

cross (road etc.), to पार करना [N]

crowd भीड़ [f]

culture, refinement तहज़ीब [f]

cup प्याला [m]

cupboard अलमारी [f]

cure इलाज [m]

current, ongoing जारी

curtain परदा [m]

cut, to काटना [N]

cycle, bike साइकिल [f]

daal, lentils दाल [f]

dacoit, bandit डाकू [m]

daily (adverb) रोज़

dance नृत्य [m], नाच [m]; to dance नाचना

dancer नर्तक [m]

dark; darkness अँधेरा; अँधेरा [m]

date तारीख़ f 8.4

daughter बेटी f

daughter-in-law बहू f

dawn उषा f

day दिन m; all day दिन भर, round the clock आठों पहर

day before yesterday/ after tomorrow परसों

dear प्रिय; (beloved) प्यारा

death देहान्त m, मौत f, मृत्यु f 16.1

degree (academic) डिगरी f

delay देर f, विलंब m

Delhi दिल्ली f, देहली f

deliberately जान-बूझकर

dense घना

depart, to छूटना, चला जाना

description वर्णन m; to describe का वर्णन करना N 16.1

despair निराशा f

detail, in विस्तार से

Devanagari script देवनागरी f

devil शैतान m

dhobi, washerman धोबी m

dial (phone), to नंबर मिलाना N

dialect बोली f

dialogue डॉयलॉग m

dictionary शब्दकोश m

die, to मरना; का देहान्त होना, की मौत/मृत्यु होना 16.1

difference फ़र्क़ m, भेद m

different भिन्न; (separate) अलग

difficult मुश्किल, कठिन

difficulty मुश्किल f, कठिनाई f

dinner डिनर m

direction तरफ़ f, ओर f

dirty गंदा, मैला

disappointment निराशा f; disappointed निराश

disciple शिष्य m

discord अनबन f

dislike, to नापसंद करना N

distant दूर

distribute, to बाँटना N

divide, to बाँटना N

divorce तलाक़ m; to become divorced का तलाक़ होना; divorced तलाक़-शुदा

do, to करना N; do not (with command) न, मत

doctor डाक्टर m

dog कुत्ता m

don't (with commands) न, मत 5.2

door दरवाज़ा m

doubt शंका f

down, downstairs नीचे

dozen दर्ज़न f

draw, to खींचना N

drawer दराज़ f

dream सपना m; to dream (of) (का) सपना देखना N 16.1

drink, to पीना N

drive, to चलाना N

driver ड्राइवर ^m

drop in, to टपकना

drown, to डूबना

drunkard शराबी ^m

each हर, हरेक

ear कान ^m

early जल्दी; (in morning) सवेरे-सवेरे

earn, to कमाना ^N

easily आसानी से, आराम से

easy आसान; simple सरल

eat, to खाना ^N

edge, shore किनारा ^m

effect असर ^m; to have an effect असर
    पड़ना

either... or या तो... या 16.6

electricity बिजली ^f

e-mail ई-पत्र ^m; ई-मेल ^f

embarrassed, to be झेंपना

embrace, to गले लगाना ^N

emerge, to निकलना

employment नौकरी ^f

end अंत ^m; in the end, after all
    आख़िर (में)

English person अँग्रेज़ ^{m, f}

enjoy, feel enjoyment आनंद आना

enough! that's all! बस

enter, to घुसना

envelope लिफ़ाफ़ा ^m

escape, to बचना

essay निबंध ^m

etc. वग़ैरह, इत्यादि

even भी (*follows* word, 2.3)

evening शाम ^f; this evening आज
    शाम (को)

every हर; every day रोज़, हर रोज़

everything सब, सब कुछ

exactly, precisely ठीक

examination परीक्षा ^f; to take (sit)
    an exam; परीक्षा देना ^N;
    to examine की परीक्षा लेना ^N

example उदाहरण ^m, नमूना ^m

except for (को) छोड़कर, के सिवाय

excuse, to माफ़ करना ^N 5.2

expensive महँगा

experience अनुभव ^m; to experience
    अनुभव/महसूस करना ^N

expert, skilled माहिर

explain, to समझाना ^N

extract, to निकालना ^N

extremely बहुत ही, निहायत

face मुँह ^m; चेहरा ^m; face to face
    रूबरू

facing, opposite के सामने

fall, to गिरना

family परिवार ^m

famous मशहूर, प्रसिद्ध

fan पंखा ^m

far away दूर

fare (taxi etc.) किराया ^m

fat मोटा

fate क़िस्मत ^f

father पिता ^m (inv.), बाप ^m, पापा ^m (inv.)

fault, guilt कसूर ^m, दोष ^m

fax फ़ैक्स ^m

fear डर ^m; to fear (से) डरना

fed up (with), to become (से) तंग आना

feel, to महसूस करना ^N; to be felt, महसूस होना; to feel at home दिल/मन लगना; I feel hungry / thirsty मुझको भूख/प्यास लगी है 13.6

fetch, to लाना, ले आना

fever बुख़ार ^m

fight, to (से) लड़ना ⁿ

film फ़िल्म ^f; film-shooting शूटिंग ^f

film-star (male) हीरो ^m

financial आर्थिक

find out, ascertain, to मालूम करना ^N

find, to पाना ^N; मिलना (with 'thing found' as subject) 13.5

fine, delicate महीन

finger उँगली ^f

finish, to ख़त्म करना ^N, समाप्त करना^N; to complete पूरा करना ^N

finished ख़त्म, समाप्त

fire आग ^f

first पहला; (adverb) पहले

fix, put right, to ठीक करना ^N

flee, to भागना

floor फ़र्श ^{m/f}

flower फूल ^m

fluency रवानी ^f

flute बाँसुरी ^f

fly (insect) मक्खी ^f

fly, to उड़ना

follow, to का पीछा करना ^N

food खाना ^m, भोजन ^m

fool मूर्ख ^m, उल्लू (lit. 'owl')

for के लिए

forbidden मना (inv.)

force, strength ज़ोर ^m

foreign विदेशी; foreign country विदेश ^m; foreigner विदेशी ^m

forest बन ^m

forget, to भूलना, भूल जाना

forgive, to माफ़ करना ^N

forgiveness माफ़ी ^f

fork (utensil) काँटा ^m

formally औपचारिक रूप से

free (vacant) ख़ाली; (gratis) मुफ़्त

free time फ़ुरसत ^f, अवकाश ^m

fresh ताज़ा

friend दोस्त ^{m, f}, मित्र ^{m, f}; girl's girlfriend सहेली ^f

from से

fruit फल ^m

full (complete) पूरा; (filled) भरा

fun मज़ा ^m

furniture सामान ^m

future भविष्य ^m

Ganges गंगा ^f

garden बग़ीचा ^m

gardener माली ^m

garland माला ^f

garlic लहसुन ^m

German जर्मन

get, to मिलना 13.5

get up, to उठना

ghost भूत ^m

gift भेंट ^f, तोहफ़ा ^m

girl लड़की ^f

give, to देना ^N; to give up छोड़ना ^N;
   to give back वापस देना ^N

glance, look नज़र ^f

glare, glower, to आँखें दिखाना ^N

glass (tumbler) गिलास ^m

glasses, spectacles चश्मा ^m; ऐनक ^f

go, to जाना

go out, emerge, to निकलना

God भगवान ^m, ख़ुदा ^m ; God knows
   भगवान/ख़ुदा जाने

gold सोना ^m

good अच्छा; decent नेक

goodbye नमस्ते, नमस्कार; (Muslim)
   ख़ुदा हाफ़िज़

good-quality बढ़िया (inv.)

gossip गप ^f, गपशप ^f

government सरकार ^f;
   governmental सरकारी

grandfather (paternal) दादा ^m
   (inv.); (maternal) नाना ^m (inv.)

grandmother (paternal) दादी ^f;
   (maternal) नानी ^m

grass घास ^f

grief दुःख ^m

grin broadly, to बत्तीसी दिखाना ^N

guest मेहमान ^m

Gujarati गुजराती

guru गुरु ^m

Gwalior ग्वालियर ^m

half आधा ^m; half past साढ़े 12.2

hand हाथ ^m; to come to hand हाथ
   आना; to lend a hand हाथ बँटाना ^N;
   to join hands हाथ मिलाना ^N

handsome ख़ूबसूरत, सुंदर

happen, to होना, हो जाना

happiness ख़ुशी ^f

happy ख़ुश

hard, difficult मुश्किल, कठिन

hardworking मेहनती

harm नुक़सान ^m

harass, hassle, to तंग करना ^N

hate नफ़रत ^f; to hate (से) नफ़रत करना ^N
   15.3

have (possess), to के पास होना 8.2;
   (be obliged), to: inf.+ पड़ना 13.3

he वह, वे

head सिर ^m

health तबियत ^f

heap ढेर ^m

hear, to सुनना ^N

heard, to be सुनाई देना/पड़ना 15b

heart दिल ^m

heat गरमी ^f

heaven स्वर्ग ^m

heavy भारी

height लंबाई ^f

hello नमस्ते, नमस्कार

help मदद ^f; to help मदद देना ^N,
की मदद करना ^N 16.1

here यहाँ, इधर

hero हीरो ^m

high ऊँचा

hill पहाड़ ^m

Hindi हिन्दी ^f

Hindu हिन्दू

history इतिहास ^m

hit, to मारना ^N

hold, to पकड़ना ^N; (phone line)
होल्ड करना ^N

Holi होली ^f

holiday छुट्टी ^f

home घर ^m; at home घर पर

Home Minister गृह मंत्री ^{m, f}

hooligan गुंडा ^m; hooliganism
गुंडागर्दी ^f

hope आशा ^f, उम्मीद ^f; I hope मुझे
उम्मीद/आशा है

horse घोड़ा ^m

hospital अस्पताल ^m

hostility वैर ^m

hot गरम

hotel होटल ^m

hour घंटा ^m

house मकान ^m, घर ^m

how (what like?) कैसा; (in what
way?) कैसे

how much/many कितना

human being मानव ^m, इनसान ^m

hunger भूख ^f

hungry भूखा; I feel hungry, मुझको
भूख लगी

hurt चोट ^f; to get hurt, चोट लगना
13.6

husband पति ^m

I मैं

ice बर्फ़ ^f

idea विचार ^m, ख़याल ^m

if अगर, यदि 10.4, 17.1

ill बीमार

immediately तुरंत

important ज़रूरी, अहम

impossible असंभव, नामुमकिन

improve, to सुधरना; सुधारना ^N

in में

in front (of) (के) आगे

inauguration उद्घाटन ^m

incomparable लाजवाब

increase, to बढ़ना

India हिन्दुस्तान ^m, भारत ^m

Indian हिन्दुस्तानी, भारतीय

individual, person व्यक्ति ^m

inferior (in quality) घटिया (inv.)

informally अनौपचारिक रूप से

injury चोट ^f; I got injured, मुझको
चोट लगी

innocent, guileless भोला

inside (के) अंदर

instead of के बजाय

intelligent होशियार, तेज़

intention इरादा [m]

interesting दिलचस्प

interrupt (की) बात काटना [N]

invite, to बुलाना [N]

iron, ironing इस्तरी [f]

irritate, to चिढ़ाना [N], तंग करना [N]

-ish -सा (redish लाल-सा)

it वह

Japanese जापानी

jewellery (item of) ज़ेवर [m]

job, employment नौकरी [f]

joke मज़ाक़ [m]; joking हँसी-मज़ाक [m]

journey यात्रा [f], सफ़र [m]

joy, enjoyment आनंद [m]

jungle जंगल [m]

just, a little ज़रा

Kanpur कानपुर [m]

kathak कथक [m]

Kathmandu काठमांडु [m]

keep, to रखना [N]

key चाबी [f]

Khan Market खाँ मार्केट [m]

kill, to मारना [N], मार डालना [N]

kind, type तरह [f], प्रकार [m]; of various kinds तरह तरह का

kindly, please मेहरबानी करके

kindness मेहरबानी [f], कृपा [f]

king राजा [m] (inv.)

kitchen रसोईघर [m]

kite (toy) पतंग [f]

knife छुरी [f]

know, to जानना [N]; मालूम होना 4.4

kurta कुरता [m]

lack, want कमी [f]

lady महिला [f]

lamp; electric light बत्ती [f]

land ज़मीन [f]

lane गली [f]

language भाषा [f], ज़बान [f]

lap गोद [f]

lass छोकरी [f]

last (previous) पिछला; (final) आख़िरी

late, delayed देर से

later बाद (में), आगे चलकर

lathi, stick लाठी [f]

laugh, to हँसना [n]; to make laugh हँसाना [N]

laughter, joking हँसी-मज़ाक [m]

laze about, to मक्खियाँ मारना [N]

lazy आलसी, कामचोर

leader, politician नेता [m]

learn, to सीखना [N]; to study पढ़ना

leave, to छोड़ना [N]

lecturer प्राध्यापक [m]

left (opp. of right) बायाँ; to the left (hand) बायें/ उलटे (हाथ)

left (remaining) बाक़ी

leisure, free time फ़ुरसत [f], अवकाश [m]

lend, to उधार देना [N]

length लंबाई ^f

lentil(s) दाल ^f

less कम

lesson, chapter पाठ ^m

letter ख़त ^m, पत्र ^m, चिट्ठी ^f

let, to: *see* 'allow, to'

lie झूठ ^m; to lie झूठ बोलना ⁿ

lie, recline, to लेटना

life ज़िंदगी ^f, जीवन ^m

lift, to उठाना ^N

light (brightness) रोशनी ^f; (lamp,
    electric light) बत्ती ^f

light (in weight) हल्का

like (in manner of) की तरह; (equal
    to) (के) समान; (such as, similar to)
    जैसा 15.4

like, to पसंद करना ^N/होना 4.4

lip होंठ ^m

listen, to सुनना ^N

literature साहित्य ^m

little छोटा; a little थोड़ा-सा 15.5

live, to (reside) रहना; (be alive,
    live life) जीना ^N

livelihood गुज़ारा ^m

load, to लादना ^N

loaded, to be लदना

loan उधार ^m

lock ताला ^m

London लंदन ^m

loneliness अकेलापन ^m

look, glance नज़र ^f

look, to देखना ^N; to look after की
    देखभाल करना ^N 16.1; to look for
    ढूँढ़ना ^N; to look like जैसा लगना 13.6

lose, to खोना ^N

lots of बहुत-से 15.5, बहुत-सारा

lout, hooligan गुंडा ^m

love प्रेम ^m, प्यार ^m; to love Raj, राज
    से प्रेम/प्यार करना ^N 15.3

lovely प्यारा; सुन्दर

low (of sound, voice) धीमा

Lucknow लखनऊ ^m

luggage सामान ^m

lunch दोपहर/दिन का खाना ^m

luxury ऐश ^m

lying (e.g. मेज़ पर) पड़ा, पड़ा हुआ 18.1

Ma माँ ^f

mad पागल

madam मैडम ^f

magnificent शानदार

Mahabharata महाभारत ^m

maharaja महाराज(ा) ^m (inv.)

mail, post डाक ^f

maintain, keep current, to जारी
    रखना ^N

make, to बनाना ^N

male, man मर्द ^m

manage (succeed), to: verb stem +
    पाना 12.3

man, person आदमी ^m

mango आम ^m

many बहुत, बहुत-से 15.5, कई

manner, way ढंग ^m; तरह ^f

market बाज़ार ^m

marriage शादी ^f, विवाह ^m

married शादी-शुदा (inv.)

marry, to शादी करना ^N; to marry Ram, राम से शादी करना ^N; to marry Ram to Sita, राम की शादी सीता से करना ^N 16.1

Maruti मारुति ^f

matter, affair मामला ^m, बात ^f

me में, मुझ

mean, miserly कंजूस

meaning मतलब ^m, अर्थ ^m

means साधन ^m

meantime, in the फ़िलहाल

meat गोश्त ^m, माँस ^m

mechanic मिस्तरी ^m

medicine दवा ^f

meet (with), to (से) मिलना 15.3

meeting मुलाक़ात ^f, भेंट ^f; (formal) मीटिंग ^f

member सदस्य ^m

memory याद ^f 16.2

middle of, in the के बीच में

middle aged अधेड़ (उमर का)

midnight आधीरात ^f

milk दूध ^m

mind मन ^m

mine मेरा

minute मिनट ^m

miracle कमाल ^m

mischief शरारत ^f

mistake ग़लती ^f, भूल ^f; to make a mistake, गलती/भूल करना ^N

mix, to मिलाना ^N

moment पल ^m, क्षण ^m; at the moment अभी

Monday सोमवार ^m

money पैसा ^m

monkey बंदर ^m

month महीना ^m

moon चाँद ^m

more और, ज़्यादा, अधिक

morning सुबह ^f; in the early morning सवेरे; this morning आज सुबह

mosquito मच्छर ^m

most ज़्यादा, अधिक; at the most अधिक से अधिक, ज़्यादा से ज़्यादा; most people ज़्यादातर लोग

mostly ज़्यादातर

mother माता ^f, माँ ^f

mountain पहाड़ ^m

mouth मुँह ^m

move, to चलना; हिलना; to move house शिफ़्ट करना ^N, घर बदलना ^N

Mr श्री, मिस्टर

Mrs श्रीमती, मिसेज़

much ज़्यादा, अधिक

Muslim मुसलमान ^{m,f}

Mussoorie मसूरी ^f

my मेरा

name नाम ^m

narrow तंग

nature, disposition स्वभाव ^m

near (के) नज़दीक, (के) पास

nearby (adv.) पास; (adj.) पास-वाला

necessary ज़रूरी, आवश्यक

necessity आवश्यकता ^f

neck गरदन ^f

need ज़रूरत ^f 7.4

need, to: see 7.4 and 13.2-3

needed चाहिए 7.4

neighbour पड़ोसी ^m

neither... nor न... न 16.6

Nepal नेपाल ^m

Nepali नेपाली

nephew भतीजा ^m

never कभी नहीं

new नया (नये/नए, नयी/नई)

news ख़बर ^f, समाचार ^m

newspaper अख़बार ^m, समाचार-पत्र ^m

next अगला

next to, close by की बग़ल में

night रात ^f; all night रात भर

no नहीं, जी नहीं

nobody कोई नहीं

noise, tumult शोर ^m

noon, afternoon दोपहर ^f

no one कोई नहीं 7.2

nose नाक ^f

not नहीं, न

note (written) नोट ^m, चिट्ठी ^f;
    (banknote) नोट ^m

nothing कुछ नहीं 7.2

novel (book) उपन्यास ^m

now अब

nowadays आजकल

nowhere कहीं नहीं

number नंबर ^m; (figure) संख्या ^f

obstinacy ज़िद ^f

obstinate, stubborn ज़िद्दी

obtain, to प्राप्त करना ^N, पाना ^N;
    (मिलना 'to be obtained' 13.5)

occur to the mind, to सूझना

ocean समुद्र ^m

o'clock बजे (e.g. तीन बजे)

of का; half of this इसका आधा; of
    course ज़रूर, अवश्य

office दफ़्तर ^m

often अक्सर

OK ठीक

old (elderly, of people) बूढ़ा; old
    man बूढ़ा ^m; old woman बुढ़िया ^f;
    (of things) पुराना

on पर; on account of के मारे; on top
    (of) के ऊपर

one एक; one and a half डेढ़; one
    and a quarter सवा; one or two, a
    couple (of) एकाध ^(sg)

oneself ख़ुद, स्वयं 15.7; of one's
    own accord अपने आप 15.7

onion प्याज़ ^m

only सिर्फ़, केवल; ही 9.4

open खुला; to open खुलना; खोलना ^N

opinion राय ^f, ख़याल ^m; in my
  opinion मेरे ख़याल में/से

opposite (के) सामने

opportunity मौक़ा ^m

or या 16.6

order (send for), to मँगवाना ^N

ordinary आम, साधारण

origin मूल ^m

other, second दूसरा

otherwise नहीं तो

our, ours हमारा

out बाहर; out of, from among में से

outside (के) बाहर

own, one's own अपना 6.3

paan पान ^m

pain दर्द ^m, दुःख ^m

paisa पैसा ^m

Pakistan पाकिस्तान ^m

Pakistani पाकिस्तानी

palace महल ^m

pale (complexioned) गोरा

pandit पंडित ^m

Panjabi पंजाबी

papa पापा ^m (inv.)

paper; piece of paper काग़ज़ ;
  newspaper अख़बार ^m

particular ख़ास, विशेष

party (political) दल ^m, पार्टी ^f

pass (exam etc.), to पास करना ^N; (of
  time), to बीतना; बिताना ^N; to pass
  away: see 'die'

passenger यात्री ^m, मुसाफ़िर ^m, सवारी ^f

pay, salary वेतन ^m

pay attention (to), to (पर) ध्यान
  देना ^N

peacock मोर ^m

pearl मोती ^m

pen क़लम ^{m/f}

pencil पेंसिल ^f

peon, orderly चपरासी ^m

people लोग ^{m pl}; the public जनता ^{f sg}

perhaps शायद

period, age ज़माना ^m, युग ^m

permanently स्थायी रूप से

Persian language फ़ारसी ^f

person, individual व्यक्ति ^m

personally व्यक्तिगत रूप से

phone फ़ोन ^m

phone, to फ़ोन करना ^N

photograph फ़ोटो ^m; to take photo
  फोटो खींचना ^N

pick up, to उठाना ^N

picture तस्वीर ^f, चित्र ^m

piece, bit टुकड़ा ^m

pile ढेर ^m

pill गोली ^f

place जगह ^f

place of, at the के यहाँ 6.4

plan योजना ^f, प्रोग्राम ^m

plane, aeroplane हवाई जहाज़ ^m

play (a game), to खेलना ⁿ

play (music etc.), to बजाना ^N

please कृपया, मेहरबानी करके

pleased खुश

pleasure खुशी^f, मज़ा^m, आनंद^m

pocket जेब^f

poem; poetry कविता^f

poet कवि^m

point, advantage फायदा^m

police पुलिस^{f. sg}

politician नेता^m

pollution प्रदूषण^m

pomp धूमधाम^m

pond तालाब^m

poor ग़रीब

popular लोकप्रिय

population आबादी^f

porter कुली^m

possible मुमकिन, संभव

post, mail डाक^f

post-office डाकघर^m

pour, to डालना^N

power शक्ति^f

practice अभ्यास^m

praise तारीफ़^f; to praise की तारीफ़
करना^N 16.1

prepare, to तैयार करना^N

present, gift तोहफ़ा^m, उपहार^m, भेंट^f

previous पिछला; previously पहले

price दाम^m, क़ीमत^f

pride गर्व^m; (arrogance) घमंड^m

prime minister प्रधान मंत्री^m

printed, to be छपना

problem समस्या^f

profession पेशा^m

profit फ़ायदा^m, लाभ^m

programme प्रोग्राम^m, कार्यक्रम^m

prohibited मना (inv.)

promising, up-and-coming होनहार

pronunciation उच्चारण^m

proper, appropriate उचित

properly ठीक से

public, the people जनता^{f sg}

published प्रकाशित

publisher प्रकाशक^m

pure, unmixed शुद्ध

put, to रखना^N

put on (wear), to पहनना^N

quarrel झगड़ा^m

quarter to the hour पौने (e.g. पौने
तीन) 12.2

question सवाल^m, प्रश्न^m

quick तेज़; quickly जल्दी

quite (fairly, very) काफ़ी;
(completely) बिलकुल

radio रेडियो^m

rain बारिश^f; to rain बारिश
होना/आना, पानी पड़ना

Rajasthan राजस्थान^m

Ramayan रामायण^m

rather (very) बहुत; (a little) कुछ,
थोड़ा; (with adj.) -सा 15.5

reach, to पहुँचना

read, to पढ़ना^N

ready तैयार

real असली

realise, to समझ जाना

really (genuinely) सचमुच; (in reality) असल में

reason कारण [m], वजह [f]

recently इधर, हाल में, अभी

recite, to सुनाना [N]

recognise, to पहचानना [N]

red लाल

reduce, to कम करना [N]

refuse (to), to (से) इनकार करना [N]

regret अफ़सोस [m], खेद [m]

regret, to पछताना [N]

relative रिश्तेदार [m,f]

remain, to रहना

remaining बाक़ी

remarkable अद्भुत

remember, to याद रखना [N]/ करना [N]/होना 16.1

remind, to याद दिलाना [N]

rent किराया [m]; to rent किराये पर लेना [N]/देना [N]

repair मरम्मत [f]; to repair की मरम्मत करना [N] 16.1

reply उत्तर [m], जवाब [m]; to reply जवाब देना [N]

request निवेदन [m]

rescue, to बचाना [N]

resemble, to (से) मिलना, मिलना-जुलना 13.5

resound, to बजना

responsibility ज़िम्मेदारी [f]

rest, ease आराम [m]; to rest आराम करना [N]

restless बेचैन

return, to लौटना, वापस आना/जाना

rice चावल [m]

rich, wealthy अमीर; rich man, 'millionaire' लखपति [m]

rickshaw रिक्शा [m]

right (opp. of left) दाहिना; to the right (hand) दाहिने/ सीधे (हाथ)

right here, in this very place यहीं 9.4

right now अभी 9.4

riot दंगा [m]

ripe पक्का

river नदी [f]

riverbank, steps घाट [m]

robbery चोरी [f]

room कमरा [m]

rudeness, impertinence गुस्ताख़ी [f]

rug दरी [f]

ruin, to बरबाद करना [N]

run (manage), to चलाना [N]

run, to दौड़ना; run away भागना

rupee रुपया [m]

Russian रूसी

sage, seer ऋषि [m]

salary वेतन [m]

salt नमक [m]

salwar qameez सलवार क़मीज़ [f]

same, the same one वही 9.4

samosa समोसा ^m

sandal चप्पल ^f

Sanskrit संस्कृत ^f

sarcasm व्यंग्य ^m

sari साड़ी ^f

satisfaction संतोष ^m; satisfied संतुष्ट

Saturday शनिवार ^m

save, to बचाना ^N

saved, left over बचा, बाक़ी

say(to), to (से) कहना ^N

scholarship छात्रवृत्ति ^f

scold, to डाँटना ^N

script (alphabet) लिपि ^f

sea समुद्र ^m

search तलाश ^f; to search for की तलाश करना ^N 16.1

seat सीट ^f

seated, sitting बैठा

see, to देखना ^N; (to visit) मिलना 15.3

seem, to लगना 13.6; मालूम होना 6.1

sell, to बेचना ^N

send, to भेजना ^N

sentence वाक्य ^m

separate, separately अलग

serious गंभीर

servant नौकर ^m

serve (food), to खिलाना ^N

several कई

shame शर्म ^f; to feel ashamed शर्म आना

she वह, वे

shiver, to काँपना

shoe; pair of shoes जूता ^m

shop दुकान ^f; shopkeeper दुकान-दार ^m; shopping दुकानदारी ^f

should: infinitive + चाहिए 13.2

shout, to चिल्लाना ^N

show, spectacle तमाशा ^m

show, to दिखाना ^N

shut बंद; to shut, बंद करना ^N

sick, ill बीमार

side, direction तरफ़ ^f, ओर ^f

sigh साँस ^f; to heave a (deep) sigh (ठंडी) साँस भरना ⁿ

silent चुप, ख़ामोश

silk रेशम ^m

silly, pointless ऊल-जलूल, बेकार

silver चाँदी ^f

simple, easy सरल

since से; since Monday सोमवार से; since the time when... since then जब से... तब से 13.1

sing, to गाना ^N

sir साहब, सर, जनाब

sister बहिन ^f

sister-in-law (elder brother's wife) भाभी ^f

sit, to बैठना; sitting बैठा, बैठा हुआ; sitting room बैठक ^f

sitar सितार ^m

situation स्थिति ^f

sky आकाश ^m, आसमान ^m

sleep नींद ^f

sleep, to सोना

slogan नारा ^m

slum बस्ती ^f

small छोटा

smile, to मुस्कराना ⁿ

smoke, to (सिग्रेट) पीना ^N

snow बर्फ़ ^f

so (then) तो, सो, इसलिए; so (+ adj.)
इतना (e.g. इतना पुराना); so that
ताकि + subjunctive

soap साबुन ^m

sold, to be बिकना

soldier जवान ^m

sole, only (child) इकलौता

solution (to problem) हल ^m

solve, to हल करना ^N; to be solved
हल होना

some (with countable noun) कोई;
(with uncountable noun) कुछ;
something कुछ; something else
कुछ और, और कुछ; something or
other कुछ न कुछ 7.2

somehow कहीं

someone कोई; someone else और
कोई, कोई और; someone or other
कोई न कोई 7.2

sometime कभी; sometimes कभी
कभी

somewhere कहीं; somewhere else

कहीं और; somewhere or other
कहीं न कहीं

son बेटा ^m

song गाना ^m, गीत ^m

soon जल्दी; as soon as जैसे ही 13.1

sorry (regret) अफ़सोस ^m; I apologise, forgive me माफ़ कीजिए

sound आवाज़ ^f

south दक्षिण ^m

speak, to बोलना ⁿ

special ख़ास

spend (time), to गुज़ारना ^N

spoon चम्मच ^m

squander, to उड़ाना ^N

stair, staircase सीढ़ी ^f

stamp टिकट ^{m/f}

standing खड़ा

star सितारा ^m

start, to: *see* 'begin, to'

state (condition) हालत ^f

state (province) प्रदेश ^m

station स्टेशन ^m

statue, image मूर्ति ^f

stay, to रहना; (e.g. in hotel) ठहरना

steal, to चोरी करना ^N

step, pace क़दम ^m

stern सख़्त

stick लकड़ी ^f; (truncheon) लाठी ^f

still (even now, up to now) अभी
(अभी तक, अभी भी)

stir up, start up, to छेड़ना ^N

stomach पेट ^m

stone पत्थर ^m

stop, to रुकना; रोकना ^N

story कहानी ^f

straight सीधा; (adv.) सीधे; straight away तुरंत, अभी; straightforward सीधा

strange अजीब

stranger अजनबी ^m

street सड़क ^f

strict सख़्त

strike, lockout हड़ताल ^f

string रस्सी ^f

stroll, to टहलना

strong मज़बूत, तेज़

stubborn ज़िद्दी

stuck, to be फँसना

student विद्यार्थी ^{m f}, छात्र ^m, छात्रा ^f

studies, studying पढ़ाई ^f

study, to पढ़ना

stupid बेवक़ूफ़; stupid person उल्लू (lit. 'owl')

subject, topic विषय ^m

success सफलता ^f; successful सफल, कामयाब

such (of such a kind) ऐसा; (so much) इतना

suddenly, unexpectedly अचानक

suggestion सुझाव ^m; to suggest सुझाव देना ^N

summer गरमियाँ ^{f pl}

sun सूरज ^m; sunlight, sunshine धूप ^f

Sunday रविवार ^m

surprise आश्चर्य ^m; I'm surprised मुझको आश्चर्य है; surprising आश्चर्यजनक

sway, to झूमना

swear, to (curse, swear at) गाली देना ^N; (make oath) क़सम खाना ^N

sweet मीठा; sweet dish मिठाई ^f

swim, to तैरना ⁿ

swindler ठग ^m

sycophancy जी-हुज़ूरी ^f

tabla तबला ^m

table मेज़ ^f

tablet, pill गोली ^f

tail पूँछ ^f

tailor दर्ज़ी ^m

Taj Mahal ताज महल ^m

take, to (receive) लेना ^N; (transport, deliver, take away) ले जाना; take care of का ख़याल/ध्यान रखना ^N 16.1; take down उतारना ^N; take off (clothes) उतारना ^N

talk, converse, to (से) बात/बातें करना ^N

tall लंबा; (of buildings etc.) ऊँचा

Tamil तमिल ^f

tap नल ^m; tapwater नल का पानी ^m

tasty स्वादिष्ट

taxi टैक्सी ^f

tea चाय ^f; teaboy चाय-वाला ^m

teach, to पढ़ाना ^N, सिखाना ^N

teacher अध्यापक ^m

tear, to फ़ाड़ना ^N

tease, to चिढ़ाना ^N

television दूरदर्शन ^m, टी० वी० ^m

tell, to बताना ^N

temple मंदिर ^m

thank you शुक्रिया, धन्यवाद

that (pronoun) वह; (conjunction) कि; (relative, 'which') जो 13.4; that is to say यानी

theft चोरी ^f

them वे, उन

then फिर, तब

there वहाँ; right there वहीं; over there उधर; there is/are है/ हैं

these ये

they ये, वे

thick (coarse) मोटा; (dense) घना

thief चोर ^m

thin पतला; (lean) दुबला-पतला

thing चीज़ ^f

think, to सोचना ^N

thirst प्यास ^f; I'm thirsty मुझको प्यास लगी है 13.6

this यह

thorn काँटा ^m

those वे

thought विचार ^m, ख़याल ^m

three days ago/ahead नरसों

three-quarters पौन, पौना

throat गला ^m

throw, to डालना ^N, फेंकना ^N

Tibetan तिब्बती

ticket टिकट ^{m/f}

time समय ^m, वक़्त ^m; age, season काल ^m; occasion बार ^f, दफ़ा ^f; what's the time? कितने बजे हैं ?; 12.2; at the time of leaving चलते समय 18.1

timid डरपोक

tired, to be थकना

tiredness थकान ^f

to को

today आज

together (in company with) एक साथ, के साथ; (jointly) मिल-जुलकर

tolerate, to बरदाश्त करना ^N

tomorrow कल

too (also) भी (*follows* word, 2.3); (excessive) बहुत ज़्यादा

tonight आज रात (को)

top of, on के ऊपर

touch, to छूना ^N, हाथ लगाना ^N

tour, to घूमना

towards की तरफ़/ओर

town शहर ^m

toy खिलौना ^m

train ट्रेन ^f, गाड़ी ^f, रेलगाड़ी ^f

translation अनुवाद ^m; to translate (का) अनुवाद करना ^N

travel यात्रा ^f, सफ़र ^m

traveller यात्री ^m, मुसाफ़िर ^m

treatment (medical) इलाज m

tree पेड़ m

trekking ट्रेकिंग f

tremble, to काँपना

trick, deceipt धोखा m; to trick धोखा देना N

trouble तकलीफ़ f, कष्ट m

troubled, upset परेशान

true सच

trust भरोसा m, विश्वास m

truth, the सच m

try, to की कोशिश करना N

tumbler गिलास m

turn, bend मोड़ m

turn, to मुड़ना, मोड़ना N

twisted टेढ़ा

two and a half ढाई

UP (Uttar Pradesh) उत्तर प्रदेश m; उ० प्र०; यू० पी०

ugly बदसूरत

umbrella छाता m

uncle अंकल m

uncle (father's younger brother) चाचा m (inv.)

understand, to समझना n

understanding समझ f

university विश्वविद्यालय m

until तक; जब तक न... 13.1

up to तक

up, upstairs ऊपर

upset परेशान

Urdu उर्दू f

urgent ज़रूरी

us हम

use, usage प्रयोग m; to use का इस्तेमाल/प्रयोग करना N 16.1

'used to': see 7.1

useless बेकार

usually आम तौर पर, अक्सर

vacant ख़ाली

vacate, to ख़ाली करना N

valuable क़ीमती

Varanasi वाराणसी f

vegetable(s) सब्ज़ी f

very बहुत

via से होकर 12.1

village गाँव m

villain बदमाश m

visible, to be दिखाई देना

voice आवाज़ f

wait, waiting इंतज़ार m; to wait (for) (का) इंतज़ार करना N

walk, to पैदल चलना/जाना

wall दीवार f

want, to चाहना 10.2 (in past , use imperfective: मैं चाहता था)

warm गरम

wash, to धोना N; (bathe) नहाना

washed, to be धुलना

washerman धोबी m

waste, to गँवाना N; (squander) उड़ाना N

watch, wristwatch घड़ी [f]

watch, to देखना [N]

watchman चौकीदार [m]

water पानी [m]

way, manner ढंग [m], तरह़ [f], प्रकार [m]

we हम

weak कमज़ोर

wear, to पहनना [N]

weather मौसम [m]

wedding शादी [f]

week हफ़्ता [m], सप्ताह [m]

weep, to रोना [n]

well, abundantly ख़ूब

well (anyway) ख़ैर; (in a good way) अच्छा, अच्छी तरह (से)

wet (soaked) भीगा; (damp) गीला

what? क्या; what like? what kind of? कैसा

wheel पहिया [m]

when... then जब... तब 13.1; when? कब

where... there जहाँ... वहाँ 14.7; where? कहाँ, किधर

whether ... or चाहे ...चाहे

which (relative pronoun) जो; which/what ever जो भी; which? कौनसा

while (on the other hand) जब कि; while doing करते समय, करते करते

whisky व्हिस्की [f]

whisper, to फुसफुसाना

white सफ़ेद; white person गोरा [m]

who (relative pronoun) जो; whoever जो भी 13.4

who? कौन; whom? किस, किन; whose? किसका, किनका

why क्यों

wife पत्नी [f]

wild, untamed जंगली

wind हवा [f]

window खिड़की [f]

with से; (in company of) के साथ

without के बिना; without doing बिना किए

woman औरत [f]

wood लकड़ी [f]

word शब्द [m]

work काम [m]; (occupation) धंधा [m]; (employment) नौकरी [f]

work, to काम करना [N]; to function (of machine) काम करना [N]; to have an effect (का) असर पड़ना

worker, labourer मज़दूर [m]

world दुनिया [f]

worth, worthy लायक़; worth doing करने लायक़

wretch, poor fellow बेचारा [m]

write, to लिखना [N]

writer लेखक [m]

wrong, incorrect ग़लत

yawn जँभाई[f]; to yawn जंभाई लेना[N]

year साल[m], वर्ष[m]; (of calendar or
  era) सन्[m]

yes हाँ, जी हाँ

yesterday कल

you (intimate) तुम; (familar) तुम;

(formal) आप 1.1

young छोटा, जवान

your, yours (intimate) तेरा;
  (familiar) तुम्हारा; (formal)
  आपका; yourself खुद

youth, young man नौजवान[m]

GLOSSARY OF GRAMMATICAL TERMS

absolutive A form of the verb such as *pahũckar* 'having arrived', whose phrase is independent of the grammar of the rest of the sentence: *ghar pahũckar maĩ ārām karū̃gā* 'having arrived home I'll rest' (= 'I'll rest when I get home').

adjective A word that describes a noun, e.g. *lāl* 'red', *baṛā* 'big'. An adjective must **agree** with its noun. An adjective is called <u>attributive</u> if it precedes the noun, (*purānā makān* 'old house'), <u>predicative</u> if it follows the noun (*makān purānā hai*) 'the house is old'.

adverb A word or phrase that describes an action, e.g. *zor se* 'loudly' in *zor se bolo* 'speak loudly'.

agree, agreement When words change to match related words, they are said to 'agree' with them: the adjective *choṭā* 'little' changes to *choṭī* to agree with the feminine noun *laṛkī* 'girl' in *choṭī laṛkī* 'little girl'.

aggregative Forms of number-words indicating a group of something: *tīnõ bacce* 'all three children', *dasõ gāṛiyã̄* 'tens of cars'.

auxiliary A verb – usually part of the verb 'to be' – that helps complete the sense of another verb (English uses the auxiliary 'will' in 'he will speak'). Hindi examples from *honā* 'to be' include *hai* and *thā* in *vah rahtā hai*, 'he lives', *vah rahtā thā* 'he used to live'.

case In English, 'I' changes to 'me' when it's the object of an action: 'He hit me'; this is a change of 'case'. Hindi has two main cases: the direct case (like *maĩ* 'I'), and the oblique case (*mujh* 'me') which is used before **postpositions** (as in *mujh ko* 'to me' etc.). See also **vocative**.

commands Forms of the verb that give commands or requests: *bolo!* 'speak!', *bolie* 'please speak'.

compound verb A verb consisting of two verbs working together: the first gives the basic meaning, the second 'colours' that meaning in some way. Thus *baiṭho!* 'sit!' can become *baiṭh jāo!* 'sit down!' (*jāo* is from *jānā* 'to go', but its literal sense 'go' is lost in a compound like this).

conditional An expression involving the sense 'if…'.

conjunct character A Devanagari character in which two consonants join to make a single syllable: in the word प्लग *plag* 'plug', a shortened form of प *pa* joins ल *la* to form the conjunct प्ल *pla*. The conjunct removes the **inherent vowel** from the first character, changing *pa* to *p*.

conjunctions Words that link clauses in a sentence: *aur* 'and', *lekin* 'but', *ki* 'that', *hālāki* 'although'.

continuous The name of '-ing' tenses that describe ongoing actions: *vah gā rahī hai / thī* 'she is/was singing'.

correlative See **relative** clauses.

direct case See **case**.

gender Nouns involving sexual gender like 'man', 'woman' are 'masculine' and 'feminine' respectively; but in Hindi all nouns have gender: *pānī* 'water' and *dūdh* 'milk' are masculine, *cāy* 'tea' and *cīnī* 'sugar' are feminine. Learn noun genders! And see **agreement**.

genitive See **possessive**.

honorific A usage that indicates the level of formality shown to a person: calling someone *tum* ('you') implies familiarity, while *āp* ('you') is more formal. Verbs and adjectives must agree with the honorific level selected: see **agreement**. The system extends to the third **person** ('he, she') also.

infinitive The basic form of the verb as used in lists, dictionaries etc. In English it includes the word 'to', while in Hindi it ends -*nā*: 'to drink' *pīnā*, 'to go' *jānā*, 'to understand' *samajhnā*.

inherent vowel A Devanagari consonant is a complete syllable that includes the vowel '*a*', called the 'inherent' vowel: thus the character न reads as '*na*', not just '*n*'. The inherent vowel can be replaced by a vowel sign, as in ने *ne*, or removed by making a **conjunct** with a second consonant, as in हिन्दी *hindī*.

imperfective verb See **perfective verb**.

intransitive verb See **transitive verb**.

nasalization A nasalized vowel is produced partly 'through the nose'.

noun A word that names something. All nouns have either masculine or feminine **gender**: *nāk* f. 'nose', *kān* m. 'ear'.

number The status of words describing things as being either 'singular' (one only) or 'plural' (more than one). When Hindi uses plural number to show respect to a singular person, this is called an **honorific** plural.

object   A person or thing to which the action of the verb is done is called the 'direct object': e.g. *gāṛī* 'car' in *maĩ gāṛī calātā hū̃* 'I drive the car'. In *maĩ tum ko tohfā dū̃gā* 'I'll give you a gift', *tohfā* 'gift' is the direct object, and *tum* 'you' is the indirect object.

oblique case   See **case**.

participle   Part of a verb like *dekhtā* 'see, seeing' (imperfective participle) or *dekhā* 'saw' (perfective participle) – the basis of various tenses etc.

passive   A construction focusing on the thing to which an action is done, rather than on the doer of the action: *gāṛī calāī jātī hai* 'the car is driven' is passive, *maĩ gāṛī calātā hū̃* 'I drive the car' is active.

perfective verb   A perfective verb describes an action that is complete, i.e. it refers to a one-off action such as *maĩ ghar gayā* 'I went home'; an imperfective verb describes an action that is not complete, such as *maĩ ghar jātā hū̃ / jātā thā* 'I go/used to go home'.

person   The person speaking ('I' / 'we') is called the 'first person'; the one spoken to ('you') is 'second person'; someone spoken about (e.g. 'he', 'she') is 'third person'.

possessive   A word describing 'possession', like *merā* 'my, mine'.

postposition   Unlike English prepositions ('in', 'on' etc.), Hindi postpositions (*mẽ* 'in', *par* 'on') <u>follow</u> the words they qualify. They take the oblique **case**: *kamre mẽ* 'in the room', *mezõ par* 'on the tables'.

presumptive   A use of the future tense to make an assumption: *bacce ṭhīk hõge?* 'I assume the kids are OK?' (lit. 'will be OK?').

pronoun   A word like *vah* 'he, she, it' which stands in place of a noun.

purpose expression   One which expresses purpose or intention by using an oblique infinitive (ending -*e*, as in *sīkhne* 'to learn') with a verb of motion: *maĩ hindī sīkhne bhārat jāū̃gā* 'I'll go to India to learn Hindi'.

reflexive   A word that refers back to the subject of a clause, like <u>khud</u> ('myself, himself' etc.) in *maĩ <u>khud</u> jāū̃gā* 'I'll go myself'.

relative–correlative   In *jab maĩ gātā hū̃ tab kutte bhaũkne lagte haĩ* 'when I sing, (then) the dogs start barking', *jab* 'when' introduces a relative clause that relates to the correlative clause beginning *tab* 'then'. Hindi has many such relative–correlative pairs .

stem   The most basic part of the verb: *bol* is the stem of *bolnā* 'to speak'. Its functions include an abrupt command – *bol!* 'Speak!'.

subject The word or words naming the doer of an action: in *merā bhāī bīyar pītā hai* 'my brother drinks beer', *merā bhāī* 'my brother' is the subject and *biyar* is the **object**.

subjunctive A form of the verb expressing what is imagined or possible: in *śāyad maĩ bhī āū̃* 'Perhaps I may come too', *āū̃* 'may come' is a subjunctive form of the verb *ānā* 'to come'.

tense The form that a verb takes to express the time-frame of an action.

transitive verb One which can take a direct object, such as *khānā* 'to eat', *paṛhnā* 'to read'. Verbs that cannot take a direct object are intransitive: examples include verbs of motion such as *jānā* 'to go' (you can 'eat something' but you cannot 'go something'). In Hindi, the two types behave differently in perfective (past) tenses, so the distinction is an important one.

vocative The **case** of words used in addressing someone: *bhāiyo bahano!* 'Brothers and sisters!'.

TAKING IT FURTHER

If you're reading this section before working through the book itself, you may like some help with learning the Hindi script. An excellent introduction to the script and its sounds is available online at the following URL: http://www.avashy.com'.

If you have access to Hindi bookshops, try the Hindi editions of the cartoon-book series 'Amar Chitra Katha', whose themes include Indian historical figures, legends and folklore.

The internet has lots of material. Many Hindi newspapers have online editions (most have to be read on a PC rather than a Macintosh); you'll find some listed in the MORE LINKS section of 'http://www.samachar.com', a useful portal for the Indian news media.

You'll need a dictionary. As mentioned in Exercise 18b.3, R.S. McGregor's *Hindi–English Dictionary* (Oxford University Press), is the best of its kind; M. Chaturvedi & B.N. Tiwari's *Practical Hindi–English Dictionary* (Delhi, National Publishing House) and Hardev Bahri's *Learner's Hindi–English Dictionary* (Delhi, Rajpal) are also excellent. English–Hindi dictionaries are more of a problem, though Bahri's enormous *Advanced English–Hindi Dictionary* (Delhi, Rajpal) is useful. I'm myself writing a short two-way dictionary that will, I hope, be published in 2003. For the latest information on online dictionaries, see the Chicago 'Digital Dictionaries of South Asia' project at 'http://dsal.uchicago.edu/dictionaries'.

A major new online resource called 'A Door Into Hindi' will eventually give a new kind of access to spoken Hindi. It is being developed by Afroz Taj and his colleagues at the State University of North Carolina. When it's finished, 'A Door into Hindi' will feature grammar lessons, short videos, custom-made dramas, shopping scenes and much else besides; and because its lessons are cross-referenced to *Teach Yourself Hindi* it will be the ideal online companion to the book in your hand. Typing the word 'Hindi' into an internet search engine such as Google will lead you to 'A Door Into Hindi' and many other sites.

I shall soon be putting some new material relating to *Teach Yourself Hindi* on the web at 'http://www.soas.ac.uk', the site of the School of Oriental and African Studies, University of London, where I teach.

INDEX